)

The Transformation of Communist Ideology

Center for International Studies, Massachusetts Institute of Technology

Studies in Communism, Revisionism, and Revolution (formerly *Studies in International Communism*)   William E. Griffith, general editor

1. Albania and the Sino-Soviet Rift   William E. Griffith (1963)

2. Communism in North Vietnam   P. J. Honey (1964)

3. The Sino-Soviet Rift   William E. Griffith (1964)

4. Communism in Europe, Vol. I   William E. Griffith, ed. (1964)

5. Nationalism and Communism in Chile   Ernst Halperin (1965)

6. Communism in Europe, Vol. 2   William E. Griffith, ed. (1966)

7. Viet Cong: The Organization and Techniques of the National Liberation Front of South Vietnam   Douglas Pike (1966)

8. Sino-Soviet Relations, 1964–1965   William E. Griffith (1967)

9. The French Communist Party and the Crisis of International Communism   François Fetjö (1967)

10. The New Rumania: From People's Democracy to Socialist Republic   Stephen Fischer-Galati (1967)

11. Economic Development in Communist Rumania   John Michael Montias (1967)

12. Cuba: Castroism and Communism, 1959–1966   Andrés Suárez (1967)

13. Unity in Diversity: Italian Communism and the Communist World   Donald L. M. Blackmer (1967)

14. Winter in Prague: Documents on Czechoslovak Communism in Crisis   Robin Alison Remington, ed. (1969)

15. The Angolan Rebellion, Vol. I: The Anatomy of an Explosion (1950–1962)   John A. Marcum (1969)

16. Radical Politics in West Bengal   Marcus F. Franda (1971)

17. The Warsaw Pact: Case Studies in Communist Conflict Resolution   Robin Alison Remington (1971)

18. The Transformation of Communist Ideology: The Yugoslav Case, 1945–1953   A. Ross Johnson (1972)

The Transformation of Communist Ideology: The Yugoslav Case, 1945–1953

A. Ross Johnson

The MIT Press   Cambridge, Massachusetts, and London, England

Copyright © 1972 by
The Massachusetts Institute of Technology

This book was set in IBM Composer Journal Roman
by C C I Compositors,
printed on Decision Offset
and bound in Columbia Millbank Linen MBL–4019
by Vail-Ballou Press, Inc.
in the United States of America.

Library of Congress Cataloging in Publication Data

Johnson, A.   Ross.
  The transformation of Communist ideology.

  (Studies in communism, revisionism, and revolution, no. 18)
  Based on the author's thesis, Columbia.
  Bibliography: p.
  1. Communism—Yugoslavia.   I. Title.   II. Series.
HX365.5.A6J57   335.43'4'09497   72–8134
ISBN 0–262–10012–6

Dedicated to Diana, Eric, and the memory of Maria Lynne

Contents

Acknowledgments

I gratefully acknowledge my debt to Zbigniew Brzezinski for his counsel and assistance in sponsoring the Ph.D. dissertation at Columbia University on which this book is based. I am indebted to William E. Griffith for urging me to publish it and, earlier, for increasing my interest in and knowledge of East European affairs. Alexander Dallin and Slobodan Stanković made many helpful comments on earlier drafts of the manuscript. Wolfgang Leonhard and Ilse Spittmann kindly talked with me openly and at length about their experiences in Yugoslavia during the period 1949–1951. I am indebted to numerous individuals and institutions in Yugoslavia for discussing ideological problems with me in 1964–1965 and making available materials that, while in the public domain, were not easily obtainable outside the country. Staff members of the Institute for the Study of the Workers' Movement, the Institute of Social Science, the High School of Political Science, and the Law Faculty, all in Belgrade, were particularly helpful. In this day of alarmingly reduced support for foreign area studies, I express my thanks to the Foreign Area Fellowship Program; this study would not have been undertaken without its financial support.

Any errors and failings are, of course, solely the responsibility of the author.

A.R.J.
Santa Monica, California
September 1971

The Transformation of Communist Ideology

3

Introduction

Organization of the Book

This is a study of the transformation of Yugoslav Communist ideology between 1945 and 1953. Part I treats the period between the end of World War II and the outbreak of open conflict with Stalin in 1948. The Yugoslav Communists have often been described in Western studies as ideologically more Stalinist than Stalin during these years, yet there has been no detailed examination of the doctrinal record. I have endeavored to undertake such a study of Yugoslav Communist theorizing about the nature of the Communist revolution in Yugoslavia during World War II, the postwar program of developing socialism, and the international situation. Such an analysis is meaningful, however, only when considered in the context of analogous doctrine formulated for the rest of Eastern Europe during these years. The first chapter has therefore been devoted to that doctrine.

Part II is concerned with the period between the outbreak of the Soviet-Yugoslav conflict and Stalin's death in March 1953. Stalin's death has been chosen as the terminal point because it was quickly followed by the revival of formal state contacts between the Soviet Union and Yugoslavia (normalization of relations began in 1954) and because 1953 was also in some respects—until the 1960s—the year of the greatest "liberalization" in Yugoslavia. I have sought to analyze the Titoist doctrine that emerged between 1948 and 1953, examining the immediate Yugoslav reaction to the break with Stalin, the critique of the Soviet system, the reappraisal of the international situation, the various elements of the doctrine of socialist democracy, and the revised view of agricultural collectivization.

In Part III, I have attempted to characterize the transformation of Yugoslav Communist ideology during the period 1945–1953 and to make explicit some conclusions about the process of ideological change in the Yugoslav case.

A Note on Methodology

A study of ideological change in Yugoslavia implies the existence of a specific body of ideas affecting the Yugoslav Communist leaders' perception of events and reaction to them; it implies the existence of a Yugoslav Communist *ideology*.

This assumption is made on the basis of the findings of previous studies of Communist ideology in general and Soviet Communist ideology in particular.[1] Zbigniew Brzezinski has suggested a useful short definition of ideology: *"Modern revolutionary ideology is essentially an action program derived from certain doctrinal assump-*

tions about the nature of reality and expressed through certain stated, not overly complex, assertions about the inadequacy of the past or present state of societal affairs. These assertions include an explicit guide to action outlining methods for changing the situation, with some general, idealized notions about the eventual state of affairs."[2] Brzezinski and Samuel Huntington have suggested four useful categories distinguishing an ideology from other sets of political ideas: (1) overtness—officially proclaimed "texts" contain the basic tenets, which are formulated very explicitly and concretely; (2) systematic nature—the official "texts" are consciously and continually updated; (3) institutionalization—the particular body of ideas is claimed to be "embodied in the ruling Communist Party, and articulated by appointed 'ideologues' "; (4) dogmatism—the ideas, no less than political directives, are binding on all Communists until officially modified by the Party.[3]

If these characteristics of an ideology, particularly Communist ideology, are accepted, it is possible further to differentiate at least three levels in a particular set of political ideas:[4] (1) general philosophical assumptions—for example, dialectical materialism; (2) doctrinal elements, indicating the general direction of political action in a given historical period—for example, the dictatorship of the proletariat; (3) "action programs": programs of political action, specifically tied to *particular* historical and socioeconomic conditions—for example, Stalin's "socialism in one country" and Mao Tse-tung's "modern revisionism." Programs of political action are always subject to revision by the political leaders, and such revision is considered to be both positive and necessary. "Action programs" are often indistinguishable from "policies" in a Communist political system; they differ from "policies" in a pragmatic political system in terms of their continuous and conscious derivation from and justification in terms of especially the doctrinal but also the philosophical elements of the ideology. "Doctrine is thus the politically crucial link between dogmatic assumptions and pragmatic action."[5]

The necessary criteria for the existence of an ideology were met, it is argued here, in Yugoslavia during the period under study. There was an official Yugoslav Communist ideology, characterized by overtness, systematic nature, institutionalization, and dogmatism. Official Party documents and, initially, all statements by Politburo members on purely "theoretical" subjects—no less than on other matters—were explicitly binding on the Party rank and file, as part of the mechanism of democratic centralism, and had to be "studied" at meetings of the basic Party organizations and, as far as possible, "implemented." One important caveat must be entered: after mid-1951, "theoretical" pronouncements of Party leaders were formally excluded from the discipline of democratic centralism, unless explicitly made binding by a Politburo decision. Nevertheless, with few exceptions the "theoretical" views of individual leaders, in fact, still remained binding. On some issues, differences of views appeared within the Party, either at the top level or among second-ranking theoreticians, which were not resolved by an authoritative Politburo-level pronouncement. On all these points, however, a Party consensus finally did emerge, and it is to this consensus that I refer when speaking of Yugoslav Communist doctrine.

I have further assumed, in dealing with cases of "theoretical" differences within the Yugoslav Party, that the range of views in fact corresponded roughly to that visible in the Party's serious public and semipublic ideological organs. Such an assumption is suggested by the previous studies of Communism and totalitarian political systems in general which have found a close correlation to exist between public statement—at the level of "esoteric communication" designed for the Party-initiated—and private expression in several cases where secret internal Party documents have subsequently come to light.[6] In the Yugoslav case, the subsequent autobiographical accounts of Djilas, Dedijer, and Vukmanović corroborate that assumption.

As these remarks suggest, I have also assumed that, by and large, the ideological "texts" of the Yugoslav Communists did not have a purely manipulative and opportunistic character. As Barrington Moore, Jr., concluded in his monumental study of the role of Soviet Communist doctrine in the Soviet political system, "cynical manipulation" of the ideology was relatively rare in Soviet behavior.[7] This general assumption does not, of course, deny the possibility that an individual ideological tenet may have a predominantly manipulative purpose. While there is no certain test for distinguishing such elements, it is possible to ask two questions about the point at issue: (1) Is it treated consistently in the context of the internal logic of the ideology, and is it expressed in corresponding terms at all levels of public expression? (2) Has a subsequent change in Party policy resulted in the publication of authentic new evidence contradicting earlier public declarations? A negative answer to the first question and a positive answer to the second make the manipulative character of the ideological tenet at issue more probable.

In this study I have attempted, first, to describe and analyze the major "doctrinal" and "action program" aspects of Yugoslav Communist ideology which were not codified in a Party program after 1948 until the Seventh Party Congress in 1958. Second, I have sought to trace the roots of the doctrines in the conflict and/or congruence of new policies with previously accepted ideological positions. The reader is cautioned, however, that political developments are traced in this study only where they are directly relevant to the examination of ideological change. I have not attempted to write a political history of Yugoslavia for the period 1945–1953. Nor have I attempted to examine institutional behavior: for example, I have formulated the Yugoslav doctrine of worker self-management and traced how and why it emerged after 1949; I have not attempted to answer the question of how the system of workers' councils operated in practice.

Even though the foregoing assumptions have been made explicit, a study of ideology like this might still be criticized on the grounds that it looks at doctrinal "shadows" instead of the "real" political world and is therefore irrelevant. Such an objection would seem to be unfounded for three reasons. First, Communist doctrine is assumed to have considerable relevance to the political behavior of Communist leaders. As Richard Lowenthal pointed out, it seems as untenable today to attempt to argue that Marxism-Leninism is a cynically manipulated catechism existing solely or primarily to rationalize and justify the political acts of its interpreters as to attempt to argue that Marxism-Leninism is a "book of rules" precisely delineating political action in any and all circumstances.[8] Brzezinski suggested that the relationship between ideology and power is contingent, not causal: ideology is "a doctrine of political power which simultaneously defines the ends, outlines the methods for their fulfillment, and mobilizes support for them."[9] I have rejected as false any sharp distinction between "ideology" and "reality" in Communist behavior; the first is an integral part of the second. I have thus assumed that the doctrine discussed in this study had significant political relevance. For to study ideology is to study how Communist leaders perceive the world—a perception that precedes and influences the course of political action—as well as how they "ideologically" justify political action in order to legitimate their power. Even in the extreme case where a point of doctrine is formulated *exclusively* as ex post facto justification of political action, it then not only becomes binding on middle-level Party cadres and the rank and file, affecting their political behavior, but also becomes part of the frame of reference in which the top Party leadership itself views "real" events.

Second, previous studies of Communism and postwar Yugoslavia have often misrepresented Yugoslav ideological developments. For example, the statement "It was at least a year [after 1948] before the [Soviet-Yugoslav] struggle was extended to the ideological plane"[10] is factually incorrect and suggests a misunderstanding of the very nature of the dispute. In fact, prior to 1948 the Tito leadership formulated a clear ideological position that was not "Stalinist" at all. Exegesis of that position in this study may serve as a reminder of how woefully underdeveloped the art of deciphering esoteric communication was twenty-five years ago. Perhaps it may also serve as a modest rebuke to scholars concerned with the empirical study of Communist systems who have succumbed to a sense of déjà vu. In the case of the East European Communist systems, at least, many "easy" analytical tasks have barely been touched.

Third, the lack of a detailed study of Yugoslav Communist ideology in the initial period after 1948 has meant that there was no frame of reference for studying Yugoslav Communist ideology and, more generally, Yugoslav politics in the crucial, present stage of Yugoslavia's development. In studying the changes in Yugoslavia after the purge of Aleksandar Ranković in July 1966, for example, it is essential to know that the promise that the Party would now act as an "ideological-political force" was fourteen years old and was, in some respects, the less radical of various formulations utilized during 1952–1953 on the changed role of the Party in society. On the other hand, statements after mid-1966 by prominent leaders that democratic centralism did not exclude the formation of different views or even "groupings" within the Party were, in the Yugoslav case, unprecedented.

In any study of Communist doctrine, the repeated, boring use of Communist terminology is unavoidable. It should go without saying that its usage for purposes of description does not imply uncritical acceptance of its meaning or the analytical categories it implies. I have hence used quotation marks only where the Communist meaning may be unclearly partisan.

Notes

[1] Among the most important: Zbigniew K. Brzezinski, *The Soviet Bloc: Unity and Conflict* (Cambridge, Mass.: Harvard University Press, rev. ed., 1967), chap. 19; idem, *Ideology and Power in Soviet Politics* (New York: Praeger, 1962); Zbigniew Brzezinski and Samuel P. Huntington, *Political Power: USA/USSR* (New York:

Viking Press, 1965), esp. chap. 1; R. W. Carew Hunt, *The Theory and Practice of Communism* (New York: Macmillan, 1960); Alfred G. Meyer, *Leninism* (Cambridge, Mass.: Harvard University Press, 1957); Barrington Moore, Jr., *Soviet Politics: The Dilemma of Power* (New York: Harper & Row, 1965); Daniel Bell, "Ideology and Soviet Politics," with comments by George Lichtheim and Carl J. Friedrich, in *Slavic Review* 24, no. 4 (December 1965): 591–621; "Ideology and Power—A Symposium," in Abraham Brumberg, ed., *Russia under Khrushchev* (New York: Praeger, 1962); Franz Schurmann, *Ideology and Organization in Communist China* (Berkeley and Los Angeles: University of California Press, 1966).

[2] Brzezinski, *The Soviet Bloc*, p. 486.

[3] Brzezinski and Huntington, *Political Power: USA/USSR*, p. 19.

[4] Ibid., p. 21; Brzezinski, *The Soviet Bloc*, pp. 489–490.

[5] *The Soviet Bloc*, pp. 489–490.

[6] An excellent summary of the studies on the role of "esoteric communication" in Communist politics is given in William O. McCagg, "Communism and Hungary" (unpublished Ph.D. dissertation, Columbia University, 1965), Introduction; also useful is Donald S. Zagoria, *The Sino-Soviet Conflict, 1956–1961* (Princeton, N.J.: Princeton University Press, 1962), pp. 24–35; Merle Fainsod, *Smolensk under Soviet Rule* (Cambridge, Mass.: Harvard University Press, 1959); Alexander George, *Propaganda Analysis: A Study of Inferences Made from Nazi Propaganda in World War II* (Evanston, Ill.: Row, Peterson & Co., 1959); Schurmann, *Ideology and Organization in Communist China*; William E. Griffith, "On Esoteric Communications," *Studies in Comparative Communism* 3, no. 1 (January 1970): 47–54.

[7] Moore, *Soviet Politics*, p. 422. See also Zagoria, *The Sino-Soviet Conflict*, p. 26; Brzezinski, *The Soviet Bloc*, pp. 490–492.

[8] Richard Lowenthal in Brumberg, ed., *Russia under Khrushchev*, pp. 27–28.

[9] Brzezinski, *The Soviet Bloc*, p. 489.

[10] R. N. Carew Hunt in Brumberg, ed., *Russia under Khrushchev*, p. 10.

I

Formulation and Defense of Specific Features of the Yugoslav Communist Revolution

"It was no accident that from the beginning, however cautiously and modestly, in order not to insult or enrage the 'Olympian' gods in the Kremlin, we observed and stressed the specific character of our revolution and the specific character of our development. . . . "

Milovan Djilas, *Savremene teme*, 1950

1

The Soviet–East European Concept of People's Democracy

The Political Situation

At the end of World War II the leaders of the Communist Parties of Poland, Germany, Hungary, Rumania, and Bulgaria returned to their countries in the baggage train of the Red Army and assumed control of the "commanding heights" of society in dependence on the Soviet occupation forces.[1] These Communist Parties were burdened with a dual weakness that limited their radicalism in the initial postwar period. All faced significant, organized opposition to the consolidation of their rule, resistance being strongest in Poland and weakest in Bulgaria. This internal situation dictated a policy of gradualism, generalized by Hugh Seton-Watson[2] as encompassing three stages: (1) a genuine coalition with the surviving socialist and peasant parties resting on a short-term program of mutually accepted "antifascist" and "democratic" reforms (lasting until early 1945 in Bulgaria and Rumania and until early 1947 in Hungary); (2) a bogus coalition with the same parties, themselves increasingly dominated by Communists, implementing more radical social reforms and more openly suppressing the non-Communist opposition (lasting until late 1947 or early 1948); at this stage, socialism was spoken of only as a distant goal; economic planning was introduced but remained limited in scope; collectivization of agriculture was not mentioned; (3) a monolithic regime that, having liquidated its opposition, set out to emulate the Soviet Union in "building socialism" through forced industrialization and collectivization.

Another aspect of the weakness of the East European Communist Parties was their great dependence on the Soviet Union and thus their subordination to the broader goals of Soviet foreign policy. During the immediate postwar period, until 1947, Soviet foreign policy sought, by playing down its maximalist goals in Eastern Europe, gradually to increase Soviet influence in the rest of the world—particularly in France and Italy—at the expense of the Western powers and without provoking their reaction.[3] Thus the requirements of Soviet foreign policy, no less than the domestic political situation, necessitated a policy of gradualism on the part of the East European Communists.

The Doctrine of People's Democracy

The dual weakness of the East European Communist Parties was reflected in a new theoretical concept markedly at odds with the Marxist-Leninist classics—the concept of "people's democracy."

Marx, Lenin, and Stalin were relatively clear and in agreement on the social order that was to follow the breakup of capitalist society. As Marx stated in the *Critique of the Gotha Program:* "Between capitalist and communist society lies the period of the revolutionary transformation of the one into the other. There is a corresponding political transition period in which the state can be nothing but the *revolutionary dictatorship of the proletariat.*"[4] Lenin devoted most of *State and Revolution* to defending this view, concluding Chapter 2 with these words: "The forms of the bourgeois state are extremely varied, but in essence they are all the same; in one way or another, in the last analysis, all these states are inevitably the dictatorship of the bourgeoisie. The transition from capitalism to communism will certainly create a great variety and abundance of political forms, but in essence there will inevitably be only one: the dictatorship of the proletariat."[5] Whatever Marx's view, the dictatorship of the proletariat was given a specific interpretation in conditions of economic underdevelopment by Lenin and Stalin. It was defined as the transitional stage between capitalism and communism in which the proletariat—led by its vanguard, the Communist Party—having overthrown the bourgeois or even pre-bourgeois order by force of arms, set out to "build socialism": to create the economic preconditions for communism which capitalism had failed to realize, while simultaneously eliminating exploitation from society.

This scheme could not be reconciled with the reality of postwar Eastern Europe. Coalition governments existed, while land reform and partial nationalization of large-scale industry were only gradually changing the prewar socioeconomic order. Moreover, the Communist Parties owed their control of the key positions of political power, not to revolution, but, with the exceptions of Yugoslavia, Albania, and Czechoslovakia, to the advance of the Red Army. Thus the concept of the dictatorship of the proletariat was theoretically inapplicable.[6] Moreover, it would have been a political liability for the East European Communists—who lacked mass support in the interwar period (except in Czechoslovakia) and were condemned as "Bolsheviks" fomenting violent revolution by the majority of their countrymen—as they sought to consolidate their power.

In this situation, Communist leaders and theoreticians set out to develop a satisfactory theoretical alternative to the "dictatorship of the proletariat." The result was the concept of "people's democracy"—albeit never systematically formulated prior to its reinterpretation beginning in 1948—which emerged first in scattered statements of East European Communist leaders in 1945 and 1946 and then in limited theoretical generalizations made by a group of Soviet academicians in 1947.

It is possible to distinguish several instrumental motivations that guided the East European Communists in developing the doctrine of people's democracy. It would seem to have reflected rather well the mood of the population, including the mass of post-1945 new Party members, which was ready for far-reaching social change in the wake of prewar dictatorship (in every country except Czechoslovakia) and wartime destruction, but which had no desire to see a Stalinist revolution repeated at home. The theory clearly also took shape in part as a result of the efforts of East European Communist leaders to convince revolutionary Communists in their own Parties—many of whom were "natives" who had remained in their countries during World War II and had, in various degrees, engaged in resistance activities—that the gradualist coalition policy was not a betrayal of socialist goals.[7]

However, it may be suggested, the East European Communist leaders were not guided solely by tactical or instrumental considerations in formulating the concept of people's democracy; such an explanation would postulate a sharp separation of ideology from action, which, as noted in the Introduction, has not been characteristic of Communist politics. It must not be forgotten that the East European Communist leaders not only had to justify their power, which was of course still limited in differing degrees in the various countries; they also had to explain their positions of power when the expected precondition and consequence of that power, proletarian revolution and the development of socialism, were lacking.

The theoretical generalization of people's democracy formulated by Soviet academicians in 1947 apparently had a somewhat different motivation. This was, in part, a natural analytical response to a new theoretical phenomenon in the international Communist movement. But in their effort to generalize, the Soviet professors sought to minimize or refute some of the very gradualist formulations of the initial postwar period—for example, the claim that a people's democracy was only a progressive form of bourgeois state. This fact suggests a more directly political motivation for their scholarship: together with possible inter-Party communications, it indirectly conveyed to East European Communists (and to proponents of a gradualist line in the

USSR itself) the position of the Soviet leadership that the "genuine coalition" phase belonged to the past and that the consolidation of Communist power in Eastern Europe must proceed apace.

In theorizing about post-1945 Eastern Europe, the Soviet and East European Communists did not break with the Marxist-Leninist "classics" on the proletarian revolution and socialist transformation as sharply and uniquely as they themselves sometimes suggested. Aside from a number of minor precedents[8] they could have returned to the "popular front" line of the Seventh Comintern Congress,[9] particularly as put into practice in the Spanish Civil War. In Spain, too, Communist domestic policy had been dictated by the foreign policy interests ("antifascism") of the Soviet state, as well as by the preponderant strength of the non-Communist Spanish Republicans. Following the line of the Seventh Comintern Congress, the Spanish Communists and International Brigades had fought for a "new type of democratic republic" (Togliatti) and a "new type of democracy" (José Díaz Ramos), as opposed to the more orthodox, revolutionary slogans of the Spanish Anarchists, Trotskyites, and Left Socialists.[10] When in 1944 Communist Parties throughout the world, including those in Eastern Europe, adopted the coalition tactics dictated by Stalin, this precedent clearly was not forgotten.

The doctrine of people's democracy was also probably influenced by Mao Tse-tung's *On New Democracy* (1940). In that work, Mao wrote that the aim of the Chinese revolution was "a state under the joint dictatorship of all revolutionary classes" including, he implied, the "national bourgeoisie," forced to back the revolution for a long period because of its opposition to foreign imperialism. The "form" of the postrevolutionary state, according to Mao, could not be "the old European-American form of capitalist republic under bourgeois dictatorship" or "socialist republics of the type of the USSR, republics of the dictatorship of the proletariat," but "only a third [state form], namely the new democracy republic."[11] In *The Chinese Revolution and the Chinese Communist Party* (1939), Mao described the "new democracy" revolution as meaning "nationalization of all big capital and big enterprises . . . distribution of the land of landlords among the peasants, and at the same time the general preservation of private capitalist enterprises."[12] Pointing out the similarities between these ideas and the later concept of people's democracy, Benjamin Schwartz convincingly argued that East European and Soviet theoreticians—in particular, Eugene Varga, who (as described later) used the very phrase "new democracy"—drew on Mao's writings.[13]

In the following pages, the concept of people's democracy as it was understood in Eastern Europe prior to 1948 will be summarized under six points.[14]

1. *Uniqueness*

The people's democracies were held to be unique historical phenomena, the consequence of the special position of the East European states at the close of World War II, and as such something previously unknown to Marxism-Leninism. In the words of the Soviet Professor A. Leont'ev, "Such a form [people's democracy] was not foreseen and could not be foreseen by Marx and Lenin, because it was created by completely specific historical circumstances, by specific conditions which could not be foreseen."[15]

It was no wonder, then, that the essential characteristics of a people's democracy were open to debate. Prior to 1948 one group of Communists regarded the postwar East European states as simply "progressive" bourgeois states. This view was expressed by the Hungarian Central Committee member Márton Horváth: "In view of the fact that a people's democracy does not destroy private ownership of the means of production, it can simply be regarded as the most progressive form of bourgeois democracy (or, more correctly, its only progressive form)."[16] Varga, too, in 1946 treated the people's democracies as part of the capitalist world, describing their economies as state capitalism.[17] *(marked Socialism?)*

A second group of theoreticians held that a people's democracy was neither a capitalist nor a socialist state but a unique, intermediate transitional form. This was the most commonly accepted view all along; in 1947 it became obligatory when Varga was criticized in Moscow for his original position. As K. V. Ostrovitianov put it: "In the states of the new democracy we have a new phenomenon in principle."[18] Varga himself now wrote: "The social structure of these states differs from all those hitherto known to us; it is something totally new in the history of mankind. It is neither a bourgeois dictatorship nor a proletarian dictatorship."[19]

One sign of the ambiguity of the notion of an "intermediate" state order was the terminological confusion that resulted. The East European leaders themselves generally used "people's democracy." Varga favored "democracy of a new type" or simply "new democracy." Professor I. P. Trainin disagreed with this usage, suggesting instead the alternative "democracy of a special type."[20]

2. *Origins*

A people's democracy was held to be a new state order resulting from a "national democratic revolution" in the individual East European countries during 1944–1945. These revolutions, it was maintained, were led by the working class and were directed not only against the foreign invader but at the leaders of the prewar societies.[21]

The national democratic revolutions were thus not considered to be classic bourgeois democratic revolutions.[22] Nor were they considered socialist revolutions.[23] They were usually treated, like the people's democracies themselves, as unique historical phenomena, as something in between bourgeois and socialist revolutions. Only occasionally were they said to be the first phase of an incipiently socialist, permanent revolution, as when Leont'ev quoted Lenin on the absence of a "Chinese wall" between the bourgeois and socialist revolutions.[24]

The concept of the national democratic revolution was developed in an effort to provide some trace of revolutionary legitimacy for the new East European regimes while attempting to explain the far-reaching social changes that in fact resulted from the presence of the Red Army. There was no attempt to deny that presence. On the contrary, the Red Army—in its role both as "liberator" from the Axis invader and as an army of occupation—was seen as the motive force of the "revolution" and was explicitly described as *the* fundamental factor giving rise to the new "popular democratic" regimes. The Polish Communist leader Władysław Gomułka, for example, noted that transformation of Polish society could begin without an internal revolution because of the presence of the Red Army.[25] The national democratic revolution was, in short, indeed unique; it was a revolution from without.

3. *State Order*

As conceived by Marx and developed by Lenin, the proletarian revolution signified the total destruction, the "smashing" of the bourgeois state machine. Both had attacked the belief that the proletariat could take over and utilize the old state machinery. In the case of the people's democracies, it was patently obvious, however, that the old state apparatus had not been destroyed. Many parliamentary institutions and much of the prewar bureaucracy survived. Hungary and Rumania even remained formally monarchies until 1947. Faced with this dilemma, the theoreticians usually responded by denying the necessity of destroying the old state. Varga formulated this point quite clearly: "The old state apparatus has not been smashed, as in the Soviet

Union, but reorganized by means of a continuous inclusion in it of the supporters of the new regime."[26]

A further problem was the form of state organization. It was easy to define it negatively: "Bulgaria will not be a soviet republic," maintained Georgi Dimitrov, "it will be a people's republic."[27] The people's democracy did not incorporate the form of state organization based on the citizens' committee, such as the Paris commune and the soviets. Positive definitions of the new state organization were much vaguer; they usually affirmed the existence of a parliamentary republic in some form. In the speech just cited, Dimitrov maintained: "Our people are for a parliamentary republic which will not be a plutocratic republic." Varga generalized Dimitrov's assertion: "The rise of the states of new democracy shows clearly that it is possible to have political rule by the working people even while the outward forms of parliamentary democracy are still maintained."[28] While the state was said to exercise functions of class repression, economic organization, and education, none of these tasks was defined as clearly, nor was the state's role in their fulfillment made as exclusive, as in Stalin's formulations of the three functions of the Soviet state.[29]

4. *Economic Structure*
Just as the people's democracies were viewed in toto as hybrid states, so their economies were viewed as neither capitalist nor socialist but as mixed economies combining elements of both.[30] The elimination of "feudal survivals," the redistribution of land, partial nationalization, and the introduction of reconstruction planning were seen as modifying the capitalist economic order without replacing it entirely. In each East European country, the coexistence of three economic sectors—the state, the peasant and handicraft, and the capitalist—was asserted. The right of private property was guaranteed, though restricted by the state in its effort to limit (not abolish) "capitalist exploitation." While the capitalist sector had lost its predominant role in the economy, its importance was not to be denied. Polish Communist leader Bolesław Bierut explained the relationship between the state and capitalist sectors in the following words: "The essence of the new social and economic order consists in the specific harmony of two factors—on one hand, the leading role of the state, which controls the large-scale means of production and which is guided in its activity by the interests of the whole people, and on the other hand, the entrepreneurship, energy, and free initiative of the mass of individuals in agriculture and the

handicrafts, just as in medium and small-scale private shops and enterprises which are based on wage labor."[31] This rationale was reflected in the East European reconstruction plans. The Polish Three-Year Plan of 1947, for example, explicitly affirmed the coexistence of the three sectors.[32]

This mixed economy was said to be developing "in the direction of socialism"—since the state sector was decisive—but not yet "building socialism"; when the latter stage was reached, it was often suggested, it would be a gradual process quite unlike the Soviet experience. In Varga's words: "[The people's democracies] may, maintaining the present state apparatus, gradually pass over to socialism, developing to an ever-increasing extent the socialist sector which already exists side by side with the simple commodity sector (peasant and artisan) and the capitalist sector, which has lost its dominant position."[33] The ultimate fate of peasant agriculture in this process was usually passed over in silence.

5. Class Structure

In classic Marxist-Leninist doctrine, it was the task of the proletarian revolution to overthrow the ruling bourgeoisie. The victorious proletarian state had only to suppress the "remnants" of the deposed ruling class.

In the people's democracies, in contrast, the "progressive" bourgeoisie was—in the Communist view—still both strong and politically active, and this fact was reflected in the theoretical conception of the new state. It could hardly be otherwise with a doctrine that still admitted an important role for capitalists in a mixed economic system. Thus people's democracy encompassed the existence of "progressive" bourgeois parties and their participation in the parliamentary state organs. As Soviet Professor N. P. Farberov was to say of the former "exploiters": ". . . . the structure of society consists not only of the toiling classes who are in power; there are still preserved exploiting *classes*, too. . . ."[34]

But while "progressive" bourgeois parties existed, as time passed less pretense was made that they really shared power. The former ruling classes, including the bourgeoisie, had been deposed, and power was said to be in the hands of the "people"—sometimes defined as including the "progressive" or "patriotic" bourgeoisie but increasingly restricted to workers, peasants, and "people's intelligentsia." In Dimitrov's words, the leading role in the people's democracy was played by "the great majority of the people—the workers, peasants, artisans, and the people's intelligentsia."[35] It was usually pointed out, with varying degrees of emphasis, that the leading force of the people, so defined, was in fact the working class.[36] While such a formulation approached the orthodox Marxist-Leninist doctrine of the leading role of the proletariat, in alliance with the peasantry, in a socialist state, there was a significant difference between the two concepts. Stalin had formulated the relationship between the proletariat and its class ally in terms of the *"hegemony* of the proletariat within this alliance."[37] In the theory of people's democracy as propounded until 1948, in contrast, the emphasis was placed on the worker-peasant alliance itself rather than on the dominance of the working class. József Révai, a leading Hungarian Communist, expressed the idea in the following words: "The essence of state power of the people's democracy is the division of power between the working class and the working peasantry. . . . State power at present is not unified, homogenous state power in the sense that state power as a whole is not in the hands of one class."[38]

This treatment of the working class as the most important but not a hegemonic element in the people's democracy was reflected in the formulation of the Communist Party's role. In contrast to Stalin's dictum on the exclusive leading role of the Communist Party,[39] it was held that the Communist Party was the most important but not a hegemonic political party in a people's democracy.

The inapplicability of the classic Marxist-Leninist concept of the dictatorship of the proletariat to the people's democracies was pointed out earlier. And, in fact, referring to this class structure of the new states, the East European Communist leaders and Soviet academicians were unanimous in explicitly denying that the people's democracies were dictatorships of the proletariat.[40] In Trainin's words: ". . . what is the social essence of the democracy of a special type? Of course it is not proletarian (socialist) democracy. Proletarian democracy is identical with the dictatorship of the proletariat, which does not share power with other classes. . . ."[41]

6. *Specific National Road to Socialism*
People's democracy, as defined by the preceding five characteristics, signified the affirmation of a specific road to socialism, quite different from that described in the classics of Marxism-Leninism. It must be repeated, however, that the people's democracies were not considered to be actively "building socialism." While socialism was "on the

agenda," as the Communists often put it, at the present stage the people's democracies were said to be engaged in creating the preconditions for the development of socialism. In Soviet leader Andrei Zhdanov's mild words, taken from his otherwise militant report at the founding of the Cominform in September 1947, the people's democracies were "paving the way for entry onto the path of socialist development."[42] The Communist regimes, backed by the Soviet military presence and proceeding from the "popular democratic" social transformation of the initial postwar period, would develop their countries in the direction of socialism. The emphasis in this process, as already pointed out with reference to the economy, was on gradual change: "An evolutionary way of social change and an evolutionary transition to a socialist order is entirely possible."[43] It was never made very clear whether socialism—that is, the "full socialism" of 1936 in the Soviet scheme of development—would be reached in this way, but the usual implication was that gradual change would characterize the whole course of socialist development; a dictatorship of the proletariat would be avoided in a people's democracy.[44]

This concept of a specific road to socialism was given a further dimension of being in harmony with the unique *national* characteristics of the respective country—an emphasis reflecting the need of the East European Communists, burdened with their pasts as Soviet agents, to present themselves to their countrymen as the "best defenders" of national sovereignty. The Hungarian Communist leader Mátyás Rákosi expressed this idea very clearly:

During the last 25 years the Communist Parties of the world learned that there are several roads which lead to socialism and, . . . although socialism utilizes a wealth of international experiences, our socialism can be created only as a result of the development of Hungarian history and Hungarian economic, political, and social forces. That will be socialism born on Hungarian soil and adapted to Hungarian conditions.[45]

Somewhat later, nearly the same thing was said about Rumania; such statements could be cited for each of the East European states. However, no Hungarian spokesman, for example, ever suggested precisely how the Hungarian road to socialism might differ from the Rumanian or the Polish road; Polish Communist leader Edward Ochab indicated in December 1945 that Polish Communists "still cannot quite define" the "Polish road."[46] The people's democracies as a group were said to be following national roads to socialism, yet there was never any attempt to differentiate the substance of this development in the individual East European countries. This was so because the "national" roads to socialism were not primarily national at all but rather non-Soviet.

These six primary characteristics of a people's democracy indicate that the very concept, as developed between 1945 and 1948, was extremely ambiguous from a Marxist point of view. Some discrepancies between the theory of people's democracy and the Marxist-Leninist "classics" have been indicated. Yet, as an aid to understanding how the theory could be accepted by theoretically inclined Communists during these years, it should be repeated that "a clear-cut, theoretical, and well-reasoned analysis of the people's democracies, made within the context of Marxian ideology, was not elucidated systematically by the East European Communist leaders,"[47] or, really, by the Soviet professors. The very vagueness of the theory, then, was one of its strengths, allowing it to serve the instrumental and analytical purposes mentioned previously.

From another point of view, however, the basic rationale of the doctrine was not entirely new or entirely at odds with Stalinism. Stalin had, after all, transformed Soviet society from above, and this fact had found suitable expression in his glorification of the Soviet state and his subsequent attribution of primacy to the superstructure instead of the economic base of society.[48] It was only one (albeit self-contradictory)[49] step further to formulating a doctrine of *initiating* such a revolutionary transformation from above, though that transformation was envisaged in this stage as gradualist and unlike the Soviet path.

More important, uncodified as it was, the doctrine of people's democracy did closely reflect the reality of the imposition of Communist regimes in Eastern Europe with the aid and under the protection of the Red Army. The people's democracies explicitly traced their origins to the westward advance of Soviet troops at the end of World War II. The doctrine thus embodied the factual dependence of the East European Communists on the Soviet Union. It also embodied an "historical" aspect of subordination to the USSR. As much as the roads to socialism were said to vary, the final goal was still socialism, and the Soviet Union, being the only country where, it was claimed, socialism had been realized, was still a historically more progressive society, whose experience, if not copied, certainly could not be ignored.[50]

Notes

[1] The best summaries of the Communist seizure of power in Eastern Europe are Hugh Seton-Watson, *The East European Revolution* (New York: Praeger, 1951); Brzezinski, *The Soviet Bloc,* chap. 1; Richard V. Burks, "Eastern Europe," in C. E. Black and T. P. Thornton, eds., *Communism and Revolution* (Princeton, N.J.: Princeton University Press, 1965).

[2] Seton-Watson, *The East European Revolution,* pp. 167–171.

[3] See Marshall D. Shulman, *Stalin's Foreign Policy Reappraised* (Cambridge, Mass.: Harvard University Press, 1963), pp. 13–20.

[4] Marx/Engels, *Ausgewählte Schriften* ([East] Berlin, 1954) 2:25.

[5] V. I. Lenin, *State and Revolution* (New York: International Publishers, 1932), p. 31.

[6] This point is made in Brzezinski, *The Soviet Bloc,* p. 26.

[7] Shortly after returning to Hungary from Moscow in late 1944, Mátyás Rákosi, invoking Stalin's authority, defended the coalition policy against the "1919-ers" or "native" revolutionary Communists in the Hungarian Party. (Speech of February 11, 1945, quoted in McCagg, "Communism and Hungary," pp. 245–246.) McCagg analyzes at length the differences between Rákosi and the "leftists" in the Hungarian Party. For a survey of similar revolutionary sentiment in the Rumanian and Czechoslovak Parties, see Burks in Black and Thornton, eds., *Communism and Revolution,* pp. 83–86. Władysław Gomułka attacked at length the "sectarian position of some comrades" in his May 27, 1945, speech to Polish Party functionaries. (Władysław Gomułka, *Artykuły i Przemówienia* [Warsaw, 1962–] 1:256–287.)

[8] The Bukharan, Khorezmian, and Far Eastern republics of the early 1920s were called "people's republics." (Richard Pipes, *The Formation of the Soviet Union* [Cambridge: Harvard University Press, 1954], pp. 254–255.) Mongolia had remained an anomaly for Soviet theoreticians; it was described in the *Politicheski Slovar'* (1940) as "a bourgeois-democratic republic of a new type, laying the foundations for a gradual transition to the path of non-capitalist development." (Quoted in H. G. Skilling, "People's Democracy in Soviet Theory," *Soviet Studies* 3, nos. 1 and 2 [July, October 1951]: 16–33, 131–149, at 22.)

[9] The Resolution of the Seventh Comintern Congress of August 28, 1935, called for the formation of "a proletarian united-front government, or an anti-fascist popular-front government, which is not yet a government of the proletarian dictatorship. . . ." (Jane Degras, ed., *The Communist International 1919–1943, Documents* [London: Oxford University Press, 1956–1965] 3:365.) This was a partial revival of the concept of "workers' government" contained in the "Theses on Tactics" adopted by the Fourth Comintern Congress on December 5, 1922. In certain circumstances, the Fourth Congress sanctioned the formation of workers' governments with non-Communists; two of three possible types were said not to be dictatorships of the proletariat, since "workers' government that is not Communist" could not be considered a dictatorship of the proletariat. (Degras, ed., *The Communist International* 1:427; see also Kermit E. McKenzie, *Comintern and World Revolution, 1928–1943* [New York: Columbia University Press, 1964], pp. 154–156; Arthur A. Cohen, *The Communism of Mao Tse-tung* [Chicago: University of Chicago Press, 1964], pp. 84–86, 94–95.)

[10] David T. Cattell, *Communism and the Spanish Civil War* (Berkeley and Los Angeles: University of California Press, 1955), pp. 90–93. Nevertheless, the "new type of democracy" was admitted to be only a transitional stage to a dictatorship of the proletariat.

[11] Mao Tse-tung, "On New Democracy," *Selected Works* (New York: International Publishers, 1954) 3: esp. 118–119. See also Cohen, *The Communism of Mao Tse-tung,* pp. 74–104.

[12] Mao Tse-tung, "The Chinese Revolution and the Chinese Communist Party," *Selected Works* 3: esp. 96–97.

[13] Benjamin Schwartz, "China and the Soviet Theory of People's Democracy," *Problems of Communism* 3, no. 5 (September–October 1954): 8–15.

[14] This section is based largely on the following studies: Skilling, "People's Democracy in Soviet Theory"; Brzezinski, *The Soviet Bloc,* chap. 2; Edvard Kardelj, "O narodnoj demokratiji u Jugoslaviji," *Komunist* 3, no. 4 (July 1949): 1–83. See also Francis J. Kase, *People's Democracy* (Leyden: A. W. Sijthoff, 1968).

[15] A. Leont'ev, "Ekonomicheskie osnovy novoi demokratii," *Planovoe khoziaistvo* no. 4 (1947): 63–79, at 69. Gomułka declared in November 1946: "Our democracy and the social order we are constructing and strengthening have no historical precedent. . . ." (*Nowe Drogi,* January 1947, pp. 4–14, at 12.)

[16] *Társadalmi Szemle* 1, no. 10 (October 1946): 693–701, at 694.

[17] E. Varga, *Izmeneniia v ekonomike kapitalizma v itoge vtoroi mirivoi voiny* (Moskow, 1946). Even after Varga modified his view, some Soviet writers still classified the people's democracies as exploitative states.

[18] *Mirovoe khoziaistvo i mirovaia politika* no. 11 (1947): supplement, p. 58.

[19] E. Varga, "Demokratiia novogo tipa," *Mirovoe khoziaistvo i mirovaia politika* no. 3 (1947): 3–14, at 3.

[20] I. P. Trainin, "Demokratiia osobogo tipa," *Sovetskoe gosudarstvo i pravo* no. 1 (1947): 1–15, and no. 3 (1947): 1–14, at no. 1:4. Trainin maintained that the first such "democracy of a special type" had been the Spanish Republic of 1936–1938 (no. 1:2–4). For a discussion of the terms applied to the world-wide Communist coalition strategy, see McCagg, "Communism and Hungary," chap. 4, who correctly notes that the Yugoslav Communists advocated the term "people's democracy" as a radical concept after mid-1945 but misinterprets the Soviet reaction to their initiative and ignores the continued use of other terms, such as "new democracy," after that date. Finnish and Hungarian Communists used the term "people's democracy" in late 1944. Its exact origin is uncertain; the earliest reference known to the author is the June 1943 proclamation of the Greek Communist Party on the dissolution of the Comintern (cited in *Komunist* 3, no. 6 [November 1949]: 31). The Czech Communist historian Kopecký claimed that when Eduard Beneš visited Moscow in December 1943, "he dropped his earlier objections to the term 'people's democracy.' " (V. Kopecký, *KSČ & ČSR* [Prague, 1957], p. 329.)

[21] Skilling, *Soviet Studies* 3, no. 1: 29.

[22] In Marxist historiography most of the area had passed through this stage in the nineteenth century.

[23] Klement Gottwald stated in a confidential speech in 1945: "We must continually remind ourselves that in the present phase we are following the line of the national and democratic, and not the line of the socialist revolution." (K. Gottwald, *Deset let* [Prague, 1948], p. 284.)

[24] *Planovoe khoziaistvo* no. 4 (1947): 79.

[25] Speech of December 7, 1945, *Artykuły i Przemówienia,* 1:512. In January 1946, attacking the "leftists" in the Hungarian Party, Rákosi denied that Hungary had experienced a revolution in any sense: "All the time people are telling me that what happened in Hungary [in 1944–1945] was really a revolution; and they are accordingly praising and criticizing everything that happened as if it were a revolution. Their error could not be greater. What happened last year was a great change. Still, the shackles which bound the Hungarian people hand and foot were not shattered by our own liberating forces, but by the Red Army. Let us never forget this. It makes a great difference, Comrades. Had we freed ourselves, as say our Yugoslav neighbors did, with a revolution, there would have been a tremendous inner strength to the Hungarian democracy. . . . He who regards the

liberation as a revolution will necessarily make rather serious mistakes." (Speech of January 19, 1946, cited in McCagg, "Communism and Hungary," p. 276.) Bolesław Bierut was later to declare that the presence of the Red Army was an integral characteristic of the Polish "people's democracy."
[26] *Mirovoe khoziaistvo i mirovaia politika* no. 3 (1947): 3. Trainin reacted differently, pointing to Yugoslavia and Bulgaria as proof of the necessity of destroying the old state machine. (Trainin, *Sovetskoe gosudarstvo i pravo* no. 1 (1947): 7, and no. 3 (1947): 6–10.)
[27] Radio address of September 7, 1946, *Sachineniia* 12 (Sofia, 1954): 292.
[28] *Mirovoe khoziaistvo i mirovaia politika* no. 3 (1947): 13.
[29] J. V. Stalin, *Problems of Leninism* (Moscow, 1954), pp. 196–197.
[30] In his 1946 book, Varga depicted the economy of a people's democracy as state capitalism, but he modified this view in his 1947 article.
[31] Kraków speech of July 1946, quoted in Kardelj, *Komunist* 3, no. 4: 12.
[32] Nicolas Spulber, *The Economics of Communist Eastern Europe* (Cambridge, Mass., and New York: Technology Press and Wiley, 1957), p. 64.
[33] *Mirovoe khoziaistvo i mirovaia politika* no. 3 (1947): 3.
[34] N. P. Farberov, *Gosudarstvennoe pravo stran narodnoi demokratii* (Moscow, 1949), p. 43 (emphasis added).
[35] Georgi Dimitrov, *Govori, članci i izjave* (Belgrade, 1947), p. 318.
[36] While Varga spoke only of the "political domination of the working people," Trainin, apparently the most extreme, affirmed that the political hegemony of the working class had in fact been achieved, although with different consequences than in the USSR. See Brzezinski, *The Soviet Bloc*, p. 30.
[37] Stalin, *Problems of Leninism*, p. 161.
[38] *Informatsionnyi biulleten'* TSK MPT, no. 8 (1948): 14, cited in Kardelj, *Komunist* 3, no. 4: 9.
[39] ". . . the leader in the state, the leader in the system of the dictatorship of the proletariat is one party, the party of the proletariat, the party of the Communists, which *does not and cannot share* leadership with other parties." (Stalin, *Problems of Leninism*, p. 160).
[40] E.g., Varga, *Mirovoe khoziaistvo i mirovaia politika* no. 3 (1947): 3; Gomułka, Speech of November 30, 1946, *Nowe Drogi*, January 1947, p. 12; Leont'ev, *Planovoe khoziaistvo* no. 4 (1947): 68–69.
[41] *Sovetskoe gosudarstvo i pravo* no. 1 (1947): 12.
[42] A. Zhdanov, *O mezhdunarodnom polozhenii* ([Moscow], 1947), p. 8.
[43] Gomułka, Speech of December 7, 1945, *Artykuły i Przemówienia*, 1: 515. Or as Révai put it: "This development toward socialism is undoubtedly slower than the tempo which we followed in 1919, but, comrades, for the good of the intelligentsia, the peasantry, the little man, for the good of the entire working people, we gladly proceed more slowly but less painfully toward socialism, instead of going faster at the price of a bloody civil war." (Speech to the Third Hungarian Party Congress, cited in Kardelj, *Komunist* 3, no. 4: 8.)
[44] Dimitrov explicitly claimed this in September 1946. (*Rabotnichesko Delo*, September 13, 1946.) Gottwald made the same claim, addressing the Central Committee of the Czechoslovak Communist Party the same month. (Gottwald, *Deset let*, p. 349.)
[45] Speech to the Third Hungarian Party Congress, cited in Kardelj, *Komunist* 3, no. 4: 7.
[46] E. Ochab, *Wieś polska na nowych drogach* (Warsaw, 1946), p. 46.
[47] Brzezinski, *The Soviet Bloc*, p. 29. Wolfgang Leonhard commented: "Until early 1948, the definition of the content and essence of the concept 'people's democracy' was one of the few unsolved problems for which there was not yet an official correct line." (Wolfgang Leonhard, *Die Revolution entlässt ihre Kinder* [Berlin: Kippenheuer & Witsch, 1955], p. 482.)

[48] See, inter alia, his *Report to the Eighteenth Congress of the CPSU* (1939), *Concerning Marxism in Linguistics* (1950), and *Economic Problems of Socialism in the USSR* (1952).

[49] See Kase, *People's Democracy,* pp. 40–41.

[50] For this point, see Brzezinski, *The Soviet Bloc,* p. 36.

2

The Yugoslav Concept of People's Democracy

The Political Situation in Yugoslavia

In the aftermath of World War II, as described at the outset of Chapter 1, Communist Parties seized power in most of Eastern Europe. The one exception was Yugoslavia (with its semisatellite Albania). The Yugoslav Communists seized power, not after the war, but during the course of the war itself.[1] The day Hitler launched his attack on the Soviet Union, June 22, 1941, the Communist Party of Yugoslavia (CPY) appealed for armed resistance "under the leadership of the Communist Party of Yugoslavia."[2] In fact, scattered opposition to the occupation powers and domestic puppet regimes had begun immediately after the collapse and fragmentation of the state apparatus in the wake of the German attack on Yugoslavia on April 6, 1941. The first organized resistance was conducted by General Draža Mihailović's *četnici* (Chetniks)—groups of the Royal Yugoslav Army who had taken to the hills rather than surrender to the Germans. The Communists, who had prepared for armed struggle prior to June 22, soon organized their own resistance groups, the *partizani* (Partisans); and the two forces—separately and in collaboration— harassed the occupation forces in Western Serbia during the second half of 1941.

The Communists enjoyed several advantages over their temporary allies in waging such guerrilla warfare: (1) Persecution at the hands of the royalist dictatorship during the 1930's had thoroughly trained them in underground operations. (2) Participation of a Yugoslav International Brigade in the Spanish Civil War had created a cadre with combat experience in an unconventional war. (3) Josip Broz Tito, appointed Secretary-General of the CPY in 1937 by Moscow with orders to create unity in the faction-ridden Party, had built up a disciplined apparatus—though no mass following—in many parts of the multinational country. (4) In a situation of national fratricide, the CPY advanced an all-Yugoslav program of "brotherhood and unity"; the Chetniks, on the other hand, were exclusively Serbian in outlook. (5) Equally important, the Communists were not deterred from fighting by mass reprisals in response to their raids. Their goal was a new social order as well as national liberation; mass reprisals had the effect of destroying the remaining shreds of the prewar social fabric while, in their view, only rallying more of the masses to their standard against the occupation powers. Mihailović, on the other hand, believed such a policy was madness, a senseless decimation of the population in the interest of a Communist-fomented civil war.

Their diverging viewpoints led the Partisans and the Chetniks into armed conflict as early as November 1941. Thereafter, as the Partisans gained strength, Mihailović entered into de facto collaboration (and some of his subordinates into open cooperation) with the Germans and Italians against them. This discredited the Chetniks in the eyes of a segment of the population; more important, it discredited them in the eyes of the British, who transferred their support from Mihailović to Tito in 1943. The subsequent Allied aid to the Partisans, coupled with their being in a position to seize surrendered Italian arms in late 1943, meant that by 1944 the military supremacy of the Partisans over the Chetniks was complete.

The growing military strength of the Partisan movement had direct domestic political repercussions. Since 1941 the Communists had been setting up "people's liberation committees" in combat zones as a means of mobilizing the local population; the committees were not only resistance organs but also—as Edvard Kardelj wrote in October 1941—"provisional organs of government."[3] A new army was also organized; the original, largely spontaneous Partisan territorial detachments were supplemented by disciplined and mobile "proletarian brigades." The Partisan movement as a whole was called the People's Liberation Movement; its activities, the People's Liberation Struggle. While its leadership included non-Communist leftist politicians, it was not—with the exception of the Slovene organization until early 1942—a coalition of political forces; only the Communist Party, which openly proclaimed its leadership role, was separately organized. The People's Liberation Movement was, in short, a classic example of the "united front from below."

By the fall of 1942, Tito was prepared to proclaim this apparatus an embryonic government; Soviet opposition forced him to wait until November 1943, when AVNOJ (the Anti-Fascist Council of the People's Liberation of Yugoslavia) proclaimed itself "the supreme legislative and executive body of Yugoslavia" without the USSR having been previously informed.[4] As the Partisans extended their control over more territory, the new state apparatus spread. It took over civil administration in the parts of Serbia occupied by the Red Army in late 1944.

Desiring Western recognition and pressured by the USSR, Tito consented—in the Tito-Šubašić agreements—to the inclusion of five representatives of the London government-in-exile in his first postwar cabinet. He had no intention of honoring the agreement,[5] however, and thus—in the absence of effective Allied intervention—it had little effect on the internal political situation. The representatives of the London government had no organizational base from which to rally political support, and, one by one, they resigned or were forced out of the cabinet. In mid-1945 the last individual anti-Communist opposition was suppressed, and single-slate elections were held in November 1945.

Thus there was a clear divergence between the Communist seizure of power in Yugoslavia and in the rest of Eastern Europe. First, the Communist take-over occurred sooner in Yugoslavia than elsewhere. Second, the CPY (with its Albanian semisatellite) came to power largely on its own, and not in the wake of Soviet occupation, as did the other East European Communist Parties (except the Czechoslovak Party, which nevertheless benefited from Soviet occupation of two-thirds of Czechoslovakia in 1945 and exploited the encirclement of the country by Soviet troops in 1948). Third, the Yugoslav Communist road to power was one of protracted armed struggle against both an occupation power and domestic opposition forces. This distinguished the Yugoslav from the Czechoslovak case; the Czechoslovak Communists seized power in a coup d'état. In these two different sets of circumstances, Tito, who was Moscow's choice to revive the dying CPY in 1937, could develop an organizational autonomy from the Kremlin; the other East European Communist leaders could not.

The Yugoslav Doctrine of People's Democracy

The uniqueness in Europe of the Communist seizure of power in Yugoslavia was reflected in the Yugoslav Communists' theorizing about their wartime struggle and the new postwar state. The CPY formulated a concept of people's democracy which was not identical with the one expounded in the rest of Eastern Europe and the Soviet Union.

Whereas Soviet and other East European spokesmen could not agree on which term best described the new states in Eastern Europe, the Yugoslavs consistently used "people's democracy."[6] In Yugoslav usage, people's democracy did not mean "something wholly new in the history of mankind." On the other hand, before the Cominform Resolution of June 28, 1948, which expelled Yugoslavia from the Soviet bloc, the term was not explicitly equated with a dictatorship of the proletariat. Thus analysis of the concept must begin with the content the Yugoslav leadership gave it between 1945 and 1948, and consideration of the relationship between the Yugoslav concept of people's democracy and the dictatorship of the proletariat must be postponed.[7] This analysis will differentiate five essential characteristics of people's democracy and examine each in turn.

1. *Origins in the People's Liberation Struggle*[8]

Since the postwar Yugoslav state was considered to be the creation of the Partisan struggle, its essence could be grasped only if the significance of the struggle itself were correctly understood. But had it been a Partisan uprising, a patriotic antifascist struggle, a civil war, or something else entirely? Tito himself posed the question: "What was the specific character of the liberation struggle and revolutionary transformation of new Yugoslavia?" In Tito's 1946 article bearing this title[9] and in a series of other articles and speeches, the CPY leaders attempted to explain and justify, in however fragmentary form, their seizure of power.

The People's Liberation Struggle was seen by the Yugoslav Communists as having been waged in a special set of domestic and international circumstances. Internally, the exploitative prewar regime culminated its oppression of the people by fleeing the country in 1941, abandoning them to the mercy of the fascist invader without any means of self-defense. The flight of the old regime and enemy invasion led to the disintegration of a large part of the state apparatus. It simultaneously exposed to the masses the unpatriotic nature of the ruling bourgeoisie.[10]

These special internal conditions were complemented—in the Yugoslav Communist view—by the special international constellation of World War II. Ignoring the role of the Western powers in the war, the Yugoslav Communists glorified the Soviet Union, whose very existence was said to have inspired the Yugoslav masses in their struggle and whose general role in the war as the chief military opponent of Nazi Germany was seen as the precondition for that struggle.[11]

Yet this praise had its limits. Although CPY spokesmen consistently spoke of the Soviet army in the standard Communist terminology of the day as the "Red Army Liberator," in fact they devoted little attention to its role on Yugoslav territory. In the first months after the war, Yugoslav statements did acknowledge the help of the Soviet army in the liberation of Belgrade and part of Serbia.[12] But after 1945 they usually neglected to include even pro forma acknowledgment of Soviet military assistance in Yugoslavia, often omitting any mention of the Soviet military presence in Eastern Europe in general.[13]

In so minimizing and even ignoring the direct Soviet military role in Yugoslavia (limited as that role in fact had been), the Yugoslav Communists sought to emphasize the autonomous nature of their struggle. In the specific circumstances of World War II, the People's Liberation Movement had itself freed the country of the invader. This was made clear in the initial postwar months when acknowledgment of Soviet (and even Western) aid was still made. Tito, for example, concluded his address to the Third Session of AVNOJ in August 1945 with these words: "The greatest and most difficult task was carried out by our glorious Army which, at the price of enormous sacrifices, fought to liberate our country and finally liberated it, aided materially by our allies and materially and militarily by the glorious Red Army."[14] Moreover, the Yugoslav People's Liberation Struggle had also affected the very character of World War II, contributing to the general victory over fascism and to its character of a war of liberation instead of an imperialist war.[15]

The Yugoslav Communists described their liberation struggle as more than a traditional national uprising against an invader. It was both a struggle for national liberation and, in its original form, a sociopolitical revolution—designated a "people's democratic revolution" or simply "people's revolution." This was true, they made clear, because in the course of the Yugoslav self-liberation qualitative social changes had occurred equal to those produced by revolution in its classic form of civil war.[16] Indeed, as Milovan Djilas pointed out, this gave the Yugoslav uprising its original character: ". . . in the course of the People's Liberation Struggle, in the course of a national war against the occupier, questions were solved for which a revolution would have been required in peaceful times (the question of power, the nationality question)."[17]

The perceived class nature of the people's democratic revolution was seldom discussed explicitly, but pronouncements on the People's Front, the mass organization through which the Party sought to mobilize the Yugoslav peoples in support of its platform, shed some light on the issue. The People's Front, described as a unique organizational form of the class alliance between the working class and its revolutionary allies, was sharply differentiated from the popular fronts of the 1930s and the postwar people's fronts elsewhere in Eastern Europe. Yugoslav doctrine stressed the absolute leading role of the Communist Party—the only separately organized force—in the Front. As Tito told the Second Congress of the People's Front, the CPY had "organized the People's Front and entered the struggle at its head."[18] Furthermore, the

People's Front, he maintained, had not been an alliance or coalition with the "progressive" bourgeoisie or other independent political forces, for the bourgeoisie *as a whole* had opposed the liberation struggle.[19] It could act no differently; its "treason" was class-motivated. This point was made by Boris Kidrič in 1945:

In old Yugoslavia. . . the anti-popular reactionaries, the social and political leaders, for *class* reasons, lost any capability of representing at all successfully the national interests of the Yugoslav state. . . . Social reaction became national reaction; the upper social strata completely disintegrated in the national realm as well, the realm which they once considered their exclusive domain. Bourgeois nationalism, as the ideology of the ruling strata—regardless of its separatist or imperialistic nauances—ended its development with capitulation and treason.[20]

The lesson was drawn by Kardelj: "An ordinary coalition among [several] parties cannot mobilize the masses, because it is based on a compromise at the top."[21] This applied not only to bourgeois parties but also to peasant or petit bourgeois parties, which—Kidrič asserted—were inevitably dominated by reactionary elements.[22] Finally, only militants could enter such a "united front from below"; the test was active struggle against the enemy, which alone could unmask the "democrats and patriots in words" who seemed to support the liberation struggle while in fact only awaiting liberation from the Western powers and the return of the domestic reactionaries.[23]

Stressing the absence of coalition, Yugoslav pronouncements on the People's Front placed emphasis on the role of the "worker-peasant alliance" in the seizure of power. While in theory Lenin sometimes affirmed the importance of the worker-peasant alliance in the overthrow of the old society, Leninism in practice, as manifested in the October Revolution, had meant that the Communist Party seized power in the major cities with the support of workers and soldiers and then, holding the keys of power, gradually consolidated its rule throughout the predominantly peasant country. In Yugoslav Communist doctrine, the worker-peasant alliance was a precondition of the seizure of power itself. The class relationship within the alliance was not in question; there could be no doubt about the leading role of the proletariat. But without the class ally the old social order could not be overthrown; the doctrine thus gave more credit than did Leninism to the revolutionary role of the peasantry, under Communist Party leadership, in an occupied underdeveloped country: "The peasantry, the broad working masses of the rural population, proved themselves between 1941 and 1945 to be truly the main army of the People's Liberation Movement, without which the movement itself would not have existed."[24]

It seems that, as Djilas later suggested, the CPY leadership was aware of the uniqueness of its interpretation. "In describing the development of the uprising in Yugoslavia," Djilas wrote of a conversation in Moscow in 1944, ". . . I made a special point of stressing the new revolutionary role of the peasantry; I practically reduced the uprising in Yugoslavia to a tie between a peasant rebellion and the Communist *avant-garde.*"[25]

As implied in the preceding analysis, the people's revolution was not considered to be a bourgeois democratic revolution under proletarian hegemony, for the revolution had been directed against the bourgeoisie. Its antibourgeois character was further stressed in commentaries on the large-scale confiscation of the property of "collaborationists" during 1944 and 1945. (Eighty percent of industry, almost all wholesale trade, and the decisive share of banking were confiscated before the enactment of the first nationalization law in December 1946.)[26] This act was not intended simply to punish German or Italian sympathizers, Boris Kidrič declared in 1946, but was also "a specific form of 'expropriation of the expropriators,' expropriation on the broadest patriotic basis in the fatherland war. . . ."[27] Nevertheless, the goals of this anticapitalist people's revolution were not originally specified; Yugoslav Communist spokesmen limited themselves to asserting that it had initiated needed social reform and was still in progress.[28]

Only with the adoption of the Five-Year Plan in early 1947 and the official proclamation of "building socialism" did the CPY indicate clearly that it considered its revolution to be a socialist one. The imperialist connections of the deposed bourgeoisie were now stressed, while it was said that a qualitative social transformation resulting from the liberation struggle had signified not only the overthrow of the old ruling class but the end of the capitalist system, "clearing the way for unhampered development toward socialism."[29]

"People's revolution" was still used instead of "socialist revolution." But the two terms were clearly synonymous in Yugoslav Communist eyes. As Kardelj put it, addressing the founding conference of the Cominform: ". . . the development of the people's liberation uprising and people's government in Yugoslavia represents a specific example of tying (and thus strengthening) a people's liberation war with the process of a people's democratic revolution—led by the working class—which has developed toward higher, socialist forms. . . . The people's democratic revolution was interlaced with socialist forms, which today predominate."[30] The implication was that the revolution, socialist in content from the beginning, had originally manifested itself in "forms" more "popular democratic" than socialist; in the postwar period the balance had shifted, with socialist forms predominating. At the same time, the Yugoslavs explicitly rejected the definition (prevalent elsewhere in Eastern Europe) of the national democratic revolution as a distinct "middle stage" between the bourgeois democratic and socialist revolutions.[31]

Clearly suggesting (after early 1947) that their revolution was socialist, the Yugoslav Communists simultaneously emphasized its specific features. It was pointed out that the October Revolution, too, had generated its own specific forms adapted to particular Russian historical conditions.[32] Thus historically conditioned forms could not be confused with the "essence" of the revolution, which was the same in both cases. "The revolution in Yugoslavia began in completely different conditions than the October Revolution; the unfolding of the revolution in Yugoslavia was different and its basic tasks were fulfilled with different means. But *in terms of its results* it had for the Yugoslav peoples the same domestic political significance that the October Revolution had for the Soviet peoples: it opened for the Yugoslav peoples the path to socialism."[33] Although the October Revolution remained the first socialist revolution, whose world historical importance could never be equaled, the socialist essence of the Yugoslav revolution was just as great—not in spite of its specific features but precisely *because* it had been adapted to Yugoslav conditions, just as the October Revolution had been suited to Russian conditions. Thus the CPY proclaimed the specific features of its revolution as merits, not liabilities, in terms of socialist legitimacy.

2. State Organs

The people's liberation committees, created during World War II, were said by the Yugoslav Communists to have been dual organs; not only were they organs of resistance; they were, at the same time, organs of government. Although until November 1943 the committees had been treated as provisional local organs of government, Moša Pijade maintained that by the end of 1942 this qualification was academic and that, because of their wartime role, they were the "only possible organs of the new people's government."[34] The people's liberation committees were, in short, the organs by means of which a new state apparatus was built up on the ruins of the old—not a spontaneous process, it was stressed, but one directed by the Communist Party.[35]

In 1946 the Communist regime enacted a new Constitution, which formally abolished the prewar Yugoslav state and proclaimed the people's committee (the adjective "liberation" was dropped) to be the basis of the new governmental structure, called a people's republic.[36] The General Law on the People's Committees, enacted later in 1946, sharply differentiated the people's republic as a form of government from the prewar bourgeois state.[37] Authoritative legal commentaries on the people's committees further stressed the distinction, maintaining that a new type of state had arisen much "higher" in form than the old.[38]

In Yugoslav writings on the people's committees, the debt to Leninist-Stalinist doctrine and the practice of the Soviet state was openly acknowledged.[39] While the people's committees were not equated with soviets, the Yugoslavs emphasized that they were not inferior institutionally. Djilas made this point in 1946 in attacking two "mistaken views" of the committees: "The present people's committees are [mistakenly] viewed either as a stage, a level toward some distant, higher—to put it frankly—soviet government or else as already finished, perfected organs of government."[40] The committees thus were not an "intermediate form" but the organs of government appropriate to the new state; they remained only to be perfected.[41]

At the same time, the Yugoslavs were quick to condemn the prevailing East European doctrine that prewar parliamentary institutions had been preserved essentially unchanged. Kardelj made this clear at the founding of the Cominform:

Sometimes it is heard from poorly informed people that the new democracy is in fact the old parliamentary democratic form with a new content. As far as Yugoslavia is concerned, such a contention does not at all correspond to reality. Characteristic of the development of people's democracy in Yugoslavia, inter alia, is precisely the fact that it did not develop through the forms of bourgeois parliamentary democracy. People's democracy in Yugoslavia . . . represents in fact a specific form of soviet democracy corresponding to our conditions.[42]

Kardelj defined this specific character as resulting primarily from the broad mass base of the committees—from the fact that, unlike the early soviets, there was no restricted franchise in their election.

The people's committees, as the political organs of the new postwar state, were complemented by a new military apparatus—the People's Army (YPA). Yugoslav Communist doctrine on the army, too, began with its revolutionary origins. The Yugoslavs rejected being characterized exclusively as "partisans." The point was that the original partisan detachments of 1941 had developed into a full-fledged army—not a conventional fighting force but, all the same, a disciplined organization of maneuverable units capable of combining guerrilla and frontal warfare. In Kardelj's words:

Comrade Tito, as Supreme Commander of the partisan detachments, from the very beginning set forth a clear course of forming regular units. The original partisan detachments were more or less restricted to a definite area and led by fixed territorial commands. . . . It was clear that to stop with the original partisan detachments would have meant to lose the battle. It was necessary to create an army which would be capable of not only harassing the enemy but of defeating him, an army able to win. It was necessary to create an army capable of waging frontal warfare, able to occupy the cities and fortifications, and to liberate the country.[43]

This army had been formed, according to the Yugoslav leaders, in the very process of fighting, and its formation was inseparable from that of the new organs of government. Originally lacking a government, territory, or resources, the army played a vital role in creating them all. It faced a dual task: "war on the front, while organizing the rear."[44] It was composed largely of peasants, since most of the people were peasants, but it was said to owe its mobility as well as its working-class direction to the "proletarian brigades" of workers who had fled the cities.

At the end of the war, Tito turned to the task of modernizing his army, drawing upon the alliance with the Soviet Union for supply of modern armaments and instruction in their use. But at the same time, he did not mean to turn the YPA into a purely conventional fighting force—a simple copy of the Red Army. Always stressing, in speeches devoted to military affairs, the need to study Soviet military experience, Tito would then mention the "second important factor," the partisan tradition, which, he insisted, was not obsolete. He thus formulated the task of the armed forces periodical, *Narodna armija*, as "imparting to our young Yugoslav Army examples of the heroic struggle of our partisan detachments and the People's Liberation Army. . . . future generations as well must use these examples . . . for only a modern army having these traits is unconquerable."[45] Djilas made the same point in 1946, stressing that there was much to learn from the Red Army, "not forgetting at the same time our valuable experience from the war, not neglecting that inexhaustible reservoir of wartime Partisan skill, bravery, dedication, and close ties with the people—all of which made us unconquerable."[46]

But the Soviet military advisers did not share the Yugoslavs' respect for the Partisan tradition; their task was to encourage the transformation of the YPA into a conventional fighting force modeled on the Red Army and, in the process, to subordinate it to Soviet control.[47] While the first manifestations of this attitude were viewed by the Yugoslavs as individual incidents, by late 1947 they were seen as part of a general pattern. At a meeting of leading Communists inside and outside the army, Svetozar Vukmanović-Tempo (wartime Political Commissar in the army and subsequently head of its Political Administration) declared that the army would continue to base itself primarily on its own Partisan experience. But the Soviet military advisers continued their effort to thwart this policy.[48] Tito chose December 22, 1947, as the occasion to take a public stand on the issue. This date was, for the first time, celebrated as Yugoslav Army Day; the public ceremonies were devoted to glorifying the Partisan heritage and proclaiming the limited applicability of Soviet military doctrine to Yugoslavia. Tito's own public words were characteristically mild, as he asserted only the need for the army to base itself "on the glorious traditions of both our army and the Soviet Army" (thus putting Soviet experience in second place).[49] It was left to Vukmanović-Tempo to speak more bluntly. After tracing the unique revolutionary origins of the YPA, Vukmanović proclaimed that its heritage was still of relevance. The YPA had to study Marxism-Leninism and Soviet military science. But this was not sufficient: " . . . without a fundamental knowledge of the political, economic, geographical, and historical conditions in our country, without a fundamental study of our wartime experiences, of the specific features in the development of our army, neither Marxism-Leninism nor Soviet military science can be understood and applied. Any other course would lead us to dogmatism, to the mechanical transfer of the experience of the Soviet Army to our conditions." This applied not only to the political aspect of the liberation struggle, but to purely military matters as well:

The military education which our People's Army received during the People's Liberation Struggle is the subject of special study. Some people think that the experience of our liberation war is exclusively of moral-political significance. This is mistaken. The moral-political significance of the People's Liberation Struggle is doubtless great, but to limit its importance to the moral-political factors would mean to neglect all the other factors which decided the final outcome of the struggle. Such an opinion in fact means narrowing the general military importance of our People's Liberation Struggle, not only with respect to our country, but with respect to all peoples who today are struggling against imperialism.[50]

The issue of the nature of the YPA thus assumed special significance, for it provided the clearest example before spring 1948 of Yugoslav Communist doctrine being affected by Soviet-Yugoslav friction. The CPY's resistance to Soviet demands found expression, in part, in renewed emphasis on the Partisan heritage; in December 1947 the Yugoslav leadership, for the first time, proclaimed that an important aspect of Soviet experience was not fully applicable to Yugoslavia.

3. *Economic Base*

The large-scale confiscation of private property notwithstanding, the Yugoslav Communists still described the Yugoslav economy at the end of the war as having "not yet emerged from the general limits of capitalism."[51] Nor, they maintained, did the 1946 constitution abolish the capitalist socioeconomic order;[52] the constitution itself provided for three types of property—state, cooperative, and private. Commentaries on the constitution noted that it guaranteed, along with the other forms, private ownership of the means of production.[53] It was pointed out that all three forms of ownership had been markedly transformed, parallel to the change in political power. State property had become "all-people's property," the basis for reconstruction planning, the instrument for controlling the economy as a whole, thus "a socialist sector in the making." Subordinated to its influence was the cooperative sector, now able—it was said—to develop in a progressive direction protected from capitalist influence.[54]

Moreover, reflecting the extent of de facto nationalization, the apparent acceptance of a role for private property was so qualified even in 1945 as to sharply differentiate Yugoslav doctrine from the prevalent East European "three sector" analysis. The CPY leaders never spoke of the three sectors in equal terms; a proposal that the Constitution affirm the equal importance of the state and private sectors was rejected,[55] while the constitution's guarantee of the right to private property was qualified by emphasis on its subordination to the state sector and by warnings that it could be expropriated in the general interest.[56] Occasionally these limits were defined more sharply, as when Tito told the Serbian Trade Union Congress in mid-1945 that he evaluated the private and state sectors differently since it was impossible to "completely protect the working class in the private sector. In order to fight heartless exploitation and receive the pay they deserve, the workers must have the means of production in their own hands."[57]

In early 1946 Tito decided to prepare for full-scale industrialization in the Stalinist manner of a Five-Year Plan. He first had to overrule the objections of Andrija Hebrang (who was to side with Stalin in 1948); Hebrang lost his positions of Politburo member, Chairman of the Economic Council, and Minister of Industry. The Yugoslavs then apparently won Soviet approval of an industrialization plan (although not of the ambitious goals of the plan eventually launched). Kidrič, who lacked training in economics, was dispatched to Moscow to study Soviet planning. Upon his return, the Five-Year Plan was drawn up and officially inaugurated on April 28, 1947.[58]

With the Five-Year Plan in preparation, Kidrič became the most frequent and authoritative Yugoslav spokesman on economic affairs. He began to speak of industrialization and "building socialism" as tasks of the immediate future. He stressed the need for new organizational forms to correspond to the increasingly socialist nature of the economy—above all, directive planning. Excluding the poor and middle peasantry and the artisans, Kidrič stated that conditions were ripe for the final elimination of the private sector.[59]

With the promulgation of the law on the Five-Year Plan, Yugoslavia officially initiated the "socialist reconstruction of the national economy," with the state clearly cast in the role of the main instrument of "socialist construction."[60] The private sector would remain only in agriculture. While capitalism had been overthrown politically and decisively weakened economically, this did not mean that the building of socialism would proceed without resistance. Kidrič pointed out in no uncertain terms in June 1947 that it was characteristic of building socialism "that it did not proceed in an atmosphere of general class reconciliation but, on the contrary, in an atmosphere of ever sharper class resistance from the remnants of the former ruling classes."[61]

Further characteristic of "building socialism" in Yugoslavia was the speed with which the leadership foresaw erecting at least its material foundations. The Five-Year Plan set fantastic goals—gross industrial production five times greater than that of 1939, with investment to account for 27 percent of national income by the end of the plan period.[62] No more modest were the predictions of how the plan would enable Yugoslavia to close the gap between itself and the advanced industrial nations. Djilas, addressing the Skupština, made the most grandiose claim: ". . . in terms of per capita production of goods, we can say with confidence that we will catch up with England in ten years."[63]

This romantic concept of the potential of socialist industrialization was accompanied by restraint in agricultural policy, where an important role was foreseen for the individual peasant for a long time to come.

This approach was only to be expected in 1945 and 1946, when land reform was carried out which limited the size of private holdings and gave half of the land thus made available to landless peasants who had supported the Partisans during the war. (The remaining land was used to organize state farms.) The first work cooperatives were formed at the time, but their number was quite small, and CPY spokesmen stressed that they were not a mass phenomenon.[64] With the launching of the Five-Year Plan, CPY leaders suggested that the socialization of agriculture would proceed much more slowly than in the USSR and, it was implied, less painfully.[65] Loose general cooperatives (in which the land was held and worked individually) would gradually encompass most peasant holdings, while a minority of the "most progressive" peasants would pool their land in work cooperatives (of several forms, only the "highest" of which was equivalent to a kolkhoz). Class struggle in the villages could not be avoided, but it would be a "sectarian mistake," Kardelj asserted, to consider the work cooperatives to be the main instrument for the socialization of agriculture.[66] The implication was that Soviet-type collectivization would not be repeated in Yugoslavia. In fact, by 1948 some economic discrimination against the individual peasant had contributed to the organization of nearly 9,000 general cooperatives. Yet work cooperatives constituted less than 3 percent of arable land. While higher than the corresponding figure for most of the other East European countries, this percentage was still very small and was matched by Bulgaria (in both countries, state farms constituted an additional 3 percent of arable land in 1948, a figure far exceeded in Poland).

4. Class Structure

The Yugoslav doctrine of the people's democratic revolution made it clear that power had been taken from the old ruling class. But what social elements now exercised power, and what was their mutual relationship? At first, the Yugoslavs sounded very much like their fellow East European Communists. Power had passed to the people, they asserted: ". . . the dominant political force in our country has changed. The antipopular, reactionary, exploitative class was deposed, and power passed into the hands of the people—in the true sense of the word, that is to say, of the great majority, the working people of the town and village.[67] Organizationally, the People's Front was said to exercise political power.[68] The Yugoslav conception of the Front as a special organizational form of the alliance between the working class and its class allies has already been outlined. After 1945, however, the Yugoslav Communists were initially ambiguous on the class composition of the Front and thus, indirectly, of the new state itself. In spite of the characterization of the bourgeoisie as traitorous, the People's Front was, before 1947, sometimes described as being broader than a worker-peasant alliance. In Tito's words: "[The People's Front] is not only an alliance of workers and peasants; it is something more. It is an alliance of all patriots, all the progressive people of our country, all those who set out on the new road of building and consolidating new Yugoslavia. It is and must remain an alliance of the working people—workers, peasants, the people's intelligentsia, and the remaining working citizens of our country."[69]

But who were the "remaining working citizens"? They were clearly not a "progressive" section of the bourgeoisie. If the term meant artisans or other "petit bourgeoisie," it was redundant, for this stratum, along with the "progressive intelligentsia," had been considered a part of the worker-peasant alliance by Lenin and Stalin. Its usage must thus be understood as tactical, an attempt to stress overwhelming mass support of the "people" for Communist policies. In fact the People's Front was apparently viewed in theoretical terms by Yugoslav ideologists as an alliance of workers and peasants only, as Kardelj clearly suggested to the First Congress of the People's Front in 1945.[70] And in 1947 the four-category analysis was dropped; Tito neglected to include it in his address to the Second Congress of the People's Front.[71] This fact alone separated the Yugoslav from the prevalent East European analysis of the class basis of the new state.

But the question remains of the doctrinal relationship that the Yugoslav Communists postulated between the working class and the peasantry and intelligentsia. On the one hand, the leading role of the Communist Party was emphasized in the postwar period, just as during the war.[72] On the other hand, Tito, in public appearances in 1945 and 1946, stressed repeatedly the equal position of the workers, peasants, and intelligentsia in the new state. On June 18, 1945, for example, he addressed a crowd in Serbia, with these words: "Peasants, workers, and the honest intelligentsia—those are the three factors, the three most important factors in our country and they are the guarantee that we can build up our country. No one of these three factors can be favored. . . . Our country must equally concern itself with all three factors."[73] In an election speech in Croatia in October 1946, Tito called the peasantry the "strongest pillar of our state"[74]—a remark later seized upon by Stalin as proof of a "pro-kulak" policy. Simultaneously, however, at a more theoretical level, the leading role of the working class was emphasized—more so than in the rest of Eastern Europe, although even the Yugoslav Communists did not yet speak openly of the "hegemony" of the proletariat.[75]

Finally in 1947 all doubt was removed that the working class was considered to be the hegemonic force within the worker-peasant alliance. "If political power in the state rests in the hands of the class whose interests correspond with the interests of the majority," wrote Boris Ziherl, quoting Lenin, "then it is truly possible to run the state in harmony with the will of the majority."[76] At the same time, the leading role of the Party was formulated more explicitly. As Tito told the Second Congress of the People's Front: "The Communist Party of Yugoslavia, as the vanguard of the working class, acquired the role of the leader of all progressive democratic forces—both during the liberation war and today in the peaceful development of the country."[77]

Parallel to the espousal of the tactical line of the "alliance of all patriots" in 1945 and 1946, "people's democracy" was described by some Yugoslav Communists as a state of an original, special type (and hence distinct from the Soviet state). "It is not a liberal bourgeois democratic republic," Pijade maintained, "but neither is it a socialist republic. The people's republic is a higher form of republic than the bourgeois democratic form, but lower than the socialist form."[78] This sounded much like the standard East European description of people's democracy. Yet even at this early date, Pijade described the people's state as "in the process of development" from the bourgeois democratic to the socialist form;[79] it was thus not, he implied, an intermediate state form with an institutional distinctiveness of its own. Furthermore, at the time other Yugoslav leaders described the Soviet Union, as well as Yugoslavia, as a "state of a new type," thus equating the two.[80]

After the launching of the Five-Year Plan, CPY spokesmen unambiguously asserted the socialist essence of the people's state; the terms "people's state" and "socialist state" were now used interchangeably with regard to Yugoslavia.[81] Yugoslav people's democracy was still not described explicitly as a dictatorship of the proletariat. But it was openly compared, though not explicitly equated, with Soviet democracy:

Democracy in Yugoslavia is not identical with Soviet democracy— neither [Soviet democracy as it existed] during the building of socialism nor [Soviet democracy as it exists] today after the victory of socialism. But it would be mistaken to view Yugoslav democracy as a special type of democracy, essentially different from Soviet democracy. *In its effect,* Yugoslav democracy is, in fact, democracy of the same type as that which existed in the Soviet Union at the beginning of socialist construction.[82]

5. *The Yugoslav Transition to Socialism*

In the first postwar months, still facing the tasks of fully consolidating power, rebuilding the economy, and gaining international recognition, the Yugoslav Communists, like Communists throughout Eastern Europe, rarely spoke of socialism. Typical was the perspective offered by Kardelj of "progressive social development" and "a better life and well-being for the working masses through democratic social reforms."[83] Even at this stage, however, without being precise, the CPY differentiated the tasks it faced from those confronting the other people's democracies. By mid-1946, with the Five-Year Plan in preparation, Party leaders began to talk openly of "socialist construction."[84] Thus, while other East European Communists saw socialism (when they spoke of it at all) as a matter of the indefinite future, for the Yugoslavs its realization was a current preoccupation. With the inauguration of the Five-Year Plan, as already indicated, the CPY officially proclaimed the beginning of the stage of building socialism.

There were other differences on this issue between the CPY and the other East European Parties. In part precisely because the stage of building socialism was at hand, the Yugoslavs, unlike other East European Communists, described their transition to socialism as similar "in essence" to the Soviet transition, stressing that it would follow basic laws of social development laid down by the classics of Marxism-Leninism and that it would inevitably "pass, in one way or another, through all the stages of development which the Soviet Union passed through."[85] It was, in short, no new road in principle, no "Yugoslav road to socialism"—a phrase that was in fact never used.

At the same time, the Yugoslav Communists suggested that their transition to socialism would not be simply a carbon copy of the Soviet experience. The CPY analysis of its revolution as socialist yet distinct from the October Revolution has been described. This outlook applied to the transition period in general, which—the Yugoslavs asserted—was unfolding in a different set of historical circumstances from those the Soviet Union had faced (the most important being precisely the prior fact of the October Revolution and the existence of the Soviet Union as the "first country of socialism").[86] Hence, Soviet experience was felt to be not totally applicable to Yugoslavia. At first the Yugoslavs cautiously suggested this by stressing that Marxism-Leninism was not dogma but a guide to action—a point that could be made by quoting the most orthodox Stalinist sources.[87] In time, as friction increased with Soviet representatives on day-to-day matters, the point was made more strongly. As Djilas put it when he delivered the commemorative address in Belgrade on the thirtieth anniversary of the October Revolution, Soviet experience had been used in every way, but not as dogma.[88] It was only natural, Kardelj asserted, that the Yugoslav transition "showed specific roads of liquidating the rule of capitalist reaction and new forms in the development toward socialism."[89]

The Yugoslav "forms" were never precisely defined. They obviously included components of the new political structure: the people's committees, the People's Front, the People's Army. The Yugoslav leaders apparently felt that all these organs rested on a distinctive, broad mass base, perceived to be a consequence of the particular strength of the class alliance between the proletariat and its allies which had permitted the successful conclusion of the Partisan struggle and the speedy consolidation of power after the war. The gradualist approach to the socialization of agriculture outlined by Kardelj—another consequence of the perceived strength of the worker-peasant alliance (that is, the role of the peasantry in the Partisan struggle)—was apparently also counted as a specific Yugoslav trait.

Before the break with Stalin in 1948, no Yugoslav Communist publicly suggested that there was any basic contradiction between the Soviet and Yugoslav transitions to socialism. Thus no Yugoslav leader or ideologue ever clearly differentiated "essence" from historically conditioned "forms" in the Soviet experience. But even before 1947 the two categories in the Soviet transition to socialism—"essence" and "forms"—had been identified in such a way as to imply that other, Yugoslav forms were, in contemporary conditions, *even more suitable* for carrying out revolutionary social change and achieving socialism.[90]

The CPY concept of the transition to socialism contained one additional element—it was offered as a model. The Yugoslav leaders chastised other Communist leaderships for not pursuing policies similar to their own during World War II. Kardelj and Djilas specifically attacked the French and Italian Communists for this failing (and for their postwar gradualist tactics) at the innaugural Cominform meeting,[91] and Tito made it clear immediately thereafter that the other East European Communists had done no better.[92] But the Yugoslav model was viewed as applicable far beyond the circumstances of World War II. Yugoslavia was not only "the classic country of the people's liberation [struggle] during World War II" but also the locus of a "typical people's liberation war in conditions of imperialist occupation."[93]

Thus, although the term was never used, there did in fact exist a concept of a "Yugoslav transition to socialism." The "Yugoslav" element denoted, not a vague "new path in principle" or a unique national approach, but rather the aspects of the Yugoslav experience which were considered to update Soviet practice since 1917 ("specific" features in this sense) and deemed suitable for application in much of the postwar world.

In contrast to the prevailing Soviet-East European theory, Yugoslav doctrine, although ambiguous on some points in 1945 and early 1946, thus affirmed that a people's democracy was a state of a new type in the sense of the Soviet Union—a socialist state. The doctrine embraced new, revolutionary state institutions, a state-dominated economy that was building socialism, and a strong worker-peasant alliance directed against an undifferentiated bourgeoisie, in which the Communist Party (and thus the working class) played the predominant role. After mid-1946, it proclaimed a course of building socialism which included the essential characteristics of, but did not copy, Soviet experience, producing its own, updated forms.

These divergent perspectives were the consequence of the different origins of the people's democracies postulated in the two concepts. In the standard doctrine, the intervention of an external factor—the Soviet Army—had led to a modification of the capitalist system. In Yugoslav theory, by contrast, the new state was the result of (and traced its socialist legitimacy to) an essentially socialist revolution, not opposed to but considered distinct from Soviet practice.

The relationship between the concepts of people's democracy and dictatorship of the proletariat provides a useful perspective on Yugoslav doctrine as a whole prior to 1948. It has been pointed out that the two concepts were not openly equated. Nevertheless, it is almost certain that (as they claimed after the break with Stalin) privately the top Yugoslav Communists did make the connection. They publicly equated people's democracy with Soviet democracy and the building of socialism, while rejecting the institutional distinctiveness of transitional forms that led other East European Communists at the time to deny the existence of proletarian dictatorship—a denial never made in Yugoslavia.

But if the CPY leadership did view the postwar political system as a dictatorship of the proletariat, why was this not spelled out? Four reasons suggest themselves: (1) Regardless of the extent to which power had been consolidated in 1945, it would have been a domestic political liability in Yugoslavia, just as in the rest of Eastern Europe, to proclaim a dictatorship of the proletariat. Minor internal opposition still existed, while international recognition of the new regime had yet to be won.[94] (2) As suggested subsequently by Yugoslav theoreticians, the leadership was preoccupied with practical matters and had simply not progressed far enough in theoretically explaining its "non-Leninist" seizure of power to elaborate on the relationship.[95] (3) Even with the full consolidation of power and greater, but still limited, attention to theory by 1947, the Soviet view denying the existence of dictatorships of the proletariat in Eastern Europe was so clear that a direct challenge to this line was unthinkable. (4) At the same time, it is possible that even to the more theoretically inclined Yugoslav leaders, such as Kardelj and Boris Ziherl, the dictatorship of the proletariat connoted Lenin's practical implementation in the USSR more than Marx's abstraction; thus, viewing their development to socialism as embodying specific forms, they avoided the term.[96]

International Radicalism

It remains to describe one additional aspect of Yugoslav doctrine before 1948, the CPY's analysis of the "nature of the epoch." As formulated by Kardelj in January 1947,[97] apparently in reaction to Varga's theses on the temporary stabilization of capitalism (and four months before Varga's public denunciation in the USSR), this analysis maintained: "To believe that in the near future the capitalist world will find an equilibrium and internal peace would mean to fall victim to a great illusion." On the contrary, "economic crises and the sharpening of all its contradictions will, in the coming years, lead the imperialist system into not only a deep economic crisis but also the strongest political convulsions."

Kardelj's analysis of the capitalist world, on which this conclusion was based, went as follows: (1) With the defeat of the Axis powers and the weakening of Western Europe, U.S. monopoly capitalism had assumed the dominant position in the capitalist world and was struggling for world hegemony. (2) This struggle was being pursued with political as well as economic means, with the state apparatus—the classic characteristic of fascism. (3) Intra-imperialist contradictions existed; the attempt to overcome them led to a more intense struggle against progressive forces, especially in the colonial world.

Opposing this capitalist world, Kardelj maintained, was the "system of socialism and people's democracy." On the one hand, the international influence of the USSR had greatly increased as a result of World War II. On the other hand, the people's democracies had dropped out of the chain of imperialism, and hence "the boundary between the two worlds, the world of socialism and the world of capitalism, in international relations is no longer so sharply drawn by the border between the USSR and the rest of the world." In other words, "the capitalist encirclement of the Soviet Union no longer exists." The existence of the people's democracies showed that the idea of socialism had won its historical victory, that the general crisis of capitalism was deepening, and that imperialism was weakening—and these developments meant that the struggle for socialism in postwar conditions assumed the most varied forms. This applied in particular to the colonial world, where—Kardelj stated—liberation movements were assuming "higher forms" as they aimed not only at "political liberation from foreign imperialism" but, *in opposition to* the (undifferentiated) national bourgeoisie, at "the victory of the anti-imperialist forces, of true people's democracy."

Thus, Kardelj maintained, the capitalist world faced an "unpeaceful, stormy period of more or less sharp conflicts" between the imperialist and progressive forces. Djilas had previously made the point more sharply, noting that "the periodic starting of wars and seizing alien territory is in the nature of capitalism, just as it is the nature of a wolf to eat sheep." While it was the task of the "forces of peace" to oppose this tendency, such a task did not deny the right of subjugated peoples (specifically Spaniards and Greeks) to fight for their freedom.[98] Nor, Kardelj added, could the people's democracies stand aloof from such conflict:

. . . in international politics, all the democratic, freedom-loving forces in the world are faced with important tasks. The outcome of the struggle between the forces of reaction and progress in each individual country depends—in the final analysis—on the accomplishment of those tasks. Above all, it is necessary for the democratic forces to cooperate as closely as possible and to extend to one another the most active support possible in the struggle for true democracy. . . . The struggle for true democracy is indivisible.[99]

This analysis applied above all to Yugoslavia itself. During World War II, Yugoslavia had considered itself the "center for the Balkan nations, both in a military and in a political sense";[100] now it proclaimed itself to be "an outpost of the democratic and anti-imperialist forces of the world (from a political as well as a geographical standpoint)."[101]

This Yugoslav Communist analysis of the international situation was "leftist" in the sense that it shared many of the assumptions of Soviet doctrine during "leftist" stages of Soviet foreign policy. Radically universalizing their own revolutionary experience, the Yugoslav Communists saw a disintegrating imperialist system creating conditions for Communist-led revolutions throughout the world. The CPY stressed that, in the colonial world as elsewhere, these revolutions had to oppose the "national bourgeoisie" as a whole—thus taking up the radical line on the national question in the underdeveloped world first formulated at the Second Comintern Congress by M. N. Roy in opposition to Lenin.[102] The doctrinal principle involved was stated precisely by a Yugoslav theoretician in 1950: "There can be no national liberation without its being tied to a socialist revolution."[103] Moreover, the Yugoslav Communists considered the support of revolution abroad to be the internationalist duty of Communists—a precept they put into practice in their support of the Greek Communist uprising.

The CPY's analysis was in many respects strikingly similar to the anti-imperialist "two camp" approach to the international situation presented by Andrei Zhdanov to the first meeting of the Cominform eight months later, which signified the beginning of a new "leftist" phase in Soviet foreign policy.[104] Yet the Yugoslav and Zhdanovian analyses differed significantly on the proper strategy to be followed by Communist Parties with respect to the national bourgeoisie and on the significance of the people's democracies themselves. The Zhadnov line was anticapitalist in a limited sense only: implicitly disavowing the vague "rightism" of the immediate postwar period which had led the Communist Party of India, for example, once to proclaim, "Nehru must not resign," Zhdanov called on Communists to rally all "really patriotic" and all "anti-fascist and freedom-loving" elements—terms so broad that (particularly in the colonial world) they did not exclude segments of the "progressive bourgoisie." E. M. Zhukov, interpreting Zhdanov's statement in *Bol'shevik* later in 1947, stated explicitly that "in many countries" the Communist Party had to unite not only the proletariat and the peasantry "but also a part of the bourgeoisie, mainly the petit and middle bourgeoisie."[105] The Yugoslav analysis, on the other hand, was explicitly militantly anticapitalist. For Zhdanov, the people's democracies were important, not because they were implementing "progressive democratic reforms," but primarily because they signified a significant shift in the balance of power between the imperialist world and the Soviet Union. For the Yugoslav Communists they signified much more than this: the emergence of new *socialist* states whose recent revolutionary experience, different from (although not opposed to) that of the USSR, was especially applicable to the rest of the world.[106]

The Ideological Aspect of Soviet-Yugoslav Relations

Not only did the Yugoslav Communists formulate a distinctive theory of people's democracy; they defended their analysis against perceived attempts of proponents of the prevalent East European doctrine to deny the validity of the Yugoslav concept by including Yugoslavia in generalizations about Eastern Europe—generalizations all the more odious since they put Yugoslavia in the same category as the ex-enemy states. As Djilas put it in October 1945: "Even those who love us are sometimes wrong in respect to the new Yugoslavia."[107] Three months later, he made clear the nature of this mistaken analysis:

Often in the foreign press which is favorably inclined toward us, Yugoslavia is compared with the other liberated countries, and general conclusions are drawn about democracy in Eastern and Southeastern Europe in which that which is specific—in fact basic—for Yugoslavia is lost. . . . It is incorrect to compare the other countries of Southeastern Europe with Yugoslavia, because there exists a difference in the basic question (i.e., the question of power). . . . It is simply incomprehensible that people who consider themselves learned, who even think they are Marxists, do not see the deep internal changes which occurred in Yugoslavia and equate it with other countries in that respect.[108]

Such polemical efforts had the effect of sharpening the distinctive features of Yugoslav doctrine. Thus Ziherl sharply attacked characterization of the "people's state" as a new historical phenomenon:

Some domestic and foreign commentators on the revolutionary transformation in new Yugoslavia, seeking a rigid framework into which to cram the revolutionary events in Yugoslavia, ignore the real content, the essence of those events. They portray people's revolution in Yugoslavia as some kind of "intermediate stage" between the bourgeois democratic and the proletarian stages of revolution and portray people's democracy—which was established in Yugoslavia as the result of a revolution—as a "third thing" floating somewhere between old bourgeois democracy and new Soviet democracy.[109]

Pijade attacked as even more erroneous the view that Yugoslavia was essentially still a bourgeois state: "Those people are wrong who do not see the elements of socialism in the countries of the new democracy, who do not see the qualitative change in the very social structure, but consider that some kind of state capitalism exists here and that the countries of the new democracy are only a special, particularly progressive form of bourgeois democracy."[110]

Similar points were made for each of the attributes of a people's democracy previously distinguished. Thus Kardelj condemned the attempt of people "either poorly informed or else mechanically implementing the teaching of Marxism-Leninism" to differentiate sharply between democratic and socialist forms of the people's democratic revolution.[111] Djilas, in an article previously quoted, attacked the view that the people's committees were an "intermediate stage" on the way to soviets.[112] Vukmanović, in words also cited earlier, attacked the view that the military significance of the Partisan army was outdated.[113] The proposition that the state sector of the economy was essentially state capitalist rather than socialist was repeatedly denounced,[114] as was the equating of the Five-Year Plan with the reconstruction plans elsewhere in Eastern Europe.[115] (At the same time, CPY leaders defended the goals of the plan against both Soviet and domestic criticism while defending gradualism in agricultural policy against impatient elements in the CPY).[116] The Yugoslavs rejected comparison of their People's Front with organizations elsewhere bearing the same name[117] and reacted sharply to downplaying of the role of the CPY in the new state. While the latter signified a defense of the primary role of the proletariat in the new state, it also amounted to criticism of a perceived unwillingness abroad to give the CPY Politburo credit for its revolutionary accomplishment. Tito's article in the first issue of *Komunist* made this point strongly; Tito here attacked the "spontaneous interpretation" of the liberation struggle by "friendly leftists" who explained everything in terms of the nationalities problem, rough terrain, and traditional fighting spirit, ignoring the "organized nature of the uprising and its correct leadership—the merit of the CPY."[118] A year later, addressing the Second Congress of the People's Front, he noted that the "spontaneous interpretation" was still prevalent abroad and reacted in even stronger words: "The political conditions for waging a struggle against the occupier were in fact the least favorable of all in Yugoslavia. . . . Thus the role of the Communist Party and the People's Front is all the more significant."[119]

The CPY thus defended its concept of people's democracy and, in so doing, emphasized the distinction between its doctrine and that espoused by other East European Communist leaders and Soviet theoreticians. But the Yugoslavs were not content to react defensively; they saw the need actively to propagate their theoretical views abroad. As the public prosecutor Josip Hrnčević told the First Congress of the Association of Lawyers, "it is the task of our lawyers to enable our friends abroad to understand our system."[120]

Whereas the polemical Yugoslav statements just quoted were doubtless aimed in part at other Communist leaderships in Eastern and Western Europe, it is clear that they extended to Soviet theoreticians as well. After all, the East European Communists concentrated on formulating their various national "roads to socialism"; it was the Soviet professors, beginning with Varga, who drew "general conclusions about democracy in Eastern and Southeastern Europe." It was symptomatic that the major Yugoslav political-legal journal, *Arhiv za pravne i društvene nauke*, which closely followed the equivalent Soviet press, ignored (with one exception) Soviet theoretical writing on people's democracy, preferring instead to review Soviet articles contrasting Soviet with bourgeois democracy; the reviewers often indirectly linked people's democracy with the former.[121]

In seeking to understand this perceived distortion of the nature of their postwar state, the Tito leadership could console itself with Yugoslavia's appeal and growing influence elsewhere in Eastern Europe. In the postwar years, Tito payed triumphant public visits to most of the East European capitals, encouraged contacts among the East European countries, and initiated a set of bilateral treaties of alliance with them well before the USSR began to construct a similar alliance structure. Albania was a de facto Yugoslav satellite, and the CPY was preparing for the inclusion of Bulgaria in Yugoslavia as a seventh republic and perhaps for a broader Southeast European federation as well.[122] The Yugoslav leadership could also reassure itself that, some specific frictions notwithstanding, there seemed to be no major problems in overall relations with the USSR and that on occasion (such as during Tito's visit to Moscow in May 1946) Stalin himself seemed to show special respect for Yugoslavia. Moreover, Yugoslavia seemed to enjoy great prestige among Soviet Party members. Ilya Ehrenburg, for example, was an early popularizer of the Partisans. Writing from Yugoslavia in late 1945, he stressed that a new army and state had emerged in Yugoslavia, distancing himself from attempts of authors abroad to "hide from their countrymen the war role of Yugo-slavia."[123] B. L. Gorbatov, another Soviet writer, concluded his visit to Yugoslavia with the words: "In the Soviet Union those who have visited Yugoslavia are envied. There is no one who would not like to come to your country. All of us who have been in Yugoslavia return to the Soviet Union as Yugoslav patriots."[124]

The Yugoslav leaders could further take heart in the fact that the theory of people's democracy was, after all, the fragmentary creation of Soviet academicians and not the official line of the Communist Party of the Soviet Union (CPSU). Yet public expressions of pro-Yugoslav feeling, at least in the USSR, also came largely from Communist intellectuals who were, as the Yugoslavs themselves later admitted, far from power.[125] The Yugoslavs were fully aware that the attitude of the Soviet political leadership and Stalin himself was far more reserved and was expressed by the writings of the Soviet professors.

During his visit to Moscow in early 1944, Djilas later related, he tried to engage lesser Soviet leaders in discussions about Yugoslavia, asserting the revolutionary nature of the liberation struggle and the formation of a new government similar in essence to Soviet rule. He described the opinion he encountered and his reaction in these words:

Everyone stubbornly talked only about the struggle against the German invaders and even more stubbornly stressed exclusively the patriotic character of that struggle, all the while conspicuously emphasizing the decisive role of the Soviet Union in the whole matter. Of course, nothing could have been further from my mind than the thought of denying the decisive role of the Soviet Party in world Communism or of the Red Army in the war against Hitler. But on the soil of my land, and under conditions of their own, the Yugoslav Communists were obviously waging a war independent of the momentary successes and defeats of the Red Army, a war, moreover, that was at the same time converting the political and social structure of the country. . . . Strangest of all was the fact that those who should have understood the best of all submissively kept still and pretended not to understand. . . . Obviously the Central Committee had not yet determined its stand; thus, as far as Soviet propaganda was concerned [the Yugoslav Communist uprising] remained simply a struggle against invaders without any real repercussions for the internal Yugoslav state or for international relations.[126]

Concrete proof of this Soviet attitude was not lacking. Djilas wrote an article about the Yugoslav uprising for *Pravda* (published on May 29, 1944), but, he relates, the editors deleted "almost everything that dealt with the character and political consequences of the struggle."[127]

Nor did the CPY leaders find greater acceptance of their views a year later, when Tito led a delegation that included Djilas to Moscow to sign the Soviet-Yugoslav mutual assistance treaty. In the course of a discussion about new phenomena in socialism, Djilas relates, "I interjected that in Yugoslavia there existed in essence a Soviet type of government; the Communist Party held all the key positions and there was no serious opposition party. But Stalin did not agree with this. 'No, your government is not Soviet—you have something in between de Gaulle's France and the Soviet Union.'"[128] Retrospective Yugoslav accounts cite many other plausible examples of Soviet reserve toward the Yugoslav Communist revolution which had direct doctrinal implications.[129] Thus direct contacts made it clear to the CPY leadership that, regardless of the official silence of the CPSU on the theory of people's democracy, through the fall of 1947 their own views had not been accepted at the highest levels in Moscow.

The founding of the Cominform in September 1947 seemed to portend a change. An international Communist forum was created, as Tito had continually urged,[130] in which Yugoslavia occupied a privileged second place, after the Soviet Union, and in which the Yugoslavs, in exercising their influence, could set forth their doctrine with Zhdanov's apparent full support.[131] Tito was quick to respond to the new atmosphere, stepping up his ties with the rest of Eastern Europe (inter alia, making a public visit to Rumania without prior notice to the Kremlin), supporting the Greek Communist uprising more openly, and urging with particular zeal Communist revolutions in Asia, probably convinced that in so doing he was acting in harmony with Stalin's wishes.[132]

At the Cominform meeting itself, however, the Yugoslavs did not find full acceptance of their views; their suggestion that the resolution adopted by the session support the Greek Communist uprising was rejected, while, as noted previously, Zhdanov himself failed to endorse fully the CPY concept of "people's democracy" (and, by Djilas's later account, hampered bilateral talks between the Yugoslav delegates and those of other Parties).[133] More seriously, the establishment of the Cominform was followed by a further deterioration of Soviet-Yugoslav relations, the best case in point being the issue of control of the Yugoslav Army. At the ideological level, the founding of the Cominform did not lead to Soviet sanctioning of the Yugoslav concepts which Belgrade had probably expected. On the one hand, the Soviet Union seemed to be encouraging Yugoslavia to present itself in the Cominform as a model; on the other hand, it abstained from the kind of praise for

Yugoslavia and acceptance of its theoretical concepts which would have constituted full endorsement. Instead, the former pattern was continued: official silence on the part of the CPSU concerning the Yugoslav revolution and the building of socialism,[134] while Soviet academicians further elaborated their theory of people's democracy, which, by virtue of generalization, was applied (with rare exceptions) to Yugoslavia as well. For example, a Soviet legal text that appeared in February 1948 under the sponsorship of the Law Institute of the Academy of Sciences examined the people's democracies in the chapter devoted to exploitative states.[135] The pattern seemed to be reversed at last with the publication of another textbook by Professor Denisov—the notes of his course at the Higher Party School in Moscow—which equated people's democracy with a dictatorship of the proletariat, using Yugoslavia as an example. But the book appeared in April 1948, while the first of Stalin's letters to Tito accusing him of anti-Soviet policies was dated March 27.[136]

In his rebuke to Dimitrov and, in absentia, to Tito over the Balkan federation scheme—the issue that precipitated the open conflict in Soviet-Yugoslav relations—Stalin declared: "Mistakes are not the issue: the issue is conceptions different from our own."[137] He was referring to different political perspectives on Balkan federation. The analysis of this chapter suggests, however, that the remark applied to doctrinal points as well. Soviet–East European doctrine on the postwar order in Eastern Europe (including Yugoslavia), though fragmentary and never officially adopted as the CPSU line, denied its socialist character and explained the gradual "revolution from above" as due primarily to the presence of the Red Army. Yugoslav doctrine, on the other hand, though equally fragmentary, affirmed the socialist character of the postwar state, tracing its legitimacy to an essentially socialist revolution that, although dependent for success on the existence of the Soviet state, had been carried out without a significant operative Soviet role on Yugoslav territory.

Moreover, as has been shown, the Yugoslav leaders were conscious of the difference between the two points of view. As with other elements of strain in the Soviet-Yugoslav relationship before the spring of 1948, however, the resulting Yugoslav criticism of the Soviet Union was concrete and limited; before the open break, dissatisfaction was not generalized, nor was Moscow's ultimate authority questioned.[138]

As for the Soviet attitude, this chapter has also suggested the extent of Soviet doctrinal reserve toward Yugoslavia, which was granted no exception in the theory of people's democracy. At the political level, it is true, Stalin may have found Yugoslav radicalism conditionally useful.[139] Before mid-1947, the Yugoslav example could encourage the consolidation of power elsewhere in Eastern Europe. After that date, qualified endorsement of Yugoslavia in the Cominform signaled the new Soviet line of creating full-fledged one-party states in Eastern Europe.[140]

Nevertheless, it may be suggested that Yugoslav doctrinal radicalism can never have been fully acceptable to Stalin and must have become increasingly suspect. For, to proclaim—in however fragmentary form—the emulation of Stalin's "building socialism in one country" with particular features on the basis of an essentially socialist revolution and to make of the Yugoslav experience a model for other countries amounted to proclaiming the existence of a new, revolution-based, and as such fully legitimate transition to socialism, thus inevitably—though unconsciously—challenging and diminishing the authority of the October Revolution and the Soviet Union's historical position as "*the country of socialism.*"

This analysis does not mean to imply that the Soviet-Yugoslav break in 1948 was the result of an ideological conflict over the interpretation of people's democracy. Open conflict came when, in the course of transforming Eastern Europe into a homogeneous bloc, Stalin could no longer tolerate the existence of an autonomous Communist power center in the area—a point hastened by the CPY's pursuit of its own foreign policy objectives, especially, Balkan federation. But the analysis of this chapter does suggest that, like intra-Party factional disputes before and like conflict among Communist states thereafter, the Soviet-Yugoslav break was accompanied by doctrinal differences and included an important ideological component. For Yugoslav doctrine (albeit unconsciously) constituted a challenge to Soviet authority. Before World War II Yugoslav Communists, like all others, had pledged total allegiance to the USSR as the only socialist state. Now a second, Yugoslav, socialist revolution had occurred, providing its leaders with direct legitimacy for the socialist transformation of Yugoslav society. Before the spring of 1948, probably no Yugoslav leader could imagine a contradiction between these two sources of historical justification. As Djilas relates, they regarded themselves as "Moscow's most consistent followers."[141] Yet a new source of legitimacy had been created; the inescapable if still undrawn conclusion was that Moscow's authority was no longer total. Unchallenged authority as the basis of un-questioning obedience was, however, the essence of the Stalinist system. In this sense, Yugoslav doctrine as formulated between 1945 and 1948 was an implicit challenge to Stalinism.

Notes

[1] The best accounts of the Yugoslav Communist seizure of power are to be found in Stephen Clissold, *Whirlwind: An Account of Marshal Tito's Rise to Power* (London: Cresset Press, 1949); Fitzroy Maclean, *Tito* (New York: Ballantine, 1957); Dinko Tomasic, *National Communism and Soviet Strategy* (Washington, D.C.: Public Affairs Press, 1957); U.S., Congress, Senate, Committee on the Judiciary, *Yugoslav Communism: A Critical Study* [by Charles Zalar] (Washington, D.C.: Government Printing Office, 1961); Seton-Watson, *The East European Revolution*, chaps. 6–8. Concise Communist accounts are given in *Pregled istorije Saveza komunista Jugoslavije* (Belgrade, 1963), chaps. 6 and 7; Vlado Strugar, *Jugoslavija 1941–1945* (Belgrade, 1970); international ramifications are examined in Dušan Plenča, *Medjunarodni odnosi Jugoslavije u toku drugog svjetskog rata* (Belgrade, 1962). A detailed Communist account of the consolidation of power from March to November 1945 is Branko Petranović, *Političke i pravne prilike za vreme privremene vlade DFJ* (Belgrade, 1964).

[2] Vladimir Dedijer, *Tito* (New York: Simon & Schuster, 1953), p. 149.

[3] Edvard Kardelj, *Borba* article of October 19, 1941, *Put nove Jugoslavije* (Belgrade, 1949), p. 238. (Page references to books published in Belgrade in both the Latin and the Cyrillic alphabets apply to the latter unless otherwise noted.)

[4] "Deklaracija Drugog zasedanja AVNOJ-a od 29 novembra 1943," *Službeni list DFJ*, February 1, 1945. Stalin reacted furiously, calling the move a "stab in the back" of the Soviet wartime coalition policy. This was only the most dramatic in a series of wartime incidents stemming from different Soviet and Yugoslav perspectives on the proper strategy for the CPY during World War II. See Moša Pijade, *About the Legend That the Yugoslav Uprising Owed Its Existence to Soviet Assistance* (London, 1950); Dedijer, *Tito*, chaps. 11–14; idem, *Izgubljena bitka J. V. Staljina* (Sarajevo, 1969), pp. 74–78, 88–89.

[5] Josip Broz Tito, Speech to the Fifth CPY Congress in July 1948, *Govori i članci* (Zagreb, 1959–) 3: 406.

[6] Several top Yugoslav Communists used the term in early 1945. (Kardelj, Speech to the First Congress of the Slovene Liberation Front, *Put nove Jugoslavije*, p. 483; Boris Kidrič, Speech of May 5, 1945, *Sabrana dela* [Belgrade, 1959–1960] 2: 283). Apparently Tito first used the term in his speech to the First Congress of the People's Front in August 1945 (*Govori i članci* 1: 358), after which it became standard.

[7] As sources for Yugoslav doctrine between 1945 and 1948, I have relied primarily upon the speeches and articles of Tito, Kardelj, Djilas, Kidrič, Pijade (all Politburo members), and Boris Ziherl (Central Committee member, leading figure in agitation-propaganda work, and later Yugoslav representative on the Cominform staff). The CPY took the first steps in transforming isolated statements of the leadership into codified doctrine before the break with Stalin. The first three issues of *Komunist*, the Party ideological journal (which appeared irregularly in 1946 and 1947), were almost exclusively devoted to exposition of the Yugoslavs' views on their people's democracy and did not contain a single article devoted to the Soviet Union. A compilation of these statements was made in early 1948 for use, along with a Soviet text, in university courses on the theory of the state and law. (R. Lukić, *O narodnoj državi* [Belgrade, 1948].) Political-legal documents from the World War II period were compiled for use in the course "History of the

People's State," introduced at the Belgrade Law Faculty in early 1948. (L. Gerškovič, *Dokumenti o razvoju narodne vlasti* [Belgrade, 1948].)

[8] *Narodni* must be translated as "people's" (or, elsewhere, as "popular"), and not as "national"; the term clearly had a strong class content. When CPY spokesmen discussed all-national coalitions, anathema to them, they consistently used *nacionalan*.

[9] T[ito], "U čemu je specifičnost oslobodilačke borbe i revolucionarnog preobražaja nove Jugoslavije," *Komunist* 1, no. 1 (October 1946): 1–9 (all references are to the Belgrade edition).

[10] Ibid., p. 3.

[11] Kardelj, Address to the First Congress of the People's Front, *Put nove Jugoslavije*, p. 98.

[12] Tito's words to the Third Session of AVNOJ were typical: "I requested of the Soviet government that the troops of the Red Army cross the border into Eastern Serbia and help our forces liberate Serbia and Belgrade. . . . With the help of the glorious Red Army, Belgrade and Serbia were quickly liberated." (Tito, *Govori i članci* 2: 10.) A rare exception were Kardelj's words of fulsome praise: "The Slovene people await with such great love the arrival of the Red Army. It is not only the liberator of the Slovene people, it is their savior." (Kardelj, "Crvena Armija na slovenačkom tlu," *Put nove Jugoslavije*, p. 482.)

[13] For praise of the USSR which ignored its operations in Yugoslavia and did not make explicit a liberation role in Eastern Europe, see Milovan Djilas, "O današnjim zadacima partije," *Borba*, January 12–14, 1946 (references are to the Zagreb edition); idem, "Tridesetogodišnjica Oktobarske revolucije," *Borba*, November 7, 1947; Moša Pijade, Speech of October 25, 1946, *Izabrani govori i članci, 1941–1947* (Belgrade, 1948) (hereafter cited as *Članci*, 1948), Latin edition, p. 349. In his speech to the Cominform in September 1947, Kardelj confined himself to acknowledging the "great liberation role of the Soviet Union" and its "unselfish aid to our liberation struggle." (*For Lasting Peace! For a People's Democracy!* November 10, 1947.) For acknowledgment of a Soviet liberation role in Eastern Europe in general, but not explicitly in Yugoslavia, see the Yugoslav speeches to the Pan-Slav Congress of 1946 (*Borba*, December 9–10, 1946).

[14] Tito, *Govori i članci* 2: 18.

[15] Kidrič, Speech of September 13, 1946, *Sabrana dela* 3: 55. See also Pijade, "O reakciji i G. Čerčilu," *Borba*, March 24, 1946.

[16] Tito, *Komunist* 1, no. 1: 5.

[17] Milovan Djilas, "O rešenju nacionalnog pitanja u Jugoslaviji," *Članci, 1941–1946* ([Belgrade], 1947), p. 232.

[18] Tito, "Narodni front kao općenarodna politička organizacija," *Komunist* 2, no. 3 (September 1947): 13–37, at 22.

[19] Tito, *Komunist* 1, no. 1: 4. An exception was granted for Slovenia, where the Liberation Front had originally been a coalition of Communist, Christian Socialist, and Sokol forces. This evaluation of the role of the bourgeoisie was spelled out clearly later by a leading Party historian: ". . . in the [People's Liberation Struggle] there was not, nor could there be, a coalition between class forces; that is to say, there was not, nor could there be, that classic form of alliance between the working class and at least a section of the bourgeoisie interested in liberation and social transformation which would have infused the liberation struggle with elements of a bourgeois democratic revolution under the hegemony of the working class. . . ." (Pero Morača, "O osnovnim karakteristikama jugoslovenskog oslobodilačkog rata i revolucije 1941–1945," *Pregled posleratnog razvitka Jugoslavije (1945–1965)* [Belgrade, 1966], pp. 15–17.)

[20] Kidrič, "Klasna logika u narodnooslobodilačkom pokretu," *Sabrana dela*

2: 301. Tito made the same point but, characteristically, in milder language. (Tito, *Komunist* 1, no. 1: 6.)

[21] Quoted by Boris Ziherl, "O nekim problemima borbe za novu Jugoslaviju," *Članci i rasprave* ([Belgrade], 1948), p. 146.

[22] Kidrič, "Klasna logika," *Sabrana dela* 2: 306.

[23] Edvard Kardelj, Speech at the inaugural meeting of the Cominform, *Problemi naše socijalističke izgradnje* (hereafter cited as *Problemi*) (Belgrade, rev. ed., 1960–) 1: 156.

[24] Ziherl, "O nekim problemima," *Članci*, p. 140.

[25] Milovan Djilas, *Conversations with Stalin* (New York: Harcourt, Brace & World, 1962), pp. 29–30.

[26] Kidrič, Speech to the Fifth CPY Congress, *Sabrana dela* 3: 349.

[27] Kidrič, "O karakteru naše privrede," *Komunist* 1, no. 1 (October 1946): 31–44, at 34.

[28] Ibid.

[29] Ziherl, "O nekim problemima," *Članci*, p. 182.

[30] Kardelj, *Problemi* 1: 160, 165–166.

[31] Ziherl, "O nekim problemima," *Članci*, p. 183.

[32] Ziherl, "Oktobarska revolucija i jugoslovenski narodi," *Članci*, p. 210.

[33] Ziherl, "O nekim problemima," *Članci*, p. 183.

[34] Pijade, Skupština address of May 18, 1946, *Članci*, 1948, Latin ed., p. 148.

[35] Ibid., p. 149.

[36] Article 6, *Constitution of the Federal People's Republic of Yugoslavia* (hereafter cited as *Constitution*, 1946) (Belgrade, 1947), p. 41.

[37] "Opći zakon o narodnim odborima od 21 maja 1946," *Službeni list FNRJ*, May 28, 1946, pp. 482–494 (references are to the Latin edition).

[38] Leo Geršković, "Karakter i struktura narodno-oslobodilačkih odbora," *Arhiv za pravne i društvene nauke* (hereafter cited as *Arhiv*) 1, nos. 1–2 (May–June 1945): 46–61; Jovan Djordjević, "Značaj i sadržina opšteg zakona o narodnim odborima," *Arhiv* 2, nos. 1–6 (January–June 1946): 41–48.

[39] Djordjević, *Arhiv* 2, nos. 1–6: 45.

[40] Djilas, "Izopačivanje karaktera narodne vlasti," *Komunist* 1, no. 1 (October 1946): 10–20, at 13.

[41] Ibid., p 14

[42] Kardelj, *Problemi* 1: 163.

[43] Ibid., p. 155.

[44] Svetozar Vukmanović-Tempo, Speech commemorating the sixth anniversary of the founding of the People's Army, *Borba*, December 22, 1947.

[45] Tito, Lead editorial, issue of October 2, 1945, *Govori i članci* 2: 39.

[46] Djilas, "O prvoj godisnjici pobjede," *Članci*, p. 263.

[47] For Yugoslav accounts, see Dedijer, *Tito*, p. 266; Hendrek Van Bergh, ed., *Genosse Feind* (Bonn: Berto Verlag, 1962), especially pp. 116–130 (a translation of *Zločinstva pod plaštom socijalizma* [Belgrade: Narodna armija, 1953], printed in September 1953 but never released). See also Harry Hodgkinson, *Challenge to the Kremlin* (New York: Praeger, [1952]), chap. 4.

[48] Svetozar Vukmanović-Tempo, *Revolucija koja teče. Memoari* (Belgrade, 1971) 2: 32.

[49] Tito, *Govori i članci* 3: 206.

[50] *Borba*, December 22, 1947. December 22 was the date the first proletarian brigade was organized in 1941. In 1945 the anniversary of this event was suitably commemorated in *Borba*. In 1946 it was almost ignored, the only mention being a reference on page 2 of the issue of December 23 to a ceremony the previous day. The issue of December 22, 1947, was entirely devoted to "Yugoslav Army Day"

and featured a eulogy of Tito as wartime Commander in Chief (with a picture only slightly smaller than Stalin's on December 21, his birthday).

[51] Kardelj, Radio address of February 13, 1945, *Put nove Jugoslavije*, p. 113.

[52] Kardelj, Skupština address of December 10, 1945, *Put nove Jugoslavije*, p. 207.

[53] Kardelj, Radio address of December 6, 1945, *Put nove Jugoslavije*, p. 199; Pijade, "O nacrtu ustava FNRJ," *Članci*, 1948, p. 67; *Constitution*, 1946, chap. 4.

[54] Kardelj, Radio address of December 6, 1945, *Put nove Jugoslavije*, pp. 195–196.

[55] Djilas, Speech of January 17, 1946, reprinted in *Constitution*, 1946, pp. 11–12.

[56] Kardelj's description of the altered position of private property was typical: "This does not mean that we suppress the private sector or reject it as one form in our economy. It only means that the private capitalist sector has to observe certain limits determined by the interests of the state and the people as a whole." (Kardelj, Skupština address of December 10, 1945, *Put nove Jugoslavije*, p. 209.)

[57] Tito, *Govori i članci* 1: 315.

[58] See Maclean, *Tito*, pp. 293–298; Ernst Halperin, *The Triumphant Heretic* (London: Heinemann, 1958), pp. 69–71; François Fejtö, *Histoire des démocraties populaires* (Paris: Editions du Seuil, 1952), pp. 165–170; see also notes 116, 129 in this chapter.

[59] Kidrič, Skupština address of July 19, 1946, *Sabrana dela* 3: 22; Kidrič, *Komunist* 1, no. 1: 39–40, 44.

[60] *Law on the Five Year Plan for the Development of the National Economy of the Federative People's Republic of Yugoslavia in the Period from 1947 to 1951* (Belgrade, [1947]).

[61] Kidrič, Speech of June 14, 1947, *Sabrana dela* 3: 219.

[62] *Law on the Five Year Plan*, p. 36.

[63] Narodna skupština FNRJ, *Treće redovno zasedanje saveznog veća i veća naroda 26 mart–26 april 1947 godine, stenografske beleške* (Belgrade, 1947), p. 438.

[64] Pijade, "O seljačkim radnim zadrugama," *Članci*, 1948, p. 339.

[65] On this issue, positions within the Party leadership were reversed: Hebrang apparently advocated radical collectivization, while the Politburo was for a gradualist course. See note 116 to this chapter.

[66] Kardelj, "Zemljoradničko zadrugarstvo u planskoj privredi," *Komunist* 2, no. 3 (September 1947): 38–90; Kardelj, Speech of September 1947 to the Cominform, *Problemi* 1: 165–170; Kardelj, "Zadaci naše lokalne privrede i komunalnog gazdinstva," *Problemi* 1: 220. "General cooperatives" were modified traditional rural cooperatives in which the peasant continued to own his land and tools but sold his crops, bought supplies, obtained credit, and participated in cottage industry. In the "work cooperative" (*seljačka radna zadruga*) the peasant turned over his land, tools, and most livestock to the cooperative. Four types of work cooperatives were later developed: in types 1 and 2, the peasant remained the owner of his land and received rent or interest for its use; in types 3 and 4, he was remunerated solely according to his "workdays," in type 4, giving up all ownership rights.

[67] Kardelj, Radio address of December 6, 1945, *Put nove Jugoslavije*, p. 195.

[68] Kardelj, Speech to the First Congress of the People's Front, *Put nove Jugoslavije*, p. 107.

[69] Tito, *Komunist* 1, no. 1: 8.

[70] ". . . its core is the alliance of workers and peasants." (*Put nove Jugoslavije*, p. 94.)

[71] Tito, *Komunist* 2, no. 3. The four-category line was apparently never clear to all the Party cadres. In an election speech on October 25, 1946, Pijade repeated

Tito's definition quoted earlier. The "crowd" responded: "Long Live the Worker-Peasant Alliance!" Pijade had to correct them, affirming that the People's Front rested on a broader basis. (Pijade, *Članci*, 1948, p. 323.)

[72] For example, Veljko Vlahović, "O liku komunista," *Komunist* 1, no. 1 (October 1946): 45–58.

[73] Tito, *Govori i članci* 1: 305.

[74] *Borba*, November 2, 1946.

[75] In February 1945, for example, Kardelj spoke of the "alliance of the . . . plebeian masses headed by the working class" and the "alliance of the popular democratic forces headed by the proletariat." (Radio address of February 13, 1945, *Put nove Jugoslavije*, pp. 114, 116.)

[76] Ziherl, "O nekim problemima," *Članci*, p. 165.

[77] Tito, *Komunist* 2, no. 3: 35.

[78] Pijade, "O nacrtu ustava FNRJ," *Članci*, 1948, p. 67. A leading constitutional lawyer characterized people's democracy as "a higher progressive form of democratic state." (Djordjević, *Arhiv* 2, nos. 1–6: 45.)

[79] Pijade, "O nacrtu ustava FNRJ," *Članci*, 1948, p. 67.

[80] Djilas, "O prvojgodišnjici pobjede," *Članci*, p. 258; Vlahović, *Komunist* 1, no. 1: 45.

[81] Kardelj, *Komunist* 2, no. 3: 45; Pijade, "Zadatak našeg krivičnog zakonodavstva," *Članci*, 1948, p. 235.

[82] Ziherl, "O nekim problemima," *Članci*, pp. 183–184. Ziherl quoted with approval Lenin's famous words "The transition from capitalism to communism will certainly bring a great variety and abundance of political forms, but the essence will inevitably be only one," leaving it to his readers to supply Lenin's concluding five words: "the dictatorship of the proletariat." In February 1948, in an article stressing that "the paths [to socialism] vary, but the goal is one," Ziherl went one step further, quoting Lenin's oft-cited words "All nations will reach socialism; this is inevitable; but they will not all reach socialism in the same way; each nation will contribute something of its own, in this or that form of democracy, in this or that different element of the dictatorship of the proletariat, in this or that tempo of socialist transformation of different elements of society." (*Članci*, p. 460.)

[83] Kardelj, Skupština address of December 10, 1945, *Put nove Jugoslavije*, p. 209.

[84] Kidrič, Skupština address of July 19, 1946 *Sabrana dela* 3: 16.

[85] Djilas, *Borba*, January 12–14, 1946; Ziherl, "O nekim problemima," *Članci*, p. 181.

[86] The specific characteristics of the Soviet transition were formulated by Ziherl as follows: (1) The revolution was born in the course of the first, imperialist (world) war. (2) It was consolidated in the struggle against the bourgeois–large landholder reactionaries who, with the direct aid of foreign imperialism, ignited a civil war. (3) The construction of socialism was begun under conditions of capitalist encirclement. (4) The Soviet Union was the pioneer of socialism. The specific characteristics of the Yugoslav transition were, in contrast: (1) The revolution was born in the course of the second, antifascist (world) war. (2) The masses were mobilized in a deeply national and simultaneously deeply "popular" liberation war against the foreign occupier and its supporter, the domestic bourgeois–large landholder reactionaries. (3) The construction of socialism was begun under conditions of encirclement by four friendly, democratic states and with close ties with the USSR. (Ziherl, "Oktobarska revolucija," *Članci*, pp. 209–210.)

[87] For example, Djilas, quoting the *History of the All-Union Communist Party*, in *Komunist* 1, no. 1: 15; Tito, *Komunist* 1, no. 1: 8–9.

[88] *Borba*, November 7, 1947.

[89] Kardelj, "Zabeleške o nekim pitanjima medjunarodnog razvitka," *Komunist* 2, no. 2 (January 1947): 12–46, at 33.

[90] From the perspective of mid-1949, Kardelj wrote revealingly and—it would seem—accurately about the Yugoslav attitude at the time. His words deserve quotation at length: ". . . that special and new road to socialism was widely discussed in all the people's democracies—except Yugoslavia. We always maintained that the issue was not new roads in principle, but various forms on the general road of socialist development—forms which can greatly differ from those known in the Soviet Union but whose essence and general direction of development must be the same. We owe the victory of our people's revolution precisely to the fact that we nurtured no illusions as to 'new paths in principle' to socialism. We were the only ones clearly to advocate this view at the first session of the Cominform. Contrary to it, the leaders of the Communist Parties of the other people's democracies constantly made 'discoveries' about their own 'new roads to socialism in principle,' about various specific harmonies between socialist and capitalist elements, and about the special worth of some vestiges of bourgeois democracy, which they glorified as a special characteristic of people's democracy.' . . . Then the Soviet professors repeated these phrases in countless variations. That is why the Soviet press always gave more prominence to opportunistic nonsense from the other people's democracies than to the facts about new Yugoslavia, which stood far ahead of the others. And we who contended that we were victorious in a socialist revolution, that our people's democracy was a democracy of the Soviet type, were told that we were narrow-minded sectarians and completely incapable of inventing something new. . . .

"However, later there was suddenly a change of course. . . . [*Bol'shevik* wrote that] the general laws [of the transition period] are not only obligatory as such, but precisely in their 'tested' and 'concretized' forms yielded by the experience of the Soviet state; the appearance of the people's democracies brought nothing new at all. And now—once again—the copyists in the people's democracies not only one after the other renounce their patented original 'discoveries' but declare that we are conceited nationalists because we hold that the process of socialist revolution in Yugoslavia brought with it a series of specific new forms which are valuable as experience not only for us but also for other countries taking the path of socialist development." (Kardelj, *Komunist* 3, no. 4: 17–18.)

[91] Dedijer, *Tito*, p. 295.

[92] Tito, *Komunist* 2, no. 3: 18.

[93] Ziherl, "O nekim problemima," *Članci*, p. 123.

[94] For an admission that Yugoslavia's international position significantly influenced the formulations on the postwar state, see Jovan Marjanović, "Forme borbe i rada KPJ u narodnooslobodilačkom ratu i narodnoj revoluciji," *Komunist* 5, no. 1 (January 1951): 117–162, at 152.

[95] Pijade spoke revealingly about this to the Fifth Congress in 1948: "We did not devote sufficient attention to the theoretical elaboration of our own experience. The practical work of building up our new state took all our strength, it is true, and the great loss of old cadres in the war is also, to be sure, one of the reasons why we did not sufficiently consider theoretical questions. But nevertheless . . . in the field of theory we did not do what we were duty-bound to do." (Moša Pijade, *Izabrani govori i članci, 1948–1949* [Zagreb, 1950], [hereafter cited as *Članci*, 1950] pp. 51–52.)

[96] In October 1948, in reply to a query by a Party member, Djilas affirmed that a dictatorship of the proletariat did exist in Yugoslavia. "If it did not, we would share power with other classes." He gave two reasons why the people's state had

not been called a dictatorship of the proletariat: (1) Tactically, it would have alarmed the peasant or petit bourgeois "class ally." "The term 'dictatorship of the proletariat' would have been rejected by a part of the masses; the deposed bourgeoisie would have been able to frighten them and mislead them into thinking that the government was not theirs, etc." (2) Theoretically, Yugoslavia lacked some of the harsh traits of the dictatorship of the proletariat as realized in the USSR immediately after the October Revolution. But this did not mean that people's democracy was different from proletarian dictatorship in Leninist theory ("Odgovor druga Djilasa na pitanja postavljena u jednom pismu," *Vojno-politič* *glasnik* 1, no. 3 [September–October 1948] : 17–22.)

[97] Kardelj, *Komunist* 2, no. 2.

[98] Djilas, "O prvoj godišnjici pobjede," *Članci*, p. 261.

[99] Kardelj, *Komunist* 2, no. 2: 44–45.

[100] Letter from Tito to Vukmanović-Tempo, October 1943, *Zbornik dokumenata i podataka o narodnooslobodilačkom ratu jugoslovenskih naroda* (Belgrade, 1949) 2, book 10: 361, as cited in Paul Shoup, *Communism and the Yugoslav National Question* (New York: Columbia University Press, 1968), p. 125.

[101] Vukmanović-Tempo, *Borba*, December 22, 1947.

[102] See Xenia Eudin and Robert C. North, eds., *Soviet Russia and The East, 1920–1927: A Documentary Survey* (Stanford, Calif.: Stanford University Press 1957) pp. 39–42, 63–67.

[103] Leo Geršković, *Historija narodne vlasti* (Belgrade, 1950) 1: 19.

[104] See Shulman, *Stalin's Foreign Policy Reappraised*, pp. 13–20; Zhdanov, *O mezhdunarodnom polozhenii.*

[105] E. Zhukov, "Obostrenie krizisa kolonial'noi sistemy," *Bol'shevik* no. 23 (December 15, 1947): 51–64, at 55. This view was, however, challenged in Moscow from a more "leftist," "Yugoslav"-like position. See John H. Kautsky, *Moscow and the Communist Party of India* (Cambridge, Mass., and New York: Technology Press and Wiley, 1956), pp. 16–45.

[106] In their analysis of the "nature of the epoch," the Yugoslav Communists thus treated the other people's democracies in Eastern Europe as new socialist states similar to Yugoslavia. Usually, however, they sharply differentiated their political order from that existing in the other East European states.

[107] Djilas, Speech of October 30, 1945, *Članci*, p. 228.

[108] *Borba*, January 12, 1946.

[109] Ziherl, "O nekim problemima," *Članci*, p. 183.

[110] Pijade, Speech of October 23, 1947, *Članci*, 1948, p. 366. See also the remarks of Josip Hrnčević, the public prosecutor, at the First Congress of the Association of Lawyers, in *Arhiv* 3, no. 2 (April–June 1947): 162–190, at 176.

[111] Kardelj, Speech of September 1947 to the Cominform, *Problemi* 1: 165–166.

[112] Djilas, *Komunist* 1, no. 1: 13.

[113] *Borba*, December 22, 1947.

[114] Hrnčević, *Arhiv* 3, no. 2: 177; Kidrič, "O nekim principijelnim pitanjima naše privrede," *Komunist* 2, no. 2 (January 1947): 47–58.

[115] See the review by V. V. of the Leont'ev article in *Arhiv* 3, no. 4 (October–December 1947): 563–566.

[116] Kidrič, *Komunist* 2, no. 2; Kardelj, Speech of August 19, 1947, *Problemi* 1: 86–87; Vladimir Bakarić, Speech to the Second Congress of the People's Front, *Borba*, September 29, 1947. Textual analysis supports the later Yugoslav claim (Kidrič, Speech to the Fifth CPY Congress, *Sabrana dela* 3: 367–373; Mile Milatović, *Slučaj Andrije Hebranga* [(Belgrade), 1952], p. 14) that Hebrang and Sretan Žujović (Central Committee member and Minister of Transport, who also refused to back Tito in 1948) opposed the superindustrialization policy while

advocating a faster rate of collectivization of agriculture. Kidrič's article of January 1947 was devoted to opposing the "mistaken theory" of the emergence of state capitalism (rather than incipient socialism) in Yugoslavia. An optimistic evaluation of the possibilities of rapid socialist development, Kidrič maintained, did not mean "adventurism" but a "higher type of economic realism." On the other hand, Djilas, in his *Borba* articles of January 12–14, 1946, in referring to the countryside, attacked "people who would like to 'leap' into socialism—not only into socialism, but into a highly developed socialist society as presently found in the Soviet Union" and noted that, while the Party had to be prepared for increasing class struggle in the village, it could not "attack our permanent class allies—the poor and middle peasant." Vladimir Bakarić, the Croatian Communist leader, attacked "those people" who saw a quick solution to the agricultural problem in "mechanization, large-scale collectivization, and struggle against the kulak." (*Borba*, September 29, 1947.)

[117] Djilas, *Borba*, January 12–14, 1946.

[118] Tito, *Komunist* 1, no. 1: 2.

[119] Tito, *Komunist* 2, no. 3: 26–27.

[120] Hrnčević, *Arhiv* 3, no. 2: 177. Evidence of such propaganda is sparse. The first three issues of *Komunist* were translated into foreign languages; Tito's articles therein were widely reprinted in the foreign Communist press. In late 1947 or early 1948, the Yugoslavs sent a large quantity of material on their wartime activities to the Academy of Social Sciences of the CPSU Central Committee. (*Voprosy istorii* no. 3 (1948): 154–156.)

[121] See the review of M. Mitin, "Sovetskaia demokratiia i demokratiia burzhuaznaia," *Bol'shevik* no. 6 (1947): 23–43, by R. L[ukič] in *Arhiv* 2, no. 2 (April–June 1947): 309–312. Mitin's article was largely devoted to contrasting bourgeois and Soviet democracy; he referred to the people's democracies as signifying "a big step forward in comparison with the bourgeois democratic states"—the standard East European–Soviet view. Lukič ignored this part of Mitin's argument, indirectly linking people's democracy with Soviet democracy. See also the review of Trainin, "O demokratii," *Sovetskoe gosudarstvo i pravo* no. 1 (1946), by R. L[ukič], in *Arhiv* 2, nos. 7–12 (July–December 1946): 238–239. The review of V. Ivanov, "Democraticheskie preobrazovaniia v Iugoslavii," *Bol'shevik* no. 2 (1947): 38–51, by R. L[ukič], in *Arhiv* 3, no. 2 (April–June 1947): 305–306, noted that Ivanov praised Yugoslavia's internal order and Balkan foreign policy, yet obliquely took exception to his analysis of "democratic *reforms* in Yugoslavia."

The only Yugoslav review of East European–Soviet writing devoted primarily to the concept of people's democracy was the review of Leont'ev's article (see note 115). This review indirectly disputed Loent'ev's thesis, objecting to his minimizing socioeconomic change in Yugoslavia and adding that the Yugoslav polity was a "specific form of Soviet democracy." After the break with Stalin, Yugoslav leaders declared that they had opposed the Soviet academicians', as well as the East European Communists', view of people's democracy. See Pijade's remarks to the Fifth CPY Congress, *Članci*, 1950, p. 52; Kardelj, as quoted in note 90.

[122] See Dedijer, *Tito*, especially pp. 300–307.

[123] Ilya Ehrenburg, *European Crossroad* (New York: Knopf, 1947), p. 68. (Published in Yugoslavia as *Putevima Evrope* [Zagreb, 1946].) For Yugoslav recognition of his role, see Dedijer, *Tito*, pp. 229–230.

[124] *Borba*, September 12, 1945.

[125] In 1951 the CPY published a book entitled *Leaders and the Press of the USSR on the PLS and Socialist Construction in Yugoslavia (before the Cominform*

Resolution), intended to show the hypocrisy of the anti-Yugoslav campaign. This book was not a very successful effort. Contradicting the title, the introduction admitted that the praise for Yugoslavia before 1948 had come from people "far from the leadership" (p. 3); the text itself was largely a compilation of statements like those of Ehrenburg and Gorbatov. From the Soviet political press, the book could quote only formal congratulatory messages or, as in the case of five articles from *Bol'shevik*, praise for Yugoslavia which still viewed it in the same framework as the other East European people's democracies. (*Rukovodioci i štampa SSSR-a o NOB-u i socijalističkoj izgradnji u Jugoslavji [pre rezolucije IB]* [Belgrade, 1951].)

[126] Djilas, *Conversations with Stalin*, pp. 27–29.

[127] Ibid, p. 44.

[128] Ibid.

[129] Inter alia, Soviet spokesmen claimed that the USSR liberated Yugoslavia, that the Partisans were militarily inferior to the Bulgarian army, that the bourgeoisie remained very strong in Yugoslavia, and that Yugoslavia was attempting "utopian industrialization." See Dedijer, *Tito*, pp. 259–283; *Genosse Feind*, pp. 136–141.

[130] Dedijer, *Tito*, pp. 291–292.

[131] Many points of Yugoslav doctrine analyzed in this chapter were expounded at the initial session of the Cominform by Kardelj and Djilas. With Zhdanov's support, the Yugoslav delegates attacked the gradualism of other Communist leaderships—particularly the parliamentarianism of the French and Italian Communists. Belgrade was chosen as the seat of the Cominform at Stalin's express direction. The CPY was always listed first in Cominform documents. The Cominform journal was published in four languages: Russian, French, English—and Serbo-Croat (ibid., pp. 259–298).

[132] See Dedijer, *Tito*, chap. 18, which, however, completely ignores the question of the relations between the Yugoslav and Greek Communists. Although the Yugoslav government, like the rest of the Soviet bloc, failed to recognize the "temporary democratic government" proclaimed by the Greek Communists in late December 1947, a Committee for Assistance to the Greek People was formed in Belgrade in January 1948 (*Borba*, January 11, 1948). See Edgar O'Ballance, *The Greek Civil War, 1944–1949* (London: Faber & Faber, 1966). In the fall of 1947, *Communist*, the journal of the Communist Party of India, began to reprint some of the radical articles from the Belgrade *Komunist* cited in this chapter. Yugoslav delegates played a key role in the Calcutta Youth Conference and the Second Congress of the Communist Party of India in early 1948, apparently influencing the adoption of a more radical "anticapitalist" line by both gatherings. See Paul N. Hehn, "Yugoslavia and the Afro-Asian Bloc," *Review* (Study Center for Yugoslav Affairs, London) no. 7 (1968): 618–642, and the references cited therein, especially Gene D. Overstreet and Marshall Windmiller, *Communism in India* (Berkeley and Los Angeles: University of California Press, 1959), pp. 265–275; Dedijer, *Izgubljena bitka*, pp. 26–35, 41–45.

[133] Vukmanović-Tempo, "KP Grčke i narodnooslobodilačka borba," *Komunist* 3, no. 6 (November 1949): 1–82, at 78; Eugenio Reale, *Avec Jacques Duclos Au Banc des Accusés à la Réunion Constitutive du Kominform à Szklarska Poreba* (Paris: Librairie Plon, 1958), pp. 32, 137; Phyllis Auty, "Yugoslavia's International Relations," in Wayne Vucinich, ed., *Contemporary Yugoslavia* (Berkeley and Los Angeles: University of California Press, 1969), p. 385, n. 35.

[134] The one partial exception was an article in *Pravda* of November 18, 1947, devoted to the first issue of the Cominform journal and reproducing from it parts of Kardelj's speech at the founding of the Cominform, but also parts of Zhdanov's "two camp" speech.

[135] *Osnovy sovetskogo gosudarstva i prava* (Moscow, 1947), as referred to by Pijade, "Neka pitanja teorije države," *Članci*, 1950, pp. 193–194. An earlier

textbook ignored the people's democracies altogether. See A. I. Denisov, *Sovetskoe gosudarstvennoe pravo: Uchebnik dlia iuridicheskikh shkol* (Moscow, 1947).

[136] A. I. Denisov, *Osnovy marksistsko-leninskoi teorii gosudarstva i prava* (Moscow, 1948), pp. 94–98, 232–237, translated as *Osnovi marksističko-lenjinističke teorije države i prava* (Belgrade, 1949). For another example, the theoretical legitimization of Yugoslavia after March 1948 by the chief of the political department of the Soviet Military Administration in East Germany, see Leonhard, *Die Revolution entlässt ihre Kinder*, pp. 483–484. Such statements suggest confusion or disagreement within the CPSU itself on the relationship to Yugoslavia. It has often been suggested (e.g., Franz Borkenau, *European Communism* [London: Faber & Faber, 1953], p. 521, and Hamilton F. Armstrong, *Tito and Goliath* [New York: Macmillan, 1951], pp. 57–60) that there was an informal Tito-Zhdanov alliance in the postwar period. There seems to have been a Titoist component to the "Leningrad affair" (see Robert Conquest, *Power and Policy in the USSR* [New York: St. Martins, 1961], pp. 101–103). If Tito had a special relationship with Zhdanov or any element within the Soviet leadership, the Soviet attitude would have been more explicable to the Yugoslavs. Yet, as noted before, although the "Zhdanov line" of fall 1947 had much in common with the Yugoslav ideological outlook, it conflicted with CPY doctrine on some key issues. Moreover, evidence from the Yugoslav side does not support the hypothesis that such an alliance existed; the Italian Communist Reale supported the later claims of Dedijer and Djilas that Zhdanov worked against them in the Cominform from its founding. (Reale, *Avec Jacques Duclos*, p. 34; Dedijer, *Tito*, p. 295; Djilas, *Conversations with Stalin*, p. 159.) Had Zhdanov sympathized with CPY policies at any time before he denounced Tito as an imperialist agent in mid-1948, the Yugoslavs would have had every reason to reveal this, as they did with East European sympathizers who turned against them—but they have not. To the extent that Yugoslavia did play a role in leadership conflict within the CPSU, that role appears to have been an unconscious one.

[137] Dedijer, *Tito*, p. 317.

[138] Denying the existence of an anti-Soviet atmosphere in Yugoslavia before the break with Stalin, Pijade wrote revealingly in October 1949 about the attitude of the leadership: "Then we were still very far from having any basis for such thoughts, or else we had little interest in thinking deeper about certain phenomena in the Soviet Union, not giving them the importance which it is only now clear they deserved and not considering these matters our business. At that time there was nothing but amazement and discomfort at certain practical measures by leaders of the Soviet Union, who did not show respect toward Yugoslavia and could not legitimize it as socialist. . . . We ascribed this in part to the psychology of a victorious power which saw only its own sacrifices and had no understanding for the sacrifices of others, and also to its large-scale needs after the devastating war." ("Veliki majstori licemerja," *Članci*, 1950, p. 315. See also Dedijer, *Izgubljena bitka*, pp. 132–136.

[139] See Brzezinski, *The Soviet Bloc*, p. 39.

[140] The possibility remains that Stalin intended the Cominform to be more an instrument to restrict Tito's autonomy than a means of harnessing Yugoslav radicalism. In Djilas's view, his intention was "to lull to sleep the Yugoslav leaders with revolutionary self-satisfaction." (*Conversations with Stalin*, p. 132.)

[141] Ibid., p. 11.

II

Emergence of the Titoist Doctrine

". . . it is necessary fundamentally to revise the scheme of development of socialism which was created in the Soviet Union on the basis of very specific forms in that country. . . . "

Edvard Kardelj, *Nova Jugoslavija u savremenom svetu*, 1950

"Socialism can develop only from the initiative of the masses properly led by the proletarian Party."

Edvard Kardelj, *O narodnoj demokratiji u Jugoslaviji*, 1949

"Shove it!" - D.A. - 1979.

3

Systematization of Yugoslav Experience and Defense of Internationalism

Open Conflict

The first explicit indications that Stalin was no longer willing to tolerate the CPY Politburo's foreign policy initiatives and organizational autonomy came in February 1948.[1] Pictures of Tito were taken down in Rumania; he was publicly insulted by the Soviet chargé d'affaires in Tirana; negotiations in Moscow for new trade and military assistance agreements were broken off by the Soviet side. When the Yugoslav leaders made it clear at a Central Committee meeting of March 1 that these measures would not induce them to agree to Stalin's demand for immediate Yugoslav-Bulgarian federation (apparently a scheme to dilute and split the CPY leadership),[2] Stalin recalled all Soviet specialists from Yugoslavia. Tito's brief letter of inquiry about this to Moscow initiated a correspondence that lasted until June. In their letters to Tito, Stalin and Molotov—in addition to citing a number of concrete incidents allegedly illustrating an anti-Soviet atmosphere in Yugoslavia—attacked the Yugoslavs for the following ideological sins: (1) failure to conduct the class struggle, particularly in the countryside, where the peasants were treated as an undifferentiated whole; (2) neglect of the leading role of the Communist Party, resulting from both its fusion with the People's Front and its "undemocratic" internal organization; (3) underestimation of the importance of Soviet experience for Yugoslavia; (4) boundless self-praise that ignored the equal merits of other Communist Parties and the fact that the Red Army had in fact liberated Yugoslavia during World War II.[3]

When the Stalin-Molotov letters, the threats of Soviet representatives in Yugoslavia, and NKVD subversion failed to bring about Yugoslav self-criticism, Moscow took the step it had twice threatened previously (in 1945, after Tito implicitly criticized the USSR for failing to support the Yugoslav claim to Trieste, and in early 1948, over the issue of Tito's Balkan policy)—public disavowal, in the form of the Cominform Resolution of June 28, 1948. The Resolution stigmatized the Yugoslavs as "outside the family of the fraternal Communist Parties," declared that their "nationalist line can only lead to Yugoslavia's degeneration into an ordinary bourgeois republic, to the loss of its independence, and to its transformation into a colony of the imperialist countries," and concluded with an appeal to the CPY for Tito's overthrow.[4] Zhdanov told the assembled Cominform delegates in Bucharest that Moscow considered Tito to be an imperialist spy.[5] When the Cominform Resolution and continued Soviet subversion, too, failed to have their intended effect, Moscow applied diplomatic, economic, and military pressure, breaking all contacts with Yugoslavia, instituting an economic embargo, and finally organizing military maneuvers of its own and its satellites' armies on Yugoslavia's borders. During this period the level of public anti-Yugoslav invective steadily mounted. A Soviet government note of August 18, 1949, accused the Yugoslav leaders of using "gestapolike methods" and of being "fascist";[6] the trial of Hungarian Communist Laśzló Rajk in September depicted the Yugoslav leaders as having been Gestapo-American spies since the days of the Spanish Civil War.[7] It came as something of an anticlimax when the Cominform, meeting again in Budapest in November 1949, adopted a resolution on "The Communist Party of Yugoslavia in the Hands of Murderers and Spies."[8]

The CPY's public response to the anti-Tito campaign was initially cautious and defensive. While the Cominform Resolution was immediately published in Yugoslavia, along with the CPY's rejoinder, the dispute was treated explicitly only briefly at the Fifth Congress of the CPY, held in July 1948, which described it as involving "differences of opinion"[9] and as a "mistake";[10] CPY leaders repeatedly expressed the hope that the dispute could and would be settled.[11] Differences with the Central Committee of the CPSU were admitted to exist;[12] yet the dispute was usually publicly treated as existing solely with the Cominform,[13] and Stalin himself, far from being criticized, was still praised. The Fifth Congress opened with the slogan "Long Live the Leader and Teacher of Progressive Mankind, Comrade Stalin,"[14] while Tito concluded his report to the Congress with the words "Long Live Stalin."[15]

Publicly de-emphasizing the dispute, the Yugoslav leaders seemed to deny the need for any special response: "building socialism" at home and militant "anti-imperialism" abroad were objective facts not affected by the abusive words from Bucharest; both policies would be continued. Kardelj made this clear in his report to the Fifth Congress:

. . . our Party and its leadership will without question do all that they can to eliminate the differences between ourselves and the CC of the CPSU, the main force of socialism. The most important means to this end is even more persistent and enthusiastic work by our Party and the entire country in building socialism here—developing our productive forces as fully as possible for both our own benefit and the benefit of the entire socialist world—and increased activity in the struggle against the forces of reaction and imperialism both at home and abroad.[16]

Continuation of this dual policy—the Yugoslav leaders maintained—precluded not only Yugoslavia's passing over to the imperialist camp, as predicted in the Cominform Resolution, but its isolation as well; the USSR, as the head of the international working-class movement, could not abandon an objectively socialist and anti-imperialist country.[17]

Thus deeds would rebuff the anti-Yugoslav campaign, and public polemics were apparently renounced. "We must work," Tito said in the fall of 1948, "we must prove with deeds what is true and what is false and not fight with phrases the lies and slander directed at us."[18] The CPY leadership did publicly deny the charges against it in the Stalin-Molotov letters and the Cominform Resolution, but it maintained that no differences of principle existed, and it treated the accusations, not as theoretical criticism, but as "slanders" and "fabrications," indicating "ignorance of the situation in Yugoslavia."[19] Characterizing the entire campaign as revealing the abandonment of Communist morals,[20] the CPY leaders initially directed their concern with matters of theory elsewhere—to further elaboration of specific features of the Yugoslav revolution and the first stage of socialist transformation. Only in early 1949 (as will be described) did they resolve on open polemics with their Soviet bloc critics, explicitly taking up the task of "defending internationalism."

This pattern of response—considering here the more ideological aspects of Yugoslav Communist behavior—should be understood as a directed rather than spontaneous reaction to the Stalin-Cominform charges. Examination of this reaction raises the question of how the CPY Politburo perceived the dispute in its initial stage. There is no question that for the rank and file of the Party, and perhaps for many members of the Central Committee as well, the Cominform Resolution (or the Stalin-Molotov letters) came as an inexplicable bombshell, which was felt to be some kind of great mistake. As one Yugoslav academician—a young Party member in 1948—put it, the dispute was at first "unbelievable and unclear."[21] The foreign affairs editor of *Borba* expected "frank explanations between comrades. . . . I would never have thought about a rupture."[22] Some top-level CPY officials were in favor of accepting the invitation to attend the upcoming Cominform meeting and there to seek a settlement of the dispute. That they were overruled[23] suggests that for Tito and his closest colleagues, the Soviet letters bearing the signature "J. V. Stalin" made it clear they faced a fundamental, long-term conflict that could not be settled by compromise. Thus it was with full awareness of the seriousness of their position that they adopted the decision to resist.

The CPY leaders themselves subsequently offered ample data in support of this interpretation. Tito himself related, in discussing his feelings in June 1948: "It was clear to me that the conflict was not a passing affair, but that it marked a conclusive breakdown, a definitive conflict."[24] Kardelj was quoted as saying in early April 1948: "There can be no turning back now. . . . I know the Russians well. I know their logic. They will even proclaim us to be fascists in order to provide in the eyes of the world the moral-political justification for the campaign against us. If they could, they would liquidate us by force."[25] On many other occasions, too, beginning in 1949, the leadership claimed that the nature of the conflict had been clear to it ever since the Soviet letters were delivered.[26]

The authenticity of such ex post facto statements is suggested by several factors. First, Tito knew perfectly well what Stalin's opposition had signified in the past, even to Communists proclaiming absolute loyalty to him. Tito was in Moscow during the period of the Great Purges and, after being appointed Secretary-General of the CPY in 1937, rebuilt the Party as real and potential rivals disappeared in the purges.[27] Second, while the Stalin-Molotov letters could not have been expected, they were also not a total surprise, for serious disagreement with the Soviet Union on a number of issues had arisen by the spring of 1948. There had been the wartime friction over the strategy of revolution in Yugoslavia.[28] Then there had been the postwar differences on various concrete issues—the Yugoslavs' superindustrialization policy, their insistence on the integrity of their military-security apparatus, and their foreign policy initiatives in Eastern Europe and elsewhere. The CPY Central Committee session of March 1, 1948, had signaled that the Tito leadership would not back down on the many issues in dispute; at that meeting individual leaders reportedly perceived the emergence of a general conflict.[29]

If Tito was not to capitulate, awareness of an approaching, irreconcilable conflict had to be matched by a feeling—if no clear perspective—that resistance was possible. This required above all an organizational base autonomous of Moscow, which in fact existed in the Yugoslav Party-military apparatus built up during the war and protected from Soviet penetration.[30] Equally important, however, resistance also required a new, non-Stalinist source of Communist legitimacy. This, as suggested in Chapter 2, the CPY had begun to create before 1948—originally quite unconsciously—in theorizing about its revolutionary experience. The dilemma "Very well, suppose you do not die; suppose by some miracle you remain alive, again what for?"[31] did not arise. The fact of an indigenous proletarian revolution and the successful building of socialism proved to most high-ranking Party members that resistance to Stalin was not equivalent to counter-revolutionary treason and abetting imperialism.[32]

It is thus suggested that in the spring of 1948, aware that he faced a life-or-death struggle with Stalin, Tito adopted a course of resistance in the belief that this policy had a chance of success. But successful defiance assumed the continued "monolithic unity" of the CPY, and, as Tito himself told the Fifth Congress, "continually and untiringly the Party—in its press and through the spoken word—educated its members and the peoples of Yugoslavia in deep belief in, love of, and loyalty to the Soviet Union, as the country of socialism."[33] How was it possible to oppose Stalin while rallying about oneself a Party some of whose members, as Tito again put it "fell in the war with Stalin's name on their lips"?[34] How was it possible to be a heretic in a doctrinally oriented movement and yet not attack the anathematizing authority?

The solution, as already indicated, was the tactical public denial of heresy, the presentation of the dispute as a "mistake" that would be corrected and in which Stalin was not involved.[35] (This was the approach taken by the leadership at meetings of primary Party organizations in late summer 1948.)[36] Meanwhile, Yugoslavia would continue full steam ahead with socialist construction and anti-imperialism. The former meant in practice continued mobilization of the population to achieve the grandiose economic goals of the Five-Year Plan. The latter policy was expressed most ostentatiously in Yugoslavia's complete solidarity with the Soviet bloc—its ostracism of Yugoslavia notwithstanding—against the West at the Danubian Conference in Belgrade in August 1948.[37] Belgrade continued to give unqualified support to Soviet positions in the United Nations. (Further details of these policies are given in Chapters 5 and 6.) At the same time, while arresting real or suspected "Cominformists," Tito attempted to increase the Party's loyalty to him by reminding it—

notably, at the Fifth Congress—of their common, successful, heroic People's Liberation Struggle and the beginnings of building socialism in Yugoslavia. In retrospect, he described these tactics as follows:

... our fundamental task was to assure ourselves of the unhampered development of the people's [Party's] knowledge of the causes of the conflict with the Soviet Union. The most important thing was that people should realize what the issue was, that they should free themselves of prejudice, of the long years of instruction, that they should understand the substance of the matter. That was not an easy job. The tremendous authority of the Soviet Union and Stalin was operating. It was with that authority, with his letters and with the Cominform Resolution, that Stalin thought he would wreck the unity of our Central Committee. ... We dared not give free rein to indignation and merely reply to all the lies and slander coming from the Soviet Union, or in the name of the Soviet Union, with sharp rejoinders. It was necessary to allow Stalin time to do such things to Yugoslavia which would move the people themselves to say: "Down with Stalin," instead of estranging ourselves from the masses by being the first to raise such a cry in a moment of fury. Practice is life's best teacher. What Stalin did during the June days of 1948, what he hinted at then, he soon confirmed with a number of his most brutal acts. From then on, at least domestically, there was no great political problem in the struggle with the Soviet Union.[38]

At the ideological level, on the one hand, this meant refraining from open polemics with Moscow and limiting theoretical discussion of its charges (which were published) within the CPY[39]—either of which would have put the Tito leadership in the position of openly challenging Moscow's authority. On the other hand, it meant further theorizing about Yugoslav revolutionary practice, which would focus the Party's attention on its heroic past under Tito's leadership and develop a substitute for Moscow's authority while still not openly challenging that authority. Yet the unexpressed challenge would exist, and this would make it clear to Moscow that renunciation of public polemics did not indicate a weakening of Tito's stand. This interpretation, it may be suggested, explained the significance of Tito's rhetorical question to the Fifth Congress: "Does anyone now have the right to expect us to remain silent about our sacrifices, to remain silent and renounce our superhuman efforts in the Great Liberation Struggle which we waged in the heart of Hitler's enslaved Europe?"[40]

Occasionally a Yugoslav source suggested more openly that the real issue was in fact a challenge to Stalin's authority. Thus Djilas wrote in *Borba* in October 1948, ".... authority is not everything—truth is above authority...."[41] Moreover, CPY leaders began to suggest that this authority was not directly operative, but was the creation of the CPY leadership. As Pijade told the Second Congress of the CP of Serbia:

The authority of the Bolshevik Party in our country is inseparable from the authority of our Party. That means, in other words, that that authority was not and could not be created directly, by the very fact of the October Revolution and the very fact of the building of socialism in the Soviet Union. It had to be transferred by means of a special transmission belt, which could only be our Party. But that authority was not created only by the untiring propaganda of our Party over thirty years . . .; it was created, consolidated and raised to such a high level primarily by our Party's own acts, . . . by victory in the liberation war which it led, by the victory of the socialist revolution which it headed. . . .[42]

Later, as will be seen, the authority of the CPSU was openly challenged as the CPY leadership took up the task of "defending internationalism" in public polemics. Thereafter, codification of Yugoslav revolutionary practice into Yugoslav Communist ideology continued—now as the source of an openly opposed alternative to Moscow's Communist authority and very legitimacy.

Systematization of Yugoslav Revolutionary Practice

The CPY began to devote greater attention to the theoretical significance of its revolutionary experience at the Fifth Congress in July 1948. The Fifth Congress (scheduled in May 1948, when an open break seemed inevitable, as a forum to mobilize the Party behind Tito) was devoted primarily to a review of the CPY's history under Tito's leadership—particularly the wartime years. In line with this focus, the Resolution adopted at the Congress proclaimed as a basic ideological task

to systematically develop work on the Marxist-Leninist study of the problems of our country. It is therefore necessary to organize work on the elaboration and study of the history of our Party, the history of the working-class movement of our country, the history of the People's Liberation Struggle and the problems of building socialism here. This task must be understood as one of the most necessary preconditions for the ideological education of Party cadres and for educating the masses in the spirit of socialism.[43]

This section of the Resolution was based on Djilas's report to the Fifth Congress on agitation-propaganda activity in which he noted that the Party's basic ideological weakness was not in the realm of Marxism-Leninism in general, but in neglect of "elaborating *our* reality and the results of *our* revolution and the paths of development of socialism *here* on the basis of Marxism-Leninism."[44] But at this point Yugoslav experience was still not directly opposed to Soviet experience, and thus Djilas added that his words did not mean that the study of Soviet practice should be neglected. Nor could the fundamentals of Marxism-Leninism be questioned. Indeed, he warned of the danger of "revisionist tendencies" appearing in the wake of the conflict with the USSR.[45]

It was easier to formulate than to implement this directive of the Fifth Congress. For example, in 1949 a translated Soviet textbook[46] (albeit with a critical introduction) had to be used in university courses on "Theory of the State and Law," for, as Pijade admitted, "Our writers are not yet in a position to work out a text based on our own socialist experience."[47] The Party propaganda apparatus was reorganized. In October 1948 the Politburo established a Historical Division in the Central Committee "to collect, collate, and publish archival and other material on the history of the Communist Party of Yugoslavia."[48] In January 1949 "History of the CPY" was introduced as a separate course in one-year Party schools; at the same time the CC Agit-Prop section directed that the course "Party Life" be made more theoretical and be based on Yugoslav as well as Bolshevik practice.[49] In February 1949 the Institute for Social Sciences was founded in Belgrade to train Party cadres in Marxism-Leninism, a task said to require both "mastery of scientific Marxist-Leninist theory" and its "concretization in harmony with the historical specifics of a given country and people."[50]

Substantively, the new ideological line resulted in the further elaboration and more systematic formulation of all the points that had come to characterize the CPY's doctrine of people's democracy by the end of 1947 (as described in Chapter 2). Particular attention was devoted to the Yugoslav Communist revolution itself. The People's Liberation Struggle was now explicitly declared to have been an autonomous "specific form of socialist revolution" from the very beginning.[51] Initially, through 1948—while the tactical public line of seeking a settlement of the dispute with the USSR was being followed—there was a return to the position of 1945 which had acknowledged Soviet military operations on Yugoslav territory as well as the decisive role of the Red Army in World War II as a whole. But this did not alter the fact of an essentially autonomous revolution. As Pijade, who dealt most directly with the issue, told the Fifth Congress:

"Of course we will not and cannot forget that we liberated our country with our own strength, through our own struggle, in our own people's revolution—with the help of the Soviet Union."[52]

The importance of this point has already been suggested. It was not just a matter of self-pride, a squabble over "who liberated Yugoslavia." The "class" character of Tito-led Yugoslavia, and hence its legitimacy, depended on how it had originated. If the CPY, under Tito, had indeed carried out a socialist revolution in the course of World War II, then the socialist legitimacy of the postwar state was traceable directly to that revolution. If, on the other hand, the People's Liberation Struggle had amounted to nothing more than a harassment of Axis military forces, if social change had come only with the advance of the Red Army onto Yugoslav territory, then socialism in Yugoslavia had to be traced directly to Moscow. In that case, Stalin remained the unchallengeable authority whose accusations could not be contested. Writing in *Borba* even before the Fifth Congress, Milentije Popović pointed out the implications of "Soviet liberation": "Of course, if you take the position of negating [the revolution of the peoples of Yugoslavia under the leadership of the CPY] then things take on their own logic, then it is possible 'logically' to maintain that the Yugoslav Communists waged their struggle from 1941 on for nationalistic reasons, that they are able to permit a 'Turkish, terrorist regime' and bureaucratic methods—then many other things, too, will be 'logical' and 'possible.' "[53]

Defending their revolution as autonomous and socialist, the CPY ideologues now also considered in greater detail the nature of the postwar state order, spelling out clearly what they had previously only hinted at— that their state, as a people's democracy, was a form of the dictatorship of the proletariat. The connection was first made publicly in the draft Program of the Fifth Congress, which proclaimed that "the leading role of the working class in the people's state guarantees it those basic characteristics of a dictatorship of the proletariat which ensure the socialist development of the country."[54] Again, however, Yugoslav Communists also emphasized specific features of their people's democracy. Quoting Lenin on the inevitability of different forms of proletarian dictatorship, Kardelj affirmed in his report to the Fifth Congress that the class alliance in Yugoslavia had been characterized by a "great mass breadth and special organizational firmness, as expressed in the People's Front," and that the leading role of the working class had expressed itself in a new way, thus "easing the building of socialism in our country."[55] Pijade, in his report to the Fifth Congress, drew the conclusion that Kardelj had left unexpressed: people's democracy was a "special *democratic* road of transition from capitalism to communism."[56] This line of reasoning was taken one step further in mid-1949, when—as will later be described—Kardelj began to differentiate the Yugoslav political system from the Soviet system precisely on this issue.

The significance of Yugoslav Communist theorizing on people's democracy as a special form of the dictatorship of the proletariat enjoying broad mass support becomes clear if the Yugoslav concept is compared with the revised Soviet-East European doctrine of people's democracy which took shape in late 1948 and 1949.[57] That revised doctrine denied most of the unique features (described in Chapter 1) which had previously been said to characterize a people's democracy. Soviet ideologues now declared that people's democracy was indeed a specific form of the dictatorship of the proletariat and, as such, was actively beginning to build a socialist society.

While the Yugoslav Communists and their Soviet bloc critics agreed on this point by the end of 1948, they still differed on what constituted the specific nature of people's democracy and, most important, on its relationship to the Soviet system. In the revised Soviet bloc theory, people's democracy differed from Soviet democracy in embodying remnants of the "bourgeois past"—especially, the formal multiparty system. The Yugoslav concept excluded parliamentarianism, distinguishing people's democracy (admittedly, never very clearly) by the special strength of the worker-peasant alliance in which, moreover, the Communist Party achieved its leading role in a new way.

The Soviet bloc concept also postulated the special, organic dependence of the people's democracies upon the Soviet Union which was lacking in Yugoslav theory. This dependence was much more than the historical subordination of a society beginning its transition to socialism to Soviet society in the advanced stage of "building communism." The main factor responsible for the rise of a people's democracy was Soviet "liberation"; the main guarantee of its continued existence was close alliance with the USSR; it was obligated to copy Soviet practice. As suggested in Chapter 1, this concept signified the theoretical justification of a revolution from without; on this point there was no change from the 1945-1947 view. Bolesław Bierut, the Polish Communist leader, expressed this relationship quite clearly:

... people's democracy is a special form of revolutionary state which arose in the new historical conditions of our epoch; it is an expression of the new relation of classes in the international arena. . . . Just as the selfless, heroic aid of the Soviet Union is the basis of our people's democracy, the basis of the specific character of our road [to socialism] in comparison with the Soviet road is the all-around aid of the Soviet Union and the utilization of the experience and achievements of its victorious dictatorship of the proletariat. Thanks to this we are able, within the framework of our people's democracy, to realize the functions of the dictatorship of the proletariat in a different form.[58]

In the revised Soviet bloc view, people's democracy was thus a special *dependent* form of the dictatorship of the proletariat. As Kardelj aptly put it, polemicizing with the first part of Bierut's statement, "people's democracy is thus not the expression of the concrete relationship of class forces inside Poland in favorable international conditions (among which the victory of the USSR abroad is, of course, the chief factor), but simply a gift from abroad."[59] The Yugoslav view, in contrast, emphasized the internal factor; it affirmed a new, revolution-based, and as such autonomously legitimate people's democracy as a form of the dictatorship of the proletariat.

At the Fifth Congress and thereafter, the Yugoslav form of the dictatorship of the proletariat was given more substance by further generalization about the special Yugoslav institutions, the people's committees,[60] the People's Army,[61] and the People's Front.[62] Now, however, the relationship of the Yugoslav forms to Soviet practice and Marxism-Leninism itself assumed greater importance. CPY spokesmen affirmed the importance of studying Soviet experience (as in Djilas's remarks to the Fifth Congress quoted earlier) but reiterated that it was incorrect to transfer Soviet experience "mechanically" to Yugoslav conditions.[63] As Djilas restated the Yugoslavs' task (in an authoritative article in *Borba*), the CPY had to utilize the theoretical as well as practical experience of the USSR—but not copy it.[64] Moreover, as early as August 1948, Tito made it clear that Soviet experiences offered negative as well as positive lessons; others, he implied, might avoid Soviet mistakes.[65] Perhaps most important, the CPY now stressed that Marxism-Leninism was not "the monopoly of any nation or any Party"[66] but the common ideology of the international working-class movement which continued to be developed outside as well as within the USSR—especially by revolutionary practice. As Djilas complained: "Our critics . . . appropriate for themselves a monopoly on Marxism by alleging—contrary to Lenin—that Marxism can be further developed only in the USSR . . . that the revolutionary practice of the working-class movements in the world does not or cannot mean the further development of Marxism."[67] Kardelj affirmed that "theory is itself enriched, supplemented, and in certain propositions even changed in the process of revolution."[68] Yugoslav revolutionary practice was the obvious case in point.

The campaign of ostracism and pressure which Stalin mounted against the Tito leadership thus led that leadership to formulate in the second half of 1948 a more emphatic statement of both the specific features and the socialist essence of the Yugoslav revolutionary experience, with no significant deviation from the theses formulated prior to the open break. This general pattern originally applied to the doctrine on the socialization of agriculture as well. During the second half of 1948, CPY statements on agriculture continued to reflect Kardelj's 1947 formulations, the only difference being a somewhat greater stress on the importance of class struggle. Implementation of a policy guided by this doctrinal perspective would refute the Cominform charge that the CPY had first "ignored class differentiation in the countryside" and subsequently, in response to Soviet criticism, adopted the adventurous line of "liquidation of the capitalist elements, and hence the kulaks, as a class."[69] Both charges were false, V. Begović wrote in Borba: "The road recommended is the road we are taking."[70] In his report to the Fifth Congress, Kardelj reiterated the CPY position that the Party's goal was the socialist transformation of agriculture; that class struggle in the countryside was sharpening; that the present phase was one of restricting capitalist elements, as a step preparing the way for their eventual elimination; that the main approach to socialization was the association of the peasantry in general cooperatives; that, while work cooperatives were important as a perspective of the future, "they do not at all represent a general peasant movement."[71]

This gradualist doctrine on the socialization of agriculture suffered a sharp reversal at the Second Central Committee Plenum of January 28–30, 1949. The Resolution of the Second Plenum formulated the basic task of agricultural policy as "strengthening the socialist sector in agriculture" through the instrument of the work cooperative, now described as the "most successful means" for the socialist transformation of the village. The Resolution directed the forming of work cooperatives "with greater boldness and at a faster tempo," giving priority to their higher types. Existing general cooperatives were to be transformed into work cooperatives by instituting common labor projects and setting up agricultural machine stations; the Resolution was silent on founding new general cooperatives. While thus adopting a policy of rapid collectivization, the Second Plenum warned of empty "anti-kulak phrase-mongering" that would only unite the enemies of socialism and induce "wavering" in the "backward segment of the working peasants."[72]

The directives of the Second Plenum remained in effect throughout 1949; they were reflected in all the Party's programmatic statements that year. Thus the May Day slogan addressed to the peasants appealed: "Enter boldly into the work cooperatives!"[73] This line signified the abandonment of the gradualist course in agriculture and the adoption of a course more closely patterned on Stalin's collectivization of Soviet agriculture. Was this not renunciation of one of the specific features of the Yugoslav transition to socialism in the face of the anti-Tito campaign and as such a compromising admission by the Yugoslav Politburo that Stalin and the Cominform had been right after all in accusing it of following an incorrect line in the countryside?

An attempt to explain this adoption of an important feature of Stalinism in the course of the conflict with Stalin must begin with the Yugoslav economic situation at the end of 1948. The Five-Year Plan was in its second year, with an ever greater influx of peasants into the cities required to supply the manpower for the grandiose industrialization projects. Yet food production was not increasing, all the efforts of the state notwithstanding. The Party leadership faced the task of achieving a marked increase in agricultural market surpluses if the Five-Year Plan was to continue. Such increased output could be realized in three hypothetical ways: (1) a neo-New Economic Policy relying on the private peasant; (2) a continuation of the gradualist line; (3) radical collectivization.

The first option had not been adopted before the break with Stalin; its adoption was precluded with socialist industrialization progressing apace and the Cominform attacking "Bukharinism" in the Yugoslav countryside. The second possibility was open to the same charge; the accusation, moreover, could not convincingly simply be denounced as a "slander" because of the adoption of a policy of forced collectivization in the rest of Eastern Eruope after June 1948. Previously, the legitimacy of the specific features of the Yugoslav transition to socialism had been enhanced by their radicalism, in comparison with the rest of Eastern Europe. Now the relationship was being reversed, yet the one thing Tito could not afford politically—at least until he was certain of the continued loyalty of the CPY—was to give the slightest substantiation to the charges of revisionism directed against himself and his close colleagues. This applied primarily to the CPY itself, especially in view of the fact that some rural activists were never happy with the gradualist policy,[74] but also to "progressive world public opinion," for the CPY was just then taking up the task of "defending internationalism," and Stalinist collectivized agriculture was still considered an attribute of socialism by Communists breaking with Stalin.[75] Thus the third option was taken, in part, to quote the authoritative CPY history, "as a result of the desire to negate the slanderous attacks expressed in the Informburo [Cominform] Resolution."[76] Supplementing this motivation was doubtless another, less instrumental rationale. The economic difficulties may have suggested to the Yugoslav Politburo that the gradualist approach to the socialization of agriculture was simply not working, in sharp contrast to the perceived success of the rest of its revolutionary program. If one aspect of Yugoslav experience proved to be defective, was the instinctive reaction not to grasp at Soviet experience at a comparable stage of development—Stalin's irreconcilable hostility notwithstanding?

There is evidence (including the proceedings of the Second Plenum itself) which suggests, however, that neither of these motivations was unanimously shared by the Party leadership. Shortly before the Plenum at least two top leaders, Vlahovic and Bakarić, condemned "the implementation of certain measures in the village under the influence of the Informburo Resolution which isolate the Party from the peasant masses, i.e., from the middle peasant, and which are premature."[77] Such remarks raise the possibility of their opposition to the radical line at the Second Plenum. At the Second Plenum itself, Kardelj noted in the introduction to his Plenum report on agriculture: "In our Party organizations and *even among leading cadres* there does not yet exist complete clarity on the forms and tempo of building socialism in the countryside. On some questions there are even certain differences of view."[78] Moreover, there was a significant difference in the treatment of general cooperatives in Kardelj's report and the Plenum Resolution. Affirming the importance of organizing more work cooperatives, Kardelj nevertheless denied that this meant neglecting general cooperatives:

Often certain of our comrades raise the question—should we take the course of rapidly developing work cooperatives or the course of developing cooperatives of the general type? The very formulation of the question in that way is completely incorrect and proof of the confusion in the heads of some of our people. It is obviously not a question of either-or, but a unified process. We must form both the one and the other in accordance with concrete possibilities and conditions.

What is more, he suggested definite limits on the establishment of work cooperatives:

We may develop work cooperatives today only within certain limits, depending on the development of the consciousness of the working peasant, but by means of the cooperative of the general type, we can today develop elements of socialist cooperative agricultural production on a mass basis.[79]

Yet, as previously indicated, the Resolution of the Second Plenum practically ignored the general cooperative, suggesting a modification of the Politburo line of relative moderation on collectivization at the insistence of more radically minded members of the Central Committee at the Plenum itself.[80]

The collectivization policy adopted by the Second Plenum failed to increase the food supply to the cities while heightening peasant discontent at a time when Tito sought to maintain the support of the country as a whole in defying Stalin. The Yugoslav leaders soon saw that the policy had to be modified. A Central Committee letter of December 20, 1949, to Party organizations condemned the tendency of forming work cooperatives "at any price and without considering whether all the necessary political and economic conditions exist."[81] A week later the Third Central Committee Plenum, while still calling for new work cooperatives in fertile areas of the country, warned the Party: "Do not place primary emphasis on the number of [work] cooperatives but on their internal consolidation; do not form unproductive work cooperatives."[82] After only eleven months, limits were thus set on radical collectivization. This marked the beginning of a reexamination of collectivization itself—a process that will be traced in Chapter 8.

Criticism of and Differentiation from the USSR

The Second Plenum of January 1949, in addition to espousing collectivization, also initiated a reformulation of the CPY's public stance in the dispute with Stalin. In a report to the Plenum on agitation and propaganda work, Djilas affirmed that a fundamental conflict with the CPSU did exist. Its origins, he stated, were traceable, not to any "misunderstanding," but to "revisionism on a whole series of questions" in the Soviet Union and its East European satellites. Djilas rejected the possibility of a settlement of the dispute, maintaining flatly that "it will inevitably sharpen."[83] The defensive line of affirming specific features of the Yugoslav revolution while abstaining from public polemics with the CPSU was to be replaced by the line of "defending internationalism." Djilas put it this way:

It is incorrect to concentrate only on denials; it is incorrect only to defend ourselves from lies and attacks. . . . It is necessary to assume a more active posture; it is necessary to reveal the lack of principle and the essence of the slanderous campaign. . . . Thus it is necessary to undertake serious work on these questions—issuing documents and writing books which not only would consider the present lies but which would—in one way or another—begin to work out the essence of the problem. . . .

The question of the approach to the problem of the so-called particular character or specific character of our development . . . has until now often been illuminated one-sidedly. . . . The new situation forces us to approach that question in a different manner. . . . Defending the specific path of our development, we in fact do not defend some kind of national independence of Yugoslavia or some kind of right of Yugoslavia to independent development. We are defending proletarian Marxist-Leninist internationalism from those who distort it, ignoring and falsely presenting the revolutionary struggle and efforts of workers in other countries—concretely, in Yugoslavia. . . . That is the essence of the problem, and not the question of our "peculiarity," "autonomous development," or "specific character."[84]

This unambiguous formulation of a new agitprop line was not unduly publicized. But, although Stalin himself was still publicly spared until later in 1949, it did initiate a new phase in the CPY's response to the conflict with Stalin.[85] The Yugoslavs now compared the dispute with the Menshevik-Bolshevik quarrel, comparing themselves, of course, with Lenin.[86] Their task, Tito declared later in 1949, was "the defense of the principles of Marxism-Leninism against anyone, even their creators, who violate them."[87] Their weapon was public polemics, which took the form of pronouncements of the leadership, articles by lesser theoreticians, and a daily column, "Against Slander and Misinformation," in *Borba*.[88]

This shift in public posture was permitted by Tito's successful consolidation of Party loyalty in the second half of 1948. It was caused by the need of the CPY leaders to explain, within a Communist framework, to the Party, to "progressive world public opinion," and to themselves *why* the conflict had arisen. If disillusionment with Stalin—above all, in the ranks of the CPY—was not to lead to disillusionment with "socialism" in general and thus to the disintegration of the Party, the Tito leadership had to offer a convincing explanation of where Stalin had gone wrong and how his mistakes were being avoided in Yugoslavia.

The first answer was that the Soviet Union had violated the principles of correct relations among socialist states. But, as Tito himself admitted, "the theoretical question of the relations among the countries which are building socialism has not been worked out."[89] Thus it became the Yugoslav ideologues' task, in explaining Stalin's behavior, to work out the normative pattern of such relations. This process unfolded gradually over the period of a year, from late 1948 to late 1949. The first contribution was a historical case study. Responding to Soviet bloc charges (especially the anti-Yugoslav invective of the First Congress of the Albanian Workers' Party in November 1948), the CPY published in January 1949 a documentary history of Yugoslav-Albanian relations until 1948. That history sought to demonstrate an unblemished record of unselfish, internationalist assistance extended by the CPY to the weaker Albanian Party. It suggested in conclusion that only on such a basis of "mutual respect and equality" could the question of proper relations among socialist states and Communist Parties in general be posed. Only a socialist system organized on this principle could continue to inspire the worldwide anti-imperialist struggle.[90]

Subsequently touched upon in public speeches, the problem received comprehensive attention in the fall of 1949 in the form of two major *Komunist* articles by Djilas and Milentije Popović.[91] Popović limited himself to the issue of economic relations among socialist states, which were said to be still essentially capitalist in nature. This conclusion was based on the argument that intrasocialist trade was carried on at capitalist world prices, which, in a Marxist-Leninist analysis, signified exploitation—including the drawing of superprofits—from a backward by a more highly developed country, even if both were socialist. Such exploitation was said to be enhanced by the Soviet joint-stock companies and other instruments of foreign trade. In contrast to this practice, Popović maintained, trade among socialist countries should be based on prices lower than world prices beneficial to less developed countries. Moreover, the latter should also be aided by an advanced socialist country through interest-free loans and outright grants. In short, it was the responsibility of a developed socialist country to aid the industrialization of backward socialist countries.[92]

Repeating this economic analysis, Djilas, in his *Komunist* article, went on to consider the political consequences. In order to guarantee its economic privileges, he said, the USSR had established "vassal regimes" in Eastern Europe. Thus there existed "imperialist exploitation" in the classic Leninist sense. Here was the root of the imperialist methods employed in the anti-Yugoslav campaign. In contrast, Djilas presented, by exegesis of Lenin's writing, a norm of economic and political equality among socialist states. He drew the following conclusion:

In socialism there are not and cannot be leading nations and leading states, for they will turn into ruling nations and states, which in fact is occurring today. Only the equality of states, peoples, and Parties can be "leading," only mutual agreement and cooperation can be "leading." . . . The leaders of the USSR . . . thought up the anti-Marxist "theory" of the leading role of the USSR—that is, the leading role of the Russian people—and made recognition of that role a condition of internationalism and Communism. They forgot that in the works of Marx, Engels, Lenin, and even, until quite recently, Stalin, there is not one word—literally, not one word—about the need for a leading state, a leading Party, and a leading nation under socialism.[93]

Only on the basis of complete equality, Djilas continued, could the international working-class movement achieve true unity. This norm of equality also had implications for the internal situation in each socialist country. Since socialism was developing autonomously beyond the borders of the USSR and since the CPSU could not claim a leading role in the Communist movement, different roads to socialism, rather than uniformity prescribed by Moscow, were inevitable. As Djilas put it:

Precisely because he discovered the law that revolutions do not break out simultaneously in all countries but break out in different periods in different countries and thus in different international conditions and with different national characteristics, Lenin clearly saw that the forms of revolution and the forms of the transition to socialism, too, are unusually rich in their diversity. . . . Different countries, going toward the same goal—socialism and communism—inevitably go toward it on different roads, at various tempos, and with different forms.[94]

The test of whether a country's internal order was socialist was not Moscow's approval but rather what Djilas described as an objective standard—the relations of production in that country.[95]

The Djilas-Popović formulation of the norm of equality in relations among socialist states and Communist Parties was the first significant new development in Yugoslav Communist ideology after the beginning of open conflict with Stalin. Determined to retain political control in Yugoslavia and believing, on the basis of their own revolutionary experience, that World War II had initiated a new stage in the "epoch of imperialism and proletarian revolution"—that is, the autonomous development of socialism beyond the borders of the USSR—the CPY leaders worked out the new doctrine, referring to Lenin as their authority.

In the course of 1949, as Soviet pressure against Yugoslavia mounted, a list of increasingly serious Soviet deviations from this norm of equality was formulated. Whereas in 1948 the USSR had been accused of "dogmatism" in ignoring the Yugoslav revolutionary development,[96] it was now accused of "systematic" and "conscious revision" of the Marxist-Leninist principle of equality among socialist states and Communist Parties.[97] At the outset of the conflict, the CPY had linked its critics with "world reactionaries" in opposing socialism in Yugoslavia. To this charge was now added—as by Djilas in his *Komunist* article—the accusation of using "imperialist methods" against Yugoslavia. The Soviet Union was condemned for "trading with the imperialists" over Yugoslavia in the cases of Trieste, Carinthia, and the Greek Communist uprising.[98] Its economic embargo was compared with that of the Austro-Hungarian Empire against Serbia;[99] its opposition to Balkan federation, with the "imperialist policy of subjugation of Russian Tsarism."[100] In November 1949, delivering the major speech commemorating Yugoslav National Day, Vlahović for the first time mentioned the threat to Yugoslavia from the Soviet Union before that from the West.[101]

Similar criticism was directed at the Soviet Union's relations with other Communist countries; by the end of 1949 it had been accused of "hegemonic aspirations toward other peoples"[102] and of pursuing a "sphere of interest policy toward Eastern Europe."[103] Moreover, CPY spokesmen began to hint that Soviet foreign policy *in general* was assuming an imperialist character. As Kardelj told the Skupština in December 1949: ". . . the moment when the government of a socialist country, such as the USSR, takes the road of hegemony over other peoples, its foreign policy begins to lose the character of principled anti-imperialist struggle and begins to transform itself into a struggle for the division of spheres of interest among the Great Powers. . . ."[104] The point was reinforced with the most notorious case from the past: in November, Pijade had subtly raised the question of the Soviet Union's motivation for concluding its 1939 pact with Hitler.[105]

In the fall of 1949 certain Yugoslav leaders expanded their criticism of Soviet foreign policy to encompass specific features of Soviet internal life. This initial questioning of the previously sacrosanct Soviet order can apparently be traced to the impact of one event—the trial of Hungarian Communist leader László Rajk. (The Rajk trial, together with the earlier trial of the pro-Yugoslav Albanian Communist leader Koci Xoxe, initiated a series of show trials throughout Eastern Europe, by means of which Stalin sought to achieve total domination over the East European Communist Parties. The defendants were usually charged with having maintained links with the Yugoslav leaders, who in turn were imperialist agents.) The absurd allegations that practically all the CPY leaders had been Gestapo-American spies since the time of the Spanish Civil War affected them, to use Dedijer's words, "like oil on fire."[106] In a polemical response to the charges from Budapest, Pijade labeled the Rajk trial "part of a police-spy provocation" and as such openly compared it with the Moscow purge trials of the late 1930s.[107] He then pointed out "various phenomena in the present-day internal life of the Soviet Union" which "needed to be explained."[108] While Pijade's articles were appearing, the literary weekly *Književne novine* published an article by Wolfgang Leonhard which pointed to "phenomena and tendencies [in the USSR] which are inexplicable and incomprehensible for a socialist country."[109]

Broaching the subject of defects in the Soviet internal order was, however, apparently not unanimously approved by the CPY leadership at this point. Pijade's approach was strongly opposed by Djilas and perhaps others whose critical reexamination of Soviet policies had not yet reached the point of questioning Soviet society itself.[110] Nevertheless, the issue of defects in Soviet domestic life was not dropped, in part for ideological reasons. Foreign policy and domestic policy were, to a Marxist, both parts of a common superstructure. If "imperialist methods" characterized the first, the second could not be the unblemished ideal of socialism—a logical progression that would repeat itself in subsequent conflicts between ruling Communist Parties, especially the Sino-Soviet conflict.

International developments, too, surely played a role. The Rajk trial was quickly followed by the "anti-Titoist" show trial of Bulgarian Communist leader Traicho Kostov in early December 1949. In the meantime, Yugoslavia felt itself threatened by a Soviet bloc military invasion and had begun the reorientation of its foreign policy toward the West (to be examined in Chapter 5). In this situation the CPY leadership as a whole became convinced that if the USSR had violated the principle of equal relations among socialist states, the internal Soviet order itself must be defective. This was first suggested explicitly in December 1949, in a key *Komunist* article by theoretician Makso Baće.[111] Maintaining that "the foreign policy of a country . . . can only be the extension of its internal policy," Baće proceeded to examine in detail one aspect of Soviet internal life—Soviet philosophy: "There are serious indications that many Soviet philosophers have left the path of the creative development of theory. What is worse, there are serious indications that many, even leading philosophers in the Soviet Union have, perhaps unconsciously, defined for themselves the task, not of developing dialectical materialism, but of formulating a new catechism." The state of Soviet philosophy, Bacé made clear, was not accidental. Examining other aspects of Soviet intellectual life, he concluded: "We found that in all branches of life in the USSR . . . there exists a strange but uniform phenomenon—strange in any case for socialism, incomprehensible for socialist society—a phenomenon, as [Soviet spokesmen] themselves say, which is not unique or accidental, and which they themselves, led by Zhdanov, call monopoly." Monopoly was a "monstrous growth" in socialist society signifying no less than "the return of one form of exploitation and suppression after the socialist revolution."

The phenomenon of bureaucratism in the USSR was criticized by Kardelj, addressing the Slovene Academy of Arts and Sciences even before Bacé's article had appeared. Taking issue with Soviet theories "making a fetish of the state," Kardelj pointed out that they were only the reflection of Soviet reality: "Such theories are, of course, in a position to cover up all kinds of undemocratic and antisocialist tendencies within the order built up in a socialist revolution—tendencies which grow either from the numerous remnants of the old class-society system or from new social contradictions, above all from the very existence of the state and the continuous tendency to perpetuate bureaucratism and thus state capitalist relations."[112] Taking Kardelj's remarks as his point of departure, S. Ljubenović, in an article entitled "Some Sources and Forms of Bureaucratism and the Struggle for Their Elimination," attacked bureaucratism in the USSR much more directly:

The phenomenon of bureaucratism is an open wound in socialist democracy, above all in the Soviet Union, where the narrowing of democratic practice in favor of an all-powerful bureaucratic apparatus and intelligence service, which suppresses criticism in internal policy, necessarily is reflected in the conceptions of foreign policy. . . . The phenomena of despotism and arbitrariness are the best sign that tendencies toward degeneration which threaten the foundation of true democracy exist in the state apparatus.[113]

In the fall of 1949, then, beginning with Pijade's condemnation of the Rajk trial, Yugoslav Communists began to question internal as well as foreign policies of the Soviet Union, suggesting vaguely that defects in the latter were to be explained in terms of the degeneration of the former.

As described in the following chapter, during the course of 1950 this criticism was developed into a fundamental reevaluation of the Soviet social system itself. On the basis of the resulting negative critique, the CPY would develop its own interpretation of Marxism-Leninism opposed to Stalinism.

The positive development of Yugoslav ideology, however, was not solely a response to negative criticism of the Soviet system. The first real criticism of the Soviet internal scene was made by Pijade in late September 1949; four months previously, in his treatise "On People's Democracy in Yugoslavia,"[114] Kardelj outlined a theoretical perspective of the transition period to socialism which contained the seed of the idea later to become known in the domestic sphere as the essence of Titoist ideology—the "withering away of the state."

Kardelj's treatise took as its point of departure the concept (formulated by Pijade at the Fifth Congress) of people's democracy as a broad, "special democratic form" of the dictatorship of the proletariat. Mocking the original Soviet–East European concept of people's democracy as a "third thing" between bourgeois and proletarian democracy, he reiterated that a people's democracy was in essence a dictatorship of the proletariat. Polemicizing with the revised (post-1948) Soviet–East European view of people's democracy as dependent (since it organically postulated subordination to the USSR) and inferior (since it embodied such "bourgeois remnants" as a formal multiparty system), Kardelj distinguished the specific character of people's democracy in Yugoslavia in the following terms:

... that which gives this state of the transition period—which, because of the undisputed leading role of the proletariat, is in essence a dictatorship of the proletariat...—the character of a *people's* democracy is the fact that is was born in historical conditions which enable it to rely on even broader masses of the working people, that is to say, on the people. It is able to rely on the daily active participation of the masses in running the state. At the present time, when the USSR has existed for more than thirty years and when the idea of socialism has won its world-historical victory, it is this popular democratic side of the transition period which ever more strongly comes to the fore, because today a socialist state can rely on a far wider segment of the masses than was possible for the dictatorship of the proletariat in Russia in the post-October period. Under these conditions, the direct participation of the masses in the entire apparatus of state administration becomes greater; democracy is deepened and further developed.[115]

People's democracy was thus a higher form of the dictatorship of the proletariat than that achieved in the post-October period in Russia since it involved the masses to a greater extent in running the affairs of the socialist state; exposition of this matter was the main subject of Kardelj's treatise. Class oppression by the victorious proletariat headed by its vanguard, the Communist Party, he asserted, was only one side of the dictatorship of the proletariat as conceived by Marx, Engels, and Lenin. Equally important was its noncoercive side, involving, in Lenin's words, "the real equal and general participation of the *whole* mass of the people in all *state* affairs."[116] This aspect of the dictatorship of the proletariat (which Kardelj consistently referred to as "socialist democracy") meant implementation after a successful socialist revolution of the principles of state organization which Marx and Engels saw embodied in the Paris Commune: (1) election and recall of all officials; (2) moderate pay for all officials; (3) "the direct drawing of the masses into state administration in such a way, as Lenin added, that everyone will be a 'bureaucrat' for a time and therefore no one will be able to become a bureaucrat."[117] This meant, Kardelj continued, nothing less than the process of the withering away of the state—a point he made by extensive quotations from Marx, Engels, and especially Lenin's *State and Revolution.*

Kardelj granted that these principles could not be fully realized immediately following a socialist revolution. But not only did they have to remain the goal; they had to be gradually implemented if a socialist society were indeed to arise.

The essential difference between bourgeois and proletarian dictatorship is, as is well known, that the first is democracy for a minority, an exploitative minority, while the second is democracy for the majority, which was until recently exploited and which liberates itself in order to create the conditions for [true] democracy, which will simultaneously mean the withering away of democracy as a state form. This means, at the same time, that the deepening and broadening of democracy in all fields of social life is a *law* of socialist development of the transition period and that violation of that law necessarily leads to serious consequences. . . .[118]

This assertion was reinforced with a warning, elaborated at great length, of the bureaucratic danger to socialism from the ranks of the proletariat itself.

From time to time voices are heard to the effect that the forms of the state are more or less immaterial, that the main thing is the fact that the state leads [the way] to socialism. The main thing is—according to such people—whom, which class, such as a state represents, and not its forms. This is, it is true, the main thing. But it is not sufficient, and whoever sees only that endangers the main objective. It must never be forgotten that not even the most perfect bureaucratic apparatus, no matter how able the leadership at its head, is capable of building socialism. Socialism can grow only from the initiative of the broad masses properly led by the proletarian Party. Therefore the development of socialism can follow no other path than the path of continually deepening socialist democracy in the sense of ever-increasing self-government of the masses, in the sense of their ever greater inclusion in the work of the state machinery—from the lowest organs to the highest, in the sense of their ever greater participation in the direct management of each individual enterprise, institution, etc.[119]

In brief, it was necessary "to safeguard the revolution—as Marx said—from its own bureaucrats." This could be achieved only by means of a "continuous struggle against bureaucratic attempts to violate the basic principles of socialist democracy . . . [which] must develop in one direction . . . in the direction of the ever greater merging of the state apparatus with the masses."[120]

The development of socialist democracy in the direction of the withering away of the state, Kardelj continued, required a special form of state organization. This was, unlike traditional state organs, the citizens' council, as embodied first in the Paris Commune, then in the soviets, and now in the Yugoslav people's committees. This instrument had to develop ever new forms of drawing the masses into public life. One concrete step in this direction in Yugoslavia, Kardelj maintained, was the revised 1949 law on the people's committees, which was intended to increase somewhat the powers of local people's committees at the expense of the central organs of state administration. Other forms, too, had to be developed; the working people would participate in running the state "through various commissions, councils, etc., attached to the people's committees; through village aktivs, people's inspectorates, and numerous other similar forms." Moreover, mass participation applied to running the economy as well as the state administration through "continuous consultation of the [enterprise] director with groups of the best workers on all questions of managing the enterprise."[121]

Kardelj's arguments have been presented in some detail because of the importance of his treatise for the subsequent development of Yugoslav Communist ideology. Pointing out the bureaucratic danger to socialism from the ranks of the proletariat itself, Kardelj outlined a vision of a socialist state that would gradually "wither away" as the masses themselves increasingly participated in state administration. This perspective signified the beginning of a return to the utopian strain of

Marxist-Leninist thought on the organization of postrevolutionary society, especially as expressed by Lenin in *State and Revolution*—the "classic" most frequently quoted by Kardelj in his treatise. The point of departure for this new line of thought was not prior explicit criticism of Soviet theory but rather Yugoslav doctrine on people's democracy as a special mass form of the dictatorship of the proletariat.

Kardelj's emphasis in mid-1949 on the need for mass participation in the affairs of the socialist state, as the substance of its "withering away," found little immediate public echo on the part of other Yugoslav Communists. The Skupština debate on the new people's committee law did include several affirmations of the need for new forms of mass participation in state affairs.[122] Yet the debate showed that the new law was not meant to change fundamentally the organization of local government; while local people's committees were given somewhat enhanced powers in relation to federal organs, this change took the form of strengthening the executive committee and administrative apparatus of the committees.[123] Moreover, aside from the people's committee law itself, Kardelj's ideas found no immediate reflection in practice.

In outlining a perspective for the correct development of the socialist state, Kardelj offered a standard against which the Soviet state could be compared. To be sure, he did not openly polemicize with the USSR. He favorably compared Yugoslav people's democracy with the Soviet order of 1918, not that of 1949. But his total silence on Stalin suggests that he was fully aware that his treatise amounted to an attack on Stalin's theory of the Soviet state. In this regard, too, Kardelj's formulations were not immediately taken up within the CPY. Before the Rajk trial, apparently the only case of openly judging the Soviet state by Kardelj's standard was the questioning, by two leading constitutional lawyers, of the theory and practice of Soviet local government.[124]

These points suggest that Kardelj began to question the Soviet doctrine on the state somewhat sooner than the rest of the leaders. While all the members of the Politburo might agree on his vision of the future and even agree in principle on the need for some change in Yugoslavia in the direction of the "withering" of the state, the other leaders were not yet prepared for a radical break with Stalinism on the doctrine of the socialist state, probably because they were not yet able to bring the Soviet internal order into question. The public prosecutor was perhaps reflecting this attitude when, in July 1949, he maintained that socialist democracy in Yugoslavia was still inferior to that in the Soviet Union, simultaneously quoting Stalin to support the point Kardelj had made on the importance of mass participation in the affairs of state![125]

Following the Rajk trial, as described previously, the Soviet internal order lost its sanctity to the Yugoslav Communists; criticism of Soviet internal affairs gradually mounted. Simultaneously, the development of socialist democracy (as defined by Kardelj) in Yugoslavia became the subject of a major intra-Party discussion. The article by Ljubenović quoted earlier, after criticizing bureaucratic tendencies in the USSR, proclaimed that the "sharpest struggle against bureaucratism has been placed on the agenda" in Yugoslavia.[126] The rationale for this "struggle" was clearly stated: "Defending the interests of the international proletariat from the bureaucratic and authoritarian methods which threaten to take root within it, the CPY is all the more duty-bound to wage a resolute struggle against such phenomena in our administration and economy, a struggle against any violation of democratic norms. This means a struggle against bureaucracy in all its forms."[127]

This was the inner logic of the subsequent development of Yugoslav Communist ideology. If Soviet foreign policy could not be separated from Soviet domestic policy, neither could the two things be separated in Yugoslavia. If Soviet society was exhibiting unhealthy bureaucratic trends, Yugoslav society had to demonstrate the process of their elimination. This involved abandoning bureaucratic institutions imported from the USSR as well as implementing the perspective Kardelj had outlined: drawing the masses more actively into state affairs—particularly through plenary sessions of the people's committees and general local "voters' meetings."[128] Simultaneously, as will be described, quiet experimentation with workers' councils began in December 1949.

To recapitulate, the first six months following the Cominform Resolution resulted in a more emphatic statement of Yugoslav doctrine formulated prior to 1948 on people's democracy. The proletarian, socialist essence of people's democracy was made explicit, while the new Yugoslav forms were further praised as an enrichment of Marxism-Leninism. The exception was the gradualist doctrine on the socialization of agriculture which was abandoned in favor of radical collectivization, in part in response to the Cominform's accusations. At the same time, the Yugoslav Politburo denied that it differed with Moscow on matters of principle. This pattern, it has been suggested, was the result of Tito's need to develop a substitute for Moscow's authority within the CPY while not challenging it openly. Once Tito had ensured the loyalty of the CPY, he had to explain where Stalin had gone wrong. In 1949, accusing the USSR of revisionism, the Yugoslav ideologues elaborated a doctrine of equality among Communist states and Parties which Stalin was said to have opposed. As Soviet pressure against Yugoslavia escalated, questioning Soviet foreign policy led to questioning of the Soviet internal scene. For most of the leadership this process apparently began with the Rajk trial; the exception was Kardelj, who in mid-1949 returned to Marx's and Lenin's analysis of the Paris Commune as the model for the organization of a socialist state before Soviet domestic policies had been publicly questioned. In December 1949 the Yugoslav ideologues began to develop a critique of the Soviet internal order and simultaneously began to differentiate their own order from the Soviet, adopting the goal, as reformulated by Kardelj, of the "withering away" of the socialist state.

Notes

[1] Accounts of the conflict are given in Maclean, *Tito*, chaps. 12–14; Halperin, *The Triumphant Heretic*, chaps. 9–10; Armstrong, *Tito and Goliath*; Adam Ulam, *Titoism and the Cominform* (Cambridge, Mass.: Harvard University Press, 1962), chaps. 3–4; George W. Hoffman and Fred Warner Neal, *Yugoslavia and the New Communism* (New York: Twentieth Century Fund, 1962) chaps. 9–10; Robert Lee Wolff, *The Balkans in Our Time* (Cambridge, Mass.: Harvard University Press, 1956), chap. 11; Josef Korbel, *Tito's Communism* (Denver: University of Denver Press, 1951), pp. 286–343; Alex N. Dragnich, *Tito's Promised Land, Yugoslavia* (New Brunswick, N. J.: Rutgers University Press, 1954), chap. 28. The authorized Yugoslav account of the initial stage is Dedijer, *Tito*, chaps. 20–23; additional details are to be found in idem, *Izgubljena bitka*; Vukmanović-Tempo, *Revolucija koja teče* 2: 60–197; Tito interview, *Borba*, May 24, 1972.

[2] Tito had proposed federation with Bulgaria as an additional Yugoslav republic; the Bulgarians advocated parity in a two-member federation. In his meeting with the top Bulgarian and Yugoslav leaders (except Tito) on February 10, 1948, Stalin rebuked Dimitrov for his public advocacy in January 1948 of a Danubian-Balkan federation, but demanded an immediate Yugoslav-Bulgarian (two-member) federation. (See Dedijer, *Tito*, pp. 304, 321, 328.)

[3] The published correspondence is translated in *The Soviet-Yugoslav Dispute* (London: Royal Institute of International Affairs, 1948); additional documents are quoted in Dedijer, *Izgubljena bitka*.

[4] *The Soviet-Yugoslav Dispute*, pp. 61–70.

[5] Dedijer, *Tito*, p. 361; Palmiro Togliatti, in *Rinascita*, February 1, 1964.

[6] *White Book on Aggressive Activities by the Governments of the USSR, Poland, Czechoslovakia, Hungary, Rumania, Bulgaria, and Albania Towards Yugoslavia* (Belgrade, 1951), p. 124.

[7] *László Rajk and His Accomplices before the People's Court* (Budapest, 1949).

[8] *White Book*, pp. 174–178. See also *White Book*, pp. 230–279; V. Kirsanov, *IUgoslavskii narod pod vlast'iu fashistskikh naimitov amerikanskogo imperializma* (Moscow, 1950).

[9] *Odluke V. kongresa Komunističke partije Jugoslavije* (Zagreb, 1948), p. 86.

[10] Tito, Speech to the Fifth Congress, *Govori i članci* 3: 421.

[11] Ibid., p. 427; Kardelj, Skupština address of December 29, 1948, *Problemi* 3: 17.

[12] *Odluke V. kongresa*, p. 86.

[13] For example, V. Begović, in *Borba*, September 9, 1948.

[14] *V. kongres Komunističke partije Jugoslavije 21-28 jula 1948. stenografske bilješke* (Zagreb, 1949), p. 1. At least one local Party organization, upon publication of the Cominform Resolution, sent one telegram of support to Tito and another to Stalin, requesting his intervention on behalf of the Yugoslav position (Dedijer, *Tito*, p. 363).

[15] *V. kongres KPJ*, p. 112.

[16] *Borba*, July 27, 1948. See also Kardelj, Speech of November 14, 1948, *Problemi* 1: 338.

[17] Pijade, in *Borba*, July 1 and 5, 1948; [Djilas], "O neistinitim i nepravednim optužbama protiv naše partije," *Borba*, October 2–4, 1948.

[18] Tito, Speech of October 15, 1948, *Govori i članci* 4: 22; CPY Central Committee letter of May 17, 1948, *The Soviet-Yugoslav Dispute*, p. 53.

[19] CPY CC Statement of June 29, 1948, *The Soviet Yugoslav Dispute*, p. 72.

[20] For example, Djilas's speech of September 1, 1948, in *Borba*, September 2, 1948.

[21] Predrag Vranicki, *Historija marksizma* (Zagreb, 1961), p. 563. Several Yugoslav theoreticians told the present author that this was their reaction. Wolfgang Leonhard, who defected from East Germany to Yugoslavia in the spring of 1949, noted the same reaction among Party intellectuals. (Interviews with Wolfgang Leonhard, Manderscheid/Eifel, West Germany, October 1965, and New Haven, Conn., June 1966.)

[22] *L'Espresso*, July 7, 1968.

[23] Dedijer, *Izgubljena bitka*, pp. 173–174.

[24] Dedijer, *Tito*, p. 377.

[25] Vladimir Dedijer, *Josip Broz Tito, Prilozi za biografiju* (Belgrade, 1953), p. 477 (omitted from English ed.).

[26] For example, Tito, Speech of October 1, 1949, *Govori i članci* 4: 301; Pijade, "Veliki majstori licemerja," *Članci*, 1950, pp. 307–308. For a different view, maintaining that in early 1949 some of the top leaders, including Tito, still believed in the possibility of a reconciliation with Stalin, see Louis Adamic, *The Eagle and the Roots* (Garden City, N.Y.: Doubleday, 1952), pp. 129–130.

[27] See Ivan Avakumović, *History of the Communist Party of Yugoslavia* (Aberdeen: Aberdeen University Press, 1964) 1: 124–137.

[28] Perhaps the most poignant example, in terms of its effect on the Yugoslavs, was Pijade's waiting on the snowbound Durmitor mountain for thirty-seven days for Soviet aid which never came. See Pijade, *About the Legend*, pp. 6–16.

[29] An account of the meeting (based on notes made by a participant) is given in Dedijer, *Tito*, pp. 326–329. Djilas was quoted as saying: "I do not believe the Russians will stop at economic pressure on our country. In my opinion the fundamental question is whether socialism is to develop freely or by the expansion of the Soviet Union" (p. 328).

[30] Thus the Yugoslav Communists fulfilled the organizational condition for resistance to which Bukharin was perhaps referring when he said at the end of his purge trial, "one must be a Trotsky not to lay down one's arms." (Robert C. Tucker and Stephen F. Cohen, eds., *The Great Purge Trial* [New York: Grosset & Dunlap, 1965], p. 667.)

[31] As posed by Bukharin, ibid., p. 666.

[32] This reasoning did not apply in all cases. Žujović, for example, was not a Soviet agent and admitted the untruth of the charges in Stalin's letters. Yet, in opposing

Tito, he acted according to the logic, "How can we convince ourselves and the people that we are on the right path, if the Soviet Party and Stalin do not approve . . .? What next and where from here? Where will Yugoslavia's place be in the struggle against imperialism?" (Dedijer, *Tito*, pp. 340–341.)

[33] Tito, *Govori i članci* 3: 320.

[34] Dedijer, *Tito*, p. 377.

[35] The tone of compromise in Tito's first letter to Stalin was added to ensure the support of some members of the Central Committee. See Tito in *Borba*, May 24, 1972; Dedijer, *Izgubljena bitka*, p. 151, and compare the partial draft of the April 13 Yugoslav letter (Dedijer, *Tito*, pp. 337–338) with the final text adopted by the Plenum (*The Soviet-Yugoslav Dispute*, pp. 18–30). When the correspondence between the CPSU and the CPY was published in Yugoslavia, Stalin's signature was omitted. Tito's position would have been far more difficult had Stalin himself publicly censured the CPY leadership.

[36] Vukmanović-Tempo, *Revolucija koja teče* 2: 86.

[37] See the account in Halperin, *The Triumphant Heretic*, pp. 79–80.

[38] Dedijer, *Tito*, pp. 377–380 (translation improved). See Tito's similar remarks to the Sixth CPY Congress, in his *Govori i članci* 7: 250–251.

[39] Thus Tito told the April 12–13 CC Plenum: "Comrades, remember that it is not a matter here of any theoretical discussions; it is not a question of errors committed by the Communist Party of Yugoslavia, of our ideological digression. We must not allow ourselves to be forced into a discussion of such things." (Dedijer, *Tito*, p. 238.) See also his attack at the Second Congress of the CP of Croatia on self-appointed "Marxist ideologues" who wanted to turn the Party into a "general discussion club." (Tito, *Govori i članci* 4: 62.)

[40] Tito, *Govori i članci* 3: 385.

[41] Borba, October 2–4, 1948. The challenge to authority was implicit in Pijade's earlier charge of an "unprincipled *fractionist* grouping of the leaders of some Communist Parties" against the CPY. (*Borba* article of July 10, 1948, *Članci*, 1950, pp. 37–38 [emphasis added] .)

[42] Pijade, *Članci*, 1950, pp. 171–172. This was previously hinted at in the CPY CC letter of April 13 (*The Soviet-Yugoslav Dispute*, p. 22) and by Tito at the Fifth Congress (*Govori i članci* 3: 320).

[43] *Odluke V. kongresa*, p. 77.

[44] *V. kongres KPJ*, p. 120.

[45] Ibid., p. 209. Djilas made the point in even stronger terms in a lead editorial in *Komunist* ("Peti kongres Komunističke partije Jugoslavije i problemi teoretskog podizanja partiskih kadrova," *Komunist* 3, no. 1 [January 1949] : 1–14, at 11).

[46] Denisov, *Osnovi marksističko-lenjinističke teorije države i prava.*

[47] Quoted from his review of Denisov's book in *Arhiv* 5, no. 3 (July–September 1949): 300–301.

[48] *Istorijski arhiv Komunističke partije Jugoslavije* 1, kn.1 (Belgrade, 1949): 5.

[49] Krsto Bulajić, "O radu godišnjih partiških škola" [report of a consultative meeting in the agitprop section of the CC, January 31, 1949], *Partiska izgradnja* 1, no. 1 (March 1949): 26–45.

[50] Remarks of the Director, Boris Ziherl, reported in "Osnivanje Instituta za društvene nauke," *Komunist* 3, no. 2 (March 1949): 196–201, at 198. The program of instruction devoted equal time to CPY and CPSU history (ibid., pp. 199–201).

[51] Kardelj, *Komunist* 3, no. 4: 3; Pijade, Speech of April 19, 1949, *Članci*, 1950, pp. 250–253.

[52] Pijade, *Članci*, 1950, p. 63. The reversion to the 1945 position on this issue first occurred in Pijade's *Borba* article of July 5, 1948. Tito indirectly adopted the same position in his report to the Fifth Congress, acknowledging a Soviet military role in the liberation of Belgrade, Eastern Serbia, and Vojvodina, but (by quoting

an article from 1944) noting that most of Yugoslav territory had previously been liberated and a new state created. Earlier in his speech, tracing the origin and battles of the People's Army, he pointedly remarked: "We were not able to receive help from anyone for three entire years of struggle." (*Govori i članci* 3: 364, 386–387.) After the Fifth Congress the Soviet military role was again ignored; in 1949 the CPY began to publicize details of Soviet opposition to its wartime policies.

[53] *Borba,* July 18, 1948.

[54] *Odluke V. kongresa,* p. 26. The draft program was first published in *Borba* (together with the Cominform Resolution) on June 30, 1948. See also Kardelj's report to the Congress (Kardelj, *Problemi* 1: 280).

[55] Kardelj, *Problemi* 1: 281, 284.

[56] Pijade, *Članci,* 1950, p. 56 (emphasis added). Kardelj drew this conclusion in November 1948. Addressing the Second Congress of the CP of Slovenia, he noted that the broad mass base not only eased the task of building socialism but gave it "much more democratic forms" than if that base were lacking. (Kardelj, *Problemi* 1: 333–334.)

[57] The doctrine is analyzed at considerable length in Skilling, *Soviet Studies* 3, nos. 1 and 2; Brzezinski, *The Soviet Bloc,* chap. 4; Kase, *People's Democracy.*

[58] Speech to the Unification Congress of the Polish United Workers' Party, *Pravda,* December 17, 1948.

[59] Kardelj, *Komunist* 3, no. 4: 25.

[60] See Kardelj's report to the Fifth Congress, *Problemi* 1: 285–292. In 1949 a documentary study of the Slovene people's committees was published (Makso Šnuderl, ed., *Dokumenti o razvoju ljudske oblasti v Sloveniji* [Ljubljana, 1949]).

[61] See Tito's report to the Fifth Congress, *Govori i članci* 3: 266–427; Koča Popović, "Za pravilnu ocenu oslobodilačkog rata naroda Jugoslavije," *Komunist* 3, no. 3 (May 1949): 12–47.

[62] See Tito's report to its Third Congress, *Govori i članci* 4: 144–189, and the Declaration of the Third Congress, *Borba,* April 12, 1949.

[63] Kidrič, Report to the Fifth Congress, *Sabrana dela* 2: 333.

[64] *Borba,* October 2–4, 1948.

[65] Tito specifically mentioned "difficulties in connection with the peasant question during the NEP and later." (Speech to a Party meeting of the First Proletarian Division, *Govori i članci* 4: 9.)

[66] Popović, *Komunist* 3, no. 3: 19.

[67] *Borba,* October 2–4, 1948. See the similar remarks by Dobrivoje Radosavljević at the Fifth Congress (*V. kongres KPJ,* p. 680).

[68] *Komunist* 3, no. 4: 19.

[69] *The Soviet-Yugoslav Dispute,* pp. 63, 66.

[70] *Borba,* August 11, 1948.

[71] Kardelj, *Problemi* 1: 301–308. See also V. Begović, in *Borba,* July 11, 1948, and September 8–9, 1948; Begović, "Naša poljoprivreda i pitanje njenog socijalističkog preobražaja," *Komunist* 3, no. 1 (January 1949): 83–111.

[72] "Rezolucija o osnovnim zadacima partije u oblasti socijalističkog preobražaja sela i unapredjenja poljoprivredne proizvodnje," *Komunist* 3, no. 2 (March 1949): 2–10.

[73] "Prvomajski proglas CK KPJ," *Borba,* May 1, 1949.

[74] See Kardelj's speech at the Fifth Congress. (Kardelj, *Problemi* 1: 303.)

[75] See Chapter 5, note 11, and the positive evaluation of the radical agricultural policy by Wolfgang Leonhard in mid-1949 in his *Kominform und Jugoslawien* (Belgrade, 1949), p. 45.

[76] *Pregled istorije SKJ,* pp. 473–474.

[77] Veljko Vlahović, "O nekin pitanjima morala u radničkom pokretu," *Komunist*

3, no. 1 (January 1949): 126–138, at 135; Vladimir Bakarić, Speech of December 1948 to Croat People's Front delegates, *O poljoprivredi i problemima sela* (Belgrade, 1960), pp. 92–93.
[78] "Zadaci naše politike na selu," *Komunist* 3, no. 2 (March 1949): 41–73, at 41 (emphasis added).
[79] Ibid., pp. 56–57.
[80] Dedijer later wrote: "In [agriculture] blind Stalinism was perhaps most damaging to Yugoslavia. Cooperatives were created after the pattern of the Soviet kolkhozes. Some Yugoslav leaders, in particular Edvard Kardelj, quickly sensed the error and insisted that cooperatives of a general type should first be created, and only later working cooperatives, but local officials, under the influence of Stalin's kolkhoz theories, raced into the creation of kolkhozes." (Dedijer, *Tito*, p. 426.) The "local officials" had their supporters at higher levels.
Bakarić—later to emerge as the major opponent of collectivization within the Central Committee—seemed to continue to disagree with the Plenum's decisions. Addressing the Second Plenum of the CP of Croatia in May 1949, he attacked "sectarianism in the question of the forms of the new work cooperatives" and envisaged complete socialization of the countryside as taking "20-50 years"—a timetable hardly in line with radical collectivization (*O poljoprivredi*, pp. 107–114).
[81] "Zadaci partije na daljem jačanju organizacionog učvršćenja seljačkih zadruga i državnih poljoprivrednih dobara," *Partiska izgradnja* 2, no. 1 (January 1950): 73–78, at 73.
[82] "Zaključci III plenuma CK KPJ o tekućim zadacima borbe za petodogišnji plan," *Komunist* 4, no. 1 (January 1950): 9–11, at 10. For a useful retrospective Yugoslav analysis, see Daniel Ivin, "Analiza 'Pregled istorije Saveza komunista Jugoslavije' u vezi sa IIi III plenumom CK KPJ u 1949 godini," *Putevi revolucije* no. 3–4 (1964): 332–336, and idem, *Revolution und Evolution in Jugoslawien* (Bern: Schweizerisches Ost-Institut, 1968), pp. 40–46.
[83] Djilas, "Aktuelna pitanja agitacije i propagande," *Partiska izgradnja* 1, no. 1 (March 1949): 14–25, at 15–16.
[84] Ibid., pp. 21–23.
[85] Djilas's report was not reflected directly in the Resolutions of the Second Plenum. Nor was it carried in *Komunist* with the other published Plenum reports, but was reprinted instead in the Party journal devoted to cadre problems. For a reflection of Djilas's analysis in public statements by the top leadership see Tito's speech of April 1, 1949, in his *Govori i članci* 4: 144–189; Pijade, "O tridesetogodišnjici KPJ," *Članci*, 1950, Latin edition, p. 255. During the first half of 1949, the CPY still sometimes publicly treated the conflict as being more with the Cominform than with the USSR. After the Soviet note of August 18, 1949, this pretense was finally abandoned. On October 4, 1949, Tito brought Stalin into the dispute, identifying him as an author of the Soviet letters of spring 1948 (Tito, *Govori i članci* 4: 301).
[86] Vlahović, "Trideset godina KPJ," *Vojno-politički glasnik* 2, no. 4 (April 1949): 28–34, at 31.
[87] Tito, Speech of August 3, 1949, *Govori i članci* 4: 240.
[88] A useful collection of these polemical statements is *O kontrarevolucionarnoj i klevetničkoj kampanji protiv socijalističke Jugoslavije* ([Belgrade], 1949–1950), 2. vols.
[89] Tito, Speech of November 16, 1948, *Govori i članci* 4: 41.
[90] Vladimir Dedijer, *Jugoslovensko-Albanski odnosi (1939–1948)* (Belgrade, 1949). This book was suggested by Ranković and written under the supervision of himself, Djilas, and other top leaders. See Dedijer, *Izgubljena bitka*, pp. 271–276.
[91] Milentije Popović, "O ekonomiskim odnosima izmedju socijalističkih država,"

Komunist 3, no. 4 (July 1949): 98–160; Djilas, "Lenjin o odnosima medju socijalističkim državama," *Komunist* 3, no. 5 (September 1949): 1–56.

[92] Popović's positive example was Yugoslav-Albanian relations prior to 1948. Yugoslavia probably did grant more aid to Albania than it received from the USSR; the goal, however, was political control of Albania. See William E. Griffith, *Albania and the Sino-Soviet Rift* (Cambridge: M.I.T. Press, 1963), pp. 14–16.

[93] *Komunist* 3, no. 5: 55–56. As late as April, Pijade had referred to the Soviet Union's "leading role" in the anti-imperialist struggle. ("O tridesetogodišnjici KPJ," *Članci*, 1950, p. 268.) This formulation was omitted from the May Day slogans, which still referred to the USSR as the "first country of socialism." (*Borba*, May 1, 1949.)

[94] Djilas, *Komunist* 3, no. 5: 28–29.

[95] *Borba* challenged the "right [of anyone] to distribute diplomas attesting to a socialist order" (August 22, 1949). See also Kardelj, Speech of November 4, 1949, *Problemi* 3: 52 (references to vol. 3 of Kardelj's works are to the 1954 edition).

[96] As in Pijade's speech of September 18, 1948, entitled "Fleeing from Reality into Dogmatism," *Članci*, 1950, pp. 94–95.

[97] Pijade, Speech of April 30, 1949, *Članci*, 1950, p. 265; Djilas, *Komunist* 3, no. 5: 5; Tito, Speech of September 11, 1949, *Govori i članci* 4: 267.

[98] Djilas, Speech of July 13, 1949, *Borba*, July 14, 1949. For an account of the effect of the Stalin-Tito conflict on these three issues see U.S., Senate, *Yugoslav Communism*, pp. 169–171.

[99] Djilas, *Komunist* 3, no. 5: 44.

[100] Pijade, "Veliki majstori licemerja," *Članci*, 1950, p. 322.

[101] *Borba*, November 29, 1949. Earlier in 1949, the Yugoslav leaders had begun to speak of the "dual encirclement" of their country (e.g., Tito, Speech of August 3, 1949, *Govori i članci* 4: 240). On December 21, 1949, when asked "which people in the world are, in your opinion, today the most dangerous for peace?" Tito replied "no comment" (ibid., p. 344).

[102] Kardelj, Speech of November 4, 1949, *Problemi* 3: 49.

[103] Principijelnost i besprincipijelnost u vanskoj politici," *Borba*, November 12, 1949.

[104] Kardelj, *Problemi* 3: 76.

[105] *Borba*, November 2, 1949.

[106] Dedijer, *Tito*, p. 396.

[107] "Veliki majstori licemerja," *Borba*, September 22, 26, and 29, October 5–6, 1949, reprinted in Pijade, *Članci*, 1950, pp. 309, 311.

[108] ". . . in which direction the local organs of government are developing, what forms the federative order of the state is assuming, the appearance of private-ownership tendencies is the kolkholz, chaos in legal writing, chaos in philosophy, etc." (Ibid., p. 354.)

[109] *Književne novine*, October 4, 1949.

[110] This is asserted by Halperin (*The Triumphant Heretic*, p. 110), at the time correspondent of the *Neue Zürcher Zeitung* in Belgrade, and corroborated by Leonhard (Leonhard interviews). Vukmanović states that the Rajk trial caused Djilas, too, to conclude that the Great Purge trials in Moscow had been staged but "one should remain silent about these matters for now" (*Revolucija koja teče*, 2: 110).

[111] Makso Baće, "O nekim pitanjima kritike i samokritike u SSSR-u," *Komunist* 3, no. 6 (November 1949): 125–167. This issue of *Komunist* appeared at the end of December.

[112] Kardelj, *Problemi* 3: 59.

[113] S. Ljubenović, "Neki izvori i oblici birokratizma i borba za njihovo iskorenjivanje," *Narodna država* 3, nos. 11–12 (November–December 1949): 3–25, at 12–13.

[114] Kardelj, *Komunist* 3, no. 4: 1–83. This article was based on an address to the Skupština on May 28, 1949.

[115] Ibid., p. 32–33.

[116] As quoted by Kardelj, ibid., p. 28.

[117] Ibid., p. 39.

[118] Ibid., p. 42.

[119] Ibid., p. 38.

[120] Ibid., pp. 42–43.

[121] Ibid., p. 56.

[122] *Narodna skupština FNRJ. Sedmo redovno zasedanje Saveznog veća i veća naroda. 25–28 maja 1949 godine. Stenografske beleške* (Belgrade, 1949), pp. 204–208.

[123] See Tito's commentary on the law, ibid., pp. 422–427. The text of the law is printed in *Službeni list FNRJ,* June 9, 1949. A legal-political analysis of the law is given in Jovan Djordjević, *Ustavno pravo FNRJ* (Belgrade, 1953), pp. 361–373. Djordjević noted the contradiction of the law: "[It] brought certain new features, which began to differentiate legislation on the people's committees from legislation on local soviets . . . parallel with this process unfolded another . . . the dualism between the people's committee . . . and its executive committee . . . led to strengthening the political power of the latter" (p. 372).

[124] Leon Geršković, "Lokalni organi vlasti u zemljama narodne demokratije" *Narodna država* 3, nos. 6–7 (June–July 1949): 5–20, at 16–17; Jovan Djordjević, "Prilog pitanju nadležnosti narodnih odbora," *Narodna država* 3, nos. 6–7 (June–July 1949): 21–60, at 35.

[125] Josip Hrnčević, "O nekim karakteristikama naše narodne demokracije," *Naša zakonitost* 3, nos. 2–3 (1949): 53–66, at 59, 66.

[126] Ljubenović, *Narodna država* 3, nos. 11–12: 5. *Narodna država* was the journal of the state bureaucracy.

[127] Ibid., p. 21.

[128] Ibid., pp. 10–11, 22.

4

Reevaluation of the Soviet Union

Continued Criticism of Soviet Specifics

Critical reappraisal of specific Soviet foreign and domestic policies in 1949 quickly led the Yugoslav Communists to the question of how such policies could be carried on by a socialist state and thus to a reconsideration of the essential character of the Soviet social system. But this questioning unfolded parallel to and derived its force from an intensified attack upon the methods of Soviet political action. During the years after 1949 when Yugoslavia de facto aligned itself politically and militarily with the United States and Western Europe against the Soviet Union, every facet of Soviet life came to be condemned in Yugoslavia in words as strong as the harshest Western anti-Soviet attacks of the period.

In 1950 Yugoslav Communists further developed their criticism of Soviet foreign policy as imperialistic, as the "direct continuation" of policies of Czarist Russia.[1] After mid-1950 they asserted that Soviet foreign policy toward Yugoslavia was no special case, no aberration of a generally progressive foreign policy, but "only one drastic manifestation of the general line of that policy."[2] As a late imperialist power, the Soviet Union—in the CPY's view—based its foreign policy on one principle: a sphere-of-interest policy that sought to achieve a new division of the world in its favor through confrontation of and bargaining with the traditional imperialist powers.

CPY leaders differed on when Soviet imperialism had arisen. Its origins were sometimes traced to the World War II four-power conferences, where the Soviet Union, a strong Great Power for the first time, attempted to share in the imperialist division of postwar Europe.[3] At other times the Nazi-Soviet Pact of 1939 was taken as the beginning, with Hitler's attack on the Soviet Union again temporarily infusing its foreign policy with a "progressive" character.[4] In either case, Soviet foreign policy before 1939 was said to have been progressive; Soviet foreign policy after 1943 was said to have been imperialistic and opposed to foreign Communist revolutions for the sake of expanding the Soviet sphere of interest.[5] In support of the latter argument, the CPY developed an extensive literature intended to expose Stalin as opposing foreign Communist revolutions (or, if this was not possible, transforming successful revolutionary Parties into Soviet tools) in Spain, Greece, China, and—above all—Yugoslavia.[6]

This general analysis of Soviet foreign policy was restated by Dedijer in an authoritative commentary on the origins of the Korean War.[7] (Diplomatically, Yugoslavia supported the defense of South Korea against aggression but opposed the counterattack of the United Nations forces into North Korea.) According to Dedijer, the Korean conflict was ultimately to be explained by the Soviet-American division of Korea into spheres of influence during World War II. The new North Korean state was able to take some "democratic" steps immediately after the war (unlike South Korea), but this progress was halted as North as well as South Korea became "ordinary executors of the will of foreign interests."[8] Soviet subordination of North Korea was explained almost entirely in terms of economic imperialism; Dedijer explicitly extended the analysis of Soviet–East European economic relations formulated by Milentije Popović to Soviet–North Korean relations. But while East and West bore equal responsibility for the fundamental cause of the war—the division of Korea—there was no such divided responsibility for its immediate outbreak. "The agents of Soviet expansionism gave the signal and the resources to the dependent North Korean government to launch the invasion of South Korea."[9] One intended consequence of this act, concluded Dedijer, was to consolidate Soviet hegemony over other liberation movements in Asia, especially to "isolate China" and "hamper the development of the Chinese Revolution."[10]

The Soviet domestic scene was subjected by CPY spokesmen to criticism no less sharp than that directed against Stalin's foreign policy. The Yugoslav Communists' profound disillusionment with the society once accepted without question to be the world's most progressive was reflected in one of Djilas's sweeping emotive attacks:

Instead of the dialectic and materialism, a new scholasticism and a "new" subjective idealism; instead of revolutionary practice, self-satisfied profit-seeking and selfish practicism. Instead of happy and free forms of spiritual and social life of working people who have thrown off the "concern" of their capitalist masters and feudal magnates for them, [there exist] gray and uniform thought, mad, inhuman, alcoholic doses of patent happiness, and a fierce and total pressure of the iron heel—[and] spies have penetrated into the most minute cell of society, into the relationship between man and wife, parents and children, the artist and his inspiration and creation—as human history has never before known. At least twice every year those who have embalmed "for the distant future" Lenin's thought and his deeds [stand atop] his embalmed body [on the Lenin mausoleum]. Dusty and forgotten uniforms have emerged from the Czarist museums—not those from the "glorious" time of Catherine but from the time of Nicholas—and with all their "new" braided splendor have fallen on the shoulders of the "socialist" marshals, generals, and policemen. Shallow and trivial lies and demagogy and arranged trials like those of heretics and witches, designed to deceive the simple, ordinary, working man—[all of] which only reveals the deep inhuman contempt for and doubt in his reason and his strength. . . .[11]

Each aspect of this comprehensive damning of Soviet reality came to be further elaborated by CPY leaders and theoreticians. The Soviet worker's low living standard had once been explained away as the price of industrialization and, in any case, as superior to that in the capitalist world. Now, both rationales were negated.[12] Secret police terror was condemned. As Tito told the Sixth CPY Congress, "They say that socialism has already been built and that they are going toward communism, but millions of Soviet citizens languish in extermination and forced labor camps."[13] Internationality relations in the Soviet Union were likewise condemned. The national question, still viewed as having been solved during Lenin's lifetime, was said to have been reopened during Stalin's rule, with nationalism in the form of Great Russian chauvinism dominating the Soviet scene. The Yugoslavs mocked the claim of a "leading" Russian nation in the march toward communism, viewing the Russians as economically exploiting the other republics of the USSR in exactly the same manner as the Soviet Union exploited its foreign satellites.[14] Soviet cultural personalities were attacked as "obedient puppets."[15]

In perhaps the most radical line of criticism, CPY leaders compared Stalin with Hitler in following a policy of genocide. Djilas first raised this point in the fall of 1950, accusing the Soviet regime of "liquidating whole nations, which not even German capitalism under Hitler was capable of carrying out."[16] Tito repeated this criticism, accusing Stalin of "genocide," of "using the same methods of national extermination once used in Fascist Germany," and (at the Sixth CPY Congress), of "completely erasing [some non-Russian nations] from the face of the earth in such a fierce manner that even Hitler could envy it."[17] Djilas subsequently maintained that the Soviet Union had passed over from a nationalistic to an openly racist policy.[18]

Reevaluation of the Soviet System
In late 1949, in the course of public polemics with Stalin, several issues raised by CPY spokesmen indicated that, in their judgment, not only was Soviet foreign policy reactionary but something was amiss in the

Soviet internal order itself. Developing further their criticism of the methods by which the Soviet Union sought to achieve its foreign and domestic goals, the Yugoslav Communists soon faced the question of whether a country that pursued an imperialistic foreign policy, that sought to subordinate the international working-class movement, and whose internal life was regimented and bureaucratized could still be considered a socialist country, let alone the "leading country of socialism."

Djilas, who was to become the most active Yugoslav public critic of the Soviet Union, first raised this question in a speech of March 18, 1950, to the assembled students of Belgrade University.[19] Drawing attention to a "classic antagonism" between the forces and relations of production in the Soviet Union and depicting the consequences of this antagonism in an emotive condemnation of Soviet life similar to that already quoted, Djilas publicly posed the question that, he implied, had arisen somewhat earlier within the CPY hierarchy:

Viewing [all the negative features of Soviet life] and drawing conclusions from the [Soviet-Yugoslav] conflict . . . and seeking a theoretical explanation both of the [Soviet] phenomena and the conflict, many comrades pose the question: whence the phenomena in every way characteristic of class formations, why do they exist, and must they exist in socialism? And further, what are in fact the real roots of these phenomena? Do we have in the Soviet Union a new class society—state capitalism—or "deviations," contradictions within socialism itself?[20]

While Soviet society was characterized by a classic antagonism between the forces and relations of production—according to Djilas as he attempted to answer the question—the form of property relations was not classic, since, although the proletariat did not control the means of production, private ownership in the class-society sense had long since disappeared. Thus the USSR gave witness to a new phenomenon—the formation of a "bureaucratic stratum" in a socialist society. Immediately after the October Revolution, according to Djilas, bureaucratic direction of society in the form of a state monopoly had been necessary and fully justified both to thwart the return of overthrown capitalism and to organize the first steps of socialist construction. But centralism had long since outlived its usefulness; the bureaucracy had divorced itself from the proletariat and consolidated a system opposed to the interests of the latter. Thus ". . . a privileged bureaucratic stratum was created, bureaucratic centralism arose which temporarily transformed the state into a force above society." The originally necessary state monopoly over the management of production had been deformed into a social monopoly over the means of production, controlling the distribution of surplus labor and, as a consequence, monopolizing all social life.

In enumerating the reasons for this triumph of bureaucratism, Djilas stressed both the objective difficulties facing the Soviet Union (the task of building socialism in one backward country encircled by capitalism) and subjective weakness of the CPSU (weak revolutionary tendencies, and the limited role of the masses in building socialism). The mounting contradictions of the system, Djilas continued, forced the Soviet leaders to attempt temporarily to compensate for domestic failures with foreign successes. The methods employed inevitably appeared to be capitalistic—a struggle for new spheres of influence and thus "a struggle for socialism only where, to the extent, and in forms suitable to the narrow hegemonic interests of the privileged stratum." But the Soviet system itself, he concluded, had to be considered as manifesting a "crisis of socialism," and not a return to capitalism. This was true for two reasons. First, the bureaucracy was not a new class but a stratum with origins in the ranks of the proletariat itself. Second, economic development was continuing; stagnation existed only with reference to possible progress (and thus not, by implication, when compared to capitalism).

The following pages will trace in some detail the reaction within the CPY to Djilas's "crisis of socialism" analysis. Such treatment is justified for two reasons. First, it is important to determine, in the light of the Soviet-Yugoslav rapprochement after 1954, to what extent the Yugoslav leaders considered that Stalin had totally liquidated socialism in the Soviet Union. Second, the issue of the nature of the Soviet system gave rise to the most obvious case of doctrinal disagreement within the Yugoslav leadership itself in the course of the conflict with Stalin.

Djilas's March 18 speech remained the most radical Yugoslav critique of the Soviet system through the summer of 1950. His basic argument was repeated by many lesser theoreticians. Echoing Djilas, Professor Jovan Djordjević, for example, speaking at the Belgrade Law Faculty on June 13, attacked the Soviet bureaucracy as an isolated stratum signifying a crisis of socialism.[21] Djilas's colleagues in the top CPY leadership, however, seemed reluctant to face squarely (at least publicly) the issue of whether or not the Soviet system itself was defective. Kardelj, in a speech also delivered on March 18, attacked "bureaucratic despotism" as the source of hegemonism and imperialism in Soviet foreign policy, but he refrained from examining its nature in detail or considering its relation to socialism.[22] Tito, in his June 26 speech announcing the introduction of workers' councils, attacked bureaucracy and "increasingly inflexible centralism" in the USSR, but he did not speak of a separate bureaucratic stratum as Djilas had done.[23]

During the same period, another, even less critical approach to the Soviet Union was occasionally reflected in the Yugoslav press. An article in the Zagreb *Vjesnik*, for example, was relatively mild in its criticism of Soviet bureaucracy, centralism, and sphere-of-interest foreign policy, placing the whole blame for the appearance of these phenomena on Western intervention, economic backwardness, and the factional struggle against Stalin within the CPSU. The Soviet order was characterized as "primitive socialism," the undesirable features of which were temporary. "Life itself will force them in the foreseeable future to correct their ways."[24]

In the fall of 1950 Djilas's disillusionment with the Soviet Union took him one step farther than he had gone in March. Influenced, no doubt, by the heightened international tension resulting from the Korean War, the introduction of workers' councils in Yugoslavia as a much-heralded attribute of socialism, and the very intra-Party differences on the nature of the Soviet Union—with some Party members denying that the Soviet social system was defective—Djilas returned to the "phenomenon and essence of the Soviet Union" in a series of articles in *Borba* entitled "Contemporary Themes."[25] In March he had concluded that the Soviet system manifested a "crisis of socialism." Eight months later, he repudiated his earlier characterization, declaring that the Soviet system was not exhibiting a "crisis of socialism" but "state capitalism, . . . a restoration and counterrevolution of a special type . . . because it does not restore the old, individual capitalist ownership . . . but state (in fact, capitalist) ownership."[26]

"State capitalism" signified to Djilas that the first socialist steps of the dictatorship of the proletariat had turned into the despotic rule of a bureaucratic stratum, with the state becoming a force above society. This much had been said in March; now, however, Djilas viewed the consequences of the bureaucracy's monopoly position in a different light. Social and economic relations characteristic of traditional state capitalism had developed, he now maintained; the laws of monopoly capitalism had once again begun to operate in a society stratified into wage-labor workers and a bureaucratic caste (as the bureaucratic stratum was now called). "In comparison with the developed capitalist countries," he maintained, "[the Soviet Union] today is no longer progressive, even in the social sense . . . it means the total negation [of socialism] and a restoration [of capitalism] in a new, particular form."[27] The measure of a socialist society was not increased production—although this was its prerequisite—but altered relations of production. "Social relations [in the Soviet Union] today," Djilas added, "are such that they represent a brake on and the most serious barrier to the further development of socialism in the world and in the Soviet Union itself."[28] The Soviet Union was thus no closer to socialism than any traditional advanced capitalist society: "Historically speaking, the order existing in the USSR today, which signifies the victory of counterrevolution and restoration of a special sort . . . , also means . . . the eve of socialism, but no more or less than monopoly capitalism means this."[29]

In Djilas's analysis of October 1950, then, the socialist achievements of the October Revolution had been totally liquidated in the USSR, with Stalin the author of capitalist restoration, albeit in state capitalist form. The Soviet Union, in his view, stood on a level with the monopoly capitalist states in terms of progress toward socialism. It was in fact state capitalism par excellence.[30] On this basis, Djilas explained the Soviet-Yugoslav conflict as inevitable and irreconcilable. Using the trappings of Marxism to conceal their true aims, the Soviet leaders, those "enemies of Marxism in power," had to oppose "true" Marxists and revolutionaries. There could be no question of a "wrong line" or "deviations" in the Soviet Union; "a social order cannot 'err' or 'deviate.'"[31] Nor was there any hope of compromise. The differences between the Soviet and Yugoslav social systems had led to an "insurmountable conflict, one no milder—and perhaps even sharper—than the conflict between capital and labor."[32] A Marxist could hardly pose the dichotomy more sharply.

Djilas's thesis of Soviet "state capitalism" was again quickly accepted as the new orthodoxy by a number of lesser Yugoslav theoreticians, who either quoted him directly or repeated the special phraseology he had employed.[33] Some of these theoreticians, repeating Djilas's argument, were even more emphatic than he had been in stressing the return of (state) capitalism in the USSR. The Macedonian theorist Kiro Hadži-Vasilev described the Soviet system as follows:

The Soviet Union carried out a number of measures that truly meant the beginning of developing socialism. But these measures were then proclaimed as "socialism" itself, showing how far from socialism they really are. To stop with these measures, if they are proclaimed a "socialist" absolute, means that the limits of the capitalist system have not been surpassed. In such conditions, even the first buds of socialism, arising with the very deposing of the bourgeoisie and the establishment of the dictatorship of the proletariat, must inevitably degenerate until they disappear entirely.[34]

Yet once again, other Yugoslav Communists did not accept Djilas's conclusions. In his article on the Korean War, Dedijer, ostensibly refusing to discuss the issue of whether the Soviet order was state capitalist, in fact based his analysis of Soviet–North Korean relations on Milentije Popović's critique of a Soviet departure from the principles of correct economic relations among *socialist* states. In the same issue of *Komunist,* another writer, too, criticized Soviet foreign economic policy from the same perspective.[35] Such analyses provoked the Croat leader Zvonko Brkić, who sided with Djilas, to lament in December 1950 that many Party members still saw the Soviet-Yugoslav conflict in terms of relations between socialist states. "It is clear only to a few," he noted, "that social relations in the Soviet Union have completely lost their socialist character. Many comrades, ignoring this, still speak of the Soviet Union as a socialist state."[36]

Djilas's "Contemporary Themes" thus provoked a debate on the essence of the Soviet system within the CPY, reflected in the pages of *Komunist,* in cafés frequented by Party intellectuals, and even in foreign "Titoist" groups.[37] Some Yugoslav Communists agreed with Djilas that the Soviet Union had totally degenerated into state capitalism; others maintained that, although badly deformed, it remained a socialist society.

For a month the debate was confined to lesser theoreticians; the rest of the top CPY leadership (with one possible exception) was silent on the subject.[38] Then, addressing the Skupština on December 29, 1950, on foreign policy, Kardelj spoke out, hinting that the Soviet order was deformed socialism, not state capitalism—the view Djilas had voiced in March.[39] "Bureaucratic-despotic political forms of the Cominform type," Kardelj asserted, "are the result of the weakness, defects, and lack of success of socialist elements in the process of socialist development."[40] Condemning indirectly Stalinist political forms, he nevertheless asserted the existence of "socialist elements" and the continuation of "socialist development" in the USSR. Depicting the strengthening of state capitalist elements in the "Informburo countries" as revealing the "weakness of the socialist elements," he saw this "bringing into danger many achievements of the socialist revolution already won"—thus maintaining that these achievements were still, by and large, intact.[41] Furthermore, while referring to "state capitalist elements, "Kardelj did not use the phrase "state capitalism," labeling the internal order of the Soviet bloc countries a "bureaucratic-despotic political system."[42]

Thus, indirectly and without polemicizing with Djilas, Kardelj made it clear that he viewed the Soviet Union, despite its deformations, as still fundamentally a socialist society; it manifested a "crisis of socialism." The relatively clear distinction between these two points of view subsequently became blurred, however, as Kardelj developed further his analysis of bureaucratic despotism. The point is illustrated by his treatment of the USSR in a major speech of April 17, 1951, to the Third Congress of the Slovene Liberation Front. Lenin's question, *kto kogo,* was temporarily answered in the Soviet Union, Kardelj maintained, "by a *third* factor—bureaucratism, which subjugated society to itself and came to exhibit hegemonic tendencies toward other peoples."[43] Kardelj viewed the significance of this development for socialism as follows: "Bureaucratism . . . takes power from the hands of the working class and the working people and creates a system which not only is not socialist—although it may take certain economic steps toward socialism—but is the direct and most dangerous obstacle to the further development of socialism."[44] In another major address of March 31, 1952, seeking the "lessons of Soviet development," Kardelj drew a similar conclusion: " . . . such a [bureaucratic] system easily produces the degeneration of the proletarian revolution into a system of bureaucratic despotism expressing a superstructure of social relations characterized by the retaining and strengthening of transitional state capitalist forms . . . When progressive economic development in that system reaches the final limits set by the state capitalist relations, the system becomes as reactionary as and leads to the internal decay of any outlived system.[45]

As had Djilas in "Contemporary Themes," Kardelj thus asserted the emergence in the USSR after Lenin's death of a bureaucratic caste which came to exercise such monopolistic control over the working class that it was no longer possible to consider the Soviet Union a socialist state. Both leaders spoke of a state capitalist superstructure in the Soviet Union. Yet, while Djilas's analysis of state capitalism implied that the Soviet Union had undergone a special type of capitalist restoration that had totally negated the October Revolution, Kardelj's analysis of bureaucratic despotism was less extreme, suggesting that, while the Soviet Union was not truly socialist, it was also not capitalist (even state capitalist) but rather a unique, "third" phenomenon derived from the former. Kardelj's terminology suggested that, as a social system, bureaucratic despotism was closer to capitalism than to socialism. But on occasion he affirmed that some achievements of the October Revolution—especially the abolition of private property—still survived in the USSR; that, in spite of the state capitalist superstructure, the economic base still exhibited socialist tendencies; and thus, while the political system was reactionary, socialism had not completely degenerated.[46]

Tito himself never undertook a comprehensive public theoretical analysis of the nature of the Soviet system under Stalin. Nevertheless, his passing references to the problem suggest that he continued to view the Soviet Union as a socialist state, albeit a degenerate one. In his speech to the Second Trade Union Congress in 1951, after condemning specific features of Soviet life, Tito added: "But I did not say, or mean to say, that achievements of the great October Revolution no longer survive [in the USSR]. They do exist! And since that is true, then we cannot quite say that it is in general not a socialist country, that is, that all the achievements of the revolution have been destroyed; rather, the leaders and responsible figures are not socialists. . . ."[47]

While the other top Party leaders were silent on the issue of the Soviet order, a small group of dogmatic theoreticians continued to adhere quite explicitly to the "crisis of socialism" analysis (although no one still spoke of "primitive socialism"). Writing in *Komunist* in 1952, the most prominent, Boris Ziherl, referred to the USSR as a state of "bureaucratic socialism . . . a bureaucratic, state capitalist distortion of a socialist state." He ruled out in priciple the possibility that this could signal capitalist restoration, for that—he said—could result only from external imperialist intervention.[48]

In 1952 two Communists publicly formulated an even more radical criticism of the Soviet system than Djilas's "state capitalism" analysis. Their point of departure was a polemical article by Djilas himself, published in April 1952, asserting that the Soviet bureaucracy had to be considered a caste, not a new class.[49] Zvonimir Kristl maintained the contrary view, noting that the criterion of a class was economic privilege based on ownership and that the Soviet bureaucracy was the collective owner of the means of production in the USSR. More significant than this allegation itself, however, were the conclusions that were drawn. The existence of the new class showed, according to Kristl, that in the Soviet Union "the working class . . . was *never*, not for one moment, *itself* the owner of the means of production. Through the revolution the working class achieved the *transfer* of ownership from the hands of the bourgeoisie and large landholders into the hands of the bureaucracy (then economically conditioned and necessary)."[50]

The initial progressive character of this bureaucratic rule was not denied; the interests of the two classes—bureaucracy and proletariat—were, Kristl maintained, essentially the same just after the October Revolution, when the bureaucracy took up the economic tasks that Russian capitalism had failed to carry out. The point was, however, that the state apparatus had been the instrument of the bureaucratic class from the very beginning. Thus it was completely erroneous to maintain (as had Djilas and all other Yugoslav critics of the Soviet system) that "the state apparatus, growing out of the working class, in specific and favorable historical circumstances separated itself from and opposed itself to society."[51]

What is more, Kristl affirmed that the situation had been no different in Yugoslavia prior to 1948. Yugoslavia, too, had first passed through a necessary period of bureaucratic rule, developing socialism only after 1948, the year that marked the beginning of the socialist revolution. Hence: "Our country differs *qualitatively* from the USSR; two different social-economic systems [exist] separated by an entire revolution."[52] This meant, moreover, that it was the "direct revolutionary task" of the Soviet proletariat to carry out a "Yugoslav revolution," which would require the "total destruction of 'their' state and the state in general." This could not be accomplished without bloodshed: "The method of rule leaves no doubt about the methods and the means required to liquidate the bureaucracy."[53] Kristl's partner in this polemic, Janez Stanovnik, went one step further, maintaining that this "required the aid of a special international constellation"[54] (that is, foreign intervention).

The emergence of a new class in the Soviet Union, Kristl continued, was as important theoretically as politically. It showed the necessity of a "dialectical critique of Marx, especially of his theory of the transition period and the dictatorship of the proletariat," for there existed "a separate social-economic system between capitalism and communism."[55]

The "new class" analysis signified a fundamental revision of the Marxist scheme of the transition period from capitalism to communism, adding one more stage—the rule of bureaucracy—to the era of class society and making the primary historical function of Communists not the overthrow of capitalism but the overthrow of bureaucracy, which followed capitalism in a backward country as inevitably as capitalism followed feudalism. Such a view totally negated the "socialist" nature of the October Revolution. Moreover, by implication it similarly negated the Yugoslav Communist revolution of 1941-1945.

It is easy to understand why no Yugoslav Communist leader could endorse this view. Such total negation of the USSR deprived a Communist of any historical justification for his actions prior to 1948. Imprisonment in prewar Yugoslavia, service in the Comintern apparatus, even the People's Liberation Struggle—all would directly signify only the endeavor to hasten the replacement of one form of class society by another. Thus Djilas, polemicizing with Kristl and Stanovnik, strongly opposed the "new class" analysis. True, he repeated his view that the Soviet system could only be described as "state capitalism."[56] But he revealingly explained why the Soviet bureaucracy had to be treated as a caste and not a class:

The truth which Marx affirmed . . . cannot lightly be ignored. He showed in *Das Kapital* that after capitalism and capitalists no new class can arise or come to power . . . . Even if we assume that Marx was wrong or that he could not see everything in advance, nevertheless the Marxist question remains: Is the formation of a new class on the basis of not only the same forces of production but the same production relations (the exploitation of labor by capital) possible after the expropriation of the capitalists? If that is possible, then why was the expropriation of the bourgeoisie a historical inevitability . . .?[57]

Djilas also rejected Kristl's concept of socialist revolution. Both the October Revolution and the People's Liberation Struggle were true socialist revolutions, he reiterated, since both signaled the overthrow of capitalism, seizure of power by the proletariat, and the introduction of new production relations. The privileges of the Soviet bureaucracy were not the direct consequence of the October Revolution; they resulted instead from the attempt to build socialism in particularly unfortunate historical circumstances.

The ambiguous posture Djilas was forced to adopt in his attempt to refute the "new class" challenge is obvious. He tried to reconcile the irreconcilable: to differentiate completely the Soviet system from the Yugoslav and from "socialism" in general while at the same time not negating the October Revolution and the Yugoslav system prior to 1948. Thus there were contradictions in his response, which maintained that the Soviet Union was a class society and yet denied the existence of a new class, which maintained that the Yugoslav economic reforms of 1950 (examined in Chapter 7) signified the first real change in production relations since the overthrow of capitalism and yet defended the October Revolution and the People's Liberation Struggle as socialist revolutions. Djilas now saw the ambiguity of his position; thereafter, while not abandoning the "state capitalist" terminology, he admitted that the Soviet economic base was, in fact, socialist after all.[58]

The "new class" analysis formulated by Kristl and Stanovnik was only the logical continuation of the "state capitalism" analysis; as such, it revealed the ambiguities of Djilas's view and indicated that the "state capitalism" analysis was, all along, more verbal bombast in the political conflict with Stalin than serious theory. This conclusion is further supported by Djilas's ambiguous approach to the question of how Soviet "state capitalism" could be overcome. While Djilas's opponents in the "class or caste" debate called for social, proletarian revolution in the USSR—a call repeated by other theoreticians propagating the "Contemporary Themes" analysis[59]—Djilas himself did not. Class struggle existed in the USSR, he affirmed, but it took the form, not of an attempt to overthrow a nonexistent ruling class, but of the working class's struggle to abolish the bureaucracy's economic privileges. His silence on the subject suggested that he thought this was not a task to be carried out by revolution.[60] On this point Djilas was in full agreement with the rest of the CPY leadership, which generally refrained from discussing how the rule of the bureaucratic caste in the USSR might be overcome, but whose occasional references to the problem suggested that the end of Stalinism required major structural changes in the Soviet political system, but not social revolution or even limited mass action "from below."[61]

In summary, the reevaluation of the Soviet system after mid-1950 led to the formulation of three distinct viewpoints within the CPY on the degeneration of the USSR. The first of these viewpoints held that objective necessity and subjective weakness had conditioned the emergence of a ruling "bureaucratic caste" that had temporarily subordinated the working class, taking over exclusive management of the means of production and expropriating the proletariat's labor surplus. The dogmatic variant of this viewpoint still openly spoke of "bureaucratic socialism," while the orthodox version spoke instead of "bureaucratic despotism." For both, the Soviet system, while not truly socialist, still had something in common with socialism since major achievements of the October Revolution—overthrow of the bourgeoisie and nationalization of the means of production—survived. However much production relations in the Soviet Union ran counter to socialist norms, this defect could be corrected within the limits of the existing social system. While political action might be required to abolish the bureaucratic caste and return the USSR to the path of socialism, a social revolution was not required.

The second viewpoint—that of Djilas in "Contemporary Themes"— was contradictory. Sharing the same analysis of the social role and origins of the Soviet bureaucratic caste, this viewpoint saw the gap between socialist norms and Soviet reality as so great that the triumph of the bureaucratic caste could be explained only as equivalent to capitalist restoration in a special, state capitalist form. The Soviet Union was thus proclaimed to be a new form of class society. Yet, reacting to the third viewpoint, the "state capitalism" view denied the logical concomitant of a class society—a ruling class—admitted that the Soviet "economic base" was still socialist, and granted that the reestablishment of socialism in the USSR did not require a new social revolution.

The third viewpoint unambiguously labeled the Soviet Union a state capitalist society; its bureaucracy, a new ruling class. The point was not that socialism had been liquidated in the USSR; it had never existed. Nor, by implication, were sprouts of the new classless society present in Yugoslavia before 1948. It was the revolutionary task of the Soviet proletariat to destroy by force the ruling Soviet bureaucracy, perhaps with foreign assistance. The October Revolution had replaced capitalist class society with bureaucratic class society. Now the Soviet Union was ripe for the real socialist revolution.

This summary suggests how the first two points of view could coexist within the CPY Politburo: the gap between the two views was simply not as great as it first appeared. Kardelj's adoption of much of Djilas's "state capitalist" terminology partially blurred the difference; Djilas's reaction to the "new class" analysis showed that he too did not totally negate the socialist character of the Soviet Union.

Djilas's ambiguous position dramatized the dilemma faced by all the Yugoslav leaders in reevaluating the Soviet system. They could defend their course of action after 1948 to the CPY, to world Marxist opinion, and to themselves only if they could show a fundamental distinction between the Yugoslav and the Soviet systems. Yet this imperative conflicted with another—that of justifying their service to the USSR prior to 1941 and their own system, modeled on Stalin's in many respects, before 1948. The second imperative limited the first. Negated totally by Stalin as Gestapo agents ruling an "ordinary bourgeois republic," the Yugoslav Communist leaders, for all the fierceness of their attacks on the Soviet Union, could not bring themselves to negate totally the Soviet system in turn.

The Question of Trotsky's Influence

Addressing the Fifth Congress of the CPY in 1948, Djilas attacked the Yugoslav Trotskyites who in the 1930s had "spread bourgeois lies and slander about the Soviet Union, about Stalin's alleged dictatorship, about the alleged power of the bureaucracy in the USSR, about the alleged falsification of the trials against the Trotskyite, Zinovievist, and Bukharinist spies."[62] Two years later the Yugoslav Communists, led by Djilas, formulated a critique of the Soviet system under Stalin which embraced all these allegations and had many other points in common with the critique formulated by Trotsky and his disciples. This led some observers to speculate that the Yugoslav Communists, needing a critique of Stalinism after their break with Stalin, turned to Trotsky and propagated his ideas as their own.[63]

Several factors argue, however, that the influence of Trotsky's ideas on the development of the CPY critique of the Soviet system under Stalin was much less than might be suggested by their common elements. First, it should be pointed out that the Yugoslav critique was not a simple copy of the critique Trotsky outlined in *The Revolution Betrayed* (1937).[64] For both the Yugoslav theoreticians and for Trotsky, the Soviet Union was ruled by a bureaucratic caste that had separated from the proletariat and, in the interest of increasing its own social privileges, had come to exercise complete economic and political control over the proletariat itself. Trotsky traced the fundamental origin of this process of the bureaucratic degeneration of the Soviet order to the failure of the Russian revolution to spread to the advanced capitalist countries after 1917 and, as a consequence of that failure, the attempt to develop socialism in conditions of "generalized want."[65] In Trotsky's view, the revolutionary opponents of that policy—that is, Trotsky himself—had been thwarted by Stalin's gradual suppression of intra-Party democracy, the mark of the degeneration of the Bolshevik Party itself.[66]

In the Yugoslav Communists' analysis, by contrast, "capitalist encirclement" and economic backwardness were only factors contributing to the emergence of the Soviet bureaucratic caste, for the Yugoslav theoreticians affirmed the possibility of achieving "socialism in one country" and placed much less emphasis than had Trotsky on the material prerequisites for the development of a socialist society. They continued to strongly oppose intra-Party factionalism—retrospectively, in the USSR, as well as in contemporary Yugoslavia. Since they insisted on viewing the Stalinist system until 1931 as not only progressive but fundamentally sound, they could never point to any basic causes for its degeneration—apart from the subjective factor of Stalin's personality.

The implications of the bureaucratic caste for the Soviet social order were also appraised somewhat differently by Trotsky and the Yugoslav theoreticians. The ruling bureaucracy was a caste, not a new class, Trotsky maintained, since it lacked the social homogeneity of a class, since it did not directly appropriate the means of production, and since it still played a partially necessary historical role in preserving socialist (state) ownership of the means of production.[67] The Yugoslavs made essentially the same argument, but they denied that the ruling caste performed any necessary function at all. Since the bureaucracy was a caste and not a new class, and since socialist ownership remained (although bourgeois norms of distribution of the labor product had revived), Trotsky argued, the Soviet Union was a transitional social system; it was not socialism, but it had not reverted to capitalism—although in time one of these two tendencies would have to prevail. The October Revolution had experienced its Thermidor; but that signified, according to Trotsky, a "phase of reaction *within* the revolution," and not a counterrevolution. Thus the Soviet Union remained a "workers' state," however deformed; Stalin had betrayed the revolution, not overthrown it.[68] But even though a social revolution was thus not necessary to return the USSR to the path of socialist development, a political revolution would be required in order to reinstitute Soviet democracy at home and a revolutionary foreign policy abroad. In the final analysis, however, progress toward socialism could be resumed in the USSR only if such an internationalist foreign policy rekindled the world revolution.[69]

The Yugoslav analysis of the degeneration of the Soviet order was formulated in somewhat different terms. None of the Yugoslav theoreticians distinguished the proletarian essence of the Soviet Union (the "workers' state") from progress toward socialism; equating the two characteristics under the continued influence of the Stalinist dogma that by 1936 the Soviet Union had become a socialist society, the varying Yugoslav views revolved around the question to what extent socialism survived there. Djilas's initial "crisis of socialism" analysis viewed Soviet society in historically more progressive terms than Trotsky's view; his "state capitalism" analysis, in historically much less progressive terms than Trotsky (but more favorably than the "bureaucratic collectivism" of the Shachtman-Burnham wing of American Trotskyism).[70] Kardelj's analysis of "bureaucratic despotism" was closer to Trotsky's analysis, but his terminology was different; he saw the contradiction in Soviet society, not as between "socialist property" and "bourgeois norms of distribution," but—again demonstrating the continued influence of Stalinist categories—as between the "socialist base" and the "state capitalist superstructure." Finally, unlike Trotsky, the CPY ideologues remained silent on how the rule of the Soviet bureaucracy could be overcome.

These distinctions indicate that the Yugoslav critique of Stalinism was not a copy of Trotsky's critique; there were important differences between the two. Moreover, Trotsky himself—along with Stalin's other major rivals within the CPSU—was never rehabilitated ideologically in Yugoslavia. In his attack on the Rajk trial, Pijade did condemn the Great Purge trials as falsifications and affirm that Trotskyism had been a "current in the international working class movement."[71] While no other CPY leader said this openly, there were no more references in Yugoslavia to Stalin's opponents as "cursed police spies," as Djilas had called them at the Fifth CPY Congress. But if this was political rehabilitation of a sort, ideological rehabilitation did not follow. Tito declared in October 1949 (granting that "innocent Communists" had been condemned for Trotskyism), "We know how much harm Trotsky did, we know that his work has been ideologically evaluated correctly as harmful."[72] Some CPY intellectuals did come to view Stalin's opponents in a different light. A lecture given in the High Party School in 1950–1951 went so far as to maintain that ". . . on a series of questions, [Stalin's opponents] were entirely correct; for example, when they demanded the democratization of Party life, when they pointed to the danger of bureaucratization . . . ."[73] But such sentiments were never repeated by any leading political figure; at that level, Tito's evaluation of October 1949 was not modified.[74]

The CPY leadership's refusal after 1948 to rehabilitate Trotsky (and Stalin's other Party opponents) can be explained in part by the tactical need to avoid being identified with Trotskyism in the eyes of the CPY rank and file and world Marxist opinion. But there were other reasons for this as well. The Yugoslav leaders saw themselves as true Leninists in the conflict with Stalin, but in their effort to negate Stalinism by returning to Leninism, they could not overcome their own Stalinist pasts. The need to justify to others and to themselves their own previous careers as Comintern agents and ideological Stalinists prevented them from negating the Stalinism of the 1930s. Pointing to "hegemonistic tendencies" in Soviet foreign policy during those years, they nevertheless continued to maintain that it had been their "internationalist" duty to support the Soviet Union and its foreign policy prior to World War II.[75] Emphasizing Stalin's role in the bureaucratization of socialism in the USSR, they never suggested that his major policies, including forced industrialization and collectivization, had been faulty. Even when, after 1951, they ideologically rehabilitated social democracy, they never granted that any of Stalin's opponents in the struggle for power after Lenin's death might have advocated correct policies after all.[76] (This point is amplified in Chapter 10.)

This burden of the past was compounded by the Yugoslav leaders' own struggle against Trotskyism and other deviations in the CPY itself in the late 1930s. Indeed, Tito's claim of merit in unifying the CPY after 1937 was in part based on his claim of successful struggle against Yugoslav Trotskyism.[77] If Trotsky himself were to be rehabilitated, that claim would be negated, and the infallibility of the CPY's policies under Tito's leadership would be brought into question.

Current international problems also contributed to the CPY's failure to reevaluate Trotsky. The publication of the June 1948 Cominform Resolution immediately led the Fourth International (the "orthodox" Trotskyites) to appraise positively the significance of the Soviet-Yugoslav conflict as a sign of the internal disintegration of Stalinism.[78] During the following two years, it openly sympathized with and sought to establish ties with Yugoslavia;[79] the CPY leaders, however, resisted the various approaches. If a possibility of an eventual informal alliance nevertheless existed, it was destroyed by differing perspectives on Soviet foreign policy—in particular, on the Korean War—and Yugoslavia's subsequent rapprochement with the Western powers. The "orthodox" Trotskyites viewed the Korean War (including the Communist Chinese intervention) as progressive and just; to the Yugoslavs, it was one more manifestation of Stalin's imperialist foreign policy. At the end of 1950, in consequence, the CPY mounted a fierce attack on the Trotskyite movement as an "objective" supporter of Soviet foreign policy. In Kardelj's words to the Skupština in December 1950: "Today we must oppose aggressive war in general . . . . We would [otherwise] become an antihistorical group like the Trotskyites, who with loud leftist phrases hide the bankruptcy of their policies and 'ideology.' In theory, that is, they fiercely . . . attack the USSR; in practice, following the tail of Soviet foreign policy . . . they objectively *became a support of that hegemonic policy.*"[80] For the Fourth International, on the other hand, Yugoslavia's stand on the Korean War showed the "rightward evolution of its foreign policy"; it subsequently became further disillusioned with the post-1950 domestic economic and political reforms, which were seen as embodying "a series of concessions to the class enemy."[81]

Hence, the CPY leaders' Stalinist pasts, including struggle against Trotsky and Trotskyism as an "anti-Party" element, and present condemnation of the Trotskyite defense of Soviet foreign policy contributed—along with more tactical considerations—to the CPY's failure to rehabilitate Trotsky ideologically and to identify with his critique of Stalinism. Moreover, it may be suggested, the burden of their Stalinist pasts, in particular, discouraged the Yugoslav ideologues from turning to Trotsky's writings as a primary source of their anti-Stalinist criticism. In time, Djilas and probably Kardelj and other ideologues read some of Trotsky's works,[82] but in 1949–1950 (as described in subsequent chapters) they devoted themselves to Marx and Lenin themselves, not to Bolshevik heretics. Rather, the Yugoslav critique of the Soviet system under Stalin would appear, at the conscious level, to have been self-generated. It is not surprising that the anti-Stalinist critiques of the CPY and Trotsky, although not identical, had some points in common. The critiques were similar responses to analogous situations. Like Trotsky, the Yugoslav Communists had to explain how the Soviet Union had degenerated under Stalin. The point of departure for both was the egalitarian goals the October Revolution was supposed to realize, the goals outlined by Lenin in *State and Revolution.* The discrepancy between those goals and Stalinism was self-evident for any Communist breaking with Stalin's ideological authority. In developing their antibureaucratic critique of the Soviet system, the CPY ideologues surely owed an intellectual debt to the antibureaucratic (but not exclusively Trotskyite) critiques of Stalinism.[83] But that debt was evidently an unconscious one; it was not only unacknowledged but, by and large, unperceived.

Notes

[1] Najdan Pašić, "Izvrtanje marksističkog učenja o državi u teoriji i praksi savremenog revizionizma," *Komunist* 5, no. 1 (January 1951): 82–116, at 113.

[2] Kardelj, U.N. address of September 25, 1950, *Problemi* 3: 136.

[3] Kardelj, "Posle pet godina," *Problemi* 3: 329–330.

[4] Tito, speech to the Sixth CPY Congress, in *Borba komunista Jugoslavije za socijalističku demokratiju. VI kongres KPJ* (Belgrade, 1952), p. 15; *Istorija medjunarodnog radničkog i socijalističkog pokreta* (Belgrade, 1952), p. 538.

[5] *Rukovodioci i štampa SSSR-a o NOB-i i socijalističkoj izgradnji u Jugoslaviji*, p. 7; Geršković, *Historija narodne vlasti*, chap. 1.

[6] For Spain: Jesus Hernandes [Hernandez], *Španija i SSSR* (Belgrade, n.d.), a Serbo-Croat edition of his *La Grande Trahison* (Paris: Fasquelle, 1953); Hernandes, "Oslobodilačka borba španskog naroda," *Istorija medjunarodnog radničkog i socijalističkog pokreta,* pp. 541–568. For Greece: Vukmanović, *Komunist* 3, no. 6: 1–82; Lj. Vukmanović, "Taktika demokratske armije Grčke u periodu od 1946–1949," *Borba*, September 7, 1949. For China: V. Teslić, *Kineska revolucija i Moskva* (Belgrade, 1953); P. Damjanović, "Razvoj revolucije u Kini i uloga komunističke partije," *Istorija medjunarodnog radničkog i socijalističkog pokreta*, pp. 569–607; Dedijer, *Tito*, pp. 322, 434–436. For Yugoslavia: inter alia, Pijade, *About the Legend*; Tito, Speech of June 26, 1950, *Govori i članci* 5: 215–216.

[7] Dedijer, "Sovjetski savez i Koreja," *Komunist* 4, no. 6 (November 1950): 143–181.

[8] Ibid., p. 169.

[9] Ibid., p. 177.

[10] Ibid., p. 178.

[11] Milovan Djilas, *Savremene teme* (Belgrade, 1950), pp. 4–5 (references are to the Latin edition).

[12] Tito, Speech to the Sixth CPY Congress, *Borba komunista Jugoslavije*, p. 29.

[13] Ibid.

[14] N. Vojanović, "O nekim karakterističnim idejnim pojavama u Sovjetskom savezu," *Komunist* 5, nos. 4–5 (July–September 1951): 159–201; Pašić, *Komunist* 5, no. 1: 109; Djilas, *Savremene teme*, Cyrillic edition, p. 24.

[15] Pašić, *Komunist* 5, no. 1: 107.

[16] Djilas, *Savremene teme*, p. 23.

[17] Tito, Speech of July 27, 1951, *Govori i članci* 6: 74; Speech of July 6, 1952, ibid., 7: 111; Speech to the Sixth CPY Congress, in *Borba komunista Jugoslavije*, p. 33.

[18] Djilas, "Antisemitizam," *Borba*, December 14, 1952.

[19] "Na novim putevima socijalizma," *Borba*, March 19, 1950.

[20] Ibid.

[21] "Diskusija o pitanjima birokratije i birokratizma," *Arhiv* 6, no. 2 (April–June 1950): 358–364. See also the similar analysis by L. Geršković, "Razvitak formi lokalnih organa narodne vlasti," *Komunist* 4, nos. 4–5 (July–September 1950): 88–124, and P. Vranicki, *O nekim pitanjima marksističke teorije u vezi sa ždanovljevom kritikom Aleksandrova* (Zagreb, 1950), chap. 1.

[22] Kardelj, *Problemi* 3: 88–114.

[23] Tito, *Govori i članci* 5: 219–221.

²⁴ G. Santo, "Uz diskusiju o uzrocima revizionističkog skretanja u SKP(b)," *Vjesnik* June 23–24, 1950. The same point was made indirectly by Z. Pečar, an editor of the *Review of International Affairs*, in the June 7, 1950, issue, where he argued that the Soviet sphere-of-influence foreign policy could not be traced to the internal Soviet structure (p. 8). He was attacked for this view by D. Blagojević in the issue of June 21, 1950 (p. 11).

²⁵ Djilas, "Savremene teme," *Borba*, November 19–20, 26, 29, 1950. Reprinted as *Savremene teme*.

²⁶ Ibid., pp. 14–15.

²⁷ Ibid., p. 16.

²⁸ Ibid., p. 21.

²⁹ Ibid., pp. 19–20.

³⁰ Conflicting Yugoslav usage of this term will be considered in the next chapter. Suffice it to say here that Djilas saw "state capitalism" as catastrophic for the working class while it lasted; the Soviet Union was the prototype, with Hitler's Germany a less-developed second example.

³¹ Djilas, *Savremene teme*, pp. 21–22.

³² Ibid., p. 24.

³³ Radomir Lukić, *Teorija države i prava* (Belgrade, 1955) 1: 409 (all references to this ed. appeared in the orignial ed. of 1953); B. Crnja, "O odumiranju državnih funkcija u privredi," *Ekonomski pregled* 1, nos. 3–4 (October–December 1950): 241–256, at 244; P. Damjanović, S. Belić, and C. Djurdjević, "Razvitak SSSR od 1921–1941 godine," *Istorija medjunarodnog radničkog i socijalističkog pokreta*, p. 509; V. Trček, in *Osvit* 1, no. 2 (March 1951): 10–23, at 23.

³⁴ K. Hadži-Vasilev, "Staljin o nacionalnom pitanju," *Komunist* 5, nos. 2–3 (March–May 1951): 182–244, at 206.

³⁵ V. Guzina, "Medjunarodni zajmovi i socijalistička izgradnja," *Komunist* 4, no. 6 (November 1950): 21–81.

³⁶ Z. Brkić, *Neprosredni političko-organizacioni zadaci partijskih organizacjija u radu s masama* (Zagreb, n.d.), pp. 59–60.

³⁷ Leonhard interviews; interview with Ilse Spittmann, Cologne, October 1965. The article was discussed at meetings of the Titoist "Independent Workers' Party" in West Germany, with opinion about equally divided on its validity.

³⁸ Kidrič seemed to support Djilas's view in "Teze o ekonomici prelaznog perioda u našoj zemlji," *Komunist* 4, no. 6 (November–December 1950): 1–20, at 6.

³⁹ Kardelj, "Nova Jugoslavija u savremenom svetu," *Problemi* 3: 174–209.

⁴⁰ Ibid., p. 181.

⁴¹ Ibid., pp. 184–185.

⁴² Ibid., p. 180.

⁴³ "Deset godina narodne revolucije," *Problemi* 2: 136.

⁴⁴ Ibid., p. 103.

⁴⁵ "Socijalizam i demokratija," *Problemi* 2: 179–180.

⁴⁶ Interview of February 22, 1952, *Problemi* 2: 150.

⁴⁷ *Govori i članci* 6: 210. See also Tito's address to the Sixth CPY Congress, *Borba komunista Jugoslavije*, p. 28, and his quoted remarks in Dedijer, *Tito*, p. 255. This analysis of differences in the Politburo on the nature of the Soviet system is supported by Dedijer's later account in *Izgubljena bitka*, pp. 406–407.

⁴⁸ B. Ziherl, "O društvenom biću i društvenoj svesti u prelaznom periodu," *Komunist* 6, nos. 1–2 (January–March 1952): 98–132, at 121, 129.

⁴⁹ Djilas, "Klasa i kasta," *Svedočanstva*, April 5, 1952, and *Borba*, April 6, 1952. The ensuing polemics were published at Djilas's initiative in *Komunist* 6, nos. 3–4 (May–August 1952): pp. 39–94. In *The New Class* (New York: Praeger, 1957), Djilas would accept the views he here combated; the controversy was revived in

1967 (see Slobodan Stanković, "Yugoslavia's Party and Economic Reforms at Turn of the Year," *Radio Free Europe Research*, January 16, 1968).

[50] Z. Kristl, *Komunist* 6, nos. 3–4: 59.

[51] Ibid., p. 63.

[52] Ibid., p. 78.

[53] Ibid., pp. 61, 71, 79.

[54] Ibid., p. 47.

[55] Ibid., p. 48.

[56] Ibid., p. 86.

[57] Ibid., pp. 87–89.

[58] Djilas, "Vrti li se Staljin u krugu?," *Komunist* 6, nos. 3–4 (May–August 1952): pp. 95–121, at 119; Djilas, in *Vjesnik*, November 7, 1952.

[59] For example, B. Horvat, "Još jedan prilog pitanju prelaznog perioda," *Ekonomist* 4, nos. 3–4 (1951): 45–55, at 52.

[60] *Komunist* 6, nos. 3–4: 91.

[61] Asked in July 1950 how he would view a "movement to overthrow" the Soviet bureaucratic caste, Tito replied: "This is a big question . . . . The question of the overthrow of such a caste is not a simple one. The moment is not at all suitable for such a matter, and I do not care to discuss the question further." (Interview in *Janata* [New Delhi], reprinted in *The Fourth International* 11, no. 6 [November –December 1950] : 188–192, at 189.) Only in 1953, after the East Berlin and Pilsen uprisings, did a Yugoslav leader endorse mass action against the Soviet bloc bureaucracy. See Kardelj, "Posle pet godina," *Problemi* 3: 334, 336.

[62] *V. kongres KPJ*, p. 182.

[63] John Plamenatz, "Deviations from Marxism," *Political Quarterly* 21, no. 1 (January–March 1950): pp. 40–55, at 55; Roy Macridis, "Stalinism and the Meaning of Titoism," *World Politics* 4, no. 2 (January 1952): 219–238, at 235–237.

[64] Analyzed at length in Isaac Deutsher, *The Prophet Outcast: Trotsky, 1929–1940* (New York: Vintage Books, 1965), pp. 298–324.

[65] Leon Trotsky, *The Revolution Betrayed* (New York: Pioneer Publishers, 1945), pp. 56–60.

[66] Ibid., pp. 94–105. Trotsky's critique of Stalinism was an extension of the criticism of increasing bureaucratization of the Party itself which he formulated in his *The New Course* (1924). See Isaac Deutscher, *The Prophet Unarmed: Trotsky, 1921–1929* (London: Oxford University Press, 1959), pp. 119–126.

[67] Trotsky, *The Revolution Betrayed*, pp. 248–252; Deutscher, *The Prophet Outcast*, pp. 304–305.

[68] Trotsky, *The Revolution Betrayed*, pp. 248–256; Deutscher, *The Prophet Outcast*, p. 314.

[69] Trotsky, *The Revolution Betrayed*, pp. 284–290. This program notwithstanding, many Yugoslav theoreticians still maintained in the 1960s that Trotsky wanted only to replace the Stalinist bureaucracy with his own.

[70] Many "sections" of the Fourth International split over the issue of the social essence of the USSR. While Trotsky continued to maintain that the USSR was a deformed workers' state (and his "orthodox" disciples continued to defend this view after his death), a number of his followers, such as Max Shachtman and James Burnham in the United States, denied that the USSR was a workers' state in any form. It was, they maintained, a completely antiprogressive "bureaucratic collectivism" bearing little relation to either capitalism or socialism (see Max Shachtman, *The Struggle for the New Course* [1943]). The "revisionist" Trotskyites were influenced by Bruno Rizzi's *La Bureaucratisation du Monde* (1939), which first used the term "bureaucratic collectivism" in depicting

the USSR as a new form of class society, and by Rudolf Hilferding and Solomon Schwarz, who—in an analogous debate in the Menshevik exile press—denied that the Soviet Union was a "workers' state." See Deutscher, *The Prophet Outcast*, pp. 457–477; Daniel Bell, "Ten Theories in Search of Reality: the Prediction of Soviet Behavior in the Social Sciences," in Alexander Dallin, ed., *Soviet Conduct in World Affairs* (New York: Columbia University Press, 1960), pp. 10–11; Lewis A. Coser, "USA: Marxists at Bay," in Leopold Labedz, ed., *Revisionism: Essays on the History of Marxist Ideas* (New York: Praeger, 1962), pp. 356–358.

[71] While still using "Trotskyite-Menshevik" as a derogatory adjective. (Pijade, "Veliki majstori licemerja," *Članci*, 1950, pp. 342, 347.)

[72] Tito, Speech of October 1, 1949, *Govori i članci* 4: 304.

[73] Damjanović, Belić, and Djurdjević, in *Istorija medjunarodnog radničkog i socijalističkog pokreta*, p. 525. Nevertheless, another lecture on the Comintern given at the High Party School implied that Trotsky opposed Stalin from antisocialist positions. (S. Belić, I. Karaivanov, and N. Vujanović, "Komunistička internacionala," ibid., p. 405.)

[74] Tito told an Indian Trotskyite in July 1950: "I do not agree with the Trotskyist Fourth International . . . . The Trotskyist movement has no chance of growing stronger. I know that amongst them there are honest people, but I do not agree with their ideology." (*The Fourth International* 11, no. 6: 191–192.) His interviewer added: "Tito, in my opinion, was still influenced by the Kremlin campaign against Trotsky. I should have thought it possible for Marxists to disagree with Trotsky without believing what Stalin and his official historians say about him." At the end of 1951, Tito told an Indian Socialist: "Stalin today is doing what Trotsky preached. A struggle for power was the issue [in their conflict] ." (*Govori i članci* 6: 266.) A later comprehensive (and on many points sympathetic) Yugoslav study of the political thought of Stalin's opponents is Predrag Vranicki, *Historija marksizma*, pp. 380–414: Party leaders objected even in the early 1960s to his treatment of Trotsky and Bukharin. Only in 1972 were Trotsky's collected works published in Yugoslavia.

[75] Dedijer, *Tito*, p. 197; Kardelj, "Posle pet godina," *Problemi* 3: 326.

[76] Even the relatively critical lecture on Soviet interwar development given at the High Party School approved the first Five-Year Plan and the policy of collectivization, objecting to undue emphasis on heavy industry in the second and third Five-Year Plans and the forced method of implementing collectivization (*Istorija medjunarodnog radničkog i socijalističkog pokreta*, pp. 477–492). This burden of the Stalinist past is strikingly portrayed in Dedijer, *Izgublijena bitka*, pp. 56–68 ("The Two Faces of Stalin"). Later, the Chinese Communists had similar difficulty in analyzing degenerate socialism in the USSR. See Schurmann, *Ideology and Organization in Communist China*, pp. 37–45.

[77] In the process, Tito himself was accused of Trotskyism (Speech of April 17, 1967, *Borba*, April 18, 1967). See Tito's condemnation of ideological and political deviations within the CPY in his speech to the Fifth Party Conference of 1940 (he called Trotskyism "not an ideological current, but an ordinary pernicious band") and his prewar article "Trockizam i njegovi pomagači" (he attacked Trotskyism as "only one form of fascism"), both reprinted in *Materijal za proučavanje linije KP Jugoslavije: Članci rezolucije i proglasi KPJ do 1941 godine* ([Belgrade], 1946), pp. 25–29. See also the retrospective accounts at the Fifth Congress by Tito (*Govori i članci* 3: 316–318) and Djilas (*V. kongres KPJ*, p. 182).

[78] See "An Open Letter to the Congress, Central Committee, and Members of the Yugoslav Communist Party" from the International Secretariat of the Fourth

International (July 13, 1948), *The Fourth International* 9, no. 6 (August 1948): 176–181, and the statement of the Political Committee of the Socialist Workers' Party [USA] of August 3, 1948, ibid., pp. 174–176.

[79] See the series of articles—especially those by Michael Pablo and E. Germain—in *The Fourth International*, 1948–1950. The International Secretariat sought to send an observer to the Fifth CPY Congress; later, it apparently sought to republish Trotsky's works in Yugoslavia at its own expense (*The Fourth International* 9, no. 6: 181, and 11, no. 5 [September–October 1951]: 156). Fourth International emissaries called at Yugoslav Embassies in various countries; the French delegation which took part in the international youth labor project in Zagreb in mid-1950 was headed by Pierre Gousset, a member of the International Secretariat (Leonhard and Spittmann interviews). See also Halperin, *The Triumphant Heretic*, pp. 112–121.

[80] Kardelj, *Problemi* 3: 186; Halperin, *The Triumphant Heretic*, pp. 116–117.

[81] "The Yugoslav Revolution" [Resolution of the Third World Congress of the Fourth International], *The Fourth International* 12, no. 6 (November–December, 1951): 202–207.

[82] In three articles published in 1952 and 1953, Djilas defensively distinguished his own analysis of the Soviet system from Trotsky's critique, thus suggesting that by that time he was rather familiar with Trotsky's arguments: "Klasa i kasta," *Svedočanstva*, April 5, 1952; "Vrti li se Staljin u krugu?" *Komunist* 6, nos. 3–4: 118; "Početak kraja i početka," *Nova misao* 1, no. 8 (August 1953): 163–205, at 189. Djilas later discussed Trotsky's ideas in *The New Class*, pp. 50–51, 54.

[83] For example, as early as 1921, Alexandra Kollontai had warned: "We are afraid of mass activity. We are afraid to give freedom to the class activity, we are afraid of criticism, we have ceased to rely on the masses, hence, *we have bureaucracy with us.*" (Quoted in Robert V. Daniels, *A Documentary History of Communism* [New York: Vintage Books, 1962] 1: 202). In 1926 the "Declaration of the Thirteen" pointed to the "bureaucratic perversion of the workers' state" (ibid., p. 283). In 1930 Christian Rakovsky depicted the Soviet state as a "bureaucratic state with proletarian-Communist survivals" (ibid., 2: 14). In 1932 the German ex-Communist Arthur Rosenberg described the Soviet order as "a peasants' and workers' state, organized in accordance with a system of state Capitalism by means of which the governing bureaucracy contrives to maintain its hold over both the basic classes in society." (Arthur Rosenberg, *A History of Bolshevism* [New York: Russell & Russell, 1965], p. 236.)

5

The Nature of the Epoch Reappraised

The Modified Doctrine

The radical appraisal of the international situation espoused by the CPY prior to 1948 was examined in Chapter 2. The Yugoslav Communists maintained, it will be recalled, that World War II had resulted in the world-historical victory of socialism. This was manifested above all in the appearance of new socialist states—the people's democracies—which ended the capitalist encirclement of the USSR. The general crisis of capitalism had deepened, creating favorable conditions throughout the capitalist and colonial world for revolutionary upheavals that could be led only by Communist Parties. In the process of carrying out revolutions and developing socialism, the CPY ideologues maintained, Communist Parties would develop new forms of militant political action.

Tito's break with Stalin in mid-1948 did not initially lead to any change in this analysis of the nature of the epoch. Throughout 1949, in spite of the newly discovered hegemonic and imperialist tendencies in Soviet foreign policy toward Yugoslavia, the Soviet Union was still viewed by the CPY as the most important member—although no longer the head—of the socialist world, the strength of which, vis-à-vis the capitalist world, was continually increasing. The seizure of power by the Chinese Communists in 1949 was interpreted as further proof of the correctness of this analysis. As Dedijer put it, writing in *Komunist* in March 1949:

The mighty successes of the Chinese revolution represent a further, large-scale weakening of the imperialist system of rule and the further sharpening and hastening of the general crisis of the capitalist system. The victory of the revolution in China signifies a fundamental, basic change in the relationship of forces in the world. With the victory of the Chinese revolution, the socialist world as a whole will, in the very near future, attain full superiority over the capitalist world as a whole.[1]

Not only did the Chinese revolution signify the strengthening of the socialist world at the expense of the imperialist world, but—in the CPY's view—it demonstrated the inevitability of immediate revolutionary upheavals in capitalist and colonial countries. It also showed, as did the Greek Communist struggle, that Communists could not shrink from revolutionary activity for fear of outside imperialist intervention:

Contemporary revolutions are an inevitable, historically determined phenomenon. Today the Chinese revolution is the strongest affirmation of that historical law discovered by Marxism-Leninism. As a result, the Chinese revolution ideologically arms revolutionaries throughout the world. The Chinese revolution has shown, in practice, on a mighty scale, that today the greatest danger for the working-class movement is to overestimate the strength of imperialism. The example of the current heroic struggle of the Greek people also confirms this fact. Over-estimating the strength of imperialism is not only seen in fear of imperialism in general but, above all, in fear of imperialist intervention if, in the struggle against the traitorous domestic bourgeoisie, more decisive, revolutionary measures should be taken.[2]

Finally, the Chinese revolution offered the Yugoslav Communists another sign that Soviet experience was not universally applicable. The Chinese revolution, too, had its "specific features," different from Soviet "forms" and similar in many respects to the Yugoslav ones. Kardelj stated this explicitly: "China and Yugoslavia have passed through similar forms of development: they liberated themselves with their own forces, and they have special state and other forms which differ from Soviet forms."[3]

The success of the Chinese Communists was, of course, a phenomenon of the colonial world. But the CPY's prognosis of the future of advanced capitalist countries was essentially the same. As formulated by a Central Committee member in May 1949: "The bourgeoisie of the Western European states have become involved in contradictions and difficulties so great that they are not able to overcome them. These contradictions and difficulties show the rottenness and anachronistic character of the entire social system. The revolutionary movements in these countries, led by the Communist Parties, the people's liberation movements in the colonies, and economic difficulties . . . are shaking the foundations of these states."[4] In the capitalist countries, too, Communist Parties would lead the masses in revolution in the foreseeable future. Their most pernicious enemies were Social Democrats, "the most fanatical enemies of the working class, the most despicable lackeys of American imperialism," whose fundamental sin was their attempt to "lull to sleep the working class with the illusion that it is possible to achieve socialism by a road other than the revolutionary road."[5]

This optimistic analysis of the strength of the socialist world and the inevitability of revolution in the capitalist and colonial world provided the Yugoslav Communist leadership with the major element of ideological self-justification necessary for its continued defiance of Stalin after 1948. This outlook reassured the Yugoslav leaders that, in resisting Stalin's hegemony, they were not automatically "objectively" aiding imperialism. For socialism was no longer the exclusive concern of the Soviet Union. It had won its world-historical victory over capitalism, spreading beyond the borders of the USSR, and was about to be further strengthened by the outbreak of new Communist-led revolutions. Since this was true, the nature of relations among socialist countries took on special importance for the further spread of socialism: revolutionaries throughout the world would be greatly emboldened if they saw that, in contrast to the imperialist world, the socialist world ordered its internal relations on the basis of full equality of its members. In resisting Stalin's attempt to deny such equality, the Yugoslav Communists thus saw themselves as in fact strengthening, not weakening, the socialist world.

In this defense of internationalism, the CPY naturally expected to find revolutionary allies. It first looked to China. Thinly disguised in the many comparisons of Chinese and Yugoslav revolutionary experience lay the hope of support from China, as another new socialist state with its own autonomous revolutionary origins, against Moscow's revisionism.[6] But support from China was not forthcoming; the Chinese Communist Party endorsed the Cominform's "slander."[7] In consequence, while never abandoning hope of future Sino-Soviet conflict that would aid it in the struggle with Stalin, the CPY concluded that, like the East European people's democracies, the People's Republic of China, too, had been subordinated to Stalin's control.[8]

The CPY also expected to find revolutionary allies within the various Stalinist Communist Parties. Here they were only slightly more successful than in the case of China. They did attract a few followers, such as Wolfgang Leonhard from East Germany, and Valdo Magnani and Aldo Cucchi from the Communist Party of Italy. Nevertheless, while latent support for the Yugoslav cause may have existed in the Communist Parties, the number of Communists who became genuine Titoists prior to Stalin's death was infinitesimally small, the so-called "anti-Titoist" purges in Eastern Europe notwithstanding.[9]

The Yugoslav Communists' greatest foreign support came from a small number of Western ex-Communist and non-Communist leftists, such as Konni Zilliacus, John Rogge, Jean Cassou, and Louis Dalmas, and an occasional ex-Socialist from the Soviet bloc, such as Bohumil Laušman of Czechoslovakia. Several Trotskyite groups, as already mentioned, also initially supported the CPY's stand. In the absence of more orthodox Communist allies, the Yugoslavs accepted, indeed, actively cultivated the support of these "little splinter groups and individuals at the fringe of the great world movement."[10] Magnifying the roles of the "Titoists" in their respective countries all out of proportion to their real political importance, the Yugoslav Communists sought to reassure themselves that they were not alone, that other true revolutionaries were to be found in the world.[11] In the process they made the first modification in their outlook on the world situation, implicitly granting that the interests of socialism need not be represented by Communists—although they could not be represented by Social Democrats.

If Tito had been engaged in a purely ideological controversy with Moscow, the radical analysis of the international situation (with the exception, just noted, made for the foreign Titoists), could and very likely would have remained the central weapon of the Yugoslav ideological arsenal. The CPY's foreign Titoist allies might have been insignificant numerically, but they prevented the demoralization that would very likely have resulted from total isolation, allowing the Yugoslav leaders to continue to wage what they saw as a struggle for principle within the international working-class movement in which—just as in the case of Lenin's struggle against the Mensheviks—the "historical" validity of their position had nothing to do with the number of their initial supporters.

The trouble was that, as fond as the Yugoslav Communists were of comparing their struggle with Stalin to the Menshevik-Bolshevik quarrel, the analogy was obviously faulty. Because it was a Communist Party in power, the CPY was engaged not only in an ideological dispute but in a very real international political conflict. While the Yugoslav leadership might not have felt isolated ideologically, by mid 1949 Stalin had very nearly succeeded in totally isolating Yugoslavia politically and economically from both East and West. It was well and good to "defend internationalism" against all odds, but Tito had to face up to the very practical problem of finding a way to overcome the increasingly effective Cominform economic embargo (prior to the break, Yugoslavia's foreign trade was overwhelmingly oriented toward the Soviet orbit) and the increasingly ominous Soviet bloc military threats.

Given a Western (especially U.S.) readiness to support Yugoslavia as an independent Communist state "under its present leadership," the solution was a gradual reconciliation with the United States and Western Europe. Following the open Soviet-Yugoslav break, Washington concluded that there were only two alternatives in Yugoslavia—

either Tito's Communist regime attempting to resist Soviet pressure or an orthodox Stalinist regime that would return the country to the Soviet bloc—and that it was in the U.S. interest to lend support to Tito. In early 1949 the U.S. government eased restrictions on exports to Yugoslavia. Previously, at the end of 1948, Yugoslavia had begun to shift its pattern of international trade by purchasing in Western Europe raw materials that the Cominform countries were refusing to deliver. By mid-1949 Belgrade began to reciprocate the U.S. interest in better relations (while seeking to avoid, prior to the outbreak of the Korean War, steps that would be viewed in Moscow as overly provocative); in July Tito terminated Yugoslav support of the Greek Communist guerrillas by denying them a sanctuary in Yugoslavia. In September 1949 the U.S. Export-Import Bank granted a Yugoslav request for a loan of $20 million. The same month, Kardelj (who became Foreign Minister in 1948) first publicly clashed with Andrei Vyshinsky at the United Nations (following which the USSR ominously broke its treaty of alliance with Yugoslavia). In October, Yugoslavia won, with U.S. backing, a seat in the U.N. Security Council in the face of Soviet opposition. In December 1949 U.S. Ambassador George Allen publicly affirmed American interest in "the retention of Yugoslavia's sovereignty," and Belgrade welcomed this declaratory position.

After 1949 the United States (and other Western countries) began to extend substantial economic assistance to Yugoslavia, whose economy threatened to flounder in the wake of the Soviet bloc embargo and a series of severe droughts. By 1955 the United States alone had extended some $600 million in economic aid to Yugoslavia. Soundings on the possibility of U.S. military assistance were made by Yugoslavia in late 1950, as Belgrade felt that the Soviet bloc military threat had increased further with the outbreak of the Korean War. A Mutual Defense Assistance agreement was negotiated in 1951; by 1955 the United States had supplied the Yugoslav armed forces with modern weapons officially worth an additional $600 million.

After 1949 Yugoslavia proceeded to normalize relations with Greece, Austria, and Italy (although the Trieste dispute continued to burden relations with Rome). The establishment of good relations with Greece and Turkey was formalized in the Treaty of Ankara of February 1953 and its military counterpart, the Balkan Pact (Treaty of Bled) of August 1954. At the same time, Yugoslavia improved its relations with more distant Western European states; in early 1953 Tito paid an official state visit to Great Britain. During these years, in the United

Nations and other international forums, Yugoslavia sided diplomatically with the West against the Soviet Union (while discovering a special communality of interest with India, Burma, and other newly independent states of the emerging Third World).[12]

The rapprochement with the Western powers ended Yugoslavia's political isolation. But it raised an obvious ideological problem. Did it not mean the final fulfillment of the dire predictions of the June 1948 Cominform Resolution? The initial Yugoslav response to the Resolution had been that continued "socialist development" at home and militant "anti-imperialism" abroad would disprove the "slanders" from Bucharest. In 1950 (as will be shown in the following chapters) the CPY could argue that the first policy, freeing itself of Stalinist distortions, was continuing apace. But if this had precluded Yugoslavia's transformation into an "ordinary bourgeois republic," what of the abandonment of militant anti-imperialism? In fighting to defend internationalism against revisionist and imperialist tendencies in the international working-class movement, had not Yugoslavia been transformed into an ally of world imperialism itself? The CPY's answer was, of course, that it had not. The justification of this answer was based on what amounted to a fundamental redefinition of the nature of the epoch.

At first glance, the revised Yugoslav analysis did not seem so different after all. As Kardelj told the Sixth CPY Congress in November 1952, in an address devoted to foreign policy:

Sometimes the opinion is heard even here that we, yes, we Yugoslavs, are the only true socialists and that socialist Yugoslavia is like a solitary island in the midst of the ocean storms. Such a view, in my opinion, does not correspond to reality. It would be a great mistake to maintain that socialism has failed because Stalin betrayed it and that it is today weaker than it was at the time of the October Revolution. We are no solitary island, for the strength of socialism in the world has never been as great as it is today. For this reason, socialist Yugoslavia was able to receive support, which greatly aided it in its resistance to the aggressive pressure of Soviet hegemonism. This is to say that the strength of socialism is such that today we can speak of a certain qualitative change in the world in the sense that precisely the problem of the further development of socialism has become the dominant problem of the present-day world.[13]

This statement displayed the same optimistic estimation of the strength of socialism as the CPY had espoused earlier, the same assertion that, as Dedijer put it a few months later, "the great battle of *kto kogo*— capitalism or socialism—has already been largely settled in the world."[14] But this evaluation, originally the basis for the radical prognosis of revolutionary upheaval throughout the world, now became the ideological justification for the rapprochement with the West. U.S. aid to Yugoslavia was to be explained, not by a pragmatic desire to exploit divisions in the Communist world, but by the alleged fact that the forces of socialism in the world—above all in the Western countries themselves—had become so strong that Western statesmen were forced by public opinion to come to Yugoslavia's aid without attempting to alter its internal socialist structure.

This amounted to a fundamental redefinition of the "forces of socialism." Originally the "forces of socialism" had a quite concrete political meaning—the "socialist world" (the USSR and the people's democracies) plus Communist-led revolutionary movements in capitalist and colonial countries. But by the end of 1950, the majority of Yugoslav Communist theoreticians were saying that the Soviet Union (and what were now termed its "satellites") had degenerated into a bureaucratic despotism or even state capitalism. Hence the geographic division between "socialist world" and "capitalist world" was re-nounced. "Two worlds in fact exist," Kardelj explained, "but they exist within each country . . . ."[15] And within each country, the forces of socialism were no longer Communist-led revolutionary movements but, it seemed, an almost spontaneous economic and ideological process creating the new classless society in the midst of the old. Kardelj first authoritatively formulated this view at the end of 1950.

. . . socialism has ceased to be the domain of "learned men" in Moscow or a tiny [Communist] avant-garde . . . . Socialism has already become a matter of the concrete practice of millions and millions of people in the whole world. Socialism today is breaking forth in numerous forms and through the most varied fissures of the old system . . . . We must not for a moment forget that socialism, especially in its present phase, is not a static social form. That is, that which we call today socialism is in fact the process of its emergence, the process of long and convulsive "birth pains"—as Marx said—in which the new is born from the old. We live in fact in the epoch of the transition of one social system into another, in which the economic factors of the new system have already won their world-historical victory and have become dominant for the entire political development of contemporary society. They place their stamp, for example, on every liberation movement, even in the most backward countries, and they become a spontaneous force which pushes through all the pores of capitalist society, even in the most developed and "firmest" capitalist countries.[16]

The forces of socialism thus became, in Yugoslav ideological state-ments, an almost abstract historical process—one that allegedly had already developed quite far. Since this was true, the roads to socialism were many and varied. The assertion of new features in the transition to socialism had been a tenet of Yugoslav doctrine since 1945. But whereas CPY spokesmen had as late as 1949 maintained the inevitability of new *revolutionary* forms in the transition to socialism, they now granted the possibility of nonrevolutionary roads as well. "Today," Kardelj declared, "indeed all roads lead to socialism."[17]

This revised view of socialism applied especially to the developed Western capitalist countries. The Yugoslav theorists now affirmed that, since the time when Lenin had analyzed monopoly capitalism, capitalism had entered a new phase of "state capitalism," signifying an immediate perspective of relative stability instead of revolutionary upheaval—although, to be sure, this would only hasten the end of capitalism as a social system. The essence of the new stage was said to be a qualitatively greater interventionist role of the state in the economy, necessitated by the development of the forces of production to such an extent that the capitalists themselves were no longer capable of maintaining the stability or ensuring the continuous growth of the capitalist economic system.[18] One consequence of the state's new role was an improvement in the economic position of the working class.

On the preceding points the CPY theoreticians were generally agreed. But they were not of one mind on the relationship between state capitalism and the capitalist class. A dogmatic minority pointed out that state intervention was still quite limited in scope and thus did not affect the bulk of private ownership of the means of production. More important, according to these theoreticians, even where the state restricted private ownership, it acted as "collective capitalist" to guarantee profits and thus in fact only strengthened the position of the bourgeoisie.[19] This was in fact the orthodox Leninist-Stalinist doctrine: whatever its increased role, the state remained solely the instrument of capitalist class oppression.[20]

A majority of CPY theoreticians, however, saw state capitalism as much more significant. "The system of state capitalism . . . ," wrote Milentije Popović, "brought a change in relation to monopoly capitalism as great as the change signified by the latter in relation to the classic liberal capitalism of the nineteenth century."[21] Intervening in the economy in order to prevent the disintegration of society through periodic economic crises, the state had become an "autonomous force."[22] The state bureaucracy had acquired an economic and political position independent of the bourgeoisie and had begun to act against its interests.[23] This was nothing less than the beginning of the expropriation of the bourgeoisie:

State capitalism wipes out, eliminates private property in capital. This means that in fact it carries out the expropriation of the bourgeois (in greater or lesser measure, in different ways, but objectively, necessarily, inevitably) and the whole class. Not only is the bourgeoisie no longer necessary; society is no longer able to live headed by it as the ruling class; thus it must be replaced by some other ruling force. However, the working class is incapable of freeing itself from the social relationships forced upon it by capital (the wage-labor relationship, etc.) and taking over the leadership of social life (first in the economy, and then in general). The state has to take up that role . . . . The system of state capitalism is therefore in essence and objectively the result of a temporary and unique compromise between the antagonistic class forces of modern society. . . .[24]

Although it meant the temporary stabilization of the capitalist system, state capitalism thus simultaneously signified—to the majority of CPY theorists—the negation of the capitalist class. (The historical analogy was absolute monarchy, as the highest stage but also the negation of feudalism.) The advanced level of the forces of production required the socialization of the means of production. Within the limits of the capitalist system, this led to etatism and to the introduction of such inherently socialist measures as economic planning. In this sense, state capitalism meant the "emergence of the new system within the old";[25] as such it was the "antechamber to socialism."[26]

However, this antechamber was not regarded as the beginning of the transition to socialism itself. While a majority of CPY theoreticians rejected the Stalinist doctrine that the "state capitalist" state was simply the old bourgeois state performing a new function for its masters, they also rejected the view that the interventionist state could act in the "fundamental interest" of the working class, as part of a process of the "peaceful growing of capitalism into socialism."[27] Emphasizing the importance of the process of the development of socialism, the Yugoslav theoreticians did not lose sight of the goal—Marx's ideal society where human exploitation had been eliminated. The achievement of communism required, however, not the restriction of private ownership of the means of production by a welfare state, but its total elimination.[28] Otherwise, exploitation remained, regardless of whether its fruits were reaped by the new state bureaucracy instead of private capitalists and notwithstanding the workers' improved economic position.

Hence, in the Yugoslav theoreticians' view, there could be no slackening of the working class's continuing political struggle for socialism. This very struggle was, indeed, an essential characteristic of state capitalism as the antechamber to socialism.[29] CPY theoreticians who viewed state capitalism as signifying the beginning of the expropriation of the bourgeoisie did not agree on whether or not the rise of the interventionist state brought greater political as well as economic rights for the working class.[30] But they were united in affirming that, in the absence of working-class political action, the historically progressive character of state capitalism would in time turn into its opposite, and the political system, no matter how democratic initially, would in time coalesce into a reactionary one.[31] This prognosis was consistent with the Yugoslav Communist analysis of the reversion to state capitalist social relations in the Soviet Union. For if the bourgeoisie was destroyed and the working class was still too weak politically to replace it, the state bureaucracy would step in and strive for total power—a position it could achieve and maintain only on the basis of terror.[32]

The preceding paragraphs should make it clear that, for all their talk about the growth of socialism inside the old capitalist society, the Yugoslav Communists continued to believe in the Leninist tenet that the old state—even if it had changed from the instrument of capitalist class oppression into a welfare state—had to be replaced eventually by a dictatorship of the proletariat. This did not necessarily mean the kind of regimented political system that had existed in the Soviet Union, or, initially, in Yugoslavia. But it did require systemic change beyond a progressive welfare state; it required a qualitative change in the position of the proletariat in relation to the means of production that would still amount to a "dictatorship" opposed to the bourgeoisie.[33] As one CPY spokesman put it in a polemic with a leading Swedish Social Democrat:

In order to achieve its aim as a class, the working class must—in one way or another—destroy the power of the bourgeoisie, establish its own rule, and transform the means of production into social property. No matter how that happens, whether through violent class conflict— through civil war—as has been the case so far wherever the working class has taken power, or through parliamentary methods, which should not be excluded as a possibility under certain conditions in certain countries, the government established will, in substance, be a dictatorship of the proletariat, although it may be unusually broad-minded and humane in form. Actually, it will be a kind of democracy that is new in terms of class substance and class goals.[34]

In developed capitalist countries such as Sweden with a firm tradition of bourgeois democracy, as suggested in the preceding quotation, the qualitative change might come about gradually, without violence, through the use of the existing parliamentary institutions. Under such conditions, a peaceful transition to socialism was possible.[35] If this road to socialism was taken, however, the parliamentary democratic institutions themselves would in time have to be modified. According to the same Party spokesman, ". . . progress toward socialism is altogether possible within the scope of parliamentary democracy . . . . But I cannot imagine a society in which 'free men work together as equals' without thoroughgoing changes in the entire social structure, and even in parliamentary democracy, which is only the political reflection of a specific social structure."[36] Yet even in an advanced capitalist democracy, a peaceful transition to socialism could not be guaranteed, for the capitalist class might in the end seek to save itself by force of arms. Just as in the case of the doctrine subsequently formulated by Khrushchev, the peaceful transition to socialism was, in the Yugoslav Communist view, only a possibility, not a certainty. The working class could therefore not renounce the armed seizure of power in advance.[37]

Still believing in the necessity of a revolutionary leap—even if it might be nonviolent—in the transition to socialism, the Yugoslav Communists continued to affirm the importance of the working-class political party. Socialism was, to be sure, no longer the exclusive concern of small revolutionary vanguards, but "a matter of concrete practice of millions and millions of people."[38] In these altered conditions, Communist Parties of the Leninist type were no longer capable of leading the working class in its struggle for socialism. This was true, of course, because the Communist Parties had become instruments of Stalin's hegemonic policy; they had turned into "fifth columns" and "dependent police spy centers [agenture] with bureaucratic leaderships."[39] But the defect ran deeper. Communist Parties in developed capitalist countries had become the tools of Moscow because they were historically outdated as a type of party.[40]

The CPY's view of which forces in the advanced capitalist countries could play the role of "conscious leader" (although not "vanguard") of the working class shifted as the conflict with Stalin continued. In 1949 and the first half of 1950, as has been described before, the Yugoslavs found a few ideological allies among defectors from the Stalinist Communist Parties and militant non-Stalinist leftists. Viewing the foreign "Titoists" as the true representatives of the international working-class movement, the Yugoslav Communists naturally also saw them as the embodiment of socialism in their respective countries. But the CPY's effort to create a "third force" within the international working-class movement, an important source of self-legitimacy in 1949, was cut short by Yugoslavia's rapprochement with the Western powers. The foreign Titoists' neutralist or pro-Soviet attitude toward world politics led to friction with the CPY from the beginning of 1950, and after the outbreak of the Korean War and the apparently increased danger of Soviet armed attack, this attitude became completely unacceptable to Belgrade.[41] Thereafter, condemning neutralism as illusory and a pro-Soviet outlook (particularly in the case of the Trotskyites) as only supporting Stalinism, the CPY turned to the only group in the West which unequivocally opposed Soviet aggression and yet still had something in common with Marxism (and was, at the same time, the political force in the West most responsive to cooperation with Yugoslavia)—the Social Democrats.[42] This move led to the ideological rehabilitation of Social Democratic Parties as a legitimate part of the international working-class movement. As Tito told a Swedish trade-union delegation in May 1952: "We are glad that today we can establish ties with very many countries through the [Social Democratic] movement. We do not view other currents in the working-class movement as enemies . . . . We believe that people may have different views, but that more or less everyone nevertheless wants somehow to achieve the same, common goal. Only the roads leading to that goal differ."[43]

Indeed, the Social Democratic Parties were now recognized to be the strongest working-class parties in the West. Since the Leninist Party was no longer applicable there, it was the task of dissident Communists, not to form new, "narrow" Parties, but to join the Social Democratic Parties.[44] Yet, in Yugoslav eyes, the Social Democrats continued to be plagued by the disease of "practicism," by a "lack of clear socialist conceptions . . . on questions of the roads and means of the struggle for socialism, the result of the existence for a long time of practical methods of political struggle."[45] Dissident Communists, along with militant Social Democrats, could play an important role in combating "practicism" within the Social Democratic Parties.[46] But for the foreseeable future, while the CPY would seek to expand its international contacts with Social Democratic Parties, this ideological weakness would prevent it from joining the Socialist International.[47]

The recognition that a Social Democratic Party could (if it overcame its ideological weaknesses) lead the working class to socialism signified an admission that the transition to socialism could begin in a multiparty political system. But this was the concomitant of the "peaceful road to socialism"; as such, it was, even in an advanced capitalist country, only a possibility.[48]

Reevaluating the "forces of socialism" in capitalist countries in the course of political rapprochement with the West, the CPY after 1949 also modified its view of the perspective facing colonial countries. It was precisely in the colonial world, it will be recalled, that the Yugoslav Communists originally saw the greatest relevance of their own revolution as a model. As late as May 1950, the old view was restated in *Komunist*: "National liberation movements of the colonial peoples, supported by the historic victory of the Chinese people, are increasingly acquiring the character of a struggle for people's democracy headed by the working class and led by the Communist Parties."[49]

The first change in this outlook occurred in the fall of 1950 following the outbreak of the Korean War, when Yugoslavia found itself adopting the same position as India, Burma, Ceylon, and other ex-colonial states in the United Nations—opposing Soviet-backed aggression in Korea but urging a cease-fire and opposing U.N. "interference" in North Korea. The radical post-1945 Yugoslav doctrine on the non-Western world had treated such anticolonial movements as that of Gandhi and Nehru in India as aiming at independence in name only, for, once "independence" had been won, the rule of the national bourgeoisie would mean the continued subordination of the ex-colony to the metropolitan power and the continued domestic exploitation of the people. In the fall of 1950, CPY spokesmen concluded that the new Asian states did possess a degree of independence which was of great international significance:

The rise of these new states . . . signifies a . . . substantial contribution in the struggle for world peace. In the comparatively brief period since they came into being, experience has shown the new states of Asia to be, to a considerable degree, composed of elements opposed to the formation of war blocs and to subjection to the great powers acting as "leaders" of such blocs. The attitude of the largest one of these states—the Republic of India—stands out with the greatest clarity in this respect. Although the ruling circles in these states need the support of imperialists, yet their divergences are clearly revealed in a series of questions. The new Asian states are struggling, even though with little consistency, for as complete independence as possible and for fuller economic development, as a safeguard of their independence, while the big metropolitan financial circles wish them to remain mere appendages of their economic system.[50]

Believing that the foreign policy of a state could only reflect its internal order, the Yugoslav theoreticians simultaneously granted that internally, too, the new Asian states—even though governed by "compromising sections of the national bourgeoisie"—had a certain progressive character. While the national bourgeoisie had succeeded in capturing the liberation movements in these countries, in the process it was forced to make economic and political concessions to the masses, partially undermining its own class positions.[51] But at this point—in the fall of 1950—the progressive character attributed to the internal order of these states was still limited: it was less than that granted in the later Soviet doctrine of "national democratic states." For the new Asian states were still viewed as developing capitalism and in the process educating the masses in the need for radical social action.[52]

In 1951 and 1952 Yugoslavia expanded its international contacts with the ex-colonial Asian and African states—the beginning of its support for a "nonaligned" grouping of countries. At the United Nations, the Yugoslav, Indian, and Egyptian delegates to the Security Council held regular consultations. In October 1951 a Yugoslav goodwill mission visited Ethiopia; in December 1951 Yugoslavia began to supply arms to Burma.[53] Now CPY spokesmen gave greater credence to the real independence of the ex-colonial states. This signified the tacit abandonment by the CPY of its earlier doctrine that national independence could not be achieved in the absence of a socialist revolution. At the same time, the progressive internal character of the new Asian states was now given more weight. State capitalist forms were seen as revealing themselves in their most progressive light in these states. But even here, just as in developed capitalist countries, state capitalist forms would in time play out their progressive role:

. . . here too, with the development of industry, the political power of the working-class movement will strengthen—a movement which will appear—or which is already appearing, although with limited strength and with an insufficiently clear orientation—with its progressive demands. On the outcome of that struggle depends whether the state capitalist forms of development, which are still progressive today, will lead in these countries to a reactionary state capitalist monopoly or whether the socialist forces will be capable of giving them a socialist direction.[54]

In the early 1950s the Yugoslav theoreticians never defined very clearly "socialist forces" in the colonial world. While Communist Parties of the Leninist type were not outdated in conditions of economic backwardness, in the CPY's view, Stalin's control over them rendered them unfit to lead the working class. In 1951 the CPY "discovered" the Asian Socialist movements—particularly in Burma. Because of their greater radicalism, the Asian Socialists were ideologically more attractive to the Yugoslavs than were the Western European Social Democrats. As one editorial on the Asian Socialist Conference of 1953 (which Djilas and Aleš Bebler attended as Yugoslav observers) commented:

. . . the Socialist Parties of Asia are devoid of the traditional sectarianism [of Socialists] in their rural policy . . . so that they regard the peasants as their closest allies. Their standpoint on the colonial issue reveals, on its part, the existence of great revolutionary possibilities within these parties. Both these issues, more than any other items dealt with at the congress, revealed the prevailing differences which distinguish and set apart the Asian Socialists from the European Socialist Parties and the present [Socialist] International.[55]

Thereafter, with Yugoslavia playing an active role in the Asian Socialist International until 1956, the CPY would affirm that socialist movements in Asia (and elsewhere outside of Europe) were pursuing genuine "working class" interests.

Political Consequences
The CPY's reevaluation of the nature of the Soviet system and the forces of socialism in the world both followed from and provided the ideological justification for Yugoslavia's altered international position after 1949. Basing themselves on this reevaluation, the CPY leaders reformulated their analysis of the concrete dispersal of political forces in the international arena. Their revised analysis may be summarized under five points.[56]

1. "The Soviet Union has reached a point in its internal development under Stalin where foreign imperialist expansion, that is, the struggle for hegemony in the world, has become the necessary and only road for the existence of the system as such."[57] This involved seizing alien territory, using the political and military means of classic imperialism. For this reason, Soviet "hegemonism" constituted the greatest threat to world peace.

2. The United States sought economic hegemony in the world in order to create markets for domestic overproduction. Because of its very economic strength and its overwhelming superiority over the other traditional imperialist powers, however, the United States no longer had

to resort to political-military measures but could rely on such purely economic instruments as "foreign aid."[58]

3. The Western European "imperialist powers," hopelessly weakened by World War II, were engaged in a struggle on three fronts— against the Soviet attempt to achieve world domination by military means, against the American attempt to achieve world economic domination, and against the liberation movements of the colonial areas.

4. Germany, Italy, and Japan, the imperialist powers defeated in World War II, were still too weak to play any significant role in the international arena.

5. The colonial and ex-colonial countries did not pursue a common foreign policy but manifested, at least potentially, "the general tendency of progressive and peace-loving humanity as a whole to put an end to both the imperialist spheres of interest and different imperialist and hegemonic aspirations."[59]

This international constellation meant, in the CPY's view, that the Soviet-American conflict had become the chief "contradiction" of international relations, far more important than contradictions among the traditional imperialist powers. World War II had not initiated a period of sharpening interimperialist contradictions; Varga (it was expressly recognized) had been right after all.[60] Instead of threatening to lead to imperialist war, "today the contradictions among the Western capitalist countries are a factor that acts in the direction of preserving peace."[61] Middle-ranking theoreticians concluded from this assertion, made by Kardelj at the Sixth CPY Congress, that, because of the strength of socialism in the world, Lenin's dictum on the inevitability of imperialist wars was no longer valid.[62]

On the basis of this analysis of the international arena, Yugoslavia could define in ideological terms its role in world politics. Its foreign policy objectives were threefold.[63] First, since international conflict in any form was judged to be contrary to the interests of socialism, Yugoslavia had to oppose the "basic causes of war"—above all, the sphere-of-interest policy pursued by all the imperialist powers of West and East. Second, since the "concrete and current danger of aggression" from the Soviet Union was the most urgent danger to socialism, it had to be opposed by a strong defensive system. In these conditions, neutralism was an untenable position for any country to adopt; countries with differing sociopolitical systems had to join together in resisting Soviet aggression.[64] Third, Yugoslavia had to oppose "aggressive tendencies" within the anti-Soviet defensive system itself. Defensive political agreements—even military arrangements such as the Balkan Pact—might be necessary, but they did not signify, according to CPY leaders, that Yugoslavia was joining a Western political bloc.

In summary, until 1950 the Yugoslav Communists continued to hold to the radical analysis of the world situation which they had formulated prior to 1948. While this radicalism could provide the ideological justification for a protracted challenge to Stalin, it could not explain or justify in Marxist terms the move toward the West which Yugoslavia was forced to make in order to overcome its political isolation. Hence the radical analysis was modified.

Parallel to the political rapprochement with the Western powers, the CPY theoreticians thus formulated a new analysis of the international situation. The basic tenet—the strength of socialism in the world—remained unchanged, but the "socialist forces" were redefined and deprived of any clear-cut meaning. On the one hand, the Soviet socialist state (along with its satellites) had degenerated. On the other hand, socialism had become the "practice of millions and millions of people" in capitalist and colonial countries. The revised analysis of socialism in the advanced capitalist countries clearly broke with Leninism, concluding that the professional revolutionary party was outdated and that the masses would, from their very role in the process of production, acquire "socialist consciousness." At the same time, much like the orthodox Marxists of the late nineteenth century, the Yugoslavs did not de-emphasize the importance of the goal of a communist society itself or the necessity of conscious political action to achieve that end. In the colonial and ex-colonial world, the CPY tacitly abandoned proclaiming its revolution as a model; it recognized the real independence of the ex-colonial states and looked upon their state capitalist internal political forms as progressive. Yet the belief in the need for eventual revolutionary political action in the transition to socialism was not abandoned by 1953.

In all three areas of the world—the Soviet bloc, the West, and the colonial world—the basic class antagonism was, according to the revised Yugoslav doctrine, no longer simply a conflict between capitalism and socialism, but a three-way struggle between capitalism, "state capitalism," and socialism. In the West and the colonial world, state capitalism was still by and large historically progressive, signaling and furthering the approach of socialism; in the Soviet bloc, in contrast, state capitalism marked its temporary defeat.

This revised analysis of the world situation provided the ideological justification for Yugoslavia's altered international position after 1949. It reassured the CPY—although not completely successfully[65]—that, in cooperating with the United States and other Western powers against the Soviet Union, Yugoslavia was not aiding world imperialism but was opposing the threat of Stalinist imperialism in a world where socialism had already won its world-historical victory over capitalism, internally transforming the traditional capitalist states. But if this new analysis could explain in appropriate Marxist terms Yugoslavia's altered international position, it did not suggest to the CPY any satisfactory ideological allies. The rapprochement with the West estranged many of the foreign "Titoists." The CPY's conception of the international working-class movement was expanded to include Social Democrats, but, although political contacts were developed, ideological rapprochement with the Social Democrats was limited. The Asian Socialists were more acceptable in this regard, but they were far away, and ties were slow to develop. At the time of Stalin's death in March 1953, the Yugoslav Communists had successfully overcome their political isolation, but ideologically they still found themselves largely alone in the world. This relative ideological isolation would subsequently play an important role both in Yugoslavia's promotion of "nonalignment" in the Third World and in its rapprochement with the USSR after 1954.

Notes

[1] Vladimir Dedijer, "O kineskoj revoluciji," *Komunist* 3, no. 2 (March 1949): 157–173, at 157.

[2] Ibid., p. 172.

[3] Kardelj, Interview of October 1, 1949, *Problemi* 3: 41–42. See also Dedijer, *Komunist* 3, no. 2. 158–159.

[4] Radoljub Čolaković, "Izdajnička politika desnih socijalista posle drugog svetskog rata," *Komunist* 3, no. 3 (May 1949): 82–104, at 90.

[5] Ibid., pp. 82, 86.

[6] The Yugoslav celebration of May Day 1949 devoted particular attention to the Chinese Communists. Pictures of Mao were displayed in Belgrade, while the CPY CC proclamation declared: "With the victory of the Chinese people's revolution, the forces of peace, democracy, and socialism will win a victory of world-historical importance." (*Borba*, May 1, 1949.) *Borba* devoted its entire third page to the Chinese Communists. Later in 1949 a volume of Mao's selected works was published in Serbo-Croat.

[7] For an example, see *Chieh Fang Jih Pao* [Liberation Daily] (Shanghai), August 29, 1949.

[8] "Povodom potpisivanja sovjetsko-kineskog ugovora," *Borba*, February 25, 1950; Dedijer, *Tito*, pp. 434–435; Teslić, *Kineska revolucija i Moskva*. The Yugoslavs' hopes were revived by a note from North Vietnam of February 15, 1950, asking for diplomatic recognition. When Yugoslavia promptly granted recognition, Hanoi

broadcast a diatribe against it. (Dedijer, *Tito*, pp. 435–436.)

[9] Halperin, *The Triumphant Heretic*, pp. 105–106.

[10] Ibid., p. 113.

[11] For positive appraisals of the foreign Titoists, see Vlahović in *Borba*, November 29, 1949, and Kardelj, Speech of March 18, 1950, *Problemi* 3: 109. For reprints of Titoists' statements, see *Borba*, April 25, 1950, and the column "Democratic Public Opinion on Yugoslavia" in the first issues of *Review of International Affairs* for 1950. The importance that the Yugoslav leaders attached to the Titoists' support at this time is suggested by the reception Louis Adamić received when he revisited Yugoslavia in early 1949, as recounted in *The Eagle and the Roots*. A brief account of the foreign Titoists' role is given in Halperin, *The Triumphant Heretic*, pp. 113–114. Their full story remains to be written; astonishingly, Dedijer later suggested they were diabolicly used by Stalin in his effort to isolate Yugoslavia (*Izgubljena bitka*, pp. 379–380).

[12] See John C. Campbell, *Tito's Separate Road* (New York: Harper & Row, 1967), pp. 14–29; Halperin, *The Triumphant Heretic*, chap. 17; Wolff, *The Balkans in Our Time*, chap. 12; Robert Owen Freedman, *Economic Warfare in the Communist Bloc* (New York: Praeger, 1970), pp. 20–37; John O. Iatrides, *Balkan Triangle* (The Hague: Mouton, 1968); Bogdan C. Novak, *Trieste, 1941–1954* (Chicago: University of Chicago Press, 1970).

[13] Kardelj, *Problemi* 3: 293–294.

[14] Vladimir Dedijer, "O problemu saradnje u medjunarodnom radničkom pokretu," *Pregled* no. 5 (May 1953): 343–348, at 343.

[15] Kardelj. Speech to the Sixth CPY Congress, *Problemi* 3: 286.

[16] Skupština address of December 29, 1950, ibid., pp. 177–178.

[17] Address of February 23, 1953, *Problemi* 2: 290.

[18] Milentije Popović, "Šta državni kapitalizam znači u društvenom razvitku," *Naša stvarnost* 7, no. 2 (February 1953): 3–34, at 5.

[19] Miladin Korač, "Neke karakteristike odnosa proizvodnje državnog kapitalizma," *Komunist* 6, nos. 3–4 (May–August 1952): 16–38; M. Perović, "O nekim problemima državnog kapitalizma," *Ekonomist* 4, no. 1 (1951): 25–42; Boris Ziherl, *Dijalektički i istorijski materijalizam* (Belgrade, 1952), pp. 331–332.

[20] This view was restated, together with an attack on Kardelj and the Yugoslav Party Program of 1958, in *Fundamentals of Marxism-Leninism* (Moscow, 1961), pp. 321–342.

[21] *Naša stvarnost* 7, no. 2: 11. Other theoreticians cautioned that "it is necessary to await further developments to judge whether or not state capitalism will really become dominant." (Lukić, *Teorija države i prava* 1: 322.)

[22] Milentije Popović, *Naša stvarnost* 7, no. 2: 10.

[23] Radomir Lukić, "Klasna priroda države u državnom kapitalizmu," *Anali pravnog fakulteta u beogradu* 2, no. 3 (July–September 1954): 257–270, at 263–266.

[24] Milentije Popović, *Naša stvarnost* 7, no. 2: 14. Similar views are expressed by Kardelj, Address to the Fourth Congress of the People's Front, *Problemi* 2: 287–291; Ljubisav Marković, *Državni kapitalizam* (Belgrade, 1953); Radoš Stamenković, *O nastanku i karakteristikama državnog kapitalizma* (Belgrade, 1953). The disagreements in Yugoslavia on the subject of "state capitalism" are analyzed by Lukić, *Teorija države i prava* 1: 317–325, and Milivoje Erić, "Državni kapitalizam i socijalizam," *Pregled* no. 2 (February 1954): 135–140.

[25] Kardelj, Speech of April 27, 1951, *Problemi* 2: 137.

[26] Djilas, "Kompartije u kapitalističkim zemljama," *Naša stvarnost* 7, no. 1 (January 1953): 1–14, at 11.

[27] Lukić, *Teorija države i prava* 1: 322.

[28] Radoljub Čolaković, "Socialism and Democracy," *Review of International*

Affairs, February 16, 1953, pp. 9–12, at 11. This was the third part of a discussion between Čolaković, representing the Commission for International Affairs of the Yugoslav Party, and Kaj Björk, Secretary for International Affairs of the Social-Democratic Workers' Party of Sweden, which indicated how far the Yugoslav Communists were from accepting the Social Democratic view of socialism in an advanced capitalist country. See also ibid., November 16, 1952, pp. 9–14, and December 16, 1952, pp. 7–10.

[29] Kardelj, Speech to the Sixth CPY Congress, *Problemi* 3: 293.

[30] For a positive evaluation, see Lukić, *Teorija države i prava* 1: 319. For a negative view, see Milentije Popović, *Naša stvarnost* 7, no. 2: 12–13.

[31] Lukić, *Teorija države i prava* 1: 319; Kardelj, Speech to the Fourth Congress of the People's Front, *Problemi* 2: 288.

[32] Djilas wrote that Stalinist state capitalism did not differ qualitatively from Western state capitalism but was only the "deepest and fullest stage of the realization of state capitalism." (*Savremene teme*, p. 18.) Other writers qualified their positive appraisal of Western state capitalism by emphasizing its transitory character; dynamically, the relatively independent bureaucracy would end up as the servant of the working class or the servant of the bourgeoisie. (Stamenković, *O nastanku i karakteristikama državnog kapitalizma*, pp. 27–28.)

[33] N. Mirković, *Socijal-demokratija u Skandinaviji* (Belgrade, 1953), p. 35.

[34] Čolaković, *Review of International Affairs*, November 16, 1952, p. 10 (style improved).

[35] Vujanović, *Komunist* 5, nos. 4–5: 174.

[36] Čolaković, *Review of International Affairs*, December 16, 1952, p. 8.

[37] See Dedijer, *Tito*, p. 422; Djilas, in *Vjesnik*, November 29, 1952.

[38] Kardelj, Speech of April 27, 1951, *Problemi* 2: 142 and Speech to the Sixth CPY Congress, *Problemi* 3: 295.

[39] Kardelj, Speech of March 10, 1951, *Problemi* 3: 235.

[40] Djilas, *Naša stvarnost* 7, no. 1: 9; Kardelj, Speech to the Sixth CPY Congress, *Problemi* 3: 292.

[41] See D. Blagojević's criticism of Zilliacus's contention that Soviet policy toward Yugoslavia could be interpreted as part of its search for security against the West. (*Review of International Affairs*, June 21, 1950, pp. 7, 11.) The divergence of view between the "neutralists" and the Yugoslavs on Soviet foreign policy was clearly manifested at the Zagreb Peace Congress in the fall of 1951. See the accounts in Halperin, *The Triumphant Heretic*, pp. 117–118; Melvin J. Lasky, "Balkan Tagebuch," *Der Monat*, 3 (December 1951): 261–269, and 4 (January 1952): 345–356. Tito pointedly remarked while the Congress was in session: "The question of aggression in Europe today is indivisible. It will be impossible for any country to remain neutral if war comes." (Tito, Press Conference of October 31, 1951, *Govori i članci* 6: 235.)

[42] According to Dedijer, the Politburo made this decision as early as (late) 1949 (*Izgubljena bitka*, p. 380). In 1950 the first Labour Party delegation, led by Sam Watson, visited Yugoslavia; in early 1951 Djilas and Pijade visited Great Britain.

[43] Tito, *Govori i članci* 7: 91–92. See also Z. Pečar, "Notes on a Trip to England," *Review of International Affairs*, October 11, 1950; Leon Geršković, in *Borba*, June 7, 1951; Kardelj interview, in *Die Neue Zeitung* (Munich), June 28, 1951.

[44] Dedijer, *Pregled*, May 1953, p. 345; Kardelj, Speech of April 27, 1951, *Problemi* 2: 142.

[45] Kardelj, Speech to the Fourth Congress of the People's Front, *Problemi* 2: 354.

[46] Kardelj, Speech to the Sixth CPY Congress, *Problemi* 3: 294.

[47] Tito, Speech to the Sixth CPY Congress, *Borba komunista Jugoslavije*, p. 48; "Šta je Socijalistička internacionala," *Vjesnik*, November 2, 1952; Dedijer, *Pregled*, May 1953, p. 345.

[48] Čolaković, *Review of International Affairs*, November 16, 1952, p. 11.

[49] Vladimir Popović, "Ravnopravnost naroda i borba za mir," *Komunist* 4, nos. 2–3 (March–May 1950): 108–123, at 118.

[50] V.B., "The Significance Underlying the Rise of New States in South and South-East Asia," *Review of International Affairs*, September 27, 1950, pp. 12–13, at 13 (style improved). The article was in response to "letters from several sources raising the question of appraisal of the significance of the emergence of new states in South and South-East Asia in the light of the prevailing differences in world opinion on the subject."

[51] Ibid., p. 12.

[52] Ibid. Djilas expressed a similar view in *Savremene teme*, pp. 31–32.

[53] Alvin Z. Rubinstein, *Yugoslavia and the Nonaligned World* (Princeton, N.J.: Princeton University Press, 1970); pp. 32–48.

[54] Kardelj, Speech to the Fourth Congress of the People's Front, *Problemi*, 2: 288.

[55] "A Good Beginning in Rangoon," *Review of International Affairs*, February 1, 1953. See also Djilas's comments upon his return, Radio Belgrade, January 20, 1953 (*Yugoslav Review* 2, no. 2 [February 1953] : 9); Rubinstein, *Yugoslavia and the Nonaligned World*, pp. 40–42. The Yugoslav Communists devoted the greatest attention to Burma. Whereas originally they had applauded the efforts of the Burmese Communist Party to overthrow U Nu's nationalist coalition by force, now they supported it, viewing the Burmese Socialists, part of the coalition, as best representing the interests of socialism. Excerpts from *The Burmese Revolution* by the moderate Socialist U Ba Swe were republished in the *Review of International Affairs*, July 1, 1952, p. 13, and August 1, 1952, pp. 12–13.

[56] Kardelj, Speech to the Fourth Congress of the People's Front, *Problemi* 2: 286–307.

[57] Ibid., p. 293.

[58] Ibid., p. 294.

[59] Ibid., p. 296.

[60] Djilas, *Savremene teme*, p. 30; Kardelj, Speech of April 27, 1951, *Problemi* 2: 137.

[61] Kardelj, Speech to the Sixth CPY Congress, *Problemi* 3: 275.

[62] S. Belić, in *Istorija medjunarodnog radničkog i socijalističkog pokreta*, p. 613. Other theoreticians saw the growth of state capitalism as only increasing the danger of interimperialist conflict. See Milentije Popović, *Naša stvarnost* 7, no. 2: 9.

[63] As formulated by Kardelj to the Fourth Congress of the People's Front, *Problemi* 2: 299, 305–306.

[64] If this justified Yugoslavia's siding with the West against the USSR, there remained the problem of Western economic "aid"—that new form of "imperialist exploitation." The best the Yugoslav theoreticians could do to justify its acceptance was an analysis purporting to show that "international loans do not have to mean economic subordination, even though they mean sending abroad a part of the surplus of production, if the country which utilizes them is developing socialism and, to that end, developing its productive forces at a faster rate. Loans do not endanger political or economic independence, either, if the country which utilizes them is truly socialist in the character of its political system and its system of production." (Guzina, *Komunist* 4, no. 6: 81.)

[65] It is clear that there was considerable resistence in the Party to the rapprochement with the West, especially U.S. military assistance. See Tito, Speech of February 16, 1951, *Govori i članci* 5: 354–358; Djilas, "Savez ili partija," *Borba*, January 4, 1954; Chapter 10, note 20.

6

The Withering Away of the State

Relaxation of Revolutionary Totalitarianism

Denounced by the Cominform in mid-1948, the CPY leadership had adopted the position that continued socialist development at home and militant anti-imperialism abroad would disprove the "slanders" and demonstrate the CPY's orthodoxy. The militant foreign policy followed by Yugoslavia during the first year after the break with Stalin has already been indicated. Domestically, through 1949 the Tito regime maintained and in some respects intensified the revolutionary totalitarianism that it had consolidated after 1945. The secret police increased its vigilance in the face of the external threat; by 1953 some 14,000 Yugoslavs had been arrested for pro-Soviet feelings. Forced collectivization of agriculture was inaugurated in January 1949. The rapid pace of forced industrialization dictated by the goals of the Five-Year Plan was maintained. As the Cominform mounted its economic embargo, the CPY sought to offset its negative effects through mass mobilization of labor, achieved in part through indirect coercion and in part through outright forced labor.

The previous chapter has recounted how Yugoslavia, forced by Stalin into a position of international political isolation, attenuated its radical foreign policy after mid-1949 and gradually achieved a rapprochement with the United States and Western Europe. Concomitantly, as the conflict with Stalin continued, Tito evidently realized that successful defiance required not just the continued loyalty of the CPY but the at least passive support of the predominantly non-Communist Yugoslav population as well and that the latter was incompatible with the more coercive measures of the postwar revolutionary totalitarianism. This perception may well have been sharpened by Yugoslavia's multinational character, which was a prime target of Soviet subversion after 1948. CPY leaders have subsequently testified to this cause-and-effect relationship between the external threat and domestic relaxation in Yugoslavia after 1949. As Kardelj declared shortly after Stalin's death: "[After 1948] the socialist forces of our country had no source of support except their own working people. Therefore, all state policies had to have the support of the majority of the people. Only such policies had, and still have, prospects of being supported with sufficient initiative by the great majority of our working people and giving Yugoslavia and its socialist development the necessary strength to resist and overcome the pressure from abroad. . . ."[1] In 1971 Marko Nikezić, head of the Serbian Party organization, made the same point: "Even though our revolution was carried out by our own forces and contained a fertile seed of democracy, I do not believe that, without the clash with the Cominform, our development would be what it is today. In the clash with Stalin, as in all decisive moments, our [Communist] movement could only survive by reliance on the masses."[2]

The CPY's endeavor to ensure itself of the support of the Yugoslav population after 1949 involved a number of piecemeal measures, including concessions to popular sentiment, which reduced tension between regime and citizenry.[3] Economic decentralization was begun in early 1950 and entailed a reduction of the higher levels of the ruling bureaucracy by some 100,000. In mid-1950 workers' councils were established in factories, while the positions of state and Party leaders were separated at the local level. In the fall of the year, at the height of the economic crisis, some of the ostentatious privileges enjoyed by the ruling Party elite (such as special shops) were abolished or reduced. The year 1951 brought the active dismantling of the command economy, a new criminal code restricting some of the arbitrary powers of the secret police, and the beginning of a reconciliation with both Orthodox and Catholic churches. Local state organs were reorganized in 1952 to enjoy more administrative authority, encourage greater involvement of the citizenry in their affairs, and permit multiple candidates in local elections. The Sixth Party Congress, which convened in November 1952, resolved to dismantle some of the Party's organizational and propaganda apparatus. Government reorganization was extended to the federal and republican levels with the passage of the Constitutional Law of 1953, which sought to make state institutions more representative in composition and less arbitrary in operation. The law restricted the prerogatives of the republican state organs, one manifestation of the CPY's post-1948 efforts to create an all-Yugoslav socialist patriotism that would serve the interrelated tasks of defending Yugoslavia against the external threat to its sovereignty while superseding ethnic-regional differences internally. Forced collectivization was abandoned in the spring of 1953 with the dissolution of most kolkhozlike work cooperatives. During these years personal freedom of expression, information, and travel was significantly increased. Where these measures were directly relevant to the transformation of Yugoslav Communist ideology, they will be discussed in more detail later; they initiated a fifteen-year process of the transformation of the postwar revolutionary totalitarianism into a still dictatorial but much less coercive one-party authoritarian political system.

The Doctrine of the "Nonstate"

As described in Chapter 3, in May 1949 Kardelj returned to the writings of Marx, Engels, and Lenin which treated the socialist state as a state that would disappear by drawing the masses into the business of running state affairs. Beginning in December 1949 this issue became a major subject of theoretical concern within the CPY. On the basis of the Marxist "classics," Yugoslav Communist theoreticians gradually developed an extensive (though never consistent) theory of the socialist state—a process initiated by an all-out attack on the Stalinist theory of the state.

Indirectly taking issue with Stalin's theory in May 1949, Kardelj in December openly condemned the "making a fetish of the state" in the USSR.[4] Tito, in his major speech of June 26, 1950, took the Soviet leaders to task for their "false interpretation and false practical implementation of Marx's and Lenin's teaching on the state."[5] Finally, following a conference of theoreticians on problems of the socialist state, in late 1950 and early 1951 Professors Leon Geršković and Najdan Pašić published the first comprehensive theoretical Yugoslav refutations of the Stalinist state doctrine.[6]

The heart of the Stalinist doctrine on the socialist state had been expressed in Stalin's address to the Sixteenth Soviet Party Congress in 1930: "We stand for the withering away of the state. At the same time, we stand for the strengthening of the dictatorship of the proletariat, which is the mightiest and strongest state power that has ever existed. The highest development of the state power with the object of preparing the conditions *for* the withering away of state power—such is the Marxist formula."[7] The socialist state, according to Stalin, had four major functions: internal repression, external defense, organization of the economy, and socialist reeducation of the people. While the first of these functions, internal repression, was said to have been eliminated by 1936 with the destruction of the last hostile class elements, the remaining three functions would continue to be exercised by the state until the higher stage of communism was reached. Moreover, the paramount importance of the state was implicit in Stalin's formulation of 1937—partially contradicting the alleged end of internal repression in the USSR—that the closer the Soviet Union came to communism, the sharper the class struggle with the "remnants of the destroyed exploiting classes" would become.[8] At the Eighteenth Party Congress in 1939, Stalin justified the prospective continued existence of the state under communism solely in terms of continued "capitalist encirclement";[9] on other occasions he made it abundantly clear, however, that only the state, in exercising its internal functions, could bring about a

Communist society. In the words of Academician Pavel IUdin, "The Soviet state is the chief force, the principal instrument for the construction of socialism and for the realization of the construction of a communist society."[10]

Hence, the "strengthening of the state by all possible means" became a primary task of Communists.[11] With the achievement of communism and the end of hostile encirclement, Stalin asserted, the state would finally disappear. By this he surely did not mean that the state would one day simply vanish, but rather that the difference between the state and society would be abolished in favor of the former. The state would be "abolished" because it would be total.

The Yugoslav Communist theoreticians set out to refute this conception of the socialist state. They attacked Stalin for equating the state bureaucracy with the state itself, for emptying both "withering" and "strengthening" of any content, and for postponing the withering process until the indefinite future. They saw all these mistaken concepts embodied in the slogan "strengthen the state by all possible means," stigmatized by Pašić as "a typical bureaucratic slogan . . . [which signifies strengthening the state] by means directly contrary to socialism."[12] Stalin's formulation of the four functions of the socialist state was rejected; of these, the Yugoslav theoreticians maintained, only the task of external defense was totally valid. The state could not be the main instrument of building socialism, let alone communism. Stalin's theory of the state, Geršković thus concluded, "is a pure theory of *etatism*, a theory which raises the state above society, a theory which maintains that society cannot develop without the state. It proceeds from a revision of the Marxist theory on the state in general and on the withering away of the state in particular."[13]

Attacking the Stalinist theory of the state, the Yugoslav theoreticians did not stop at merely quoting from the Marxist "classics" but attempted to work out, from the perspective of a Communist Party in power, a detailed substitute theory. This doctrine was officially formulated only in the Party Program of 1958. Nevertheless, a study of the pronouncements of ideologues and lesser theoreticians between 1950 and 1953 reveals the emergence of a widely accepted theoretical conception, as well as a number of extreme formulations never incorporated in Yugoslav doctrine.[14]

Rejecting Stalin's formulation of the four functions of a socialist state, the Yugoslav theoreticians redefined these functions as follows:

1. *External defense.* This function was said to exist and even to be strengthened. On this point, the only difference with Stalin was that, in the concrete Yugoslav case, the state had to defend the socialist order against the hostile, "state capitalist" East as well as the capitalist West.

2. *Internal repression.* This task was viewed as slowly disappearing as the socialist order strengthened. In the Yugoslav case, since the danger of at least partial capitalist or "state capitalist" restoration was postulated, "administrative restriction of political activity directed against socialism is unavoidable in our state order."[15]

3. *Organization of the economy.* The state was denied the role, attributed to it by Stalin, of exclusive management of the economy. Nevertheless, decentralization of the Yugoslav command economy notwithstanding, the state was still said to play an important economic role, although no clear-cut, positive theoretical definition of its proper function in this sphere was offered. One academician saw its task as being "to defend and develop the socialist mode of production."[16] Some theoreticians seemed to deny the need for any *direct* state *administrative* role in the economy.[17] Others, led by Kidrič (who was most directly responsible for running the economy), initially affirmed that the state continued to exercise "administrative-operational leadership" of the economy, a function that, he maintained, was being decentralized but not liquidated.[18]

4. *Socialist reeducation.* The Yugoslav theoreticians unanimously denied that the state had any responsibilities in this sphere.

In accordance with this modification of Stalinist theory, the Yugoslav theoreticians declared that the state could not be the main instrument for achieving either the lower or the higher stage of communism: ". . . it is not the task of the workers' state to 'create' socialism, to conceive and construct it. Its task is to clear the way for socialism so that it can freely develop. In other words, its task is to clear the way for social and economic forces which by their inner essence are necessarily socialist and therefore, developing freely, must inevitably create socialism."[19] Thus the state did not "build" socialism or communism. But how did it "clear the way" for inherently socialist forces? No clear answer was given. In his commentary on the Constitutional Law of 1953, Kardelj said only that this meant "defense of the socialist system" and "regulating the legal order in harmony with the needs of socialist development."[20] He had previously declared that it entailed "[state] intervention in the backward social sectors to ease and speed up as much as possible the development of socialist elements" and "guaranteeing a certain measure of social discipline."[21] In short, while CPY theoreticians denied the state the total control over society ascribed to it in theory (just as in practice) by Stalin, no clear-cut positive definition of its proper role was offered.

The preceding paragraphs have dealt with the static aspect of Yugoslav doctrine on the state. The dynamic aspect of the doctrine was, however, more important. After all, the Yugoslav state had exhibited, between 1945 and 1948, most of the features characteristic of the Stalinist state on which the Yugoslav critique of the Soviet system was based. Attempting to account for these similarities, the CPY did not admit any major past mistakes of theoretical conception or policy, however. Rather, it tried to explain away the period of centralized state rule. So when Tito himself proclaimed, "Marx, Engels, and Lenin taught that the state begins to wither away from the moment when the proletariat comes to power," he added lamely, "Of course, this means that the proletariat should really be in power in every respect."[22] More theoretical approaches to the problem granted the necessity of a preliminary period of "administrative socialism" or "state socialism" immediately following the proletarian revolution in a backward country, during which the state bureaucracy indeed exercised monopolistic control over society. Some theoreticians attempted to characterize this system as "incomparably higher than state capitalism" since it entailed the end of private ownership and increased produc- tion[23]—ignoring Kardelj's and Djilas's admonitions that, in the Soviet case, bureaucratic control of the means of production negated such claims. Other (more honest) theoreticians granted the similarity. As Milentije Popović pointed out, "Some comrades . . . call our earlier economic system state socialism. It seems to me that this is unnecessary and perhaps even harmful. The system was not socialist . . . , at one point of development the whole system had to be exchanged, abolished. Why abolished? Because it was not socialist but state capitalist, because it stifled the forces of socialism."[24]

The only difference was thus in the stage of development; what was historically progressive in the immediate postrevolutionary period would (as in the USSR) turn into its opposite if not subsequently modified. To quote Kardelj: "[State capitalist] forms were inevitable in the first revolutionary phase. That necessity resulted from the relatively low level of development of the forces of production in our country . . . and from the insufficiently developed consciousness of the working masses. It is obvious that in those conditions the role of the state ... was very great and necessary; as such it was progressive. . . ."[25] The point where progress turned into reaction was, however, never spelled out. Nor could it be, for the "antibureaucratic" changes in the political system after 1949 were the consequence neither of increased production nor of heightened mass "socialist consciousness" but, fundamentally, of the break with Stalin.

Affirming the initial necessity of the period of administrative socialism, CPY theoreticians generally held (contrary to Popović's assertion) that it had not been abolished but gradually superseded. As a consequence, it was unavoidable that remnants of the state's monopolistic position continued to manifest themselves at the beginning of the new phase. The important point, the Yugoslavs maintained, was the direction of development—the fact that, in Yugoslavia, the state had *begun* the process of dying out prescribed by the Marxist classics. But what did it in fact mean to speak of the "withering away of the state"?

The CPY's definition of the process, as it emerged in the early 1950s, distinguished the following three categories of what had once been considered to be state tasks:

1. *True state functions.* For the foreseeable future, the state would continue to exercise certain tasks of a purely *class* nature, including external defense and internal repression in the sense of "defending the socialist order." The proletarian state thus remained, in a restricted sphere, a state in the Marxist sense—an instrument of class repression possessing a monopoly of physical force.

2. *Former state functions.* Some of the state's initial functions were later abolished outright; others were transferred to economic units or public organizations of society itself. In the Yugoslav case, the obvious example was the transfer of state economic functions to workers' councils. Professor Lukić explained this transfer of functions as follows:

... it is necessary to differentiate that state activity which is properly the state's function from that which is not and which the state more or less accidentally exercises. The state exercises these public functions because it is the strongest public organization, but a free [nonstate] public organization can also exercise them. The process of the withering away of the state unfolds first in the transfer of these public functions from the state to free public organizations, which do not exercise power through the use of physical force. . . .[26]

3. *"Nonstate" functions.* The majority of state functions would continue to be exercised by the existing state apparatus, which, drawing ordinary citizens into running its affairs, would gradually merge with

society itself. This process, the most complex aspect of the doctrine, was often called the "democratization of state functions" and required, first of all, decentralization. "Decentralization itself," Tito declared, ". . . not only has a deeply democratic character but contains the seed of the withering of centralism and the state in general."[27] Parallel to doctrinal and institutional changes in the sphere of economic management (to be taken up in the next chapter), Yugoslav doctrine consequently placed new emphasis on the powers and authority of the local state organs, the people's committees.[28] This emphasis was reflected in practice in a new law on the people's committees of 1952 and the Constitutional Law of 1953, which abolished much of the federal ministerial structure and transformed the people's committees into the primary administrative units of Yugoslavia.[29]

But the CPY theoreticians held that decentralization itself was only a prerequisite for the merging of the state apparatus with society. "Although it is true that decentralization of certain functions—and rather extensive decentralization at that—is involved," Kardelj explained, "nevertheless that word does not signify at all the essence of the process; . . . . in fact we are achieving such forms of state administration which will allow and guarantee the most direct participation and decision-making of the working masses in all branches of administration and the economy."[30]

Therefore, it became the task of the CPY to work out both in theory and in practice the correct organizational forms for achieving such mass participation. The people's committees themselves, formerly compared with the Paris Commune and soviets as the epitome of proletarian democracy, were now admitted to be inadequate in themselves to achieve true participatory democracy. Hence, a series of supplementary organs was established. The most important of these were electors' meetings (gatherings of local citizens to discuss issues and nominate candidates); citizens' committees (advisory functional organs attached to the people's committee which replaced its executive committee); and—after 1953—public governing boards of educational, cultural, and scientific institutions.[31] (After 1955, local administrative districts were reorganized into communes (opštine) that—according to CPY ideologues—manifested many "nonstate" attributes. This aspect of the doctrine on the state was later developed into a distinct subdoctrine of "social self-management.")

In post-1949 Yugoslav Communist doctrine, then, the socialist state remained a state in terms of the first category of tasks; in terms of the second and third categories, it was the state that was withering away. In Gerškovič's formulation, the process of withering away "should be understood as ever less state intervention in specific areas of social life and ever greater mass participation in exercising the state functions which remain."[32] Yet CPY theoreticians were not agreed on the relative emphasis to be placed on these two aspects of the withering process. A "radical" minority maintained that mass participation in the work of state organs was of secondary importance. The heart of the process, such theoreticians held, was the surrender of state responsibilities to public organizations. This view was formulated most clearly by Professor Lukić:

The democratic organization of the proletarian state apparatus is not enough—it must disappear. . . . Every state organ [must be] surrounded by certain other organs which are not state but public organs, that is, free mass organs. . . . These organs exercise control over the work of the state organs, give them directions for work, help them in their work, and take sanctions against them if they function poorly. . . . [In time] the [state] functions are transferred to the free, public organs, to the free citizens.[33]

In this view, the essence of the withering away of the state was the *transfer of functions* from state to nonstate public organs. The state, proletarian as well as bourgeois, remained a class instrument that could never really be democratized.

The CPY leadership (and the great majority of theoreticians) was understandably more cautious. It put the emphasis in the withering process on the "democratization" of the state organs themselves. Drawing the masses into their operations, in this view, the organs of government would gradually undergo a qualitative change, until one day, representing the interests of all of society and involving, in turn, all the citizens in their affairs, these organs would cease to exhibit "state" attributes. Kardelj formulated this conception as follows:

It would be incorrect to think that the process of the withering away of the state consists of the state organs simply transferring one function after another to some kind of "nonstate" organs. In that case only the form and name would change; the essence would remain the same. What is involved is thus not the state "relinquishing" some "rights" to the people, but the internal development of the whole social mechanism of management—and the state organism, too, is a component part of that mechanism—which becomes ever more the organ of popular self-management in the basic cells of social life (the factory, enterprise, institution, community, district) just as in the higher social (state) organs (main [economic] directorates, economic associations, the

Government, the People's Assembly). In short, it is a process in which the difference between "state" and "nonstate" disappears.[34]

In this orthodox view, the *"democratization"* of state organs thus took precedence over the surrender of state functions. The point was reinforced by repeated warnings against anarchist conceptions of abolishing the state. As an editorial in the most authoritative political-legal journal declared, "The process of the withering away of the state does not and cannot take the line of blind and doctrinaire negation of the state, but the line of gradual and conscious permeation of the state apparatus with the masses. . . ."[35] On the contrary, CPY theoreticians often said, the withering away of the state did not exclude its becoming stronger. Professor Pašić sought to explain this seeming paradox as follows:

. . . it is not difficult to understand how the socialist state becomes stronger and *at the same time* withers. The state becomes stronger as the true representative of the interests of the whole society . . . but this process, this transformation by means of ever broader democratization into the organization of the [workers] themselves simultaneously signifies its withering as a special apparatus of class force separated from society, [the characteristic] which was inseparably connected with the very concept of the state.[36]

The majority of CPY theoreticians thus did not in fact disagree with Stalin on the need for strengthening the state. Their objection was that Stalin had reduced this process exclusively to strengthening the "bureaucratic state apparatus." The correct Marxist concept of strengthening the state as part of its withering away, the Yugoslav theorists maintained, involved increased mass participation in running state affairs. It also meant ensuring the representative character of the state organs that had not yet begun to loose their "state" quality as a result of participatory democracy. Indeed, it was admitted that, at least at the higher levels of government, this would be the main feature of state development in Yugoslavia for the foreseeable future. Kardelj formulated this perspective as follows:

A small but highly skilled apparatus [will function] in the center as a technical apparatus subordinated to the central public representative organs, with strictly determined rights and duties. The primary locus of public activity [will be] 'below'—in the sense of Marx's commune—in public organs of the district and community, factory, institution, etc. Qualified technical apparatuses responsible to these organs [will] carry out their tasks within the limits of exactly determined rights and duties. This is the general course of the organizational development of our state system. In this way the system not only assumes an ever-increasing democratic character . . . but the element of the withering away of the state becomes ever more important. . . .[37]

In addition to promising increased mass participation in running state affairs, this vision embodied three important features. First, it did not deny the necessity of professional bureaucrats, provided they did not have arbitrary powers. As Kardelj said earlier in the same speech, "a skilled technical apparatus can by no means be replaced with 'voluntarism.' "[38] Second, it assumed—at least at the higher level—the continuation of traditional representative state bodies. These bodies, however, had to be based on economic as well as traditional political principles. This was the reasoning behind the "councils of producers" elected by the collectives of economic organizations; in 1952 the councils were established as second chambers of local people's committees and in 1953 as the second chamber of the Federal Assembly.[39] Third, it did not portend the disintegration of modern society. While the goal at lower levels was the transformation of state organs into public bodies, this did not mean, Kardelj emphasized, "that we splinter society into some kind of federation of autonomous communes. . . ."[40]

To recapitulate, Yugoslav Communist doctrine on the withering away of the state excluded from the withering process certain categories of state functions. It recognized the necessity of the continued existence of central representative state bodies (which were still described as such even in areas where they were said no longer to carry out functions of class oppression). At lower levels, it foresaw a qualitative change in the essence of state bodies as ordinary citizens participated more and more in state affairs. At both the central and local levels it assumed that separately organized bodies, staffed by professionals, would continue to exist as instruments of political decision making. These bodies would enjoy, at least for the foreseeable future, a monopoly of physical force, even if there would be increasingly less need for its application.

Yugoslav doctrine on the withering away of the state was, in short, not completely utopian. It foresaw no rapid transfer of state functions to society itself, let alone an anarchistlike "dismantling of the state." Engels's phrase, "the withering away of the state," became the slogan of the day in Yugoslavia in reaction to Stalinism. But "withering away" was defined to mean a change in the state's internal essence, not the abolition of its external forms. "It must cease to be a classic, absolute state; it must become not a 'new type' but a 'nontype' of state," wrote Professor Djordjević.[41] But, even as viewed by Yugoslav theoreticians, this "nonstate" remained very much a state. Separately organized decision-making bodies of society would remain and even become stronger. But these bodies would no longer be called state organs—since Marx had reserved the term "state" for an instrument of class repression—but "sociopolitical organs."

Significance of the Doctrine

Yugoslav Communist doctrine on the "withering away of the state" took shape primarily in the pronouncements of Kardelj and in the writings of a number of academicians. After the issue of the withering away of the state became a subject of intra-Party discussion in December 1949, a variety of viewpoints appeared, ranging from the "dogmatic," which was essentially the Stalinist conception, to the "utopian," which foresaw the large-scale surrender of state functions to public bodies. In 1951 Kardelj formulated the essentials of an orthodox CPY position. This by no means brought a return to the same uniformity of thought on the subject that had existed prior to 1950, however. "Dogmatic" and "utopian" interpretations of the doctrine continued to appear.[42]

The CPY doctrine took as its point of departure the utopian prescriptions of the Marxist-Leninist classics—especially Engels's *Anti-Dühring* and Lenin's *State and Revolution*—on the withering away of the state. The CPY ideologues devoted renewed attention to the prescriptions of Engels and Lenin after their disillusionment in Stalin enabled them to perceive the discrepancy between Stalinist doctrine and the earlier Marxist-Leninist texts. Indeed, available evidence suggests that the writings of Marx, Engels, and Lenin provided the primary source of inspiration for the initial development of the doctrine on the state. There is no sign that at this stage the CPY theoreticians were familiar with the works of Soviet academicians, led by Pashukhanis, who had at an earlier date dealt with the problem of the withering of the state. It also seems unlikely that, at this time, the Yugoslav theoreticians were directly influenced by nineteenth-century Serbian radical thought, which, as expounded most prominently by Svetozar Marković, glorified *samouprava,* or local peasant self-government.[43] As with the CPY's critique of the nature of the Soviet system, the doctrine of the withering away of the state was apparently self-generated.

The past two decades have shown that many postulates of the doctrine, including direct participation by the citizenry in state affairs on a large scale, could not easily be implemented in Yugoslavia. In this sense, the formulation of the doctrine was responsible for creating a gap between theory and practice—a gap that CPY spokesmen attempted to account for but in fact simply acknowledged. In his speech of April 27, 1951 (which formulated many aspects of the CPY doctrine on the state), Kardelj added the following words of caution:

Of course it is a long process and it would by no means be correct excessively to flaunt such phrases as "withering away of the state," "community of producers," etc. When we speak about that, we are thinking of the perspective which must remain before us if we are not to depart from the correct path and find ourselves on reactionary positions. Nevertheless, we must keep a firm foothold in present reality. We dare not run ahead where neither the working class nor the remaining masses can yet follow and for which neither objective nor subjective conditions have ripened. Struggling for the future, we should not create fantasies. We must not squander the present in dreaming about the future.[44]

The state had to wither away, in the sense already described, after the proletarian revolution, CPY doctrine declared. Yet, according to Kardelj, in Yugoslavia the state could die out only in conjunction with the ripening of "objective" and "subjective" conditions. This major qualification became the standard justification for the gap between theory and practice. For example, notwithstanding the CPY's insistence on the necessity of the withering away of the state, Kidrič (citing objective and subjective weaknesses of socialism) maintained at the end of 1951:

Our state economic apparatus bore on its back an enormous burden in the course of our socialist construction. Hostile tendencies exist which would like to distort the struggle against bureaucracy into a struggle against the state apparatus in general. The state apparatus, however, is still very much needed, not only to thwart all kinds of counter-revolutionary elements, but also to ensure the normal functioning of our economic system.[45]

The divergence between theory and practice notwithstanding, post-1949 Yugoslav Communist doctrine on the state nevertheless embodied a serious ideological effort to give some content to the brief and vague references of Marx, Engels, and Lenin on postrevolutionary state development. The most important institutional consequence of the doctrine was the workers' council (which will be examined in the next chapter); while conditioning the pattern of decentralization, the doctrine also hastened introduction of functional representation and expansion of citizen participation in the machinery of government. The doctrine broke with Stalin's claim that the state was the exclusive institution responsible for postrevolutionary change, the "builder" of socialist and communist society. In so doing it gave new life to the ideal of communism itself—which meant, in the view of the CPY, Marx's "free community of producers," and not Stalin's "society of uniformed plebes."[46]

Yet the gap between theory and practice should not be over-estimated. CPY doctrine on the state, formulated from the standpoint of a Communist Party in power, turned Engels's quixotic reference to "the withering away of the state" into an action program. In the process of formulating the means by which this ideal could be implemented, the ideal itself was concretized, and its original utopian character was diluted. Emphasizing the internal transformation of the state's essence, rather than the transfer of state functions to society, in the early 1950s CPY theoreticians could thus elaborate the instruments of participatory democracy without being required, at the same time, to draw up a blueprint for the disappearance of state organs themselves.

Notes

[1] Kardelj, Speech of November 10, 1953, *Problemi* 4: 77.

[2] Nikezić interview, *Politika*, January 3, 1971.

[3] See Hoffman and Neal, *Yugoslavia and the New Communism*; Charles P. McVicker, *Titoism* (New York: St. Martin's Press, 1957); Frits W. Hondius, *The Yugoslav Community of Nations* (The Hague: Mouton, 1968), pp. 194–209, 337–338.

[4] Kardelj, Speech of December 12, 1949, *Problemi* 3: 58.

[5] Tito, *Govori i članci* 5: 221.

[6] Geršković, *Komunist* 4, nos. 4–5; Pašić, *Komunist* 5, no. 1.

[7] J. V. Stalin, *Works* 12 (Moscow, 1953): 381.

[8] Report to the Soviet Party Plenum of February–March 1937, *Pravda*, March 29, 1937.

[9] Stalin, *Problems of Leninism*, pp. 790–797.

[10] *O sovetskom sotsialisticheskom obshchestve* (Moscow, 1949), p.22.

[11] Ibid., p. 7.

[12] Pašić, *Komunist* 5, no. 1: 102.

[13] Geršković, *Komunist* 4, nos. 4–5: 97.

[14] The main sources of the doctrine on the state, in addition to the words previously cited in this chapter, were Kardelj, "Deset godina narodne revolucije" [April 27, 1951], *Problemi* 2: 51–147; Kardelj, "Socijalizam i demokratija" [March 31, 1952], *Problemi* 2: 176–220; Kardelj, *Borba* article of November 29, 1952, reprinted in *Problemi* 2: 221–223; Kardelj, Speech of December 28, 1952, *Problemi* 2: 234–248; Kardelj, "O društvenim i političkim osnovama FNRJ i Saveznim organima vlasti" [January 12, 1953], *Problemi* 2: 249–285; Črnja, *Ekonomski pregled* 1, nos. 3–4; Djordjević, *Ustavno pravo FNRJ*; Ivo Krbek,

Odumiranje države (Zagreb, 1951); Lukić, *Teorija države i prava* 1; "Neka nova pitanja naše teorije o socijalističkoj državi i pravu," *Arhiv* 6, no. 3 (July–September 1950): 385–402.

[15] Kardelj, *Problemi* 2: 227.
[16] Lukić, *Teorija države i prava* 1: 373.
[17] Djilas, in *Borba*, March 18, 1951.
[18] Kidrič, *Komunist* 4, no. 6: 8.
[19] Kardelj, *Problemi* 2: 223.
[20] Ibid., p. 253.
[21] Ibid., pp. 223, 225
[22] Tito, *Govori i članci* 5: 221.
[23] Črnja, *Ekonomski pregled* 1, nos. 3–4: 248.
[24] Milentije Popović, *Naša stvarnost* 7, no. 2: 15.
[25] Kardelj, *Problemi* 2: 235. This remains the orthodox Yugoslav Communist view, but it has subsequently been disputed by individual theoreticians. For a statement that the "withering" process might have begun in 1946 see Veljko Cvjetičanin, "Odumiranje države kao proces razvoja samoupravljanja u Jugoslaviji," *Praxis* 3, nos. 4–6 (July–December 1966): 743–756, esp. 747.
[26] Lukić, *Teorija države i prava* 1: 408.
[27] Tito, *Govori i članci* 5: 218.
[28] Geršković, *Komunist* 4: 4–5; Djordjević, *Ustavno pravo*, pp. 354–379.
[29] See the description in McVicker, *Titoism*, pp. 145–175; Fred Warner Neal, *Titoism in Action: The Reforms in Yugoslavia after 1948* (Berkeley and Los Angeles: University of California Press, 1958), pp. 89–117, 160–184.
[30] Kardelj, *Problemi* 2: 113.
[31] Radomir Lukić, "Napomene o zborevima birača, savetima gradjana i lokalnom referendumu," *Arhiv* 6, no. 4 (October–December 1950): pp. 617–630; Djordjević, *Ustavno pravo*, pp. 354–379; "Za što šire učešće masa u radu narodne vlasti," *Borba*, January 14, 1950. Accounts of the operation of these organs are given in the sources cited in note 29.
[32] Geršković, *Komunist* 4, nos. 4–5: 94.
[33] Radomir Lukić, *Materijal za izučavanje teorije države i prava* 1 (Belgrade, 1952): 219; J. Smiljan, "Problemi birokratizma u socijalizmu," *Vojno-politički glasnik* 3, no. 6 (June 1950). 89 105, at 103.
[34] Kardelj, *Problemi* 2: 111. See also Pašić, *Komunist* 5, no. 1: 84.
[35] *Arhiv* 6, no. 3: 393.
[36] Pašić, *Komunist* 5, no. 1: 85.
[37] Kardelj, *Problemi* 2: 116.
[38] Ibid., p. 115. Lukić wrote: "Socialism does not exclude bureaucracy . . .; what is essential is that the bureaucracy is not exploitative." (*Teorija države i prava* 1: 370.)
[39] See the sources cited in note 29.
[40] Kardelj, *Problemi* 2: 241.
[41] Djordjević, *Ustavno pravo*, p. 85.
[42] A "dogmatic" viewpoint is adopted in Ziherl, *Dijalektički i istorijski materijalizam*. A "utopian" viewpoint is still expressed in part in Lukić, *Teorija države i prava* 1: esp. 401–410.
[43] These conclusions are based on study of the documentary record and the author's interviews in Yugoslavia. The only known reference to the Soviet academicians is the statement in a lecture at the High Party School (in the context of a discussion of Stalin's "revisionism" on the state) that "the last theoreticians of the Leninist school were liquidated" prior to the Eighteenth Congress (Damjanović, Belić, and Djurdjević, in *Istorija medjunarodnog radničkog i socijalističkog pokreta*, p. 511). In later years, CPY theoreticians developed a

certain interest in Marković; his ideas probably had some influence on the development of the commune system after 1954. In the immediate postwar period, his philosophy was viewed as "not only not signifying any real enrichment of the scientific world outlook but, in comparison with dialectical materialism, a step backward." (Djilas, "O nacionalnoj istoriji kao vaspitnom predmetu," *Komunist* 3, no. 1 [January 1949]: 57–82, at 62.) In the 1960s Yugoslav Communists regarded Marković as at best "a well-intentioned but misguided utopian socialist." (W. D. McClellen, *Svetozar Marković and the Origins of Balkan Socialism* [Princeton, N.J.: Princeton University Press, 1964], pp. 273–274.) See also Viktor Meier, "Yugoslav Communism," in William E. Griffith, ed., *Communism in Europe* 1 (Cambridge, Mass.: M.I.T. Press, 1964): 21–22.

[44] Kardelj, *Problemi* 2: 117.

[45] Kidrič, Skupština address of December 28, 1951, *Borba*, December 29, 1951. Two other approaches to the gap between the abstract theory and practice should be mentioned. The first proclaimed simply that institutions based on state force were, willy-nilly, examples of the withering process. The best illustration was the case of the peasant work cooperatives, characterized by one theoretician as an example of "the whole society in miniature" marking the "beginning of the withering away of the state in agriculture." (M. Vučković, "O nekim novim elementima odumiranja države kod nas," *Socijalistička poljoprivreda* 2, no. 6 [June 1951]: 1–16, at 15.) The second approach, put forward by "dogmatic" theoreticians before the orthodox position became clear-cut, was simply to reject the theory. Attacking Stalin for glorifying the state bureaucracy, these theoreticians propagated essentially unchanged the Stalinist theory of the state. Perhaps the best example was Josip Brnčić, who wrote at the end of 1950: "... the state must become stronger in order to execute its [four Stalinist] functions as soon as possible and through this to wither away ... [Marxism-Leninism teaches that] the state is absolutely needed by the victorious proletariat, that its functions must be strengthened continually, but that the state withers away precisely through its becoming stronger, through the execution of its functions." (Josip Brnčić, "Kratka objašnjenja Osnovnog zakona o upravljanju državnim privrednim poduzećima i višim privrednim udruženjima od strane radnih kolektiva," *Naša zakonitost* 4, nos. 3–4 [1950]: 115–124, at 122 [This article is presented as representing the general Yugoslav view in Ivo Lapenna, *State and Law: Soviet and Yugoslav Theory* (New Haven: Yale University Press, 1964), p. 50.]) In the 1960s, all the approaches presented in this chapter would be criticized as "inadequately developed theoretical conceptions." (Cvjetičanin, *Praxis* 3, nos. 4–6: p. 753).

[46] Pašić, *Komunist* 5, no. 1: 101.

7

"The Factories to the Workers"

The Doctrine of Worker Self-management

Prior to 1949, as pointed out in the preceding chapter, the Yugoslav Communists regarded the socialist state as the "builder" of socialist society in the Stalinist sense. This belief was reflected in the establishment of a rigidly centralized command economy on the Soviet model.[1] At the level of the economic enterprise, the principle of *edinonachalie* (one-man management) was unambiguously adopted in the Basic Law on State Economic Enterprises of July 1946.[2] Firmly rejecting the principle of "collective leadership"[3] in the enterprise, Boris Kidrič, in presenting this law to the Skupština, revealingly described the organization of the enterprise in military terms: "Just like our army, our economy—and especially our industrial production—demands a single line of command—i.e., sufficiently authoritative leadership."[4]

Kidrič maintained in his report that one-man management did not negate "control by the production workers" and the "comprehensive initiative of the trade union organization."[5] But this claim was quite at odds with the rights in fact granted to the workers and the trade union within the enterprise. True, a 1945 law had provided for the election of workers' representatives (*radnički poverenici*) in state enterprises (as well as in the remaining private factories), but they were empowered only to be in "permanent contact with the authorities of the people's state, the enterprise management, and the trade union organization" and to advise the enterprise director on the workers' social and economic conditions.[6] Later (apparently in 1947), "production conferences" were organized in enterprises with management and "shock worker" representation, but they had advisory powers only and were strictly subordinated to the control of the enterprise's Party organization.[7]

The trade union organization was empowered by the Basic Law on State Economic Enterprises to make suggestions to the director, but—quite apart from the reality of Party control of the trade union—such suggestions were to deal primarily with "raising the productivity and the efficiency of labor" and only secondarily with improving working conditions.[8] The same note was struck by the First Congress of the United Trade Unions in October 1948, which, in its final resolution, called on all trade union organizations to develop "a

socialist relationship to work" and "socialist emulation" and to strive
for "the realization of daily production tasks."[9] Thus even in theory
the institutions presumably most concerned with articulating the
workers' interests were granted only vague rights of advising the
enterprise director on peripheral matters; in fact, his word was law.

The lack of any direct channel for the expression of worker interests
within the enterprise was in harmony with the Stalinist tenet that (in
Kidrič's words) "where a government of the working people is in
power, the state [economic] sector is in essence explicitly a *social*
sector."[10] In this view, with the nationalization of private property,
exploitation was, ipso facto, eliminated. The worker might be subject to
labor discipline far stricter than he had experienced under capitalism,
but his labor was now harnessed to the industrialization of a backward
country directed by a Party-state bureaucracy endowed with exclusive
consciousness of the workers' historical interest. Before 1949 this line
of reasoning was beyond question for the Yugoslav Communists—
simon-pure Stalinists in this respect. Even after they had developed the
doctrine of "worker self-management," they still stubbornly defended
it—in line with their justification of the period of administrative
socialism in general—as historically progressive at the time.[11]

The Stalinist view that advocated the strict hierarchical internal
organization of the economic enterprise was challenged by the critique
of Soviet bureaucratism which the Yugoslav leadership began to
develop in 1949. As already described, in May 1949 Kardelj returned to
pre-Stalinist Marxist texts—particularly Lenin's *State and Revolution*—for ideological guidance on the organization of society in a
country that was building socialism, indirectly challenging the Stalinist
pattern. Kardelj explicitly applied his general analysis to the problem of
management of state economic enterprises. One-man management had
in fact been carried to an extreme in Yugoslavia, he hinted. Speaking in
general of personal responsibility of state officials, he noted:

Here too, bureaucratic distortion of the principle of personal responsibility occurs, consisting in the tendency to abolish control of the
manager from below. If we would take that path, we would strengthen
bureaucratism and prevent the possibility of broad development of
mass initiative. That would be a bureaucratic-administrative method of
management, which would greatly hamper the progress of socialist
development.[12]

Control from below could be developed and the bureaucratic danger
avoided, Kardelj continued, by cultivating the workers' consultative

production conferences. "This underdeveloped, spontaneous form must be further developed and transformed into a continuous form of direct cooperation of the workers in the management of our enterprises."[13]

This was the ideological inspiration for the subsequent development of the workers' councils. The exact process by which Kardelj's injunction came to be adopted as CPY policy remains a matter of speculation. The production conferences established in some factories prior to 1949 had clearly been conceived as an additional Party-dominated instrument—along with "shock work," "socialist emulation," and forced labor—to increase output. The mounting economic problems created by the Cominform embargo in 1949 made some suitable means of stimulating production all the more desirable to the Yugoslav leadership. Yet the increasing Soviet pressure on Yugoslavia at the time required an all-Yugoslav consensus to resist the external threat. Such a consensus was incompatible with the coercive mobilizing instruments of "agitation" and compulsion—in the factory as in society in general—which threatened (as Kidrič recognized at the time) "open conflict" with the workers.[14] Developing the consultative workers' meetings into workers' councils, as regular advisory bodies elected by the entire work force of an enterprise, offered a novel, noncoercive, and less overt method of mobilizing the worker to raise the output of his plant.

This practical motivation was supplemented by ideological considerations, and the timing and substance of the decision to develop workers' councils suggest that the latter were as important as the former. Following the Rajk trial, as has been pointed out, the Soviet system lost its sanctity for the CPY leaders. As first Pijade and then other leaders came to feel that Soviet internal life was marred by "bureaucracy" and "hegemonism," they were faced with the problem of differentiating their own internal order—so similar in many respects—from the Soviet one. Kardelj's theoretical analysis of socialist democracy of May 1949 suggested how they might begin. There was surely no place more appropriate to begin freeing themselves from Soviet dogma and attempting to encourage mass participation in state affairs than the critical economic sphere. It was perhaps a result of this line of reasoning that in December 1949—just at the moment when the public critique of Soviet internal bureaucratism was launched—the CPY Politburo ordered the establishment, on an experimental basis, of workers' councils as advisory bodies in 215 large industrial enterprises.[15]

Yet the advisory workers' councils initially received very little publicity. Antibureaucratic theoretical commentaries published in Yugoslavia in early 1950 either ignored them entirely or mentioned them only in passing—apparently to the dismay of officials involved in their development.[16] Perhaps the CPY leadership wanted to test its innovation in practice before committing itself publicly to emphasizing the councils' ideological importance. In any case, the performance of the initial 215 workers' councils was apparently quite satisfactory; by June 1950, workers' councils had been established in a total of 520 enterprises.[17] More important, in spring 1950, Tito accepted a proposal of Djilas, Kardelj, and Kidrič to endow the workers' councils with ultimate legal control of the enterprises and, in so doing, to make them potentially the key institution distinguishing the Yugoslav political system from the Soviet system. The workers would not just participate in the management of the enterprise; they would be the managers.[18] The consequence was Tito's Skupština address of June 26, 1950, in which he introduced a law establishing workers' councils as management organs in all industrial and mining enterprises.[19]

Tito's Skupština address was also the first step in the public formulation of the doctrine of "worker self-management" (*radničko samoupravljanje*), which constituted a major subtheory of the doctrine of the withering away of the state. While industrial management of the Stalinist type had originally been necessary in Yugoslavia, the CPY now maintained that if this system had not been modified after a short period, it would have perpetuated essentially unchanged capitalist relationships at the workplace. In that situation, the bench worker would remain a wage laborer, and the resulting surplus labor would be disposed of as surplus value by the state bureaucrats, beginning with the enterprise director. This was, indeed, the situation in the USSR, where the exploitation of the worker in the factory by the state apparatus was the point of departure for its development into an exploitative bureaucratic caste.[20] This could not be concealed by grandiose declarative claims of the creation of socialism. For the development of socialism required not only a change at the vortex of the political system but concrete changes in social relations at the level of the individual factory or workshop—indeed, the Yugoslav theoreticians later came to believe (complementing the doctrine of worker self-management with the doctrine of "social self-management" [*društveno samoupravljanje*]), in all the basic cells of society.[21]

The June 1950 workers' council law was interpreted as signifying the beginning of such altered social relations in Yugoslavia, the first step toward realizing in practice the slogan "The Factories to the Workers."[22] For the first time in history, workers' councils were said to create the perspective for bridging the gap between the creation and the control of surplus labor, between production and the management of production. The essence of the doctrine was subsequently concisely formulated as follows:

[Workers' councils] . . . represent and guarantee a change of social relations in a consistently socialist direction. That is to say, by this instrument the producers [workers], for the first time in history, simultaneously become managers, which means that the historical division and contradiction of class society, the division between mental and physical labor, between managers and producers, begins to be overcome. This signifies, at the same time, the beginning of the solution of the historical contradiction and limitation of every class society— that the direct producers create the material goods for the entire society, yet they do not manage these goods in any way or decide on their distribution and appropriation to the least extent. These tasks are carried out [instead] by the property-owning, ruling classes or by forces alienated from society and raised above it—the state, bureaucracy. What is involved, therefore, is an essential change in property relations, in the relation between production and the distribution of the labor product . . . .[23]

This doctrine incorporated a revised view of the progressiveness of state ownership. According to the Stalinist conception, with the nationalization of private property, the state took over the property rights of the former owners and exercised them in the name of society. In the revised Yugoslav view, state property could be considered to be only the "lowest form of social property . . . only indirectly socialist property."[24] Postrevolutionary society had to transfer management of the enterprise from the state apparatus to the collective of the enterprise itself. This did not, however, mean that the collective became a new owner; it was entrusted with the management of the enterprise ("right of use") by society in the interest of society as a whole. In Yugoslav doctrine this was described as the transformation of "state property" into "social property," which was, as Professor Djordjević pointed out, a sociological, not a legal term.[25] In this view, which was disputed by other theoreticians, worker self-management meant that property itself, as a historical category, was superseded.[26]

It is evident from the preceding exposition that worker self-management was by no means viewed as a unique Yugoslav characteristic. On the contrary, the CPY viewed it as an essential trait of every socialist society. In Kardelj's words, "Workers' councils are not only a specific feature of our development, but they are—in one form or another—a necessary element of the mechanism of socialist democracy in the transition from capitalism to socialism in general."[27] Endowed with such importance, workers' councils indeed became, for the Yugoslav Communists, the most convincing indication of the distinction between the Yugoslav and Soviet social systems.

The CPY's desire to magnify the ideological significance of the workers' councils led some Yugoslav commentators on the 1950 workers' council law to treat it as signifying an immediate, qualitative change in the position of the existing experimental councils from advisory bodies to management organs.[28] This was indeed the goal of the 1950 law. In mid-1950, however, the command economy was still essentially intact;[29] plan targets formulated in Belgrade were still binding on the enterprise director. This meant that the 1950 law could not in fact introduce worker self-management, and indeed the CPY leadership itself readily admitted this. Interpreting the law, Tito stressed that the state would continue to manage the enterprises; only it would no longer be the exclusive manager.[30] Kidrič, writing in *Komunist* a few months later, was even more emphatic: "The institution of workers' councils ... introduces the process of the de-etatization and democratization, but not the liquidation of [state] administrative-operative or planning-operative [economic] management."[31]

Thus, regardless of exaggerated claims made in its behalf, the 1950 workers' council law did not signify even in theory a qualitative change in the position of the workers in terms of enterprise management. In practice, as the Croat leader Zvonko Brkić was to admit, "Initially the workers' councils played more or less a formal role."[32] This was readily acknowledged in a later case study of worker self-management in one plant.

The whole of 1950 and 1951 were years of searching for proper methods of work and the endeavor of the workers' council to establish itself as the actual manager of the enterprise. The meetings of the workers' council were meetings at which the members of this body made proposals, made suggestions; but in most cases no concrete decisions were adopted, much less was their enforcement requested and supervised. Various opinions were expressed ... but there was no enforcement of decisions.[33]

The workers' councils were institutionalized by the 1950 law, not as management organs (although this was the eventual goal), but as advisory organs intended to encourage the development of worker interest in the business of the enterprise and thus to teach him the art of management. The magnitude of this task in an underdeveloped country like Yugoslavia was admitted. "An enormous number of peasants, or half-peasants–half-workers, are entering our enterprises. First they must acquire the traits of workers, and then be educated as worker-managers. This is not a short-run or an easy task. . . ."[34]

Even before June 1950, however, reform of the Yugoslav economic system had begun. The strict centralism of the postwar system began to be relaxed in the spring of 1950, when administrative control of several economic sectors was transferred from the federal to the republican level.[35] As the economic situation worsened as a consequence of the overambitious industrialization program, forced collectivization of agriculture, severe drought, and the Soviet bloc economic embargo, decentralization was quickly overshadowed by reform of the basic structure of the command economic system itself. This is not the place to trace that process in detail; important steps were a law of January 1951 which made some prices responsive to demand and a law of December 1951 which replaced directive central planning with a system of general "social plans" of basic "economic proportions," many of which were not legally binding on individual enterprises. Accompanied by much organizational experimentation, a new, market-oriented economic system gradually emerged in which the enterprise enjoyed significant economic independence. The firm was free to plan its production and to sell its products on the market, within the framework of a centrally determined macroeconomic preference scale imposed by what became a regulative instead of directive state economic bureaucracy. Integrally related to this structural change was the abandonment of forced industrialization in favor of more balanced economic growth.

Development of this decentralized and market-oriented socialist economic system led to a corresponding theoretical reevaluation. At the end of 1950, Kidrič pioneered the concept of "socialist commodity production," which sought to reconcile socialist ownership of the means of production with enterprise autonomy. In his exposition in mid-1951 of legal measures affecting the economy, Kidrič distinguished between various aspects of economic planning in a manner that constituted acceptance of the market as a useful economic mechanism. Addressing the Sixth CPY Congress in late 1952, Kidrič argued that the new economic system had to be based on "objective economic laws," the operation of which could not be stifled by administrative decree but could be limited only for the purpose of "giving general direction to the economic development of the country." Worker self-management, Kidrič continued, had to encompass control of enterprise profits. This imperative could be harmonized with central regulation of economic accumulation, inter alia, by a credit system based on payment of interest—which was proclaimed to be a characteristic of commodity production in general, not exclusively capitalism.[36]

The central importance of the workers' councils in this theoretical construct is obvious. In Kidrič's analysis, they had not only to direct the day-to-day operation of the enterprise but to play a decisive part in controlling its investments as well. This meant that the perspective of "worker self-management" raised by the 1950 law had to be realized immediately in practice—far sooner than originally contemplated. On this issue, the Yugoslav leaders were caught in a dilemma of their own making. If the state bureaucracy no longer directly controlled the enterprise, and if the enterprise director was not to be endowed, legally and ideologically, with powers suggestive of new ownership rights, it was necessary to proclaim that the workers themselves were now fully empowered to run the enterprise—their semiliterate, half-peasant status in much of the country notwithstanding. Thus Kardelj flatly stated in 1954: "It has been proved that workers' councils, in cooperation with the commune, are able *completely* to replace both the capitalists and the state administrative apparatus in directly managing production."[37]

Taken literally, this claim was greatly exaggerated and over-simplified, ignoring both the continued role of state and Party organs in the economy and the prerogatives of the enterprise management.[38] In fact, such claims were qualified by other aspects of CPY doctrine on worker self-management. Proclaiming after 1952 that in Yugoslavia the workers had achieved the full right to manage production directly, the Yugoslav Communists simultaneously pointed to limits on the power of the individual collective in the interests of the working class as a whole. When workers' councils were first granted some control over enterprise funds in 1952, the not surprising result was the allotment of excessive funds to wage increases. The Yugoslav leadership quickly moved to combat such manifestations of "particularism." Stricter legal regulations were one answer, giving local people's committees more control over such matters.[39] Equally important was the attention now devoted to "social control" of the individual collective. The need for such control was one important theme of a major speech by Kardelj in the spring of 1953, entitled "The Further Development of Our Economic System."

. . . we must boldly continue on the road which we have taken . . . . Are
there dangers on that road? Of course . . . . Such dangers are a narrow
outlook on things, particularism, and other similar phenomena . . . .
They cannot undermine our system, but they can harm it, slow down
its development. Therefore it is necessary to struggle stubbornly against
them. To a certain extent, we will struggle against these phenomena
with laws and social plans. Nevertheless, we also need the activity of all
conscious socialist forces. The trade unions, the [People's Front], [the
CPY], and other public organizations must be active. If that kind of
social control is present, then we have almost nothing to fear if we
boldly continue developing our economic system on the basis of
producer [worker] self-management.[40]

The first instrument of "social control" to be considered here was
the trade union. During the period of central planning, as already
indicated, the trade union was charged primarily with striving for
increased production; its second task—far more declarative than
real—was to defend workers' socioeconomic rights. The introduction of
the workers' council system seemed to undercut the rationale of either
function. If the workers were indeed themselves to manage the
enterprise, they would not require a separate working-class organization
in the enterprise to see that their own rights were protected. As Tito
declared in his June 1950 address, "In connection with the participation of the workers in the management of the enterprise and
production in general, the task of the trade union related to defending
the workers' interests weakens, for now the workers themselves decide
such things in their councils or [enterprise] management boards."[41]

What had previously been the trade union's primary task—directly
encouraging increased production—was now also weakened, but, the
CPY leadership insisted, this did not render the organization superfluous, as many Communists seemed to think in 1950.[42] The trade
union would henceforth concentrate on "educating" the workers to
manage economic affairs.[43] Commentaries on this new educational task
stressed not only raising the general and technical educational level of
the workers so that they would be capable of participating in enterprise
management, but, equally important, raising their "socialist consciousness" so that they would exercise their powers of management, not in
the "particularist" interest of their own collective, but in the interest of
socialist society as a whole. "The factories to the workers" was indeed
the goal, but the workers of a *particular* factory could not run it for
their own personal advantage to the detriment of general "working-
class interests"—that is, the higher interests of the country as defined by
the state and Party leadership. Tito made this point as early as June
1950,[44] but when the functioning of the more market-oriented eco-

nomic system brought home to the Yugoslav leadership the economic dangers of "particularism," it began to emphasize the trade union's function of "social control" more sharply. Now the trade union was increasingly referred to by CPY spokesmen as the organization within an enterprise representing the interests of the working class as a whole. In his Oslo address of 1954, Kardelj authoritatively formulated this regulative task of the trade union as follows: "The trade union . . . contributes to the harmonizing of the direct economic interests of all workers with the interests of an individual collective, since it struggles to see that the material and other rights of the workers are enjoyed everywhere in the same manner and since it struggles against possible egoistic tendencies of an individual collective which may harm other collectives."[45]

The second instrument of social control over the workers' councils was the system of councils of producers—as described in the previous chapter, the second parliamentary chamber introduced at the local level in 1952 and at the republican and federal level in early 1953. Composed of representatives directly delegated by workers' councils, the councils of producers were granted equality with the political chamber in dealing with economic and social questions.[46] Their primary rationale was said to be the extension of the worker's control over the product of his labor from direct management of his enterprise to local, republican, and federal political organs, where major economic decisions were still made. But the councils of producers were also intended to play a second important function: not only to assure control from below but to achieve regulation (if not control) from above. As Kardelj put it, in an authoritative commentary on the councils of producers:

With the introduction of councils of producers we will, on the one hand, guarantee full inspection and control by our working people with regard to the use and distribution of their surplus labor and maximum mobilization of their initiative. On the other hand, we will also guarantee the necessary control of the community over the activity of individual enterprises and their collectives . . . without interfering in a bureaucratic way in their daily work.[47]

With the development of the commune system after 1955, a social control function was ascribed to all communal organs, not just the commune council of producers. Later, too, vertical economic associations were set up on a functional basis to exercise "social control" over the enterprise.

Third, the People's Front was charged with responsibility for political activity within the enterprise, which inevitably included a strong element of "social control." Initially almost nothing was said about the role of the Party itself, although in fact many workers' councils were initially completely subordinated to the enterprise's Party organization.[48] This was perhaps a consequence of the confusion within the CPY resulting from the attempt to redefine its role in society in general—a problem that will be taken up in Chapter 9. Later, after the Djilas affair and the general reemphasis on the leading political role of the Party in society which followed, Tito himself made it perfectly clear in early 1954 that enterprise's Party organizations themselves had a very important role to play in the management of the enterprise:

... Communists may not interfere in the technical management of the enterprise .... But Communists in the enterprise cannot limit themselves to education and raising the consciousness of the unconscious or weakly conscious workers to a higher level. That is insufficient. They must see what general policies are pursued in the enterprises and how the workers' council functions. They must give the tone to the work of the workers' council. They must ... be vigilant and guard against various kinds of criminal activity and damage ... they must work so well that they disarm all those elements which would like to prevent and weaken the correct development of self-management in the enterprises. That is an enormous task; there is much to be done; that work is all-encompassing.[49]

In summary, when faced with the practical need to replace Stalinist instruments for stimulating economic production with less coercive means and the ideological necessity of distinguishing their own system from the Soviet system in 1949, the Yugoslav leaders began experimenting with advisory workers' councils. In June 1950 workers' councils were declared to be potential management organs; with the emergence of the new market-oriented socialist economic system in 1952, the councils were said to be actually managing the factories. The new doctrine of "worker self-management" which defined their role was an elaboration in the sphere of industrial management of the theory of the withering away of the socialist state. According to the Yugoslav doctrine, with the inauguration of workers' councils, the workers in an enterprise began to act as the managers of the production process as well as producers, overcoming the historical division of labor between the two functions. Simultaneously, however, the doctrine stressed the importance of "social control" of individual workers' councils. The realization in practice of the slogan "The factories to the workers" was proclaimed, but this did not mean that the work force of an enterprise was transformed into a new collective owner.

Significance of the Doctrine

In late 1952 Tito told the Sixth CPY Congress:

It would be incorrect to think, as do many people both here and abroad, that ... giving the factories and enterprises to the workers to manage is some kind of epochal discovery which we have made in the further development of the science of Marxism-Leninism or some kind of new experiment on the road to developing socialism, etc. No, the essence of that act is part of [Marxism-Leninism] ... but that act does have epochal importance because, on the one hand, Marxist science ascribes to it the greatest importance in changing social relations of production and distribution of the labor product and, on the other hand, since it is being realized for the first time in history—what is more, during a very short period of revolutionary development in a small and backward country such as ours.[50]

These words reveal two things about the Yugoslav Communist view of the significance of worker self-management. First, the Yugoslav leadership claimed great credit for implementing, for the first time in history, a system of direct worker management through workers' councils. Second, it took great pains to legitimize the inauguration of the workers' council system as only the realization in practice of an essential element of Marxism-Leninism—one that Stalin had blatantly ignored.

The Yugoslav Communist Party viewed its system of worker self-management as the direct continuation of the experience of the Paris Commune. Addressing the Skupština in December 1951, Kidrič devoted his opening remarks to the history of the struggle for worker self-management: "The revolutionary Paris Commune of 1871 by its practical example in fact formulated an entire historical program of socialist management in the enterprise, as well as discovering the essence of associating the working people in a socialist unity."[51] As suggested earlier, the Yugoslav theoreticians "rediscovered" the Commune through the writings of Marx, Engels, and Lenin. In this sense, it was true that the workers' councils were a realization in practice of an "element of Marxism-Leninism." But the specific writings of Marx, Engels, and Lenin to which the Yugoslav Communist theoreticians most frequently referred in their attempt to legitimize the workers' councils—above all, Marx's *Civil War in France* and Lenin's *State and Revolution*—had in fact been reactions to spontaneous mass action beyond the control and contrary to the expectation of their authors—in the one case, the syndicalism of the Commune; in the other, the forces of industrial anarchism released in Russia by the February Revolution.[52] These particular Marxist writings actually incorporated an ideological current that, at a critical historical juncture, both Marx and Lenin were influenced by and sought to utilize but could never fundamentally accept: anarcho-syndicalism. Hence, it was to the anarcho-syndicalist movement, as transmitted through these atypical Marxist "classics," that a precedent and source of ideological inspiration for the Yugoslav workers' councils is to be traced.[53] For, as a student of workers' councils in various forms has pointed out, "Syndicalism, rather than Marxian communism, has been the origin of the movement to make self-governing workers the managers of their plant."[54] But the CPY ideologues apparently had little direct knowledge of anarcho-syndicalism, which was considered then (and much later) to be an "anti-Marxist" ideological deviation.[55] (Similarly, the CPY ideologues evidently had little knowledge of the theories of market socialism developed by Socialists in the 1930s.)[56]

It would be wrong to overstress[57] the anarcho-syndicalist character of the Yugoslav industrial management system itself—in theory no less than in practice. The Yugoslav Communist leaders did not, of course, proclaim the trade union itself the vehicle of worker management. This would have meant open acceptance of syndicalism—a heresy that continued to be roundly condemned. If trade union industrial management could have come to life, it would have meant the creation of a powerful all-Yugoslav organization in competition with the Party apparatus. Also, the Yugoslav leadership quite likely felt that, given the previous role of the trade union organization as the handmaiden of the state bureaucracy in attempting to increase production, the worker would not be much inclined to accept it as "his" instrument of management.

Moreover, while proclaiming that workers' councils were to manage the enterprises, the CPY simultaneously stressed the necessity of "social control" of the individual workers' council. The Party ideologues made abundantly clear that the goal was not a society splintered into independent communes;[58] in the economic sphere, in consequence, they fundamentally excluded the development of a Proudhonist economy with collective factory owners—the workers—mutually exchanging their goods.[59] The individual collective was not the new owner of the enterprise, but only society's trustee in its management. The unexpressed consequence of this conception was that, in Marxian economic terms, a significant part—indeed, the bulk—of the workers' surplus labor would still be disposed of *outside* the factory.[60] While Yugoslav theoreticians claimed that the institution of councils of producers guaranteed worker influence at higher levels of decision making as well, this very contention was indirect evidence of the limits of "worker self-management."

The character of the new system of economic management, taken as a whole, was indeed predetermined by the fact that the workers' councils were initiated and developed exclusively from above. Where managerial-type workers' councils have arisen from below—the Soviet *fabzavkomy*, the Catalonian workers' councils of the Spanish Civil War,[61] or, more recently, Polish, Hungarian,[62] and Algerian workers' councils—they have generally striven for the anarcho-syndicalist goal of collective ownership. Anarcho-syndicalist goals are, however, in terms of their emphasis on spontaneity and denial of central authority, by definition incapable of being formulated from above. Certainly the Yugoslav Communist leadership, in establishing workers' councils, had no intention of abolishing central economic authority or the Party's own "leading role" in the economy.

Notes

[1] This chapter does not attempt to describe the organization or functioning of the Yugoslav economy, either before or after the introduction of workers' councils. Accounts are given in Harry Schleicher, *Das System der betrieblichen Selbsverwaltung in Jugoslawien* (Berlin: Duncker & Humblot, 1961); Viktor Meier, *Das neue jugoslawische Wirtschaftssystem* (Zurich and St. Gallen: Polygraphischer Verlag, 1956); Albert Waterston, *Planning in Yugoslavia* (Baltimore: Johns Hopkins Press, 1962); International Labour Office, *Workers' Management in Yugoslavia* (Geneva: ILO, 1962); George Macesich, *Yugoslavia: The Theory and Practice of Development Planning* (Charlottesville: University Press of Virginia, 1964); Deborah D. Milenkovitch, *Plan and Market in Yugoslav Economic Thought* (New Haven: Yale University Press, 1971); Benjamin N. Ward, Jr., "From Marx to Barone: Socialism and the Postwar Yugoslav Industrial Firm" (unpublished Ph.D. dissertation, University of California, Berkeley, 1956). Representative Yugoslav accounts are Dj. Miljević, S. Blagojević, and M. Nikolić, *Razvoj privrednog sistema FNRJ* (Belgrade, 1955); J. Sirotković, *Novi privredni sistem FNRJ* (Zagreb, 1954); Dušan Bilandžić, *Management of Yugoslav Economy (1945–1966)* (Belgrade, 1967).
[2] "Osnovni zakon o državnim privrednim poduzećima" of July 24, 1946, *Službeni list FNRJ* no. 62 (1946). Article 40 read: "The director is responsible only to the administrative-operative manager of the enterprise [in the state economic bureaucracy] for its management."
[3] As the term was used in the early debates on industrial management in the USSR. See Robert V. Daniels, *The Conscience of the Revolution* (Cambridge Mass.: Harvard University Press, 1960), pp. 107–110, and Maurice Dobb, *Soviet Economic Development Since 1917* (London: Routledge & Kegan Paul, 1960), pp. 91–98.
[4] Kidrič, "O osnovnom zakonu o državnim privrednim preduzećima," *Dela* 3: 24.
[5] Ibid., pp. 24–25.

6 "Zakon o radničkim povjerenicima," of July 31, 1945, *Službeni list FNRJ* no. 54 (1945). See also Kidrič, "Exposition of the Basic Law on State Economic Enterprises," *Dela*, 3: 36.
7 D. Marković, M. Mimica, and Lj. Ristović, *Fabrike radnicima—Hronika o radničkom samoupravljanju u Jugoslaviji* (Belgrade, 1964), p. 76.
8 Article 43.
9 *Borba*, October 30, 1948. See also Tito's address to the Congress, *Govori i članci* 4: 25–26. A later Yugoslav study noted that in 1945–1946 the Party had to combat two deviations in the trade union organizations: *economism*, "defense of the narrow and apparently direct interests of the working class, leading to the opposing of the interests of the state and the workers," and *trade union avant-gardism*, "appropriating certain functions which did not belong to the trade union organization: interfering in the business of the enterprise, replacing managers, forcing salary increases, improving work conditions beyond justified measures." (Branko Petranović, "Narodna vlast u periodu administrativnog rukovodjenja privredom," *Pregled posleratnog razvitka Jugoslavije*, p. 81.)
10 Kidrič, "O osnovnom zakonu" *Dela* 3: 16.
11 See Miljević, Blagojević, and Nikolić, *Razvoj privrednog sistema FNRJ*, pp. 19–20.
12 Kardelj, *Komunist* 3, no. 4: 60.
13 Ibid., p. 56.
14 Vukmanović-Tempo, *Revolucija koja teče* 2: 120.
15 The idea of new worker organs was discussed as early as "mid-1949" at a joint Central Committee–government meeting. The authoritative Party history dates the Politburo decision as "fall" 1949. On December 23, 1949, a joint Instruction of the Government Economic Council and the trade union Central Committee ordered the establishment of experimental workers' councils. The councils were production-oriented; if the enterprise director disagreed with a council's recommendations, he was required to refer the matter to higher state authorities. See Marković, Mimica, and Ristović, *Fabrike Radnicima*, pp. 87–92 (the Instruction is reproduced following page 100); *Pregled istorije SKJ*, p. 477. The formation and operation of the advisory councils are described in some detail in *Fabrike Radnicima*, pp. 92–100.
16 Explaining the first measure of economic decentralization to the Skupština as a blow against bureaucratism, Kidrič omitted any mention of the workers' councils (*Borba*, February 8, 1950). He referred to them in passing in a speech of March 21, 1950 (*Borba*, March 22, 1950). The trade union organ *Sindikati* devoted a lead article to the workers' councils and complained that they were being ignored in the press. (M. Pavičević, "O radničkim savetima," *Sindikati* 2, no. 2 [April 1950] : 3–12.)
17 *Borba*, June 28, 1950.
18 Dedijer implied that Kidrič played the primary role in the enunciation of self-management (*Izgubljena bitka*, pp. 405–408). Djilas attributed primacy to himself and Kardelj, reporting that after a brief period of initial skepticism, Kardelj and Kidrič joined him in working out the concept in spring 1950. It was then presented to Tito, who, after initial hesitation, enthusiastically adopted the project. (Milovan Djilas, *The Unperfect Society: Beyond the New Class* [New York: Harcourt, Brace & World, 1969], pp. 220–223.
19 "Osnovni zakon o upravljanju državnim privrednim preduzećima i višim privrednim udruženjima od strane radnih kolektiva" of July 2, 1950, *Službeni list FNRJ* no. 43 (1950).
20 Kardelj, Speech to the Fourth Congress of the People's Front, *Problemi* 2: 317–320.

[21] As discussed in Chapter 6.

[22] Tito, Speech of June 26, 1950, *Govori i članci* 5: 205. In the same sentence, Yugoslav leaders could speak of peasant self-management in the work cooperatives. This incongruity will be examined in the next chapter.

[23] M. Perović's postscript to *Društveno upravljanje u Jugoslaviji* (Zagreb, 1960), pp. 476–477.

[24] Tito, Speech of June 26, 1950, *Govori i članci* 5: 234.

[25] Djordjević, *Ustavno pravo FNRJ*, p. 107.

[26] See also Ljubislav Marković, "Svojina i njena negacija u FNRJ," *Naša stvarnost* 7, no. 12 (December 1953): 24–42. Another group of Yugoslav theorists continued to maintain, however, that "social property" was a meaningful legal expression. See Meier, *Das neue jugoslawische Wirtschaftssystem*, pp. 60–64.

[27] Kardelj, "Četiri godine iskustva," *Problemi* 4: 185.

[28] "Izraz naše snage i napretka," *Borba*, June 28, 1950.

[29] Decrees of February and April 1950 initiated some decentralization of economic administration, but the republics continued to exercise the administrative functions previously exercised at the federal level. See Schleicher, *Das System der betrieblichen Selbstverwaltung in Jugoslawien*, pp. 34–35.

[30] Tito, *Govori i članci* 5: 225.

[31] Kidrič, *Komunist* 4, no. 6: 8.

[32] Z. Brkić, *O političkom radu partijskih organizacija u novim uvjetima; referat održan na IX proširenom plenumu CK KPH* (Split, [1952]), p. 25.

[33] M. Bogosavljević and M. Pešaković, *Workers' Management of a Factory in Yugoslavia* (Belgrade, 1959), p. 52 (style improved).

[34] Tito, Speech of June 26, 1950, *Govori i članci* 5: 226.

[35] See note 29.

[36] Kidrič, *Komunist* 4, no. 6; Kidrič, "O nacrtima novih ekonomskih zakona," *Komunist* 5, nos. 4–5 (July–September 1951): 1–27; Kidrič, Speech to the Sixth CPY Congress, *VI kongres Komunističke partije Jugoslavije (Saveza komunista Jugoslavije) 2–7 novembra 1952; stenografske beleške* [Belgrade], [1952], pp. 129–137. For fuller treatment of the CPY's revised economic theories, see Milenkovitch, *Plan and Market in Yugoslav Economic Thought*, pp. 77–120.

[37] Kardelj, "Četiri godine iskustva," *Problemi* 4: 185 (emphasis added).

[38] See Schleicher, *Das System der beltrieblichen Selbstverwaltung in Jugoslawien*; Jiri Kolaja, *Workers' Councils: The Yugoslav Experience* (New York: Praeger, 1966). A useful example of the extensive self-critical Yugoslav literature on the initial period of worker self-management is a report by the Center on Worker Self-Management, "Radničko samoupravljanje u Jugoslaviji," *Jugoslovenski pregled*, November 1969, pp. 427–448.

[39] See the reports in *Komunist*, June 1953, pp. 368, 373, and in *Naša stvarnost* 7, no. 2 (February 1953): 41; Meier, *Das neue jugoslawische Wirtschaftssystem*, pp. 57–59, 137–138, 146–169.

[40] *Komunist*, April 1953, pp. 235–254, at 243.

[41] Tito, *Govori i članci* 5: 231.

[42] *Pregled istorije SKJ*, p. 489.

[43] See the address of Djuro Salaj, head of the trade union, to the Second Trade Union Congress in October 1951, *Drugi kongres Saverza sindikata Jugoslavije* (Belgrade, 1951), p. 92.

[44] Tito, *Govori i članci* 5: 231.

[45] Kardelj, *Problemi* 4: 217.

[46] See Schleicher, *Das System der betrieblichen Selbstverwaltung in Jugoslawien*, pp. 43–77.

[47] Kardelj, Speech of March 31, 1952, *Problemi* 2: 195.

[48] *Pregled istorije SKJ*, p. 489.

[49] Tito, Remarks to the Fourth CC Plenum, *Govori i članci* 9: 103.

[50] Tito, *Govori i članci* 7: 226.

[51] *Borba*, December 29, 1951. The Yugoslav workers' councils are also traced back to the Paris Commune in Miljević, Blagojević, and Nikolić, *Razvoj privrednog sistema FNRJ*, pp. 29–33. For a later Yugoslav study, see Pero Damjanović, "Pariska komuna," *Priručnik za istoriju medjunarodnog radničkog pokreta* (Belgrade, 1964), pp. 235–278.

[52] The Russian Revolution unleashed a powerful movement for worker management of industry, manifested in the appearance of the *fabzavkomy* (which, largely spontaneously, took over control of capitalist enterprises) and given legal expression by the Soviet regime in its decree of November 1917 on workers' control. But by 1918, faced with near chaos in the economy, Lenin—repudiating the demand for mass industrial management which he had made in *State and Revolution*—was calling for the return to traditional principles of industrial organization. When Shiliapnikov and Kollontai then took up the advocacy of greater worker participation in enterprise management through the trade unions (i.e., the essence of syndicalism), this was expressed through an avowedly factional Workers' Opposition to Lenin. (Accounts of the developments are given in Daniels, *The Conscience of the Revolution*, pp. 81–87; Dobb, *Soviet Economic Development Since 1917*, pp. 77–89.)

[53] For later Yugoslav acknowledgements of this influence, see A. Deleon, "Fabrike radnicima," *Zbornik o radničkom samoupravljanju* (Belgrade, 1957), pp. 215–219; and P. Romac and J. Franić, *Workers' Self-Management in Factories* (Belgrade, 1962), pp. 6–7.

[54] Adolf F. Sturmthal, *Workers Councils: A Study of the Workplace Organization on Both Sides of the Iron Curtain* (Cambridge, Mass.: Harvard University Press, 1964), p. 58.

[55] For example, in 1949–1950 the Yugoslav theoreticians did not closely study (and were not greatly influenced by) the experience of the Russian *fabzavkomy* of 1917 (Leonhard interviews). Until the late 1960s, they universally condemned the Workers' Opposition. Ignoring the real Russian precedent, CPY ideologues argued that after 1917 Lenin continued to hold to the views expressed in *State and Revolution* but was prevented by the force of circumstances from implementing them. See Kidrič, Speech of December 28, 1951, *Borba*, December 29, 1951.

[56] See Milenkovitch, *Plan and Market in Yugoslav Economic Thought*, p. 101, note 34.

[57] As Halperin seemed to do in *The Triumphant Heretic*, pp. 132–138.

[58] See Kardelj, *Problemi* 2: 241, and Kidrič, in *Borba*, June 22–24, 1952.

[59] Meier, *Das neue jugoslawische Wirtschaftssystem*, pp. 102–104.

[60] By 1957 it could only be claimed that workers' councils disposed of 30 percent of total national income (Blagojević and Pešaković, *Workers' Management of a Factory in Yugoslavia*, p. 51).

[61] The Spanish Communists bitterly opposed the syndicalist-dominated workers' councils. See Cattell, *Communism and the Spanish Civil War*, pp. 88–90.

[62] The Polish and Hungarian workers' councils of 1956 were significantly influenced by the Yugoslav councils. While acknowledging this debt, a Polish commentary drew attention to the essential difference in the two movements: "[Self-management] was initiated in Yugoslavia essentially as an initiative from above, in the form of a decree . . . . In our country, as we all know, it was wrested from the ministers by the workers' themselves." (*Po prostu*, October 28, 1956, quoted in Labedz, ed., *Revisionism*, p. 220.)

8

Socialization of the Countryside Redefined

The Doctrine Modified

The history of the Yugoslav approach to the socialization of agriculture through the end of 1949 was presented in Chapter 3. To recapitulate, the Second Plenum of January 1949 reversed the previous policy of relative gradualism, which had emphasized the loose general co-operative, and called for intensified collectivization through the establishment of kolkhozlike peasant work cooperatives. (Even in 1949, however, collectivization in Yugoslavia did not approach the pace or the degree of violence of Soviet collectivization.) This policy, as originally formulated, lasted only eleven months. At the end of December 1949, after increased scarcities of foodstuffs and peasant resistance, the Third Plenum set limits on the pace of collectivization. The resolution of the Third Plenum, adopted on the basis of Kidrič's report on economic affairs, warned Party activists: "Do not put primary emphasis on the number of [work] cooperatives, but on their internal consolidation." It also cautioned against forming new un-productive cooperatives in rugged mountainous country.[1]

An authoritative commentary on the Third Plenum declared that Yugoslavia could not simply copy Soviet collectivization experience, reaffirmed that the present stage was one of "pressuring and restrict-ing" and not "liquidating" the kulak, and defended the correctness of admitting even kulaks into work cooperatives if they had fought with the Partisans or had otherwise proved their loyalty to socialism.[2]

On the other hand, published materials make it clear that the Third Plenum did not question the peasant work cooperative as the proper institution for further collectivization. While the final socialization of agriculture awaited industrialization and an abundance of agricultural machinery, Kidrič told the Plenum, it was possible to increase agricultural production "*now*, on the basis of more limited measures of rationalization, on the basis of simple *cooperative labor*, of better and more correct organization of the labor process on the basis of the *present* level of the forces of production in agriculture." Thus the work cooperative remained "the most efficient lever ... for the socialist reconstruction of our countryside. . . ."[3] The problems encountered in 1949 were attributed to the "present initial phase of collectivization."[4]

The fact that the Third Plenum resolution remained the authorita-tive guideline for CPY policy until November 1951 showed that the dogmatic conceptions prevailing at the Second Plenum remained dominant within the Party. Like Stalin in 1930, the Yugoslav leaders blamed the difficulties they had encountered on the excessive zeal of lower officials.[5] Although a slower pace of collectivization was consequently adopted, the goal of collectivization by means of work cooperatives remained unchanged.

Nevertheless, the problems created by forced collectivization reinforced doubts within the Party about the wisdom of the Second Plenum's decisions. The slowdown in the process of collectivization ordered by the Third Plenum, coupled with the admission that mistakes had been made in the countryside, made it easier for the doubters to speak out without directly challenging the Party line. In the following year and a half, two distinct lines of criticism of the collectivization policy of the Second Plenum gradually emerged.

The first approach placed renewed stress on the general cooperative as an instrument of the socialist transformation of the countryside. General cooperatives were not mentioned in the published materials of the Third Plenum. But in late January 1950, at a session of the Executive Committee of the People's Front, Kardelj again took up the advocacy of that form of cooperative.

. . . in the first draft of the resolution [on the Front's future tasks], much attention is devoted to work cooperatives. I think that is necessary. But it is also necessary to emphasize again that we must struggle to consolidate cooperative agriculture in general, that is, in all its forms. The fact is that a certain dizziness with success has appeared here. We have perhaps a fifth of our agriculture in the socialist sector, and yet we very easily renounce the lower forms [of cooperatives]. The tendency in cooperative agriculture for only work cooperatives to be formed is, I think, mistaken . . . . I believe that it would be necessary to say something in the resolution to the effect that the People's Front must continue to struggle for the consolidation of general agricultural cooperatives . . . .[6]

Kardelj's intervention was effective. The final text of the "Resolution on the Future Tasks of the People's Front" repeated the Third Plenum's directive to put primary emphasis on the consolidation of work cooperatives but declared: "It is also necessary to wage a decisive struggle for the consolidation of agricultural cooperatives of the general type."[7] This injunction was subsequently repeated by other CPY spokesmen in the course of 1950.[8]

Nevertheless, at this point there was no reversion to the view (accepted until the end of 1948) that the general cooperative should be considered the *main* instrument for achieving socialism in agriculture. That role was still assigned uniformly to the work cooperatives. For example, when the Minister of Agriculture, Mijalko Todorović, claimed in May 1950 that the Second Plenum had not de-emphasized the general cooperative (as it obviously had), he was quick to add that present conditions still required the "forming of work cooperatives on a large scale."[9] It was thus no wonder that the renewed verbal emphasis on the general cooperative had almost no effect in practice. While the rate of forming new work cooperatives did fall drastically in 1950, in comparison with 1949, the number of general cooperatives declined—though their total membership increased slightly. (See Tables 8.1 and 8.2.)

The revival of interest in the general cooperative within the CPY signified an incipient return to the gradualist policy of achieving socialism in the countryside which had prevailed prior to 1949. Parallel to that approach, a second dissident view on the socialization of agriculture emerged. This was a "technocratic" criticism, which sought, not to reemphasize looser cooperatives, but to rationalize the internal organization of existing work cooperatives. This line of criticism was developed in Croatia, where the Party Secretary, Vladimir Bakarić,

Table 8.1
Postwar Development of Peasant Work Cooperatives

Year	Number	Number of Members
1945	31	—
1946	454	75,186
1947	779	174,518
1948	1,318	286,234
1949	6,626	1,707,073
1950	6,964	2,128,839
1951	6,797	2,003,644
1952	4,679	1,504,874
1953	1,152	192,582

Sources: Jozo Tomasevich, "Collectivization of Agriculture in Yugoslavia," in Irwin T. Sanders, ed., *Collectivization of Agriculture in Eastern Europe* (Lexington, Ky.: University of Kentucky Press, 1958), p. 173; Ranko M. Brashich, *Land Reform and Ownership in Yugoslavia, 1919–1953* (New York: Free Europe Committee, 1954), pp. 7, 109.

Table 8.2
Postwar Development of General Agricultural Cooperatives

Year	Number	Number of Members
1945	5,041	492,800
1946	8,011	1,807,798
1947	6,632	2,535,408
1948	8,666	3,127,464
1949	9,060	3,250,000
1950	8.004	3,540,339
1951	7,581	3,476,876
1952	7,266	3,242,819
1953	7,061	3,297,771

Sources: Same as for Table 8.1.

accepted the view of several agricultural specialists that work co-operatives run according to the organizational principles of a kolkhoz were economically unviable.[10] Formally basing his stand on the Third Plenum's edict to "consolidate" the work cooperative, Bakarić elaborated, in the course of 1950 and 1951, a scheme for their economic rationalization that in fact signified a fundamental break with the kolkhoz model.

The first incipient formulation of this view appeared in early 1950, in a *Komunist* article entitled "Problems of Land Rent in the Transition Period." In this article, Bakarić took issue with the twin Soviet "dogmas" that land nationalization was in itself a socialist measure and that a collective farm could not pay rent to the peasant for the use of his land. The significance of the article, however, lay not so much in its specific criticisms of Soviet theory but in its general approach and the conclusion that Bakarić drew:

This examination [of Soviet collectivization doctrine] was much more important for our situation [than for an explanation of Soviet reality]. Above all in order to free ourselves from the conceptions which such [Soviet] theories have forced upon us and, then, to see and evaluate what concrete policy we should follow . . .It was necessary . . . to depict the kolkhoz system as a *transitional system* and explain . . . its limits . . . . That knowledge forces us to study more carefully our own problems . . . . It may enable us to find still newer forms . . . .[11]

Bakarić's article signified the beginning of a general reexamination of the kolkhoz model. Unlike the antibureaucratic critique of the Soviet social system, theory of the state, and system of industrial management, this critical attitude was not the result of an ideological reexamination of the Soviet scene after the break with Stalin in the light of earlier Marxist-Leninist writings. This critique arose from practice, and more specifically, as Bakarić himself explained,[12] from an awareness that the Yugoslav work cooperatives lacked any economic stimulus for increasing wheat production.

Bakarić carried his critique a step further in January 1951, when he published a second article in *Komunist*. Again criticizing the kolkhoz organizational model (and the Yugoslav Ministry of Agriculture for defending its correctness), he called for the introduction of a system of economic accounting in work cooperatives.[13] Two months later, addressing the Third Congress of the Croatian People's Front,[14] he repeated his criticism. "It is obvious," he told the assembled delegates, "that the organization of [work] cooperatives is today a barrier to the further development of cooperative farming and thus a barrier to the further socialist transformation of the village." He proposed three specific departures from the kolkhoz model: (1) abolition of the brigade system of labor; (2) introduction of cost accounting in work cooperatives and their branches; (3) abolition of the *trudodan* system (calculating equal labor units for all work in the cooperative, regardless of its economic importance, and paying a large share of the resulting wages in kind). Bakarić again attacked Federal Ministry of Agriculture officials who, "lacking the most basic knowledge of political economy" and "still under the influence of Soveit conceptions of the problem," were resisting these proposed innovations. What was required, he concluded, was less concern with theoretical constructs and more attention to daily problems. "The proof of the pudding is in the eating, and not in evaluating it and measuring it."

The preceding pages have traced the development of three different views on the socialization of agriculture within the CPY following the Third Plenum. The dominant view, that laid down as the Party line by the Plenum, called for a continuation of collectivization through work cooperatives except in infertile mountainous regions of the country (while stressing that internal consolidation was more important than the number of new work cooperatives). In this view, the pace of collectivization attempted in 1949 had been excessive; nevertheless, the kolkhoz model remained (to quote Todorović) "in the main, correct" for Yugoslav work cooperatives.[15] One dissenting view (voiced most prominently by Kardelj), while not taking exception to this view of the internal organization of work cooperatives, advocated paying more attention to the general cooperative as a transitional form. The second dissenting view (articulated most prominently by Bakarić) ignored the general cooperative but demanded the internal reorganization of work cooperatives on rational economic principles.

The CPY officials who found fault with the Party's agricultural line were spurred on in formulating and advocating their views by increased practical problems in the agricultural sphere.[16] A severe drought in 1950 reinforced the detrimental effects of collectivization on agricultural output. The state authorities nevertheless attempted to fulfill delivery quotas, and this led to peasant resistance, including scattered riots.[17] This peasant discontent, in conjunction with U.S. assistance in supplying surplus foodstuffs and the initial modifications of the global economic system, led to the gradual elimination of compulsory deliveries of agricultural products and the abolishment of Machine Tractor Stations in September 1950. In the context of the general political relaxation, these developments reinforced peasant resistance to collectivization; members of work cooperatives devoted more attention to cultivation of private plots and increasingly requested to withdraw from the work cooperatives entirely. The latter form of resistance developed into a major political crisis in mid-1951, when a large proportion of peasants who had entered the lower types of work cooperatives in 1948 sought to exercise their legal right to leave after a three-year period. While some work cooperatives were dissolved at this time, the majority were preserved with "administrative measures."[18] Nevertheless, the withdrawal crisis led the Party leaders to reexamine the policy of collectivization itself.

The result of their reexamination was a Central Committee directive of November 24, 1951, "On the Further Paths of the Socialist Transformation of the Countryside."[19] The directive confirmed the Politburo's intention of preserving the majority of existing work cooperatives—a point on which, in view of the seriousness of the withdrawal crisis, it may be assumed that the Party leadership was united. Yet the leadership now did concede the folly of trying to maintain work cooperatives in the mountains; the directive ordered their abandonment; equally important, it called for the internal economic rationalization of remaining work cooperatives along the lines Bakarić had advocated. The principle of profitability was to be introduced in each cooperative and its branches, and regular cash wages were henceforth to be paid to the cooperative members. Management of the work cooperatives was to be harmonized with management of other sectors of the economy through the introduction of "producer self-management." These measures would bring the "final liquidation of elements of the kolkhoz system." In terms of the internal structure of the work cooperatives, Bakarić's "technocratic" line of criticism had triumphed.[20]

Ordering the abandonment of the most unproductive work cooperatives and the economic rationalization of the majority, the November 1951 directive signaled an even more fundamental reversal of agricultural policy by de-emphasizing the establishment of new work cooperatives and proclaiming that "consolidation and gradual expansion of cooperatives of the general type is, in present conditions, the basic method of the further socialist transformation in the countryside." This signified a return in principle to the gradualist agricultural line that had prevailed prior to 1949. Kardelj had then been the chief spokesman in the CPY leadership for that policy; his influence was apparently decisive in its revival.

But in fact the command to concentrate again on general cooperatives remained, initially, a dead letter. In 1952 Yugoslavia was hit by a drought worse than that of 1950, causing many peasants to slaughter their livestock. At the same time, the freeing of agricultural prices and the adoption of credit and taxation policies intended to stimulate individual peasant output had the effect of increasing pressure from cooperative peasants to leave the work cooperatives. In this situation, rural Party cadres were too preoccupied with problems of the existing work cooperatives to worry about the "further paths of the socialist transformation of the countryside." The year 1951 marked the peak of the socialization of agriculture in Yugoslavia, with 18.5 percent of agricultural land incorporated in the work cooperatives (and an additional 6 percent incorporated in state farms). Party slogans continued to emphasize development of general cooperatives,[21] but intra-Party discussions on agricultural matters remained focused on internal difficulties of work cooperatives.

In these discussions, the "technocrats" at first limited themselves to urging the speedy implementation of their scheme of economic rationalization incorporated in the November 1951 directive.[22] But despite its gradual introduction, in the face of passive resistance of many rural activists,[23] in 1952, the "technocrats'" victory was a hollow one. They had advocated economic accounting as a means of reorganizing work cooperatives on sound principles. But once this policy began to be implemented, it quickly showed that the work cooperatives, in anything like their existing forms, were incapable of being rationalized. It became apparent that they suffered, not from faulty internal organization, but from what was frankly admitted to be "surplus labor."[24] At the same time, the disparity between the initial measures of liberalization in the country as a whole and the perpetuation of a Stalinist institution in agriculture became more uncomfortable.

By June 1952 (perhaps before) Bakarić himself had come to realize this, as he revealed in a major speech that month to the executive committee of the Zagreb region Party organization. He did claim that introduction of the principles of economic accounting had, in some cases, uncovered "tremendous material reserves" that had allegedly made possible the preservation of some cooperatives. In other cases, however, the new economic principles had merely shown the unviability of the cooperatives. "If you begin to apply the same economic accounting to cooperatives which were called weak cooperatives, then it assumes a completely different form. You will be able to calculate that, in their present form, those cooperatives are not very productive, etc. What kind of a cooperative is it which directly consumes all its output? What kind of a cooperative is it that lives at state expense? Such cooperatives are not needed. That is not socialism"[25] While Bakarić loyally declared his support for the Party's policy of "preserving every cooperative," he made quite evident his conviction that the majority of work cooperatives were incapable of serving as an instrument of the socialization of agriculture. His support for their preservation was temporary and defensive, dictated by the necessity of warding off the total demoralization of the rural Party cadres threatened by the increasingly self-evident failure of collectivization. As he told the session:

If we would today give up the [work] cooperatives, the result would be general demoralization. Therefore we emphasized that we will not give up the [work] cooperatives. That would be the main reason, as we said, why it is necessary to fight stubbornly for every cooperative. This, of course, means something quite different from saying: let's collectivize the countryside, let's create [work] cooperatives where objective, if not subjective, conditions exist. The preservation of every [work] co-operative is, so to speak, a defensive measure which we support only so that demoralization does not occur. Nevertheless, if the present state of affairs continues very long, then demoralization will follow anyway and will be worse than if we had immediately dissolved the cooperatives. We must therefore work very quickly.[26]

The solution to the problem of the work cooperatives, as Bakarić outlined it at this point, was twofold. First, it was necessary to make a model of the (implicitly few) work cooperatives that could prosper. Second, it was necessary to take seriously the November 1951 directive's injunction to develop general cooperatives. When these two tasks had been carried out with some degree of success, thus creating a new perspective for the continued development of socialism in the countryside, then peasants would have to be allowed to leave the work cooperatives if they so desired.

We will, perhaps in the immediate future, have to openly tell people who don't wish to remain in the cooperatives to leave. We will say this when we have a number of cooperatives in which people desire to stay and which will have a decisive influence on agricultural production. I mention this because our general economic development is forcing us to take that course. A general democratization is being carried out here; greater freedom of association within individual collectives, etc., is developing. Thus it is logical that this leads to a point where there cannot exist a disharmony in development [between industry and agriculture]. We will have to say: let those who want to stay, stay, and those who want to leave can leave. It will happen that the unproductive cooperatives will fail. That means that it is better that they break up of their own accord than fail under our protection.[27]

But the strength of the dogma that collective farms were the major "socialist achievement" in the countryside, coupled with the CPY leadership's determination not to reverse a past policy in the face of opposition from the "class enemy," meant that initially such arguments, no matter how persuasive economically, fell on deaf ears within the Party hierarchy. Majority sentiment in the Party continued to defend the work cooperatives, maintaining that in their internal organization they differed fundamentally from kolkhozes—not so much because of the implementation of "economic accounting" (by which the "technocrats" had originally sought to distinguish them), but because of the alleged introduction of "producer self-management" in agriculture corresponding to worker self-management in industry. As one spokesman for this view claimed:

The peasant work cooperatives in Yugoslavia have practically no connection with the kolkhoz system in the USSR . . . . The Yugoslav cooperatives have sprung up and developed on a voluntary basis and not by means of compulsion, as did the kolkhozes They are run by the peasants themselves through their cooperative assemblies and conferences and their elected management committee, without the right of the governmental authorities to interfere in any of their internal affairs, while the kolkhozes have an appointed president-manager. The Yugo-slav cooperatives develop as complex cooperative farms with their own equipment, while all mechanized work in the Soviet kolkhozes is done through the state Machine Tractor Stations. . . .[28]

Tito himself, at public meetings in Serbia and Croatia in July 1952, reaffirmed his view that the work cooperatives could not be abandoned—no matter what. Referring to the disastrous drought of mid-1952, he said: "Probably because of that, people will seek to leave the [work] cooperatives. But that is not the solution. Cooperatives are a good thing, and they must continue to exist and further develop." In another speech he declared: "The cooperatives which are able to exist must be preserved like the apple of our eye, while new work cooperatives should be created."[29] Privately, Tito expressed the same viewpoint: much remained to be done to improve the internal structure of the cooperatives, but their radical abolition was unthinkable.[30]

This dogmatic belief in the progressive character of the work cooperatives still prevailed at the Sixth CPY Congress (November 1952). The Congress proceedings contained no exhortations to struggle for socialism in agriculture, whether through work cooperatives or any other means, and this very silence was an indirect admission that the policy of collectivization had reached a dead end. Tito did refer to the issue in his Congress report, lamenting: "It is not an easy and quick task to create socialism in the countryside." But the only solution he could offer was a reaffirmation of the old dogma: "[work cooperatives] represent the most important element of the victory of socialism in the countryside."[31]

Nevertheless, two leaders raised objections in the course of the Sixth Congress. Openly admitting in a public session that he had a "different viewpoint from the [other] comrades in the Central Committee," Bakarić told his colleagues: "What is important is not that we made mistakes . . . . We must seek the reasons why we could make mistakes."[32] The main cause of the problems in agriculture, he seemed to say, was the mistaken acceptance of the work cooperative as the main instrument of socialism in agriculture. While he did not say so outright, his comments on work cooperatives (which he called "almost reaction-ary") indicated clearly enough his view that they had to be abandoned. Todorović (still in charge of agriculture in the state apparatus) now seemed to support Bakarić's stand. Noting, in his remarks to the Sixth Congress, that overemphasis on "certain organizational forms" had resulted in a neglect of "total economic policy" in the countryside,

Todorović regretted the fact that "the Soviet kolkhoz theory leads many people to see the possibility of socializing small-owner production only through the direct joining of peasant holdings."[33]

The Sixth CPY Congress did not modify the Party line on peasant work cooperatives. But the opponents of that policy, led by Bakarić (who was elevated to the supreme Party leadership at the Sixth Congress) and Kardelj, evidently succeeded sometime shortly thereafter in winning over Tito and a majority of top leaders to their view. A hint of the pending change was given by Kardelj in his address to the Fourth Congress of the People's Front in February 1953, in which he declared: "Practice has shown that every use of force, every creation of artificial structures in [agriculture] has only resulted in negative economic consequences . . . only if something is economically justified can it be considered socialist."[34] A month later the "Regulation on Property Relations and the Reorganization of Peasant Work Cooperatives" was issued which (despite the wording of its title) sanctioned the dissolving of the great majority of work cooperatives.[35]

A commentary on the Third Plenum had justified the work cooperatives on three grounds: (1) to increase agricultural production; (2) to strengthen the "worker-peasant alliance"; (3) to develop socialism in the countryside.[36] But as a consequence of collectivization and adverse weather, agricultural output had stagnated or fallen, necessitating import of American foodstuffs worth 170 million dollars by 1953.[37] The peasant had been driven to resistance on such a scale that, in the eyes of the Yugoslav leadership, it was threatening to undermine the broad non-Party support for the regime required by the international situation. Tito revealingly expressed these rationales in May 1953:

That which we wanted to attain, to have more bread, more agricultural products, we did not achieve. Instead we had less . . . when today some of our working people—I am speaking of Communists—say that we have no [policy] line and that, since we issued the Regulation, we will destroy cooperative farming, I answer: what would happen if war came? Then, too, the cooperatives would disintegrate, but not only that. We would lack the [support of the] people and the necessary unity to fight.[38]

Moreover, work cooperatives had incorporated less than 20 percent of agricultural land. A creation of the "administrative phase" of development, they were an economic anachronism in the decentralized, market-oriented economy of 1953. Finally, repudiation of centralized bureaucratic management in the rest of the economy led to increasing skepticism within the CPY as to whether work cooperatives could be considered "socialist" at all. These factors were decisive in the decision to abandon work cooperatives. As the authoritative Party history later stated, "Putting the emphasis in the struggle for the socialist reconstruction of agriculture on the creation of peasant work cooperatives led to serious stagnation and failure . . . . Moreover, that path in the struggle for the socialist reconstruction of agriculture came into sharp conflict with the conceptions which developed in the Party after the introduction of worker self-management."[39]

It fell to Kardelj to provide an authoritative theoretical explanation of the March 30 regulation. Admitting the harm that had resulted from the Soviet dogma on collectivization, Kardelj told the Party: "It is no longer necessary to rely only on general [Marxist-Leninist] theoretical propositions and foreign [Soviet] experience. We have our own experience; from it we must, without prejudice, draw clear conclusions. . . ." The most important conclusion was that work cooperatives had come into contradiction with the rest of the socioeconomic system. Publicly justifying their utility during the earlier "administrative" period, Kardelj declared that they had long since outlived their time. The attempt to preserve them by force would only make matters worse: For ". . . every artificial, administrative retention of outlived forms or imagined constructions in economic life must result in a contradiction between the tendency of the development of the forces of production and the artificial preservation of economic relations . . . . Such a contradiction engenders both negative economic and political consequences."[40] Hence it was necessary "to implement consistently the principle of voluntarism" in connection with the work cooperatives. While some could be reorganized on a sound economic basis, their membership would sharply decrease, and many would have to be disbanded outright.

Nevertheless, Kardelj affirmed, giving up the work cooperatives did not mean "that we abandon peasant agricultural production to spontaneous development, independent of the socialist sector of our economy, or that we forfeit the perspective of its socialist transformation." The socialist transformation of the countryside would be achieved as the result of natural economic development instead of by political force: "We must free our agriculture in general and our agricultural cooperatives in particular from administrative ties and pressures and clear the way for economic forces in agriculture. On that basis we must establish suitable *economic relations* between the

socialist sector and individual peasant production which will . . . increasingly strengthen socialist elements . . . in the countryside."[41]
Given the dominant position of the socialist industrial sector and the
application of appropriate price, tax, and credit policies, the individual
peasant would be motivated, in his own economic self-interest, to
expand his participation in the manifold activities of the general
cooperatives. In consequence, although calling for "the development of
agricultural cooperatives—in their various forms, from the lowest to
developed producers' cooperatives," Kardelj made it clear that the
Party henceforth had to concentrate on the loose general cooperative
that "*today* can directly encompass, so to speak, the entire mass of the
working peasantry, associate it in the most simple forms of cooperation, and bind it economically to the socialist economy."

While the CPY leadership thus sanctioned the abandonment of
peasant work cooperatives, it restated its continued adherence to the
goal of the socialization of agriculture.[42] The primary instrument in
pursuing that goal would be the general cooperative. Freeing itself of
the dogmatism that had triumphed in 1949, Yugoslav doctrine seemed
to be returning to its previous emphasis on the loose general
cooperative.

But, as events quickly showed, a simple reversion to the old doctrine
was impossible. The first problem was, as the leadership had feared, the
demoralization of rural Party activists. The Party leadership, in
sanctioning the disbanding of the work cooperatives, seemed to have
been unprepared for the speed with which that process unfolded after
March 1953 and the proportions it assumed. The situation became most
critical in the fertile Vojvodina region (in which collectivization had
been considerably greater than elsewhere in the country), where the
withdrawal of peasants with land from the work cooperatives
threatened their total collapse. This would have forced the one hundred
thousand landless peasants, the majority of whom were ex-Partisans
who had been resettled in the region after World War II from
mountainous areas, to become laborers for landed peasants. That
prospect, in particular, portended the total demoralization of Party
activists in the region.[43] To prevent this development, the Vojvodina
Party leader, Jovan Veselinov, proposed a further restriction in the size
of individual holdings from the twenty-five hectares permitted by the
1945 land reform law to ten hectares. This measure, Veselinov declared,
would prevent the growth of "capitalist tendencies" in the countryside
and allow the creation of a socialist land fund for the landless

peasants.[44] It would simultaneously provide Party activists in the region with a sorely needed demonstration that the "kulaks" had not triumphed and that they themselves had not become superfluous.

The proposed land restriction was apparently opposed by a faction within the Party headed by Bakarić which denied that a peasant owning twenty-five hectares of land could exhibit "capitalist tendencies" and argued that the measure would only add to the difficulty of increasing agricultural production.[45] But for Tito the critical issue was not an economic one but a political one. Demoralization of the rural cadres as a result of the breakup of the peasant work cooperatives came at just the moment when the Party's leading role in Yugoslav society in general seemed to be called into question—a problem to be examined in the following chapter. Hence, the CPY leadership evidently felt it had to convince the Party rank and file that it had not abandoned the goal of socialism in the countryside. Veselinov's proposal was immediately supported by Kardelj, who saw the primary importance of the political issue involved,[46] and was subsequently adopted as Party policy; on May 27, 1953, the Skupština approved the "Law on the Agricultural Land Fund," which limited the size of individual peasant holdings to ten hectares.[47]

Although this further restriction on the size of peasant holdings helped to prevent the total demoralization of the Party cadres, it greatly contributed to an atmosphere that fostered continued economic discrimination against the individual peasant. Discrimination against the peasant had been an integral part of the pre-1949 policy of fostering general cooperatives. However, it was incompatible with the new policy that, while renouncing work cooperatives and again emphasizing general cooperatives, envisaged the socialization of the countryside as a gradual, exclusively *economic* process and recognized that the private peasantry would, for a long time to come, provide most of the increasing quantities of foodstuffs the country required. Cognizance of this relationship was not totally lacking in the CPY. As Kardelj declared in April 1953, in a second authoritative commentary on the new agricultural policy, "... socialist society must allow the individual peasant freedom of action within the limits of his economic possibilities and also help him in his efforts to raise the productivity of labor on his holding."

But this awareness of the need to increase peasant agricultural output was neutralized by an unchanged, ideologically determined fear of the individual peasant. Kardelj's own words (which immediately followed the passage just quoted) were quite characteristic: ". . . at the same time, conditions must be created with economic means which will prevent the development of capitalist elements and, further, will increasingly bind economically individual peasant production to the socialist economy, which will transform every step forward in [agricultural output] into a step forward in socialist relations, and, finally, which will continually increase the economic strength of the socialist forces in the countryside."[48] The latter attitude was the operative one in practice.[49] Ideologically, the upshot was a doctrine that was internally inconsistent. Renouncing the work cooperative, Yugoslav Communist doctrine recognized, on the one hand, the necessity of allowing the peasant to become an efficient producer on his own land. On the other hand, it viewed increased private peasant production as signifying the growth of "capitalist tendencies" in the countryside. This was the situation at the end of 1953; a coherent doctrine on the socialization of agriculture was lacking.

Only in the late 1950s did the CPY come to see that it could not rely on the private peasant for the bulk of agricultural output for the foreseeable future while simultaneously discriminating against him economically. The essence of the view, advocated by Bakarić, which finally triumphed was contained in his speech to the Third Congress of the Croatian Party in 1954:

Our peasant's immediate perspective is to be the most modern farmer possible on his land, relying on his own labor, the labor of his family, and modern technical implements. Such a perspective must be opened before him; he must be assisted in realizing it. Not only is there no danger of the return of capitalism in such a perspective, but it will help us to mobilize our forces in the countryside in developing the forces of production and broadening the market for socialist industry.[50]

Even in the 1960s, however, agriculture would remain the neglected stepchild of the Yugoslav economy.

To recapitulate, Yugoslav doctrine on the socialist transformation of agriculture underwent major changes after 1948. The Second Plenum of January 1949 adopted a course of radical collectivization through kolkhozlike work cooperatives, but the pace of collectivization was slowed by the Third Plenum at the end of 1949. After criticism of the organizational principles of work cooperatives and renewed interest in general cooperatives appeared within the CPY, the November 1951 directive on agriculture reaffirmed the general cooperative to be the basic instrument for achieving socialism in the countryside. In practice, however, the Party continued to be fully occupied with problems of the existing work cooperatives, stubbornly preserving them in the face of mounting economic and political liabilities until finally, in March 1953, they were abandoned. Thereafter, a policy of helping the smallholding peasant to produce more efficiently was eventually adopted.

Significance of the Doctrine

The changes in Yugoslav Communist doctrine on the socialization of agriculture which have been traced in this chapter signified the fundamental renunciation of *collectivization* of agriculture (although this was not absolutely clear until later in the 1950s).[51] After 1953 the Yugoslav leadership, prodded on by Bakarić and others, came to feel that individual peasant production not only had to be tolerated but had to be actively encouraged—with the qualification that large-scale private holdings were excluded. Nevertheless, the socialist transformation of agriculture remained the goal. Writing in 1959, Kardelj gave an authoritative explanation of the revised Yugoslav Communist conception of that process:

In connection with the question of our acceptance or rejection of collectivization, it is first necessary to be clear what is understood by that term. Is it a specific, historically determined method identified with collectivization of the Stalinist type, or is it the general socioeconomic goal of socialism in the sphere of agriculture, that is, the socialization of the basic means of production and land? If it is the former, we do not see the possibility or the need for its implementation in our conditions, for we consider that that method would produce negative economic and political results. If it is the latter, we could not call ourselves a socialist movement if that were not our goal and if our entire social activity were not directed to that end . . . . The problem of unifying and socializing land—in a country with backward agriculture such as ours—can thus be approached in two ways, by two methods: [1] general collectivization of land on the basis of simple cooperation of labor, with the perspective of the later gradual technical reconstruction of agriculture; or [2] making social investments, through suitable forms of cooperative organizations, in modern means of production, with suitable methods of unifying land parallel to the growth of the scope and economic role of these means of production in agricultural production. We have resolved on the second method. . . .[52]

Elimination of the private peasant as a major agricultural producer remained the long-term goal. Industrialization would draw the bulk of the peasantry into the cities, while its former economic role would be taken over by agricultural enterprises organized on the same basis as enterprises in other sectors of the economy.

With regard to the process of ideological change, Chapter 3 suggested that the CPY's decision to adopt radical collectivization at the Second Plenum was not reached without opposition. Once the Third Plenum had reduced the pace of collectivization and admitted that mistakes had been made in its implementation, opponents of radical collectivization could again seek to influence Party policy. One dissenting view (associated with Kardelj), while not doubting the eventual necessity of work cooperatives, advocated a more gradualist approach emphasizing the general cooperatives as transitional forms. This signified an attempt to return to the pre-1949 gradualism that had been considered a specific feature of the transition to socialism in Yugoslavia. The other, "technocratic" view (identified with Bakarić) sought initially to rationalize economically the work cooperatives but, in 1952, came to view the peasant work cooperative as an economic (and political) liability that had to be abandoned. This viewpoint finally prevailed in March 1953, when permission was given to dissolve most work cooperatives.

It should be noted that this line of criticism arose in Croatia, which was the more economically developed and culturally Western of the two major agricultural surplus regions of the country (the Vojvodina being the other). The peasant movement had been stronger in Croatia prior to World War II than in any other part of Yugoslavia. Hence Bakarić himself had devoted special interest to the peasant question in the interwar period.[53] These factors may account for the strength of the reservations about work cooperatives in Croatia.

As significant as the process by which opposition to the collectivization policy emerged was the degree of resistance it encountered within the CPY, despite the increasing practical agricultural problems. This resistance demonstrated the strength of the Stalinist dogma that only extensive agriculture in the form of large-scale collective farms could achieve socialism in the countryside, simultaneously increasing agricultural production and "reeducating" the peasant. In no other field did the old dogma resist change so strongly. As Dedijer correctly observed, "In this field, blind Stalinism was perhaps most damaging to Yugoslavia."[54] The irony was that it was an aspect of Stalinism that was accepted as Yugoslav doctrine only after the break with Stalin.

The tenacity of the dogma that only collective farms could bring about socialism in the countryside surely stemmed in part from politically motivated fear of the peasant on the part of Communist leaders in a country where peasants accounted for 60 percent of the population in 1953. This fear was evident in the Party's interpretation of the withdrawal crisis of mid-1951 as primarily a *political* challenge to its policies, as proof that the "class enemy" was still strong in the countryside.

The tenacity of the Stalinist dogma on agriculture was, however, further enhanced by the very process of ideological transformation. The doctrine of the socialist essence of state industrial management and the doctrine of collectivization of agriculture were both Stalinist concepts that the Yugoslav Communist leadership, faced with the economic and political pressures resulting from the break with Stalin, finally had to renounce. But the process of ideological change unfolded quite differently in the two cases. Outside the agricultural sphere the break with Stalin led to the formulation, on the basis of a new exegesis of Marxist-Leninist texts, of an antibureaucratic critique prior to the implementation of institutional reforms, justifying and explaining them ideologically. In the case of agriculture, this ideological perspective was totally lacking and could not have been formulated. The withering away of the state and worker self-management were postulated or suggested in the more utopian writings of Marx, Engels, and Lenin; for all three, however, large-scale farms were assumed to be ipso facto superior to small farms and a necessary attribute of socialism.[55]

These factors help to explain why kolkhozes were still in effect being praised in Yugoslavia in 1951, when almost every other feature of the Soviet system had been subjected to a withering ideological critique, and why the criticism of peasant work cooperatives which had been formulated within the CPY by that date had its origins, not in theoretical criticism of Soviet collectivization, but in practical problems of Yugoslav agriculture. This relationship was to characterize the entire course away from Stalinist dogma in agriculture. As Bakarić himself was later to admit, in referring to the agricultural question, "The criticism of practice was—this must be recognized—faster than our theoretical criticism."[56]

Notes

[1] "Zaključci III plenuma CK KPJ o tekućim zadacima borbe za petogodišnji plan," *Komunist* 4, no. 1 (January–February 1950): 9–11, at 10; Kidrič, "O tekućim zadacima borbe za petogodišnji plan," ibid., pp. 46–56.

[2] Petar Stambolić, "Neka pitanja socijalističkog preobražaja naše poljoprivrede," ibid., pp. 57–80, at 59, 66–68.

[3] Kidrič, *Komunist* 4, no. 1: 52–53, 55.

[4] Stambolić, ibid., p. 60.

[5] Tito, Speech of January 1, 1950, *Govori i članci* 4: 353–354.

[6] Kardelj, *Problemi* 2: 14–15 (omitted in the account of the speech first published in *Borba*, January 25, 1950).

[7] *Borba*, January 25, 1950. The authoritative Party history later acknowledged the importance of this session in reviving interest in the general cooperative (*Pregled istorije SKJ*, p. 479).

[8] See the address of Minister of Agriculture Mijalko Todorović to the May 1950 meeting of the Main Cooperative Alliance, the report of Dušan Calić to the Fourth Plenum of the Croatian Party, and the article by Ljubomir Veljković in *Narodna država*, May 1950, all reprinted in M. Todorović, *Za pravilan odnos prema općim poljoprivrednim zadrugama* (Zagreb, 1950). General cooperatives were ignored in the 1950 May Day Proclamation but mentioned again in the 1951 Proclamation (*Borba*, May 1, 1950 and May 1, 1951).

[9] Todorović, *Za pravilan odnos*, p. 7.

[10] Bakarić was by his own account most influenced by the views of Zvonko Sirola, Advisor on Agriculture in the Porec region people's committee, and Ivan Buković, Minister for State Supplies in Croatia (interview in *Politika,* December 24, 1951, reprinted in *O poljoprivredi*, pp. 305–306). Buković first expressed his views in print in a series of articles in *Vjesnik* in early 1951.

[11] Bakarić, "Problem zemljišne rente u prelaznoj etapi," *Komunist* 4, nos. 2–3 (March–May 1950): 1–107, reprinted in *O poljoprivredi*, 241.

[12] In October 1951, in an address to the Croatian Cooperative Alliance (*O poljoprivredi*, p. 295).

[13] Bakarić, "K pitanju privrednog računa i kalkulacije u seljačkim radnim zadrugama," *Komunist* 5, no. 1 (January 1951): 34–56, reprinted in *O poljoprivredi*, pp. 263–287.

[14] Ibid., pp. 288–293. In his address to the Croatian Cooperative Alliance, Bakarić again attacked "bureaucratic" resistance to his proposals (ibid., pp. 305–306).

[15] Todorović, Speech of July 14, 1951, reprinted as *O problemima zadrugarstva i odnosima na selu* (Zagreb, 1951), p. 4.

[16] See the accounts by Tomasevich in Sanders, ed., *Collectivization of Agriculture in Eastern Europe*, pp. 166–192; Brashich, *Land Reform and Ownership in Yugoslavia 1919–1953*, pp. 61–125.

[17] See the graphic account by Vojvodina Communist leader Jovan Veselinov to the Federal Economic Council ("peasants have been arrested and tried by the thousand. There have been fatalities"), as reported in Vukmanovic-Tempo, *Revolucija koja teče* 2: 127–128.

[18] Todorović, *O problemima zadrugarstva i odnosima na selu*, p. 8.

[19] "Uputstvo CK KPJ partiskim organizacijama i rukovodstvima o daljim putevima socijalističkog preobražaja sela," *Partiska izgradnja* 4, no. 1 (February 1952): 36–45.

[20] According to McVicker (*Titoism*, p. 132), at the end of 1950 the Politburo had ordered Todorović's Ministry of Agriculture to consider practical reforms in the organization of the work cooperatives.

[21] General cooperatives were stressed in the 1952 May Day Proclamation (*Borba*, May 1, 1952), while work cooperatives were not mentioned.

[22] This was the theme of the Eighth Plenum of the Croatian Central Committee, held in December 1951. See especially the speeches by Slavko Komar (then emerging as Bakarić's most influential advisor on agriculture) and Ivan Buković (the father of the "economic accounting" scheme), *Vjesnik*, December 12, 1951. See also Ivan Buković, *Prilog pitanju privrednog računa i organizacije rada seljačke radne zadruge* (Zagreb, 1951).

[23] Komar, *Vjesnik,* December 12, 1951; "Ubrzati rad na uvodjenju privrednog računa u zadrugama," *Naprijed,* February 1952.

[24] Bakarić, "Aktuelni problemi našeg zadrugarstva," *O poljoprivredi,* p. 316; D. Pavić, in *Ekonomski pregled* 3, no. 6 (1952): 331.

[25] Bakarić, *O poljoprivredi,* p. 316.

[26] Ibid.

[27] Ibid., p. 320.

[28] M. Ivanović, "The Development of Yugoslav Agriculture," *Review of International Affairs,* October 1, 1952, p. 18 (style improved). Similar views are expressed by Todorović, "O radnoj zadruzi," *Komunist* 6, nos. 1–2 (January–March 1952): 70–97; Krbek, *Odumiranje države,* pp. 15–16.

[29] Tito, Glina speeches of July 27, 1952, *Govori i članci* 7: 137, 153. See Tito's similar remarks in Niš on July 6, 1952, ibid., pp. 118–121.

[30] Dedijer, *Izgubljena bitka,* pp. 411–412, quoting the stenographic record of a personal discussion with Tito on July 1, 1952.

[31] Tito, *Govori i članci* 7: 248–249.

[32] *VI kongres KPJ,* p. 330. See also Bakarić's frank comments at the Zagreb Party school in December 1952, where he explicitly stated that unproductive work cooperatives would have to be abandoned. (*O poljoprivredi,* pp. 331–348.)

[33] *VI kongres KPJ,* pp. 324–328. Todorović formulated an even more radical criticism of the work cooperatives in *Naša stvarnost* 7, no. 1 (January 1953): 15–37.

[34] Kardelj, *Problemi* 2: 315–316. It was apparently at about this time that Kardelj chaired a series of meetings of Party leaders in which he elaborated the point (Vukmanović-Tempo, *Revolucija koja teče* 2: 165–168). As late as February 28, 1953, Tito publicly denied that work cooperatives would be renounced (*Govori i članci* 8: 26–27).

[35] The Regulation allowed peasants to leave with their equipment and land, although they could not withdraw land they had received in the 1945 land reform and had to assume a share of the cooperative's debt. The entire work cooperative could be disbanded if all its members desired; this was mandatory in the case of clearly unproductive ones. Work cooperatives that remained had to be further rationalized economically. See the text in *Službeni list FNRJ,* March 30, 1953, and the account in Neal, *Titoism in Action,* p. 195.

[36] Stambolić, *Komunist* 4, no. 1: 63.

[37] Wheat and corn production, for example, had still not reached the 1934–1938 average by 1953; in 1950 and 1952 (the drought years) it fell below 50 percent of the prewar average. See Doreen Warriner, "Urban Thinkers and Peasant Policy in Yugoslavia, 1918–1959," *Slavonic and East European Review* 38 (1959): 70.

[38] Tito, *Govori i članci* 8: 80.

[39] *Pregled istorije SKJ,* p. 485.

[40] "O nekim problemima naše politike na selu," *Borba,* March 30, 1953, and *Komunist,* April 1953, pp. 223–234, at 227.

[41] Ibid, p.228.

[42] See, inter alia, Tito's interview in *U.S. News and World Report,* April 6, 1953, and his interview of May 22, 1953, *Govori i članci* 8: 92.

[43] A consultative meeting of the Vojvodina Party organization of April 1, 1953, condemned "passivity" and "demoralization" that had appeared in its ranks as a result of the March 30 decree being interpreted as a "retreat." (*Komunist,* April 1953, pp. 290–292.) For a similar report from Macedonia, see ibid., pp. 282–289; for Bosnia-Herzegovina, see *Komunist* May–June 1953, p. 383.

[44] Jovan Veselinov, *Obrazloženje predloga zakona o poljoprivrednom zemljišnom fondu* [speech to the Skupština of May 21, 1953], (Belgrade, 1953), p. 3; partial text in *Borba,* May 22, 1953. This and the following paragraph rely heavily on the

excellent analysis (based on conversations with Kardelj, Veselinov, and other leaders) by Richard Lowenthal, "Modellfall Jugoslawien," *Der Monat* 5 (November 1953): 125–134.

[45] According to Lowenthal, the faction included the top Slovene leaders and the leadership of the Serbian Cooperative Alliance. In the Skupština, Veselinov attacked the "skeptics and critics" of the proposal, calling them "technocrats" who mistakenly saw the small peasant as the bearer of agricultural progress. (*Obrazloženje predloga zakona.*)

[46] As early as April 7, Kardelj publicly hinted at the need for "other measures which would prevent the exploitation of the poor peasantry." ("Dalji razvitak našeg privrednog sistema," *Komunist*, April 1953, pp. 235–254, at 251.) On April 27 he attacked "glorification of the 'economic advantages' of individual peasant production" and "various theories about the profitability of individual holdings." ("Još nešto o našoj politici na selu," *Komunist*, May–June 1953, pp. 333–342, at 336.)

[47] *Službeni list FNRJ*, May 27, 1953.

[48] *Komunist*, May–June 1953, p. 339. See also Djilas's attack on the individual peasant, "Izmjene u politici prema selu," *Nova misao*, 1, no. 5 (May 1953): 677–683.

[49] See Neal, *Titoism in Action*, p. 199.

[50] Bakarić, *O poljoprivredi*, pp. 384–385.

[51] Renouncing collectivization by force, Kardelj told Fred Warner Neal in late 1954, "It may be that we will never develop the kolkholz-type agricultural collective in Yugoslavia. I don't know." (Fred Warner Neal, "Yugoslav Communist Theory," *American Universities Field Staff Reports*, FWN-5-1954, p. 13.)

[52] Edvard Kardelj, *Problemi socijalističke politike na selu* (Belgrade, 1959), pp. 12–13, 17.

[53] Three of Bakarić's prewar articles devoted to agriculture are reprinted in *O poljoprivredi*, pp. 11–51.

[54] Dedijer, *Tito*, p. 426.

[55] See Warriner, *Slavonic and East European Review* 38: 75.

[56] Bakarić, *O poljoprivredi*, p. 10.

9
The New Role of the Party

The Leninist-Stalinist Conception

The doctrine of the elitist Party was Lenin's most significant theoretical contribution to Marxism. Only a well-organized, highly disciplined organization of professional revolutionaries, he maintained in *What Is to Be Done,* could bring about the proletarian revolution. This doctrine rested on the premise that the proletarian's role in the production process alone did not, as Marx and Engels had thought, make him a revolutionary. Only a professional apparatus could transform workers' economic grievances into political demands. The chief instrument of this apparatus was "agitation," which, with whatever distortion of existing reality, would turn the workers against the capitalist system. The historical consciousness of the professional revolutionary thus replaced proletarian class consciousness, and the Party of professional revolutionaries became the general staff of revolution.

It fell to Stalin to first develop a comprehensive doctrine of the postrevolutionary Party, the Communist Party in power. As the "highest form of class organization" of the proletariat and as its "organized vanguard," the Communist Party was—Stalin declared—the "main guiding force in the system of the dictatorship of the proletariat."[1] As such it could not share power with any other party, while it opposed with force enemies of the revolution. It also controlled the state apparatus and mass organizations, guiding them in building socialism. "*In this sense,*" Stalin declared, "it could be said that the dictatorship of the proletariat is, *in essence,* the 'dictatorship' of its vanguard, the 'dictatorship' of the Party."[2] The quotation marks were meant to indicate that the Party did not exercise a dictatorship over the proletariat itself. Yet Stalin himself made perfectly clear the subordination of class to Party when he stated: "The dictatorship of the proletariat consists of the guiding directives of the Party, plus the carrying out of these directives by the mass organizations of the proletariat, plus their fulfillment by the population."[3]

The Party could achieve this hegemonic position in the dictatorship of the proletariat, however, only if it was internally completely united. The doctrine of democratic centralism, which was first formulated by Lenin, purported to combine free intra-Party discussion with absolute unity of action. Lower Party organs would elect higher organs but were subsequently bound to implement their directives. Policies would be discussed within the Party, but once a decision had been made, debate was cut off, and those Communists who had opposed the policy were required to accept it and to work as diligently as its supporters for its implementation. On both points, however, the doctrine itself put the whole emphasis on centralism. The Tenth Soviet Party Congress ban on factions prevented any organized challenge to the Party leadership, guaranteeing that it would be self-renewing. The assumption that there was only one historically correct solution to every problem and the fact that responses to new issues inevitably involved past Party decisions meant that the Party leadership itself set the limits of intra-Party discussion, distinguishing between constructive and destructive criticism and thus reducing the right of free discussion to almost nothing. In Stalinist practice, "democratic centralism" became the justification for the strictist dictatorial centralism.

Before the break with Stalin, and for almost two years thereafter, the Yugoslav Communists unreservedly adhered to the Leninist-Stalinist doctrine of the Party. The CPY's conception of its leading role in postwar Yugoslavia has been outlined in Chapter 2. This doctrine proclaimed not only the leading role of the proletarian class in the new state but also the Communist Party's absolute directive role in mass organizations—the purely proletarian trade union as well as the broader People's Front—and in the state apparatus. Pijade emphasized this point in 1948, in an article comparing the mechanism of people's democracy in Yugoslavia with that of the dictatorship of the proletariat as outlined by Stalin in *Concerning Questions of Leninism* (January 1926). He described the role of the Communist Party in Yugoslavia as follows:

The Communist Party [is] the vanguard of the working class. It is the fundamental leading and guiding force of all mass state and public organizations of the working people of the town and village. It leads the entire working people—the working class, the working peasantry, and the working intelligentsia—united in the People's Front in the struggle for building a socialist society. . . . It runs the state through the organs of people's government. . . . Only the Party of the working class, only the Communist Party is able to unite the work of all mass organizations of the working people and direct them to one goal—building a socialist society.[4]

The internal organization of the CPY, as formulated in the Party statute adopted at the Fifth Congress, was based on Stalinist principles of "democratic centralism."[5]

The Initial Reevaluation

In late 1949, when the Yugoslav Communists began to reexamine the Stalinist doctrine of the transition period from capitalism to communism, they did not exclude consideration of the role of the Party. Tito saw the total identification of Party and state in the USSR as one of the factors responsible for exploitation of the working class by the bureaucratized state.[6] The lesson, Kardelj pointed out, was that a Communist Party in power had to maintain a certain distance from the state apparatus and act as its socialist critic.[7]

In consequence, the proper relation of the CPY itself to the state apparatus in Yugoslavia began to be redefined. The Party, one theoretician explained, would replace its administrative control with "general control of the policies of economic and state organs." The difference, he explained, was that while the Party bore historical responsibility for state policies, it was not required to determine in advance each individual state act. Party leadership (*rukovodjenje*) remained, but this role excluded the "operative, everyday, practical execution of all kinds of minor tasks."[8] Organizational changes prescribed by a Central Committee directive of June 22, 1950, to prevent excessive Party interference in state matters included separating the positions of Party secretary and president of the people's committee at the district level and substituting "collective leadership" for the practice of entrusting individual local Party executive committee members with responsibility for state organs.[9]

Doctrinal restriction of the Party's operative control over the state apparatus was formulated hand in hand with heightened emphasis on political work by the Party and the People's Front among the masses. As the resolution adopted by the Federal Council of the People's Front in January 1950 proclaimed: "Some Front organizations have forgotten that raising the political consciousness of the masses is their most important task."[10] The June 1950 Central Committee directive ordered local Party organizations "to direct all their work to mobilizing the masses, attracting the masses to the business of managing economic affairs, raising the socialist consciousness of the masses."[11]

Mobilization of the masses was considered a necessary condition for engaging them in the affairs of the socialist state, as part of the process of its withering away, and only the Party could carry out this mobilization. The June directive stated:

It is not sufficient merely to foresee new organizational forms and consider that this solves the problem of the masses in managing state affairs. It is necessary to continually develop the creative initiative of the masses, to continually raise the socialist consciousness of the masses. . . . whether or not our measures will represent a mighty revolutionary step in developing the socialist state depends on the ability of the Party organizations to continually develop the creative capacities of the masses and to guide them in conscious participation in managing [state] affairs. . . .[12]

This was true, Djilas explained a few months later, because socialist democracy signified, not a relaxation, but a "further strengthening of the revolution in new forms, . . . a further development of the class struggle." As such, he continued, "the struggle for socialist democracy itself . . . obviously must not and cannot (if it is to be victorious) unfold spontaneously. It must be the organized struggle of the conscious and disciplined vanguard and the conscious and disciplined masses."[13] The withering away of the state, it seemed, required a corresponding strengthening of the Party's mobilizing role among the population.

The Yugoslav Communists started to rethink the Party's role in order to distinguish their system from Stalinism and because the measures of decentralization initiated in 1950 eliminated part of the centralized administrative apparatus through which the Party had exercised control. Yet the exhortation to concentrate on political work among the masses might have suggested that, just as the phase of administrative socialism had necessitated total Party control of society through the state machinery, so socialist democracy could develop only under a differently focused but equally total Party control.

But continuation of the same degree of total Party control of society was neither what in fact occurred nor what was intended by the CPY leadership. By 1950, as has been pointed out, Tito felt that the Soviet threat required a narrowing of the gap between Party and people in Yugoslavia and initiated a series of measures that signified, not heightened "class struggle," but concessions to popular feelings.

This development was, in turn, reflected quite early in the CPY's attempt to rethink theoretically its leading position. A lessening of Party control was in fact implicit in the proclaimed limits on the Party's operative control of the state apparatus, which meant restricting its use of the most powerful instrument of mass mobilization. It was also implicit in the Party's admission that political work among the masses had a second purpose (besides organizing mass participation in state affairs): explaining the conflict with Moscow to ensure continued popular support for Tito's stand.[14]

In the course of 1951 and 1952, CPY spokesmen declared more explicitly that, while Party control was still essential to the system of socialist democracy, the Party could no longer exercise the total social control which it had once enjoyed. This was true functionally; strict "Party-mindedness" (*partajnost*) in literary works, for example, was renounced.[15] The theoretical relationship between Party and class was also reexamined. Writing on the occasion of May Day, 1952, Djilas stressed that the main force of socialism was the working class itself, not (as Stalin held) the apparatus of the state or Party.[16] "Socialism in a backward country is above all a matter of the physical labor of the working class." To be sure, the workers would require their state and Party in some form until the realization of communist society, but neither instrument could replace the working class itself. Moreover, the roles of the two had to be differentiated. While the state would continue to exhibit elements of an instrument of force against the enemies of socialism, the Party had to act primarily as a factor of consciousness, imbuing the working class with its ideals by persuasion.

References to the future withering away of the Party which began to appear in Yugoslavia at this time suggested the same distinction. Kardelj was the first to raise the issue, maintaining in his speech of April 27, 1951, that political parties in general were creatures of capitalist society. While the proletariat required a strong Party to carry out and consolidate its revolution, the one-party system, too, had to wither away as socialist democracy expanded.[17] As Tito put it later in 1951, "When socialism is developed, then the Communist Party too will gradually disappear as a party."[18] This concept followed logically from the CPY ideal of a "free community of producers" that, having abolished the state and classes, would have no need of a political party.

But this talk of the withering away of the Party was not as radical as it might have sounded. Just as in the case of the withering away of the state, by "withering away," the CPY meant, not the end of the Party, but a change in its essence. And even so qualified, no CPY spokesman claimed that the process had yet begun in Yugoslavia. Moreover, the context of the remarks on the withering away of the Party must be borne in mind. They were advanced defensively, usually in contacts with Social Democrats or other non-Communists, to illustrate why socialist democracy, at least in an economically backward country, precluded the existence of a multiparty system. Kardelj's reply to "very progressive people and honest socialists who cannot imagine socialist democracy without a multiparty system" was characteristic.

"We are not such unrealistic formalists that, for the sake of this or that external democratic form, we would be ready to lose the substance, that is, socialism. As long as the historical conditions under which socialism is developing in our country require, the working class headed by its revolutionary Party will ensure, with state means, the un-hampered development of socialism."[19] The references to the wither-ing away of the Party thus did not detract from its present importance; on the contrary, they served to justify its necessity—even if it would no longer exercise total control over society.

These halting steps toward a reformulation of the Communist Party's social role were matched by a certain verbal reemphasis on intra-Party democracy. Tito touched on the subject in early 1951. Reaffirming that Party decisions had to be unconditionally carried out by every member, he nevertheless emphasized the importance of "broad discussion" prior to the formulation of the Party line: "Always keep in mind, comrades, that discussion must be allowed, that Party members must say what they think and that, until a decision is reached, no member can be characterized as a foreign element, a saboteur, or an enemy of the Party."[20] The context of his remarks made clear, however, that he was referring to one particular issue—theoretical questions—and that he was less concerned with encouraging discussion in lower Party organizations than limiting the disorienting effects of theoretical differences in the Party leadership itself—the most obvious case being the different approaches to the Soviet system examined in Chapter 4.

The point of Tito's remarks became the Party line four months later, when the Fourth CPY Plenum resolved: "The works of individual leading members of the Party whcih have a clearly theoretical character must be studied by Party organizations only if the CPY Politburo expressly passes a resolution to that effect. . . . The development of new theoretical views in the CPY unfolds on the basis of discussion and the struggle of opinions."[21] Yet Djilas, in his report to the Plenum, made it quite clear that the Party leadership would continue to set struct limits to intra-Party discusɔion:

. . . every [Party member] has the right to express freely his opinion, orally or in writing, but the Party majority has the right to take appropriate measures against those individuals who depart from the basic principles of internal life or the program of the Party, who break its internal regulations, oppose its line, or refuse to carry out its directives. . . . no one can dispute the Party's right to undertake propa-gandistic and organizational measures as soon as some viewpoint or its advocate in one way or another obviously comes into conflict with the ideological or organizational bases on which the very Party is built or with the decisions and conclusions of its organizations and forums.[22]

The Sixth CPY Congress

Reformulating the role of the Party in the system of socialist democracy and clarification of its principles of internal organization were major concerns of the Sixth CPY Congress (November 1952).

The Sixth Congress confirmed what had been suggested by various CPY sources since 1950: After successfully carrying out the revolution and consolidating it in the phase of administrative socialism, a Communist Party had to turn its primary attention from the administrative-operative task of running the state apparatus to the political task of raising the socialist consciousness of the masses and engaging them in the management of state affairs. In order to distinguish the Party's role in the new stage from its previous role (and even more important, to distinguish it from the Soviet-dominated Communist Parties), the CPY changed its very name to the League of Communists of Yugoslavia (LCY, *Savez komunista Jogoslavije*). (Informally, the name Communists Party was still widely used in Yugoslavia.) The role of the League of Communists was defined by the Sixth Congress resolution as follows: "The Congress considers that, as a result of the development of social relations in the direction of ever more democratic forms of rule, the basic duty and role of Communists is political and ideological work in educating the masses. . . . The League of Communists is not and cannot be the direct operative manager and commander in economic, state, or social life."[23]

Hence the Congress proscribed the total identification of Party and state which Yugoslav Communist critics had previously identified as a major factor in the degeneration of the Soviet socialist order. This doctrinal point found organizational expression in the new Party statute, which abolished basic Party organizations (but not Party aktivs) in the state bureaucracy and in public (that is, formally nonstate) organs.[24] Party members affected by this change would be included in the basic territorial Party organizations. Aleksandar Ranković, interpreting the new statute at the Congress, stressed that the separation of Party and state leadership positions at the local level, which had been ordered in 1950, would continue.[25] (The size and powers of the CC Secretariat were also reduced.)

Limiting their duties of administrative control would free Party organizations for political work among the masses, now usually described by LCY spokesmen as "educating" them. This meant raising their socialist consciousness, or as the new statute put it, "raising the political-ideological consciousness of the workers to the level of consciousness of the Party."[26] This task involved ideological struggle, viewed as all the more important owing to the danger of the spread of

"Western ideas" engendered by the internal political relaxation and rapproachement with the West. "The further democratization progresses," Tito warned the Sixth Congress, "the greater the vigilance of the Party must be."[27]

But educating the masses was clearly considered to be a political as well as an ideological task. As the new Party statute declared, it was the task of the League of Communists "to develop the initiative and activity of the masses for their broadest possible participation in the economic, social, and political life of the country."[28] It was also its task, according to the Sixth Congress resolution, to directly influence state and public organs, not by means of formal directives from Party organs, but through the activity of individual Communists within these bodies. "By means of its political and ideological activity—primarily persuasion—[the LCY] acts in all organizations, organs, and institutions for the adoption of its line and views, or the views of its individual members."[29] The importance placed on that influence in workers' councils, in particular, was evident from the fact that the Congress rejected a proposal to dissolve basic Party organizations in economic enterprises.[30]

This reformulation of the Party's role did not mean that the Party ceased to claim historical responsibility for the proper unfolding of the process of socialist development in Yugoslavia. "The League of Communists not only does not reduce its role in and its responsibility for the successful development of socialism," Tito affirmed, "but further increases its role and responsibility."[31] Tito still described the League of Communists as playing the "leading role" in society, although Ranković claimed that it would achieve this role "on the basis of correct work and broad knowledge of social laws," and not by self-decree.[32] Some of the military terminology of Bolshevism suggesting a hierarchical relationship to society was dropped. The new statute described the League of Communists as the "conscious and most progressive organized section of the working class" (instead of the "vanguard of the working class," as the 1948 statute read) and as "the organized political force of the working class" (instead of its "leading organized detachment"). Yet the new statute still charged the League of Communists with "imparting consciousness to the broad mass of the working class and the working people in general," while Tito told the Sixth Congress that the LCY "correctly guides and organizes our entire social life."[33] As further evidence of the continued importance of the Party, there was no mention at the Sixth Congress of its withering away.[34]

The League of Communists thus affirmed at the Sixth Congress that it would still play the "leading role" in Yugoslav society, although this role would be achieved in a novel, non-Stalinist way. Yet Tito pointed out that its role could not be reduced entirely to an "educational" one. "When I said that in the future the most important role of the CPY will be of an ideological-educational character," he noted, "I did not mean by that that all its other leading functions end. No!" Communists would, he suggested, continue to occupy important state and other public offices "according to their abilities."[35] Ranković further warned that the task of political work among the masses did not end the Communists' responsibility for quite specific daily problems. Attacking the "old practical methods" as the chief danger to proper Party work, he continued:

The second weakness, which has been widespread and which, after the danger of the bureaucratic method of work had been pointed out, led to the other extreme, is that some Party organizations have not displayed an interest in many problems with which they must be familiar and in the solution of which they must participate, in the factory, the institution, and the village. The view has been widespread among many Party members, for example, that all their previous work was no good at all. They understood the primary emphasis on political work to mean that Party organizations should be engaged only in some general and highbrow political problems, not delving into basic problems of the enterprise, village, institution, school, etc. The result has been that some Party organizations remained passive during elections of workers' councils and leaderships of certain mass organizations, as well as during the solving of certain very important political and economic problems in some towns, villages, enterprises, and universities.[36]

The reformulation of the Party's leading role was further complicated by the Party's attempt to redefine its relationship to the People's Front. The resolution of the Sixth Congress defined the Front as a "united and active political organization of conscious fighters for socialism."[37] Reaffirming the doctrine on its wartime role, both Tito and Kardelj admitted to the Sixth Congress that the Front had subsequently stagnated; especially since the inauguration of the Five-Year Plan, it had confined itself largely to mobilizing the population for "voluntary" labor projects. Now the Front would truly become the active political organization of the people. As such, it would provide the organizational framework for the "reeducation" of the masses, which had been proclaimed the Party's chief task. As the Sixth Congress resolution declared, "[the People's Front] is the chief, basic organization in which and through which [Communists'] political and ideological activity must develop."[38]

Three months later the People's Front met in its Fourth Congress (where it changed its name to the Socialist Alliance of the Working People of Yugoslavia). The Fourth Congress seemed to claim a political significance for the Socialist Alliance far beyond what had been said about its role at the preceding Party Congress. In his major speech to the Fourth Congress, Kardelj described the Socialist Alliance as the organization that would determine the basic line of political struggle itself and would exercise control over state and other public organs: ". . . concrete political and other social questions should be solved directly in the organizations of the Socialist Alliance. . . . [The Socialist Alliance] is the political alliance of the working class and the entire working people, who are the ruling force in this socialist land. Through the Alliance they realize their rule politically and determine the socialist policies of their government and of other social organs."[39]

The League of Communists was not granted any "leading role" within the Socialist Alliance; it was, Kardelj maintained, only its "ideologically most consistent section," whose ideological role was clearly distinguished from the political tasks of the Socialist Alliance itself. While it had to struggle ideologically for acceptance of its views, Kardelj said, "the LCY does not consider determination of the political line of struggle for developing socialist relations in our country to be its monopoly." What was more, it did not even claim a monopoly on progressive socialist thought.

These claims went considerably beyond any that had been made at the Sixth Party Congress. For all its ambiguity, the Sixth Congress had suggested that the Socialist Alliance would be an instrument of mass mobilization where, once Party organizations had taken a stand on questions of political importance, individual Communists would seek to "persuade" the masses of the correctness of Party decisions. The Fourth Congress of the Socialist Alliance, on the other hand, seemed to call for an end to the Party's political monopoly and transformation of the Socialist Alliance into the most important political institution in Yugoslavia.

This definition of the role of the Socialist Alliance, it may be suggested, should be viewed, not as a correction of the Sixth Party Congress line, but rather in contradiction to it. The Fourth Congress of the Socialist Alliance concentrated on problems of the Alliance itself, to the exclusion of a balanced view of the total political system. This limited focus, in a situation where the Yugoslav Communists sought to maximize the differences between their new system and Stalinism, led to overemphasis on the role of the Socialist Alliance. A further factor contributing to this overemphasis was the fact that it was Kardelj who defined the role of the Socialist Alliance at the Fourth Congress. The chief ideologue of the new system of socialist democracy, Kardelj was inclined to describe it in very abstract terms. The result was that what he viewed as a future perspective could be interpreted as his prescription for the present—although his other writings from this period reveal that he believed this was impossible.

But there was another, instrumental reason for the overemphasis of the role of the Socialist Alliance at its Fourth Congress. Driven by their international position to expand cooperation with Social Democratic and other non-Communist leftist movements, the Yugoslav leaders recognized that the Party itself—even in the form of the League of Communists—was not a suitable instrument for the task. As a Leninist cadre organization, it was viewed with suspicion by foreign Socialists. On the other hand, if closer international contacts were nevertheless established, penetration of alien "reformist" ideas into the Party itself would greatly increase. Both problems would be solved if the Socialist Alliance were to serve as the instrument of international cooperation. Yet the Socialist Alliance would be taken seriously abroad only if it seemed to play a real political role within Yugoslavia. Thus, it is suggested, with representatives of several European and Asian Socialist parties in attendance, the Fourth Congress intentionally overemphasized the political importance of the Socialist Alliance. (Thereafter the Socialist Alliance in fact represented Yugoslavia in dealings with Social Democrats, including participation in the Asian Socialist International.)

The Party's internal organization was also examined by the Sixth Party Congress. Tito told the Congress in no uncertain terms that the reformulation of the Party's role in society "does not affect the organizational structure of the Party, its democratic centralism."[40] Yet the proclaimed break with the Stalinist conception of the Party was said to require greater intra-Party democracy, which the new Party statute was intended to foster.

The new statute put greater verbal emphasis on a Party member's right to participate in the making of decisions, as well as his duty to execute them. Whereas the 1948 statute had granted the right "to participate in . . . the free discussion of practical questions of Party

policy and influence their solution," the 1952 statute provided for the
right "to participate in the discussion of all questions of League policy
and in the making of its decisions."

The new statute also provided for a certain relaxation of the rigid
organizational centralism sanctioned by the 1948 statute. Republican
congresses were now given the right to determine the "political line" of
the republican Communist organizations, within the framework of the
general LCY political line; the 1948 statute had empowered the
republican congresses to determine only the "tactical line" at the
republican level. The new statute also expressed the desirability of
greater autonomy for the basic Party organizations. It abolished the
right of the Central Committee to appoint local Party organizers
directly responsible to it and gave the basic organizations the power to
accept and expel Party members without reference to higher organs.[41]

At the level of the basic Party organization itself, the new statute
sought to expand the activity of the rank and file, replacing the
political bureaus with a single Party secretary (or, in larger organizations, a three-man secretariat). The statute also gave expression to the
desire to bridge the gulf between the basic Party organization and the
masses, simplifying the admissions procedure (abolishing elaborate
requirements of candidacy and multiple recommendations) and providing for open meetings of the basic organization.[42]

It must be emphasized that these changes in the Party statute, while
sanctioning more intra-Party discussion and a certain autonomous
sphere of action of basic organizations, did not signify, even in theory,
a departure from the doctrine of democratic centralism. The new
statute reaffirmed that, while lower organs should elect higher ones, the
lower bodies were then required to implement the decisions of the
higher organs and that, participating in the making of decisions, all
League members had to "implement them consistently and with
discipline."[43]

The continued validity of the principles of democratic centralism
was particularly stressed at the Sixth Congress by Ranković (who was in
charge of Party organizational affairs). This emphasis was necessary, he
maintained, because many Communists had misunderstood the political
relaxation in Yugoslavia to mean that the doctrine was no longer
applicable. "Lately the phenomenon of petit bourgeois spontaneity has
appeared to a considerable extent in many Party organizations," he
lamented. This had led to the following "monstrous conceptions"
about intra-Party democracy: ". . . that democracy means only the

right of secret ballot on all questions, that democracy means the right
to attend or not attend Party meetings, to pay or not pay [Party] dues,
to carry out or not carry out assignments, and, finally, the right to
discuss the correctness of the Party line."[44] Ranković's defense of
democratic centralism against "petit bourgeois spontaneity" was an
example of an admission made several times in the course of the Sixth
Congress: the political relaxation and turn toward the West had
nurtured the spread of revisionist ideas within the Party itself, just as in
the country at large.[45]

In summary, the Sixth Party Congress confirmed both the League of
Communists' continued historical responsibility for the achievement of
socialism in Yugoslavia and its continued organization on the principles
of democratic centralism. The change of name to the League of
Communists signified, not the surrender of its "leading role," but the
intention to exercise that role in a new way, by "persuasion," and not
command, "abandoning certain harmful methods which originated in
Soviet practice"[46] and focusing on "political and ideological education
of the masses." Yet "education" was never clearly defined. At
times—particularly at the Fourth Congress of the Socialist Alliance—it
was given an almost exclusively ideological content that seemed to deny
the need for political action at all. But if this were to be the essence of
Party work, how could Party *apparatchiki*, whose ideological level was
admittedly very low, be transformed into masters of persuasion? More
often during the Sixth Congress "reeducation of the masses" was
described as a political and organizational, as well as ideological, task.
But if this were to be the essence of Party work, what political and
organizational means were to be used? How could Communists avoid
Stalinist methods and yet not—as Ranković had warned was in fact
occurring—surrender their control entirely at the local level? Whether
the essence of Party work was primarily ideological or political, what if
the masses were not "persuaded" of the correctness of Communist
policies? Did the League of Communists modify its line, did it extend
the timetable for achieving its goals, or did it openly resort to the old
methods? All these questions were raised by the attempt to reformulate
theoretically the special role of a Communist Party in power. Only
practice could provide the answers.

The Aftermath of the Sixth Congress
"The Communist Party has found its true place, its correct role, as the
educator and organizer of the masses," *Partiska izgradnja* editorially

declared on the eve of the Sixth Congress.[47] This confident statement proved to be premature. Party spokesmen could not even agree on what the Sixth Congress had signified. A majority of commentaries in the Party press accurately reproduced the ambiguities of the Congress itself. A good example was a book, *The League of Communists of Yugoslavia and the Marx-Engels League of Communists*, which declared that the Party's "direct leading function" had been replaced by "ideological-educational work."[48] It clearly distinguished the ideological tasks of the League of Communists from the political tasks of the Socialist Alliance, while denying that the League enjoyed a monopoly on socialist consciousness. "Our League of Communists," it proclaimed, "plays as the most perfect instrument and with the purest socialist tones in an orchestra which, in its entirety, plays the melody of socialism."[49] Yet the book declared that the "general leading role" of the League of Communists had increased, that it had to continue to exert direct influence on state and public organizations, and that Communists would continue to occupy the important leadership posts of the country. Withering away of the Party was again mentioned, but as a development that would occur in the historical period of communism.

In another view, the League of Communists remained unambiguously the conductor of the socialist orchestra. Such a "dogmatic" interpretation of the Sixth Congress was expressed by Moma Marković (editor of the Party journal for organizational questions).

In organizations of the League of Communists throughout the country, discussions are being held about political-educational work as the basic task of Communists. Nevertheless, to draw the conclusion that "political-educational work in the masses is the basic task of Communists" is at least insufficient, especially if that phrase is understood to mean that today Communists ought to concern themselves with some kind of general agitation and propaganda, not delving into concrete reality and concrete problems.[50]

Marković cited with approval Ranković's warning to the Sixth Congress that the Party must not ignore daily practical problems; it seems quite likely that a large number of Party *apparatchiki* were similarly attracted to Ranković's words. Even if they could accept verbally the end of the practice of Party organizations' issuing formal directives to state and public bodies, they could not accept the description of their role in society as primarily "educational," for such a term minimized their responsibility for decision making at even the lowest levels of society.

A third viewpoint began to be expressed in the writings of Djilas in the months following the Sixth Congress. In a series of articles,[51] he began to develop those formulations of the LCY and Socialist Alliance Congress proceedings which were most at odds with Stalinism. Dealing with the philosophical concepts of consciousness and spontaneity, Djilas wrote in January 1953 that, while the former was necessary in revolutionary periods, "spontaneity is still and undoubtedly will be for a long time the main force responsible for [historical] development."[52] This was the unexpressed rationale for his affirmation, in another article, that the Leninist type of Party had played out its historical role in Yugoslavia. Once the revolution had been consolidated, he declared, "the *whole* system of [Party] work must change."[53] But that had not yet happened, he implied, the Sixth Congress notwithstanding. Hence the continued danger of *Yugoslav* bureaucratism, which Djilas now began to attack in terms by no other Yugoslav leader: "Bureaucratic conceit, haughtiness, and despotism . . . have appeared on many sides, in more or less all areas of social life [in Yugoslavia]."[54]

The Sixth LCY Congress thus gave rise to differing interpretations of the Party's proper role in society. On the one hand, certain ideologues—Kardelj and Djilas above all—put special emphasis on the Party's ideological role. The real creators of the doctrine of socialist democracy, the ideologues seem to have been carried on by the internal logic of their scheme. However necessary the Party's political role at the moment, they implied, it was important not to stress this but to concentrate on the not-too-distant future, when socialist ideals would prevail in Yugoslavia without ideological differences or even major political disputes. In Kardelj's words, "People will not decide on this or that ideological conception; they will decide the current concrete questions of their lives, and in the process they will in practice develop socialist relations. Here, the common interest of the working man will, undoubtedly, prevail over all other influences."[55] Under these circumstances, the Party would indeed act primarily as the "ideological educator" of the masses. This did not mean, however, that the Party would surrender power; it signified instead a utopian belief in the superseding of political power itself. As Djilas himself explained, ". . . to renounce power is possible and progressive and socialist, but only insofar as that renounced power does not come into someone else's hands, insofar as simply nobody (no other class, party) seizes it."[56]

Many *apparatchiki*, on the other hand, saw that "political power exists—the question is, who exercises it."[57] They consequently believed that Communists must continue to bear responsiblity for quite specific, everyday problems at the local level. This was partially the consequence of the desire of Party activists to retain their own positions of power and prestige. It also reflected a less sanguine—and, as it turned out, far more realistic—estimate than that of the ideologues of the masses' commitment to "socialism" and willingness to follow, without compulsion or even excessive guidance, the policies of the LCY leadership. Having experienced at first hand resistance to Party directives, the *apparatchiki* saw that to "renounce power" at the local level would lead, not to a surge of popular enthusiasm for socialist goals, but to apathy, localism, and a host of other deviations from them.

Either interpretation of the Sixth Congress formulations on the role of the Party portended passivity on the part of the rank and file. If a Party activist took seriously the injunction to be an "ideological educator," he found that he did not know how to persuade. If he heeded Ranković's warning not to stop concerning himself with specific political problems at the local level, he did not know how to do this without falling into the more serious danger, from the Party leadership's point of view, of continuing to employ Stalinist methods.

In practice, such passivity became widespread at the local level in the aftermath of the Sixth Congress, while at the district level and above the old instruments of Party control remained largely intact. The secretary of the executive committee of one district Party organization later described the resulting situation.

When we talk about [executive] committees, especially at the district level, then it must be said openly that the essence of work in them has not changed much, even after the Sixth Congress . . . . Whether we wish it or not, the district committees in most cases have the final and decisive word. Of course, this occupies our political cadres, so that their political work in the Socialist Alliance—among the masses—has been very limited. On the other hand, very often meetings of basic [Party] organizations are forced to invent an agenda . . . . Anything at all is placed on the agenda of the basic organization so that it can have something to discuss and then be able to say: we held so many meetings.[58]

The general validity of this description was confirmed by reports from a series of consultative meetings held in the republican Party Central Committees in spring 1953.[59] These meetings attempted to reaffirm and make more concrete the new conception of the Party's role formulated at the Sixth Congress. They called for less frequent meetings of the basic Party organizations, with their agenda limited to general political and economic questions, excluding specific operational problems of enterprises, mass organizations, and state bodies. It was a Communist's duty to engage himself in political activity primarily *outside* the basic Party organization. Moreover, the old practice of Party "assignments" to non-Party organizations had to be discontinued; each Communist had to be active, not as a Party "delegate," but autonomously, in his enterprise, government office, or mass organization.

Yet the reported conclusion of each of the republican consultative meetings was that this ideal was not being realized. In many places, district Communist leaders continued to employ the old methods of direct control. The meeting in Croatia, for example, discussed many cases of such infractions of the Sixth Congress directives: a district executive committee replacing an enterprise director by telephone, another executive committee opposing a legitimate decision of the local people's committee, a third ensuring its own reelection by improper means, a fourth attacking "good members" of the Socialist Alliance as enemies for rejecting the Party organization's candidates in an election.[60]

At the same time, the Party rank and file, who "were ordered to be active, but no longer knew how," became passive and demoralized.[61] The republican consultative meetings noted that the rank-and-file members were not fulfilling their intended role as autonomous political activists. Each meeting noted that the Party organizations had failed to adjust to the new situation; they faced what Yugoslav theoreticians later quite aptly called the "crisis of the content of work."[62] With the end of the Stalinist pattern of militant campaigns in Party work, the rank and file simply did not know what to do—except to discuss what to do.

This passivity, reinforced by the shock of the abandonment of work cooperatives in the countryside in March 1953, resulted in demoralization in the LCY of such proportions that it threatened to neutralize the ability of the LCY to serve as an instrument of social control. In 1948 Tito had to prevent the Party from being turned into a Soviet instrument; in 1953 he faced the danger of its internal disintegration. In order to counteract that danger, he sought to make absolutely clear that the League of Communists had not abandoned its claim to exercise political control at *all* levels. This was the task of the Second (Brioni)

Plenum (June 1953), which issued an authoritative reinterpretation of the Sixth Congress formulations on the role of the Party. (At the time, LCY spokesmen said that the Brioni Plenum authoritatively explained what the Sixth Congress had resolved. Later, the LCY criticized the Sixth Congress resolution itself for overemphasizing the purely ideological aspects of its "leading role.")[63]

The Brioni Plenum was also influenced by another event of the greatest importance—Stalin's death in March 1953. Soon thereafter, both Tito and Stalin's successors began, slowly and cautiously, to envisage a lessening of the total hostility that had characterized Soviet-Yugoslav relations since 1949—a process that finally led to Khrushchev's apologetic visit to Belgrade in 1955 and the short-lived Soviet-Yugoslav rapprochement of 1956. This altered international situation certainly acted as a brake on political liberalization in Yugoslavia, including a further relaxation of Party control. Although no evidence has come to light, it seems likely that LCY *apparatchiki*, headed by Ranković, argued in Party councils with considerable success that, with Stalin's death, Soviet pressure on Yugoslavia would ease and hence the leadership could now—without returning to Stalinist methods—politically afford stricter Party control.

Nevertheless, it may be suggested, it would be a mistake to attribute the Brioni Plenum's emphasis on increased Party control primarily to Stalin's death. Stronger emphasis on the leading role of the Party would seem to have been necessary in any case, for practice quickly disproved the optimistic assumptions of the Sixth Congress, not that the Party should be removed from power, but that it was capable of achieving its leading role in society in a new way, by "persuasion," and that the population was ready and willing to follow it under such conditions in achieving a socialist society. To be sure, had Stalin lived five years longer and Soviet bloc pressure against Yugoslavia continued unabated, internal change away from Stalinism would probably have proceeded much faster. It seems doubtful, however, that the second stage in the LCY's redefinition of its leading role which began in 1966 with the purge of Ranković could have begun in Yugoslavia in 1953 or 1954, even had Stalin lived. The rapprochement with the West had not entailed significant external pressure on the Tito leadership to modify its Communist institutions.[64] Moreover, the second stage of redefining the Party's role was conditioned not only by the more advanced economic level that Yugoslavia had attained by 1966 (which, inter alia, sharpened acutely the contradiction between modern economic management and Party control in the decentralized, market-oriented economy and exacerbated regional differences in the circumstances of regionally unbalanced growth) but also by the very experience of thirteen years of attempting unsuccessfully to reconcile the twin goals of relaxing and redirecting the Party's leading role while not abandoning control at all levels of society.

Hence it was primarily for internal reasons and only secondarily as a consequence of Stalin's death that the Brioni Plenum of June 1953 underlined the League of Communists' continued responsiblity for the development of socialism in Yugoslavia and placed new emphasis on the need for direct political action by LCY activists. Warning that "individual Communists have ceased to think politically and to react politically," the Plenum, in a directive to all Party organizations, described this passivity as the main distortion of the decisions of the Sixth Congress. As evidence, it pointed to the appearance of the following "negative conceptions":

... that now Communists free themselves of responsiblity for the further development of socialism; that the role of Communists is now reduced to giving lectures; that the development of democratization means that it is no longer necessary to fight antisocialist tendencies and phenomena; that Communists are no longer bound by the positions of organizations and the leadership of the League of Communists in questions of political struggle and socialist development; that abolishing the methods of commanding in the work of Communists means that Communists renounce the struggle for their conceptions and their goals; that Communists do not need to have their own positions, etc.[65]

The directive proclaimed that Communists must raise the "socialist consciousness" of the masses. But this required the prior "ideological elevation of the Communists . . . as conscious political fighters in daily practical struggle and action, and not only by means of general Marxist education." It also meant consolidating the ranks of the LCY in a struggle against "foreign [Western] manifestations" and purging it of "negative" elements.

Significance of the Doctrine

The Brioni Plenum of mid-1953 signaled the end of the first phase of the Yugoslav Communists' post-1948 attempt to reformulate the proper role of a Communist Party in power. The need to distinguish the Yugoslav system from Stalinism, the felt need to reduce the distance between Party and people, and the abolition of some of the centralized state machinery through which the Party had operated—all contributed to that doctrinal effort. The Communist Party renamed itself the League of Communists and declared that, in contrast to Stalinist "administrative-operative" control, it would henceforth focus on "educational" work among the masses. Yet that term remained abstract; when Party spokesmen attempted to give it some content, they did not agree. Some of the ideologues, apparently caught up in the logic of their theory of socialist democracy, stressed the purely ideological role of the League of Communists—an emphasis carried to the extreme in the special circumstances of the Fourth Congress of the Socialist Alliance. On the other hand, leading *apparatchiki*, while considering themselves to be equally anti-Stalinist, believed that Party goals could not be achieved without continued application of direct influence by Party organizations, and hence they emphasized the direct political nature of the new role of the League of Communists. But they provided little guidance on how that role could be carried out in a new, non-Stalinist manner.

The reexamination of the role of the Communist Party in Yugoslavia at this time did not break with the essence of the Leninist conception of the Party as the necessary factor of historical consciousness. While the ideologues were fond of proclaiming that the working class could develop nothing but socialism, they never granted that the working class alone—without its Party—could develop socialism. The LCY doctrine did modify, to a certain extent, the Stalinist relationship between the Party, on the one hand, and the working class and the masses, on the other hand. Yet this difference was more one of practice than theory, for Stalin too had declared, "[the Party] must not command but primarily convince the masses."[66]

Yugoslav Communist doctrine certainly did not diminish the social importance of the Party in relation to the Stalinist conception. The Yugoslav critique of Stalin was not that he had overemphasized the Party but, on the contrary, that he had neglected it, permitting the merger of the Party with an all-powerful state apparatus. Hence, in the LCY view, the Party retained its leading role in society, and this required its continued internal organization on the principle of democratic centralism. ["The question is not whether after the revolution the most conscious forces (the Party) will be the leading forces. The question is how to lead."[67] The attempt to answer this question in doctrinal terms at the Sixth LCY Congress and the Fourth Congress of the Socialist Alliance led to a threat in practice to the leading role itself. Hence the Brioni Plenum, which authoritatively reinterpreted the Sixth Congress, stressed anew the importance of daily political struggle on the part of Communists.

However, the Brioni Plenum resolution did not signify a definitive formulation of the proper role of the Party. Djilas, who had made a special point of criticizing bureaucratism in Yugoslavia in his articles of early 1953, did not agree with the Brioni Plenum's emphasis on greater Party control. Convinced that the Plenum was "one-sided, that it forgot the struggle against bureaucratism, and . . . had somehow to be corrected to a degree,"[68] in the fall of 1953 Djilas began to publish a series of articles that were increasingly critical of the bureaucratic danger to socialism in Yugoslavia and concluded that the Leninist type of Communist Party had become outdated there (and that the once-revolutionary LCY leadership was degenerating into a self-serving bureaucratic caste).[69] Djilas's ideas immediately achieved considerable popularity, and after he refused to retract his sharpest formulations, Tito decided that he would have to be repudiated. The Third CC Plenum, hastily convened in January 1954, condemned Djilas's conceptions as "revisionism" (and his personal attack on the Party leadership as immoral slander) and ousted him from all his Party offices. The Third Plenum (and the related Fourth Plenum, which met two months later) emphasized in stronger terms than had the Brioni Plenum the necessity of continued political control by the LCY. As Tito declared, the "class enemy" would continue to threaten socialism in Yugoslavia for a very long period; dissemination of Djilas's "anarchist" ideas would mean that "in a year our socialist reality would not exist without a bloody battle." In these circumstances, "there can be no question that today Communists have the same responsibility . . . for the correct development of socialism as they had earlier in preparing and carrying out the revolution."[70]

But the Third and Fourth Plenums did not resolve the issue of the Party's leading role either. It would be discussed again in much the same terms at the Seventh LCY Congress in 1958 and at the Eighth Congress in 1964. As Kardelj declared in 1967, ". . . because of unsatisfactory practical solutions, we repeatedly return to discuss anew decisions of principle, instead of finding better solutions for concrete problems."[71] In short, for well over a decade after 1953, the Yugoslav Communists never succeeded in formulating a conception of the proper role of a Communist Party in power consistent and coherent enough to be called a doctrine. As a CC Secretary noted with regret in mid-1966, "it has not been made sufficiently clear what is really meant by the ideological-guiding role of the League of Communists, what it originates in, how it should be exercised, what effect it will have on the organizational forms of the League of Communists, and so forth."[72] For, theory could not resolve the dilemma of the continued existence of a totalitarian Party in a nontotalitarian state. The Party's leading role was continually affirmed, but it could not be defined. Only after 1966, following the purge of Ranković and the devolution of power from the central Party apparatus to the republican Party organizations, were the terms of reference of the Sixth CPY Congress superseded as the foundations of the Leninist Party itself were challenged in theory and practice.

Notes

[1] Stalin, *Problems of Leninism,* pp. 96–102, 197.
[2] Ibid., p. 168.
[3] Ibid., p. 170.
[4] Pijade, "Sistem (mehanizam) narodne demokratije u Jugoslaviji," *Članci,* 1950, p. 12.
[5] "Statut Komunističke partije Jugoslavije," *Odluke V. kongresa,* pp. 49–68 (hereafter cited as *Statut* 1948). In *Izgubljena bitka* (p. 290), Dedijer related how the statute was quickly drafted, with the Soviet Party statute the model.
[6] Tito, Speech of June 26, 1950, *Govori i članci* 5: 224.
[7] Kardelj, Speech of June 25, 1950, *Problemi* 2: 45.
[8] Drago Vučinić, "Partija—politički organizator i vaspitač," *Partiska izgradnja,* 3, no. 1 (February 1951): 29–41, at 31–33.
[9] "Svim centralnim komitetima KP republika," *Partiska izgradnja* 2, no. 6 July 1950): 52–56.
[10] *Borba,* January 24–25, 1950. Vlahović had previously similarly criticized "agitation-propaganda" work ("O radu odeljenja za agitaciju i propagandu," *Partiska izgradnja* 1, nos. 9-10 [November–December 1949] : 13-19).
[11] *Partiska izgradnja* 2, no. 6: 52.
[12] Ibid.
[13] Djilas, *Savremene teme,* p. 49.
[14] For example, "Rezolucija II Zemaljske konferencije KP Hrvatske," in Brkić, *Neposredni političko-organizacioni zadaci,* p. 61.
[15] Milovan Djilas, *Razmišljanja o raznim pitanjima* ([Zagreb], [1951]), p. 23.
[16] "Glavna snaga socijalizma," *Borba,* May 1–3, 1952.
[17] Kardelj, *Problemi* 2: 120–121.
[18] Tito, Interview of November 9, 1951, *Govori i članci* 6: 265.
[19] Kardelj, *Politika* article of October 10, 1951, reprinted in *Problemi* 2: 165.
[20] Tito, Speech of February 16, 1951, *Govori i članci* 5: 351. See Dedijer, *Izgubljena bitka,* p. 407.
[21] "Rezolucija Četvrtog plenuma CK KPJ o teoretskom radu u KPJ," *Komunist* 5, nos. 2–3 (March–May 1951): 5.
[22] Djilas, "O nekim pitanjima teoretskog rada Partije," *Komunist* 5, nos. 2–3 (March–May 1951): 43–51, at 49.
[23] "Rezolucija Šestog kongresa KPJ o zadacima i ulozi Saveza komunista Jugoslavije," *Komunist* 6, nos. 5–6 (September–December 1952): 1–8, at 7–8.

[24] Article 14, "Statut Saveza komunista Jugoslavije," *Komunist* 6, nos. 5–6: 163–174 (hereafter cited as *Statut* 1952).
[25] Ranković, "O predlogu novog statuta KPJ i nekim organizacionim pitanjima Partije," *Komunist* 6, nos. 5–6: 98–129, at 120.
[26] Article 17.
[27] Tito, *Govori i članci* 7: 258.
[28] *Statut* 1952, article 1.
[29] *Komunist* 6, nos. 5–6: 8.
[30] Ranković, ibid., p. 109.
[31] Tito, *Govori i članci* 7: 284.
[32] *Komunist* 6, nos. 5–6: 107.
[33] *Statut* 1952, article 1; *Statut* 1948, pp. 49, 63; Tito, *Govori i članci* 7: 283.
[34] After the Congress, Djilas did claim that "individual functions of the Party . . . should wither away." (*Vjesnik,* November 29, 1952.) In the foreign editions of his biography of Tito (published in early 1953), Dedijer related a conversation with a Western Socialist in which Tito and Kardelj spoke of the withering of the Party (Dedijer, *Tito,* pp. 430–431).
[35] Tito, *Govori i članci* 7: 284.
[36] *Komunist* 6, nos. 5–6: 127–128.
[37] Ibid., p. 7.
[38] Ibid.
[39] Kardelj, "Uloga i zadaci Socijalističkog saveza radnog naroda Jugoslavije u borbi za socijalizam," *Problemi* 2: 340.
[40] Tito, *Govori i članci* 7: 284.
[41] *Statut* 1952, articles 2, 7; *Statut* 1948, pp. 51, 61; Ranković, *Komunist* 6, nos. 5–6: 103.
[42] *Statut* 1952, article 4; Ranković, *Komunist* 6, nos. 5–6: 102.
[43] *Statut* 1952, Articles 6, 2.
[44] Ranković, *Komunist* 6, nos. 5–6: 123.
[45] Tito, *Govori i članci* 7: 257; Djilas in *VI kongres KPJ,* pp. 190–192.
[46] Tito, Speech to the Sixth CPY Congress, *Govori i članci* 7: 284.
[47] "Pred Šesti kongres KPJ," *Partiska izgradnja* 4, no. 4 (September 1952): 277–279, at 278.
[48] Pero Damjanović, *Savez komunista Jogoslavije i Marks-Engelsov Savez komunista* (Belgrade, 1953). A similar interpretation of the Sixth Congress is given in Djordjević, *Ustavno pravo FNRJ,* pp. 89–91.
[49] Damjanović, *Savez komunista Jogoslavije,* p. 89.
[50] Moma Marković, "O stilu rada Saveza komunista Jugoslavije," *Komunist,* January 1953, pp. 19–24, at 21.
[51] "Dvostruka 'filozofska' uloga profesora Nedeljkovića." *Nova misao* 1, no. 1 (January 1953): 37–67; "Kompartije u kapitalističkim zemljama," *Naša stvarnost,* 7, no. 1; "Iskustva Jugoslavije u borbi za socijalizam" [his speech to the Asian Socialist Conference in Rangoon in January 1953], ibid., 7, no. 4 (April 1953): 45–54.
[52] *Nova misao* 1, no. 1: 58.
[53] *Nasa stvarnost* 7, no. 1:7.
[54] *Nova misao* 1, no. 1: 67.
[55] Kardelj, Speech of September 18, 1953, *Problemi* 4: 38.
[56] Djilas, "Početak kraja i početka," *Nova misao* 1, no. 8: 192.
[57] As a then Central Committee member put it in a conversation with the present author.
[58] *Oslobodjenje,* January 8, 1954.
[59] Reports from the meetings in Serbia, Croatia, Slovenia, and Macedonia are in *Komunist,* April 1953, pp. 261–289. The report from the meeting in Bosnia-

Herzegovina is in *Komunist,* May–June 1953, pp. 380–383.

[60] *Komunist,* April 1953, pp. 270–271.

[61] Richard Lowenthal, "Djilas Crisis," *Twentieth Century,* April 1954, pp. 316–326, at 322.

[62] Mito Hadži-Vasilev, "Razvitak društvene uloge komunista," *Komunist,* November 12, 1964.

[63] *Pregled istorije SKJ,* p. 510.

[64] The contrary is argued in Halperin, *The Triumphant Heretic* (p. 215), who stresses the importance of Stalin's death in the LCY leadership's decision to limit internal liberalization.

[65] "Svim organizacijama Saveza komunista Jugoslvije," *Komunist,* July 1953, pp. 451–456, at 451.

[66] Stalin, *Problems of Leninism,* p. 174.

[67] Vranicki, *Historija marksizma,* p. 586.

[68] Remarks to the Third CC Plenum, *Komunist,* January–February, 1954, p. 157.

[69] Collected and translated in Rothberg, ed., *Anatomy of a Moral.*

[70] Tito, *Govori i članci* 9: 14–30, 101–108. See the accounts of the "Djilas affair" in Hoffman and Neal, *Yugoslavia and the New Communism,* pp. 186–196; Halperin, *The Triumphant Heretic,* pp. 216–244; Vukmanović-Tempo, *Revolucija koja teče* 2: 180–191.

[71] Interview in *Borba,* January 15, 1967, reprinted in *Socialist Thought and Practice* no. 25 (January–March 1967): 30–39, at 34.

[72] Mijalko Todorović, speech to the Fifth Plenum, reprinted in *Socialist Thought and Practice* no. 24 (October–December 1966): 30–59, at 36.

III

Conclusion

"The fierceness of the struggle against Stalin and the monstrousness of his methods not only aroused distrust and disappointment among Yugoslav Communists—at least the most idealistic among them—but also spurred them on to strive for a society where such occurrences would be an impossibility. They sought a society that would have to be freer and more permissive toward critical opinions. Yet they remained dogmatists, and it was inevitable, in view of the forces that had produced them and the social realities in which they had fought, that any ideas and practical means which to their minds appeared different from Stalin's had *ipso facto* to become a more faithful interpretation and application of Marx's teaching. To reject Stalin, they had to reaffirm their Marxist faith. First of all, there was a return to Lenin, and, soon after that, to Marx."

Milovan Djilas, *The Unperfect Society*, 1969

10

The Dynamics of Ideological Change

This book has traced the development of Yugoslav Communist ideology from 1945 to 1953, examining in detail the six most important tenets of post-1948 doctrine: the critique of the Soviet system, the re-examination of the nature of the epoch, the withering away of the state, worker self-management, the renunciation of collectivization in agriculture, and the new conception of the leading role of the Party. This final chapter will make explicit conclusions about the *process* of ideological transformation in Yugoslavia.

Emergence of the New Doctrine

Prior to 1948 and the outbreak of open conflict with Stalin, the Yugoslav Communists, after their largely autonomous seizure of power, espoused a doctrine of revolutionary radicalism. Domestically (after a brief interlude devoted to consolidating power and gaining international recognition), they openly proclaimed the socialist character of the people's revolution, the leading role of the Communist Party in the new state, and their socialist goals, which operationally signified centrally directed superindustrialization. The Yugoslav doctrine of people's democracy indicated Tito's intention to repeat immediately in Yugoslavia the forced industrialization campaign of Stalin's "second revolution" at a time when (as manifested in the orthodox theory of people's democracy) Stalin and the other East European Communist leaders considered that conditions had not matured for the radical transformation of the East European societies. In this sense, the Yugoslav Communists were overly zealous programmatic Stalinists.[1]

While this Stalinist orthodoxy was the most visible element of Yugoslav Communist ideology in the immediate postwar period (and the aspect that has been stressed almost exclusively in Western analyses),[2] it was not the only element. While the CPY stressed the relevance of Soviet experience far more than any other East European Communist Party at the time, this did not mean that it viewed the transition to socialism in Yugoslavia as a carbon copy of the Soviet record. Soviet experience had to be studied carefully for its socialist essence, but the Yugoslav transition would embody its own specific features, just as the Soviet transition had included specific Soviet traits. These specific Yugoslav features included three institutions: the People's Front, as a special organized form of the proletarian-peasant class alliance; the People's Army, as a full-fledged fighting force created largely from peasants in the course of Partisan warfare; and the people's committees, as universal, mass organs of government replacing the old state apparatus. The gradualist approach to the socialization of agriculture was also apparently considered a specific Yugoslav feature. These forms were part of a general conception of a specific type of revolution, socialist in terms of its goals and proletarian in terms of its leading force, the Communist Party, but quite un-Leninist in terms of the role of the proletarian-peasant class alliance—in fact, a Communist Party–peasant alliance—in the carrying out of the revolution itself.

The Yugoslav Communist analysis of the international scene in the immediate postwar years was characterized by a degree of radicalness and militancy as great as that manifested internally. According to this analysis, with the deepening general crisis of imperialism resulting from World War II, the world was ripe for revolutions, led by Communist Parties, directed against the domestic bourgeoisie as well as foreign imperialism. Foreign Communist support of such revolutions was seen as a sacred international duty. This was a much more radical approach than the "two camp" analysis formulated by Zhdanov in the fall of 1947; it was the product of a radical, dogmatic, antihistorical universalizing of the Yugoslav Communist revolutionary experience. The specific features of the Yugoslav revolution were in fact viewed by the CPY, not as specifically Yugoslav at all, but as applicable to much of the world; indeed, the Yugoslav revolution was proclaimed to be a model for the expected new wave of worldwide revolutions.

The Yugoslav Communists stressed, on the one hand, the importance of Soviet experience and, on the other hand, the international significance of their own revolution. The two were never considered contradictory; indeed, they were never clearly distinguished prior to 1948. But underlying the Yugoslavs' radical international outlook lay the belief that their own recent revolutionary experience, while incorporating the essential socialist elements of Soviet development, constituted an updating of Soviet experience which was particularly relevant to the post-World War II world.

This doctrinal belief was one sign of an attitude toward the USSR which implicitly differed from that which the Yugoslav Communist leaders had held prior to 1941. Then, they had had no doubts about the validity of Stalin's dictum: "He is an internationalist who unreservedly, unhesitatingly, and unconditionally is prepared to defend the USSR, because the USSR is the base of the world revolutionary movement."[3] But after 1945, proletarian internationalism took on a new meaning for the CPY leaders, if not for Stalin. The Soviet Union had won the total loyalty of so many foreign Communists between the wars precisely because it was regarded as the "base of the world revolutionary movement." Now, in the Yugoslav Communist mind, with the rise of new socialist states—among which Yugoslavia itself had advanced the furthest toward socialism—the world revolutionary movement had at last spread beyond the borders of the Soviet Union. As Kardelj said in 1947, "the capitalist encirclement of the Soviet Union no longer exists." The CPY traced the legitimacy of the new Yugoslav socialist state to a basically autonomous socialist revolution. This meant that, while the Yugoslav Communist leaders never questioned Stalin's ultimate authority prior to the spring of 1948, they had nevertheless created an additional source of Communist authority. Moreover, Yugoslavia was viewed by its Communist leaders as not just another autonomously legitimate socialist state but a *new* socialist state, one with recent revolutionary experience applicable abroad. As such, Yugoslavia was viewed as a revolutionary outpost of the Soviet-led "socialist camp"; it was "an outpost of the democratic and anti-imperialist forces of the world." Yugoslavia's loyalty to the Soviet Union, as the center and "head" of the socialist camp was unquestioned. But, in turn, it expected support from the center, both for rapid industrialization at home and in pursuing its Balkan foreign policy objectives (including assistance to the Greek Communist uprising). Before 1948 the Yugoslav Communist leaders considered themselves to be "Stalin's best disciples." As the author of that phrase, Djilas, put it in 1952: "I believed that everything said about the USSR by its leaders was true, and I honestly and devotedly fought for it just as much as for . . . our revolutionary movement."[4] But the essence of Stalinism was undivided authority and exclusive loyalty; Yugoslav Communist doctrine as formulated between 1945 and 1948 was thus, in spite of the intentions of its authors, a challenge to Stalinism.

The doctrine of an autonomous socialist revolution provided the Yugoslav Communist leadership with the necessary ideological self-justification to resist Stalin in 1948. But defiance of Stalin required the continued support of the CPY, whose members were largely ignorant of the events that led to the June 1948 Cominform resolution but had been thoroughly indoctrinated with the belief that Stalin was infallible. Hence, although the impossibility of compromise must have been rather clear to most Yugoslav Politburo members with Stalin's first letters, the Soviet leader could not be openly opposed. The initial Yugoslav response had to be ostensibly purely defensive. Continued socialist development at home and militant anti-imperialism abroad, the CPY leadership said, would disprove the "slanders" and show that the anti-Yugoslav campaign was a terrible "mistake." But simultaneously with their protestations of continued loyalty to Stalin, the Tito leadership elaborated doctrinally on the specific features of the Yugoslav revolution and socialist transformation, making more explicit both the socialist essence of the revolutionary experience and its specific, mass features. This theoretical activity served to develop an alternative, non-Stalinist source of Communist authority for the CPY, while simultaneously indicating to Stalin that Tito's stand was not weakening.

Once the Party was over the shock of the Cominform Resolution, the Politburo could (and had to) abandon its ostensibly purely defensive posture and pursue an active policy of "defending internationalism." What had been publicly treated as an incomprehensible attack by Stalin on his most devoted followers was now proclaimed to be a conflict of the utmost international and historical importance, a struggle for the principle of equality in relations among socialist states and Communist Parties. That struggle had to be waged in the theoretical as well as the political field. As Djilas told the Second Plenum in January 1949: "It is necessary to undertake serious work on these questions . . . issuing documents and writing books which will . . . begin to work out the essence of the problem."

In this effort to "defend internationalism," the Yugoslav Communist leadership developed, on the basis of its radical international analysis, a revolutionary critique of Soviet foreign policy. In the Yugoslav view, not only had Stalin replaced the Leninist norm of equality among socialist countries with his own practice of complete subordination of other countries to the USSR, but the Soviet Union had abandoned support of foreign revolutionary movements in the interest of consolidating a new imperialist sphere of interest.

The Yugoslav ideologues subsequently extended this revolutionary criticism of Soviet foreign policy to the Soviet internal scene. Pointing first to disturbing signs of "bureaucratism" and "hegemonism" in various areas of Soviet internal affairs, CPY ideologues subsequently challenged the socialist legitimacy of the Soviet system itself. Yugoslav criticism of Soviet internal affairs emerged only in the fall of 1949, with the further sharpening of the Soviet-Yugoslav conflict and after extensive criticism of Soviet foreign policy in itself had raised, for

Marxists convinced of the strict interdependence of foreign and domestic policy, the question of the nature of the Soviet internal system. While the CPY's criticism of the Soviet internal order developed in this indirect way, the normative standard it postulated had been made explicit somewhat earlier. The Yugoslav condemnations in December 1949 of "bureaucratism" and "hegemonism" in Soviet society raised the question of the principles on which a socialist society should be based. The answer had been hinted at several months earlier by Kardelj, in his treatise "On People's Democracy in Yugoslavia," which stressed the necessity of mass participation in the affairs of a socialist state.

Kardelj's treatise signaled a partial revival of the utopian current in earlier Marxist thought which had emphasized the importance of large-scale participation of the citizenry in political affairs in the postrevolutionary period and had warned of the danger to socialist goals posed by the apparatus of the proletarian Party-state itself. This was the view espoused by Lenin himself just before the October Revolution. When, after seizing power, he abandoned the principles he had advocated in *State and Revolution*, their advocacy was taken up, in turn, by the Left Opposition, the Workers' Truth Group, the Workers' Opposition, and the Bolshevik-Leninist Opposition. Rosa Luxemburg, another outstanding Marxist who held such views, wrote: "[The dictatorship of the proletariat] must be the work of the class, and not of a small, leading minority in the name of the class; i.e., it must originate from the continuous active participation of the masses, must be directly influenced by them, must be subordinate to the control of the whole people, and must be borne by the increasing political education of the masses."[5] These words could have been written by a Yugoslav Communist; it was from this revolutionary utopian perspective that the Yugoslav criticism of Soviet internal affairs was formulated. This outlook was, in terms of Communist history, not at all at odds with the radical Yugoslav international analysis. Support for foreign revolution coupled with demands for ensuring real mass participation in running the postrevolutionary socialist state had been the essence of the position of the "Left Opposition" in 1918.

The origin of the revolutionary Yugoslav critique of Soviet foreign policy is clear; it was only the extension of the radical international analysis formulated prior to 1948. The genesis of the antibureaucratic critique of the Soviet internal scene is, on the other hand, far less easy to establish. The antiauthoritarian, egalitarian, utopian current in

Marxism had, of course, never been completely repudiated. Instead, the goals that the Russian Revolution was supposed to achieve had, under Lenin, been postponed and, under Stalin, been increasingly ritualized.[6] The mass mobilization of the Yugoslav Communist revolution brought a certain revival of this tradition. But the revival was partial indeed, more a matter of form than of substance, for while Yugoslav Communist doctrine again emphasized the role of the masses,[7] it placed equal or greater importance on the absolute leading role of the CPY, organized on Bolshevik principles. After 1945 this consciousness of the importance of the masses, while retained to some extent in the theorizing on the Yugoslav revolution, was increasingly neglected in the interest of consolidating total power and under the influence of the Stalinist dogma that socialism meant above all else centrally directed forced industrialization.

After the break with Stalin, the necessity of further developing the doctrine of specific features of the Yugoslav revolution led the CPY ideologues to place renewed emphasis on its mass base. It was at this point that Pijade and Kardelj described the Yugoslav people's democracy as a special *mass* form of a dictatorship of the proletariat. It was only one step further to Kardelj's formulation of May 1949: the mass character of a people's democracy made it a *higher* form of dictatorship of the proletariat than that achieved in the USSR after 1917, since it involved the masses to a greater extent in running the socialist state. Once Stalin's ideological authority had faded, as it evidently had for Kardelj by this time, the contradiction between Stalin's pronouncements on the strengthening of the Soviet state and the teachings of earlier Marxist-Leninist texts—especially *State and Revolution*—about the necessity of mass participation in the affairs of a socialist state was perceived. This process was probably hastened by the importance that Yugoslav doctrine had placed previously on the role of the masses during the revolution.

In the fall of 1949, when the Soviet internal order lost its sanctity for the rest of the CPY leadership, the gap between Stalin's statements and the Marxist-Leninist classics on the issue of the socialist state was generally perceived, and Kardelj's perspective was in principle adopted as a guideline for the future development of Yugoslav society. Emphasis on the importance of mass participation in the affairs of the socialist state has served Communist leaderships in a variety of ways in different political contexts. Antibureaucratic campaigns in the USSR in the mid-1920s served only to further consolidate the power of the central Party apparatus over the state apparatus. Similar campaigns in

Communist China, culminating in the Great Proletarian Cultural Revolution, and in Albania have served as the doctrinal basis for coerced mass mobilization directed against an entrenched Party apparatus. In Yugoslavia in 1949–1950, in contrast, emphasis on mass participation in the affairs of state served as a Marxist framework in which to initiate the limited political decompression that the Tito leadership evidently felt was necessary to ensure itself of the continued support of the predominantly non-Communist Yugoslav population in the protracted conflict with Stalin. This ideological approach justified political relaxation, not as a retreat from socialist goals, not as some kind of neo-NEP, but precisely as a necessary step toward the realization of socialist goals, as a *revolutionary* measure that would decisively differentiate the Yugoslav from the Soviet system in terms of socialist legitimacy.

Hence there developed the doctrine of socialist democracy, the three major components of which—the doctrine of the withering away of the state, worker self-management, and the new conception of the Party's leading role—have been described in considerable detail. Socialist democracy was markedly at odds with the Stalinist concept of the transition period to socialism; it reintroduced into Communist ideology as an operative aim the reign of new social relations which Marx had promised would follow the overthrow of capitalism. Socialism, Yugoslav doctrine asserted, could not be reduced to economic development, although that task had to be carried out in a backward country where capitalism had failed to fulfill its "historical" function. Socialism meant above all achieving new social relations; it was nothing but the process of bringing about a communist society.

As such, Yugoslav doctrine had many points in common with the views of the opposition factions to Lenin and (to a much lesser extent) Stalin, which had rebelled at the abandonment of the ideals of the October Revolution. Yet this element of Marxist thought was revived in Yugoslavia, not from below, but exclusively from above. This explained the emphasis in Yugoslav doctrine, not on mass spontaneity, but on *controlled* mass activity—as manifested in the doctrinal limits to the withering away of the state, the doctrinal requirements of social control of the workers' councils, and, above all, the doctrinal emphasis on the necessity of the Party's continued (albeit redefined) leading role in society.

The CPY revised its doctrine on the socialization of the countryside quite separately from the process of formulating the body of doctrine related to socialist democracy. Renunciation of collectivization had little connection with the new, antibureaucratic ideological conceptions. On the contrary, the dogma that collectivization was synonymous with creating socialism in the countryside led many Yugoslav theoreticians to assume, in the initial stage of working out their anti-Stalinist doctrines, that worker self-management in the factories would be complemented by peasant self-management in the kolkhozlike work cooperatives. It took three years after the organization of workers' councils for practical economic and political difficulties to convince the CPY leadership that the work cooperatives were not viable, not compatible with the new economic system, and not a step toward socialism at all.

Yugoslav doctrine on the nature of the epoch, too, underwent a dramatic change largely unrelated to the emergence of the doctrine of socialist democracy. Beginning in 1950, the CPY's radical international analysis gave way to a more moderate outlook. Directly responsible for this changed view was the rapprochement with the United States and Western Europe after 1949, which was the only way to overcome the almost total political isolation that Stalin had succeeded in imposing on Yugoslavia by the fall of 1949. In Kardelj's words, ". . . it was necessary . . . to find our way in the changed international circumstances."[8] To justify and explain the move toward the West, the CPY formulated a revised analysis of the nature of the epoch by redefining the forces of socialism in the world and in the process denying that they need be exclusivist or militant. In advanced capitalist countries, state capitalism was viewed as the antechamber to socialism, although the need for working-class political action and eventual systemic change was not renounced. State capitalist forms in newly independent and colonial countries—that is, military dictatorships or other non-Communist regimes aiming at modernization—were viewed even more favorably in terms of their role in advancing socialism. Although the CPY's international analysis changed suddenly and dramatically after 1949, the outlooks of 1949 and 1953 proceeded from the same basic assumption: the strength of socialism in the world, the belief that World War II had resulted in its world-historic victory over capitalism. This assumption permitted the forces of socialism to be redefined after 1950. As would be demonstrated again after 1960 in the polemics between the Soviet and Chinese Communist Parties, a confident analysis of the strength of socialism in the world could serve as the basis of an optimistic and more passive gradualism as well as the basis of a militant revolutionary activism.

Theory and Practice

Earlier studies of Yugoslav Communism have often stressed, along with the CPY's Stalinist orthodoxy prior to 1950, the ex post facto nature of post-1948 Yugoslav Communist ideology. It has been suggested that, as such, the transformed ideology was a tool of the leadership in its political struggle with Stalin, something apart from its perception of real events—in brief, not an *ideology*.[9]

The transformed Yugoslav Communist doctrine on domestic and foreign affairs followed and ultimately resulted from Tito's break with Stalin in 1948 and the altered international situation in which the CPY leadership then found itself. As such, post-1948 Yugoslav doctrine as a whole might be termed ex post facto. But such usage is misleading, for it implies that Yugoslav ideology was unique in this respect (more ex post facto than, say, the standard doctrine of people's democracy or later Albanian "dogmatism") and that it had a largely manipulative function, justifying to Party subordinates (strongly motivated by ideology?) the behavior of Party leaders not so motivated. Moreover, the ex post facto explanation ignores the differentiated—indeed, contradictory—process of transformation of various doctrinal components of Yugoslav Communist ideology.

It was shown in Chapter 2 that the doctrine of an autonomously legitimate, new socialist state in Yugoslavia *preceded* Tito's break with Stalin in 1948, as did the related radical international analysis. These doctrines provided the Yugoslav Communist leaders with a source of necessary ideological authority in resisting Stalin—a factor as important for the success of that endeavor as the independent Yugoslav Party and secret police apparatus.

Socialist democracy—the core of "Titoism"—was first articulated in incipient form in 1949 before the CPY leadership had any thought of systemic political reform. As a normative standard, socialist democracy influenced the emerging Yugoslav critique of Stalinism. That critique was useful in the political struggle with Stalin. It was, at the same time, a serious theoretical effort, for it was necessary for the Yugoslav leaders—given their Stalinist past and ideological commitment—to explain, not only to the Party they controlled and the non-Stalinist leftists they attempted to cultivate but also to *themselves*, where Stalin had gone wrong. Yet (as Djilas's self-contradictory position best illustrated), precisely because of that Stalinist past and the derivation of the Yugoslav political system from Stalinism, the CPY was unable to formulate a comprehensive critique of the roots of the degeneration of the Soviet social system.

Enunciated in embryonic form before and elaborated parallel to institutional change, the Yugoslav Communist doctrines associated with the concept of socialist democracy strongly influenced the course of political and institutional change in Yugoslavia after 1948. If political liberalization in some form was necessary for Tito's continued defiance of Stalin, given the international situation of 1948–1953, the doctrines of the withering away of the state, worker self-management, and the new role of the Party suggested, within a Marxist framework, *how* such political decompression could be carried out (and how it could be limited). Without this ideological factor, it would be difficult to explain the establishment of workers' councils, councils of producers, and other organs of mass participation.

It has been argued that in the German Social Democratic movement, utopian elements of Marxism were revived to compensate for the prior emergence of a less militant, more gradualist action program, giving rise to a gap between theory and practice. In the case of the CPY, a radical movement that had assumed power, the revival of ideological utopianism strongly influenced the gradualist transformation of key policies. This led, in turn, to a more concrete and less radical form of that utopianism. With regard to the elements of the ideology related to socialist democracy, the Yugoslav case was characterized neither by ex post facto justification of policy decisions nor by the emergence of a compensatory gap between theory and practice but rather by the interdependent development of theory and practice. Yugoslav Communist ideology was deradicalized; it was transformed, not abolished.[10]

On the other hand, the reactive and synthetic character of other Yugoslav ideological tenets was much stronger. The attempt to reformulate in theoretical terms the role of the Party was in part a case of derivative ideological change. It was developed both as part of the conception of socialist democracy and as a consequence of the institutional changes that eliminated some of the state apparatus through which the Party originally exercised control.

The revised Yugoslav analysis of the nature of the epoch was more clearly ex post facto; the forces of socialism in the world, the perceived strength of which had originally served as the doctrinal basis for a radical foreign policy, were redefined, almost overnight, to justify collaboration with the West in resisting Stalin. This did not mean that the previous ·doctrine was not taken seriously. The CPY's original revolutionary radicalism was one factor postponing such a course of action for two years; only after disavowal by the Chinese (and Vietnamese) Communists and a fruitless search for a "third force" was the rapprochement with the West pursued as a last resort.[11] If Chinese Communist support had materialized, Yugoslavia might have taken the road Albania was to follow ten years later.

Finally, Yugoslav doctrine on the socialization of the countryside was transformed almost exclusively by the "criticism of practice." The CPY made a reluctant, gradual retreat from the dogma of collectivization which triumphed in January 1949 under the sustained pressure of mounting economic and political problems in the countryside. The lack of any preexisting doctrinal perspective of socialized small-scale farming delayed that process considerably—further testimony to the significance of the ideological factor.

In terms of the typology of ideology employed in the Introduction, socialist democracy—especially worker self-management and the withering away of the state—obviously signified a transformation of "action programs." It simultaneously embodied a modification of normative "doctrine" on the nature of socialist society itself, a process that revived (but then limited) the dormant utopian elements of Stalinist Marxism. The revised conception of the Party's role was, in part, a derivative case of such a development. The abandonment of collectivization represented a much more pragmatically induced transformation of an "action program" which only after 1953 involved a change of "doctrine" on the socialization of the countryside. Another, similarly pragmatically induced transformation of an "action program"—the revised approach to Yugoslavia's international position—was related to a reappraisal of the nature of the epoch that modfied fundamental Leninist "doctrine" on the nature of imperialism. This suggests that there is no simple relationship between the primary immediate cause of ideological transformation and its scope. In the Yugoslav case, both more ideological and more pragmatic immediate determinants struck at the "doctrinal" core of Leninism-Stalinism.

Whatever insight it may offer into ideological deradicalization in general, the Yugoslav pattern of ideological transformation is almost certain to prove unique in the history of Communism. The very categories utilized in previous studies of ideological change shed little light on the Yugoslav developments. Ideological change in Yugoslavia was not a case of the initial adjustment of a revolutionary ideology to the demands of social organization and the requirements of political power, when an attempt was first made to establish a political system based on that ideology.[12] It was not a case of a gradual (and largely internal) challenge to the ideology of an established political system from new social forces and competing intellectual concepts.[13] Nor was it an instance of deradicalization of a radical movement either as a result of "worldly success" linked with leadership change (the case of German Social Democracy)[14] or from "worldly failure" (for example, the case of the Swedish Communist Party). In Yugoslavia, rapid deradicalization of revolutionary ideology of a Communist Party in power derived utlimately from a strong external threat in the unique bipolar international system of 1948–1953, when it was doubtful that the CPY leadership could have remained in power without internal relaxation and rapprochement with the Western powers. In quite different circumstances, Albania, faced with a less serious economic, political, and military threat than Yugoslavia faced in 1948 and able to win the Chinese Communist support Tito had sought in vain, would follow an opposite course of ideological and political change after 1959.

Creators of Theory
The post-1948 ideological innovations in Yugoslavia, no less than the political and institutional changes, were introduced exclusively from above. But the new doctrines could not simply be decreed by the Politburo and then passed on in directives to lower Party organizations. This was due to the inherent difficulty of rethinking doctrines which had seemed infallible. The difficult process of working out the new doctrines inevitably gave them something of an inchoate and provisional character; although overt, they were codified only in 1958, in the Party program adopted at the Seventh LCY Congress.[15] Many of the pre-1948 conceptions were rejected, but alternative programmatic formulations could not quickly be devised. This was admitted at the Sixth CPY Congress, which constituted the logical occasion to replace the Stalinist program adopted at the Fifth Congress in 1948. But, as Djilas told the Sixth Congress, a new program could not yet be written:

When the preparations for this congress were discussed in the CPY CC Politburo, the conclusion was reached that too little time had passed to work out [a program] ; moreover, the paths not only of our socialist development but of international events have not yet been outlined completely . . . . It was and still is necessary completely to free ourselves of bureaucratic illusions, both "Soviet" and our own, as well as all kinds of bourgeois democratic confusion . . . .[16]

The inherent difficulty of a sudden ideological reevaluation was compounded by the fact that Tito himself did not play a major innovative role in working out the new doctrines; the label of "Titoism," so often applied to post-1948 Yugoslav Communist doctrine, was in this sense a misnomer. A brilliant revolutionary strategist like Lenin, Mao, and Ho, Tito's background differed from theirs: he was an industrial worker turned Party worker, not a revolutionary intellectual. The task of theoretical innovation thus fell to the ideologue-intellectuals (although, to be sure, Tito had to accept the new ideas before they could qualify as CPY doctrine).[17] Between 1945 and 1948, it is true, Tito himself did play an important role in the CPY's first tentative attempts to explain in theoretical terms the revolution of which he had been the master strategist. Even then, however, most top-level theoretical commentaries were by Kardelj, Pijade, Ziherl, and Djilas—roughly in that order of importance—while Kidrič became the authoritative spokesman on economic theory after early 1946.

The same division of labor continued in the period immediately following the outbreak of open Soviet-Yugoslav conflict, with Pijade distinguishing himself as the CPY's most brilliant—and witty—polemicist. But with the emergence of the doctrine of socialist democracy and the more moderate international analysis, the roles shifted. Thereafter, Kardelj emerged as the undisputed chief Party ideologue on both foreign and internal matters—including, after the abandonment of collectivization, agriculture. Bakarić, who played such an important role in the decision to renounce the peasant work cooperatives, continued to be the chief advocate of the view that the private peasant should not just be tolerated but should be encouraged to become an efficient producer on his small holding. Djilas took the lead in formulating the Yugoslav critique of the Soviet system, but his extreme conclusions were not universally shared in the Party leadership; thereafter, with the exception of his writings on the proper role of the Party, he made little contribution to the working out of the new doctrines until the fall of 1953, when he extended his antibureaucratic analysis of Stalinism to the Yugoslav scene. Kidrič remained the authoritative ideologue on economic matters until his death in early 1953, outlining the rudiments of the theory of the market-oriented economic system. Pijade and Ziherl, on the other hand, made almost no contribution to the new doctrines. (Indeed, Ziherl became known for a time as a prominent Yugoslav dogmatist.)

In contrast to the role of these ideologues, all of whom were active Communist publicists prior to World War II, the other top Party leaders contributed very little to the creation of the new doctrine. One looks in vain through the speeches of General Ivan Gošnjak, France Leskošek, and Blagoje Nešković (the other members of the 1948 Politburo) for any contribution to the development of the new theories. The same was true for Ranković, with the exceptions of his exposé of past secret police excesses in 1951 (which was coupled with a semitheoretical explanation of the importance of "socialist legality")[18] and his speech on Party organizational matters at the Sixth Congress (which was quite significant in defining the new conception of the proper role of the Party).

It was thus a handful of Partisan ideologues who were responsible for the construction of a new Yugoslav Communist theoretical edifice after 1948. It was they who experienced what was at times the agony of changing beliefs previously held to be infallible.[19] The result of their labors testified to the ability of revolutionary intellectuals to influence the course of events in one consolidated revolutionary system.

The inherent difficulty of trying to work out a Yugoslav Communist ideological alternative to Stalinism, coupled with Tito's personally relatively limited innovating role in the process, meant that while (with one exception)[20] the Party leadership remained politically closely united between mid-1948 and mid-1953, political solidarity did not mean complete ideological unanimity. Earlier chapters have pointed out the different approaches to the questions of the critique of the Soviet system, the dogma of collectivization, and the role of the Party which emerged within the top leadership, as well as the differences of opinion among lesser theoreticians on the issues of the withering away of the state and state capitalism. The original appearance of these theoretical differences led to the Fourth Plenum's decision to partly remove purely theoretical matters from the binding discipline of democratic central-ism. That decision, in turn, greatly facilitated the subsequent emergence of divergent theoretical views within the CPY. This was demonstrated most clearly after 1953, in the Djilas affair. It was only as a consequence of the Fourth Plenum that Djilas's articles critical of the Yugoslav system could continue to appear in *Borba* at the end of 1953 even after Tito, Kardelj, and Ranković had privately expressed disagreement with much of their content. The Djilas affair also suggested that ideological transformation was likely to involve acute leadership conflict; it was the strong external threat to Yugoslavia through spring 1953 which initially permitted resolution of that conflict without major personnel changes.

The Relationship to the Marxist Pact

Many aspects of the Yugoslav Communist doctrines developed after 1948 had precursors in earlier Marxist thought. Trotsky was the original author of the concept that the Soviet ruling elite was a bureaucratic caste that had betrayed the proletarian revolution. Karl Renner had described state capitalism in an economically developed country in terms much like those used by Yugoslav theoreticians.[21] During the 1920s a group of Soviet legal theoreticians led by Pashukhanis had theorized about the withering away of the state.[22] Workers' councils not only were a long-standing anarcho-syndicalist demand but had been advocated as management organs after World War I by such Marxists as Antonio Gramsci in Italy and Karl Korsch in Germany.[23] Oskar Lange and other Socialists had developed theories of market socialism in the 1930s. Bakarić's approach to the private peasant in a society proceeding toward socialism had much in common with the views held by Bukharin.

While post-1948 Yugoslav Communist ideology paralleled pre-existing Marxist ideas in many respects, the *direct* influence of earlier Marxist theorists on the development of Yugoslav doctrine was apparently slight in the 1948-1953 period. Exact tracing of intellectual influence is, of course, an impossible task; the ideas of one thinker may eventually influence others in a variety of ways, and it cannot be ruled out that any of the Marxist precursors mentioned here indirectly influenced the development of CPY doctrine after 1948. Apparently, however, the Stalinist ideological heritage of the Yugoslav Communist leaders precluded their being directly influenced by non-Stalinist Marxists in the crucial initial years after 1948. The CPY leaders seem to have had very limited knowledge of the non-Stalinist Marxist tradition (apart, of course, from writings of Marx, Engels, and Lenin themselves), and if they did have some idea (from Stalinist counterpolemics, if from no other source) of what a Renner or a Bukharin had written, they had little motivation to turn to those ideas for ideological inspiration.

Stalin's political attack on the Tito leadership in the spring of 1948 undermined his ideological authority with the Yugoslav leaders—

immediately, in terms of the doctrine of proletarian internationalism, and after mid-1949 in a general sense. But the break with Stalinism did not for a moment bring into question for the Yugoslav Communists the superiority of Leninism over Bernsteinism, Bolshevism over Menshevism, or the Third International over the Second. It did not even lead them to reevaluate ideologically the views of Stalin's opponents in the struggle for power in the USSR after Lenin's death. That this did not happen was testimony to the ideological burden of the CPY leaders' Stalinist pasts.

That past may be recalled briefly. Pijade and Tito himself, both born around 1890, were active in the Social Democratic movement prior to World War I, but they became Communists after the October Revolution and ideological Stalinists in the 1930s. The other important Party ideologues were born too late to have been directly exposed to pre-Stalinist Marxist influence. Kardelj, Kidrič, and Djilas were born in 1910, 1911, and 1912, respectively; the first two joined the CPY in 1928 at the age of eighteen; Djilas joined in 1932 at the age of twenty-one. They thus simultaneously came of age and joined the Communist movement—not as sympathizers, but as disciplined Party members entrusted with increasingly important organizational tasks—in the years when Stalin was taking the final steps to consolidate his power in the USSR and control over the Comintern.

There is ample evidence that in the 1930s the future CPY ideologues' belief in Stalinist dogma was unquestioning. Consider, for example, the case of Djilas. After spending three years in Sremska Mitrovica prison (where the Party continued the ideological education of its cadres in relative freedom), Djilas became a watchdog of Party orthodoxy in literature, engaging in violent polemics with Yugoslav intellectuals who, although considering themselves Marxists or even Communists, refused unthinkingly to follow the Party line. Djilas's warning to Dedijer not to help the leftist surrealist poet Oskar Davičo, who had just served five years in prison for Communist activity, seems to have been typical of his dogmatic orthodoxy at the time: "Vlado, I understand that you have been selling the poems of Oskar Davičo. He is no longer a good comrade . . . . Davičo is basically a surrealist . . . . Don't you know that the Party creates men but it can also destroy them, when they leave the Party line. Oskar is a [Trotskyite], he is dangerous to the Party, and you will have to do what the Party is asking of you."[24]

After his appointment as Secretary-General of the CPY in 1937, Tito set out to "Bolshevize" the Party, to rid it of its bickering factionalism while consolidating his own power. During these last interwar years, the CPY became even more intolerant of the least sign of independent Marxist thought.[25] In the following four years of war and revolution, the new Party cadres were raised almost exclusively on the Stalinist *History of the All-Union Communist Party (b) Short Course.*[26]

The hypothesis that this Stalinist past had largely isolated the Yugoslav Communist leaders from the earlier Marxist heritage is supported by the testimony of former foreign "Titoists" who went with them through the experience of breaking with Stalinism.[27] It is corroborated by Yugoslav theoreticians and academicians in testimony given, not in the days when the leaders had, in any case, to justify themselves as orthodox Leninists, but from the perspective of the 1960s, when a considerable diversity of Marxist thought had developed in Yugoslavia, when a very intensive study of Marsixt thinkers ranging from Bernstein to Mao had begun, and when Lenin himself, while still respected, had almost vanished from the scene as a source of ideological authority. The Zagreb academician Predrag Vranicki, concluding a thorough study of Marxist thought in all its varieties published in 1961, faced up to the fact that many of the ideas which the Yugoslav leaders had claimed great merit for elaborating were in fact very old. "Nevertheless, it must not be forgotten that . . . for thirty years the entire Marxist movement stood in the shadow of theses proclaimed by Stalin and stubbornly repeated in all publications, discussions, books and directives, and that the international practice of the proletariat was directed according to them. Precisely because this was the situation . . . the old ideas had to be creatively [re] discovered on the basis of new historical experience."[28]

Hence, post-1948 Yugoslav Communist ideology was not a direct and conscious revival of its various Marxist precursors but began instead with a new, largely independent exegesis of the writings of Marx, Engels, and Lenin. This exegesis was quite fundamentalist and unsophisticated, resting primarily on a few of the best-known classics— above all, Lenin's *State and Revolution.* Only much later did Yugoslav theoreticians turn to the "young Marx" as a source of legitimacy for their system of self-management; they never devoted particular attention to Lenin's last writings as an eleventh-hour warning of what was to become Stalinism. "Back to Marx and Lenin" was the slogan of the day in the struggle with Stalin. It was also an apt five-word description of what happened initially in the theoretical sphere. Dedijer has recounted how the works of Marx and Engels appeared on the desks of Djilas, Kardelj, and Kidrič in 1949; Djilas (in a passage quoted in full at the beginning of Part III) has attested to this "return to Lenin and, soon after that, to Marx." Vukmanović has revealingly described his own rereading of Marx and Lenin:

Utilizing the experience of the Paris Commune [in the revised law of 1949 on the people's committees] awakened in me a desire to read again the classics of Marxism. Oddly, many things seemed new to me, as if I had never read them. Earlier I had not understood some things and had passed over them, not realizing their importance. Now, however, they seemed somehow closer and more understandable . . . . I found an answer to many questions which appeared in daily life. I saw for the first time that there was a divergence between what the classics had considered to be a socialist society and what Stalin had developed in the Soviet Union . . . .[29]

This return to Marx and Lenin indicated that the CPY's defense of Communist purity after 1948 was not just good tactics; the Yugoslav Communist leaders—Communists in power who sought to perpetuate their position—indeed saw themselves as revolutionary defenders of "Marxism-Leninism." As Wolfgang Leonhard wrote, on the basis of his own experience in breaking with Stalinism: "In the case of officials who have grown up in the Stalinist system, and been educated in its ideology, opposition took its origin from a Marxist standpoint; it was a defense of the doctrines of Marx, Engels, and Lenin against the corruptions of Stalin."[30] And for those who saw themselves as true disciples, the writings of earlier heretics could hold little attraction.

The Doctrine in Perspective

The CPY's doctrine of an autonomous socialist revolution which was formulated prior to 1948 (and is still espoused in essentially the same terms) was a concept of "people's war" which differed from Lenin's theory of revolution and had much in common with Mao Tse-tung's concept of popular revolutionary guerrilla war. Both the Yugoslav and the Chinese concepts stressed the indigenous character of the uprising, the necessity of creating a mobile military force on liberated territory capable of guerrilla and frontal warfare, the importance of the peasantry, an optimistic evaluation of the weakness of imperialism, and the universalization of domestic experience as a model for other countries. These close doctrinal similarities suggested the importance of protracted armed struggle for the radicalization of Communist doctrine.[31]

The doctrine of equal relations among socialist states and Communist Parties which Djilas and Milentije Popović worked out in mid-1949, the first such formulation in Communist history, was a clear alternative to "proletarian internationalism" in the Stalinist sense and the basis of the conception of independent roads to socialism. The concept has remained a cardinal tenet of Yugoslav Communism; after 1956, it was selectively taken over by other Communist states, such as Rumania; it influenced Khrushchev's conception of a less monolithic Soviet bloc, but was opposed anew by the USSR with the enunciation of the Brezhnev Doctrine in 1968.

The Yugoslav critique of Stalinism represented a revolutionary Marxist critique of the Soviet social system under Stalin. After 1955 and the improvement of Soviet-Yugoslav relations, the LCY dropped its extreme interpretations of the Stalinist system as "state capitalism" or "bureaucratic despotism," granting again that some form of socialism did exist in the USSR. This revision notwithstanding, the Yugoslav Communist critique of Stalinism has remained (along with that later formulated by the Communist Party of Italy) the most comprehensive in the Communist world.

The normative doctrine of socialist democracy which complemented the Yugoslav critique of Stalinism, also first elaborated in Yugoslavia, represented a major qualification of the Leninist conception of the dictatorship of the proletariat. After 1956 it influenced the ideological framework of other East European Communist Parties (especially the Hungarian Party since the mid-1960s), although in much-diluted form and with much-reduced implications for liberalization of the political system. The doctrine of the withering away of the state, the first post-Leninist Communist alternative to Stalin's theory of the state, was in some respects a precursor of Khrushchev's "state of the whole people." This doctrine, too, is still affirmed in Yugoslavia, although in recent years LCY theoreticians have shifted their focus to elaboration on the system of socialist self-management as a whole. The doctrine of worker self-management represented the first Communist attempt since Stalin's rise to power to require more of socialism in the economic sphere than simply state ownership; this concept has remained a central tenet of Yugoslav Communist ideology. The revised doctrine of the Party's leading role was the most ambiguous of all the points of doctrine at the conclusion of the period under study. The new concept went beyond Lenin's eleventh-hour warnings of the dangers of Party monopoly, but in the 1948–1953 period, it did not supersede Leninism itself. Only after an interval of thirteen years and the purge of Ranković did the LCY attempt to draw conclusions from its conception of self-managing socialism for the leading role of the Party.

Stalinist dogma on the collectivization of agriculture was gradually renounced in Yugoslavia after 1949; the existence for the foreseeable future of small private farms was declared to be not incompatible with socialism. After 1958 a more systematic conception of the eventual socialization of agriculture by osmosis, as a gradual economic process, was worked out, a scheme that had something in common with the post-1956 Polish Communist views.

The redefined Yugoslav Communist doctrine on the forces of socialism in the international arena broke sharply with the Stalinist "two camp" conception of socialism as a besieged fortress and with Leninist doctrine on the nature of imperialism and the inevitability of imperialist wars. Rejecting Leninist Parties as irrelevant to the capitalist world, the LCY affirmed the desirability of cooperating with Social Democrats and, five years before Khrushchev, granted the possibility of a peaceful transition to socialism. This doctrine was the theoretical foundation for the international posture of nonalignment and active coexistence adopted by Yugoslavia since the mid-1950s.

After 1953 Yugoslav Communist ideology developed a more integral, codified conception of socialist self-management, with its own philosophical assumptions, analytical categories, and terminology— much of which must often have seemed as unfamiliar to Soviet or Chinese Communist theorists as to Western non-Marxists. After 1953 the philosophical component of the ideology underwent a major transformation matching the doctrinal transformation examined in this study. Stalinist dialectical materialism and historical materialism were revised as Yugoslav philosophers drew increasingly on the non-Marxist philosophical tradition.

However, by 1966, when the most recent stage of political and economic reform in Yugoslavia was initiated, it was perhaps questionable whether a Yugoslav Communist *ideology* still existed at all, in the sense that ideology was defined in the Introduction. Certainly Yugoslav Communist thought became increasingly less doctrinaire, more secularized and internalized. Self-management itself became a term of self-legitimization for a number of contending groups within the LCY (including the "conservatives" around Ranković purged in 1966).

Under the rubric of self-management, the doctrine of socialist democracy, in particular, became so secularized that it lost most of its character as an ideological "action program" and was absorbed into a new Yugoslav political culture.[32] In the ensuing search for new theories in the 1960s, many of the doctrines that emerged between 1948 and 1953 were themselves subjected to a critical reappraisal. As one leading Yugoslav ideologue wrote in 1967: "It is at least today sufficiently clear that socialism is a higher and more complex system than merely a struggle against bureaucratic *etatism* . . . . [Hence] it is necessary to 'revalue' theories which, in the preceding phase of the [socialist] transformation, opened the road for new [social] relations. This is why a specific relativization of all 'hard' theories is unavoidable. . . ."[33]

Notes

[1] The adjective "leftist" is best avoided because of the confusion arising from its dual meaning in Western studies of Communism, a duality taken over from Communist literature. The utopian "leftism" of the Left Opposition to Lenin was quite different from the totalitarian "leftism" of Stalin's post-1928 policies. Similarly, in latter-day Poland, the utopian "leftism" of Karol Modzelewski and Jacek Kuroń's "Open Letter" to the Party was quite different from the Stalinist-Maoist "leftism" of the conspiratorial "Communist Party of Poland."

[2] For example, Ulam, *Titoism and the Cominform*, chap. 5; Sherman in Labedz, ed., *Revisionism*, p. 258.

[3] I. V. Stalin, *Sochineniia* 10 (Moscow, 1948): 51.

[4] Djilas, Speech to the Sixth CPY Congress, *VI kongres KPJ*, p. 234.

[5] Rosa Luxemburg, *Die russische Revolution* (Berlin, 1922), pp. 116–117, quoted from F. L. Carsten, "Freedom and Revolution: Rosa Luxemburg," in Labedz, ed., *Revisionism*, p. 63.

[6] These categories were suggested by the discussion in Moore, *Soviet Politics*, pp. 418–425.

[7] The best example was Kardelj's 1945 article "Snaga narodnih masa" ["The Strength of the Popular Masses"] (*Put nove Jugoslavije*, pp. 126–152), which incorporated a strong warning against the danger of "socialist" bureaucracy. Later, however, in an attempt to stress continuity between the wartime and post-1948 periods, Yugoslav theoreticians overemphasized the "antibureaucratic" character of the former, terming it a period of "revolutionary democratic self-management." (Kardelj, "10 godina nove Jugoslavije," *Problemi* 4: 131.)

[8] Kardelj, Speech of April 2, 1951, *Problemi* 2: 144.

[9] For example, Sherman in Labedz, ed., *Revisionism*, p. 257; Halperin, *The Triumphant Heretic*, chap. 13.

[10] This paragraph was stimulated by Robert C. Tucker, "The Deradicalization of Marxist Movements," *American Political Science Review* 61, no. 2 (June 1967): 343–358.

[11] A similar point is made in Ulam, *Titoism and the Cominform*, p. 221.

[12] Moore pointed out five possible fates of the original doctrine in this case: (1) outright repudiation; (2) incorporation of old symbols; (3) postponement; (4) ritualization; (5) implementation (*Soviet Politics*, pp. 422–425).

[13] Bell pointed to four factors challenging the ideology in this case: (1) inherent contradictions; (2) differentiation of Communist-ruled society; (3) influence of Western thought; (4) crumbling of the "walls of faith" (*Slavic Review* 24, no. 4: 599–600).

[14] Tucker, *American Political Science Review* 61, no. 2.

[15] *Yugoslavia's Way: the Program of the League of Communists of Yugoslavia* (New York: All Nations' Press, 1958).

[16] *VI kongres KPJ*, p. 234.

[17] Dedijer and Djilas retrospectively described this process with respect to the idea of worker self-management (see Chapter 7, note 18), while Vukmanović recounted how Tito accepted Kidrič's arguments that (in economic theory) interest need not be regarded as an attribute of capitalism (*Revolucija koja teče*, 2: 151).

[18] Aleksandar Ranković, "Za dalje jačanje pravosudja i zakonitosti," *Komunist* 5, nos. 2–3 (March–May 1951): 6–42.

[19] This is stressed in Neal, *Titoism in Action*, pp. 3–4.

[20] Nešković was dropped from the leadership at the Sixth Congress for opposing the extent of the reconciliation with the West. See Halperin, *The Triumphant Heretic*, p. 174; Vukmanović-Tempo, *Revolucija koja teče* 2: 125–126.

[21] *Marxismus, Krieg and Internationale* (1918) and *Wege der Verwirklichung* (1929).

[22] See Lapena, *State and Law: Soviet and Yugoslav Theory*, pp. 28–32.

[23] See Giorgio Galli, "Italy: The Choice for the Left," in Labedz, ed., *Revisionism*, p. 327. Korsch outlined his views in *Arbeitsrecht für Betriebsräte* (1922).

[24] Vladimir Dedijer, *The Beloved Land* (New York: Simon & Schuster, 1961), p. 267. See also Avakumović, *History of the Communist Party of Yugoslavia* 1: 100, 105; Manès Sperber, "Milovan Djilas," *The New Leader*, July 9, 1962, pp. 11–17.

[25] See Chapter 4, notes 62, 77.

[26] Djilas, Report to the Fifth CPY Congress, *V kongres KPJ*, pp. 191–195. The importance of this text in the training of new cadres was stressed in a wartime article, "Za teoretsko uzdizanje partijskih kadrova," *Borba*, December 13, 1942, reprinted in *Istorijski arhiv Komunističke partije Jugoslavije* 1, no. 2 (Belgrade, 1949): 275–278.

[27] Leonhard and Spittmann interviews.

[28] Vranicki, *Historija marksizma*, pp. 568–569.

[29] Vukmanović-Tempo, *Revolucija koja teče* 2: 141; Dedijer, *Izgubljena bitka*, p. 406; Djilas, *The Unperfect Society*, p. 218.

[30] Wolfgang Leonhard, *Child of the Revolution* (Chicago: Regnery, 1958), p. 426.

[31] The Yugoslav Communists were more radical than the Chinese Communists, however, in terms of their totally negative attitude toward the "liberal bourgeoisie." Posing the question "Who are the 'people'?" in 1949, Mao explained: "At the present stage in China they are the working class, the peasantry, the petty bourgeoisie, and the national bourgeoisie." (*On the People's Democratic Dictatorship*, quoted in Cohen, *The Communism of Mao Tse-tung*, p. 80.) In terms of the postrevolutionary state, as pointed out in Chapter 1, Maoist doctrine was similar to the standard, pre-1948 doctrine of people's democracy.

[32] As suggested in William N. Dunn, "Yugoslavia: National Communist Ideology and Political Integration," unpublished Ph.D. dissertation, Claremont College, 1969, pp. 286 ff.

[33] Mito Hadži-Vasilev, in *Komunist*, January 12, 1967.

Bibliography

This study is based primarily on the following public Yugoslav Communist sources, listed in decreasing order of authoritativeness:
1. The stenographic records of the Fifth CPY Congress (1948) and the Sixth CPY Congress (1952).
2. Central Committee directives and letters, published in *Komunist/ Naša stvarnost* and *Partiska izgradnja/Komunist.* *
3. Doctrinal pronouncements and ideologically significant statements by Party leaders, usually as reprinted in selected or collected works published since the period under study.[†]
4. Ideologically important works by second-level theoreticians and academicians; that is, editorials and articles, primarily in *Komunist/ Naša stvarnost, Partiska izgradnja/Komunist* and *Vojnopolitički glasnik* (organ of the army's Main Political Directorate), and books.

The following other sources have also been used:
1. The autobiographical-historical accounts of Vladimir Dedijer, Milovan Djilas, and Svetozar Vukmanović-Tempo.
2. Retrospective Yugoslav monographs—for example, the authoritative *Pregled istorije Saveza komunista Jugoslavije.* Such studies are somewhat more critical of the past than in other Communist countries; nevertheless, a strong tendency remains to justify all past policies as proper at the time.
3. Personal interviews and conversations with some twenty-five academicians and Party theoreticians in 1964–1965 in Belgrade, Zagreb, Skopje, and Ljubljana, as well as interviews with two German ex-"Titoists."
4. Previous Western studies of Yugoslav developments.

Yugoslav Sources

Books, Pamphlets, and Articles
Bakaric, Vladimir. *O poljoprivredi i problemima sela (Govori i clanci).* Belgrade, 1960.

---

*The title of the CPY ideological journal was changed from *Komunist* to *Naša stvarnost* in 1953, while the title of the journal for organizational matters was changed from *Partiska izgradnja* to *Komunist* the same year. (The "ideological" *Komunist* for 1951–1952 bears the same volume numbers as the "organizational" *Komunist* for 1953–1954, vols. 5 and 6.) In 1957, *Komunist* became a weekly publication of the LCY.

[†]These works are generally reliable, with the exception of the omission (almost always indicated by ellipses) of strongly pro-Stalinist statements in the pre-1948 period. (Posthumously published works are entirely free of such omissions.) Where a pre-1948 or other questionable text is cited from a collected work, it has been compared with the text as originally published.

Bartoš, Milan. "Yugoslavia's Struggle for Equality." *Foreign Affairs* 28, no. 3 (April 1950): 427–440.

Bilandžić, Dušan. *Borba za samoupravni socijalizam u Jugoslaviji, 1945–1969.* Zagreb, 1969.

———. *Management of Yugoslav Economy.* Belgrade, 1967.

Bogosavljević, M., and Pešaković, M. *Workers' Management of a Factory in Yugoslavia.* Belgrade, 1959.

Brkić, Zvonko. *Neposredni političko-organizacioni zadaci partijskih organizacija u radu sa masama. Referat na II. zemaljskoj konferenciji KPH* and *Rezolucija II. zemaljske konferencije KP Hrvatske.* Zagreb, n.d.

———. *O političkom radu partijskih organizacija u novim uvjetima; referat održan na IX proširenom plenumu CK KPH.* Split, [1952].

Buković, Ivan. *Prilog pitanju privrednog računa i organizacije rada seljačke radne zadruge.* Zagreb, 1951.

Četrdeset godina revolucionarne borbe Komunističke partije Jugoslavije; govori rukovodilaca o proslavi 40-godišnjice KPJ. Belgrade, 1959.

Constitution of the Federal People's Republic of Yugoslavia. Belgrade, 1947.

Damjanović, Pero. *Savez komunista Jugoslavije i Marks-Engelsov Savez komunista.* Belgrade, 1953.

———. *Tito na čelu Partije.* Belgrade, 1968.

Dedijer, Vladimir. *The Beloved Land.* New York: Simon & Schuster, 1961.

———. *Izgubljena bitka J. V. Staljina.* Sarajevo, 1969.

———. *Josip Broz Tito, Prilozi za biografiju.* Belgrade, 1953.

———. *Jugoslovensko-Albanski odnosi (1939–1948).* Belgrade, 1949.

———. *Tito.* New York: Simon & Schuster, 1953.

Deleon, A., and Mijatović, Lj. *Kongres radničkih saveta Jugoslavije 25–27 jun 1957.* Belgrade, 1957.

Djilas, Milovan. *Anatomy of a Moral; the Political Essays of Milovan Djilas.* New York: Praeger Publishers, [1959].

———. *Borba za socijalizam u Jugoslaviji i Peti kongres KPJ.* Zagreb, 1948.

———. *Članci, 1941–1946.* [Belgrade], 1947.

———. *Conversations with Stalin.* New York: Harcourt, Brace & World, 1962.

_____ . *Govor u političkom komitetu Organizacije ujedinjenih nacija.* Zagreb, 1949.

_____ . "Klasa ili kasta." *Svedočanstva.* April 5, 1952.

_____ . *The New Class: An Analysis of the Communist System.* New York: Praeger Publishers, [1957].

_____ . *O današnjim zadacima partije.* Belgrade, 1946.

_____ . *On New Roads of Socialism.* Belgrade, 1950.

_____ . *Razmišljanja o raznim pitanjima.* [Zagreb], [1951].

_____ . *Savremene teme.* Belgrade, 1950.

_____ . *Tridesetogodišnjica oktobarske revolucije.* Zagreb, 1947.

_____ . *The Unperfect Society: Beyond the New Class.* New York: Harcourt, Brace & World, 1969.

Djordjević, Jovan. "Local Self-Government in Yugoslavia." *American Slavic and East European Review* 12, no. 2 (April 1953): 188–200.

_____ . *Naše državno uredjenje.* [Belgrade], 1950.

_____ . *Novi ustavni sistem.* Belgrade, 1965.

_____ . "Status and Role of the Executive Organs During the First Stage of Yugoslavia's Political and Constitutional Development." *International Social Science Bulletin* 10, no. 2 (1958): 259–269.

_____ . *Ustavno pravo FNRJ.* Belgrade, 1953.

Dragomanović, Vladimir. *Obeležja Komunističke partije Sovjetskog Saveza danas.* Belgrade, 1953.

Društveno upravljanje u Jugoslaviji; Zbornik članaka i govora 1950–1960. Zagreb, 1960.

Dvadeset godina radničkog samoupravljanja u Jugoslaviji, 1950–1970. Belgrade, 1970.

"Evolution du système d'auto-gestion ouvrière," *Questions actuelles du socialisme* no. 41 (March–April 1951): 101–134.

Geršković, Leon. *Dokumenti o razvoju narodne vlasti.* Belgrade, 1948.

_____ . *Historija narodne vlasti.* Belgrade, 1950–1955. 2 vols.

_____ . *Historija narodne vlasti; predavanja i materijali.* Belgrade, 1954.

_____ . *Historija narodne vlasti (udžbenik za studente Pravnog fakulteta).* Belgrade, 1957.

Hernandes [Hernández], Jesus. *Španija i SSSR.* Belgrade, n.d. (translation of *La Grande Trahison.* Paris: Fasquelle, 1953.)

Istorija medjunarodnog radničkog i socijalističkog pokreta. Belgrade, 1952.

Ivin, Daniel. *Revolution und Evolution in Jugoslawien.* Bern: Schweizerisches Ost-Institut, 1968.

Karaivanov, Ivan. *Kominterna i Kominform.* Belgrade, n.d..

Kardelj, Edvard. *Borba KPJ za Novu Jugoslaviju; informacioni referat na savjetovanju komunističkih partija u Poljskoj.* Belgrade, [1948].

_____. *The Communist Party of Yugoslavia in the Struggle for New Yugoslavia, for People's Authority and for Socialism. (Report to the Fifth CPY Congress.)* Belgrade, 1948.

_____. *Problemi naše socijalističke izgradnje.* Belgrade, 1960–, rev. ed.

_____. *Problemi socijalističke politike na selu.* Belgrade, 1959.

_____. *Put nove Jugoslavije, članci i govori iz Narodno-oslobodilačke borbe 1941–1945.* [Belgrade], 1949.

_____. *Snaga narodnih masa.* Zagreb, 1945.

_____. *Speech Held at the General Assembly of the United Nations Organization.* [September 29, 1948]. [Belgrade], [1948].

Kardelj, Edvard, and Djilas, Milovan. *O agresivnom pritisku vlada sovjetskog bloka na Jugoslaviju; govori održani na VI. zasijedanju Organizacije ujedinjenih naroda.* Zagreb, 1951.

Kidrič, Boris. *O novom finansiskom i planskom sistemu.* Belgrade, 1951.

_____. *Privredni problemi FNRJ.* Zagreb, 1948.

_____. *Sabrana dela.* Belgrade, 1959–1960. 3 vols.

Ko je ko u Jugoslaviji; biografski podaci o jugoslovenskim savremenicima. Belgrade, 1957.

Krbek, Ivo. *Odumiranje države.* Zagreb, 1951.

Lača, Ivan. *O marksističkom učenju.* Belgrade, 1950.

_____. *Uloga svesti u borbi za socijalizam.* Belgrade, 1953.

Laušman, Bohumil. *Kako je umirala čehoslovačka sloboda.* Sarajevo, 1953. (Translation of *Kdo byl vinen?* Vienna, 1953.)

Law on the Five Year Plan for the Development of the National Economy of the Federal People's Republic of Yugoslavia in the Period from 1947–1951; with Speeches by Josip Broz Tito, Andrija Hebrang, Boris Kidrič. Belgrade, 1947.

Leonhard, Wolfgang. *Die Wahrheit über das sozialistisches Jugoslawien.* Belgrade, 1949, 2nd ed.

_____. *Kominform und Jugoslawien.* Belgrade, 1949.

Lewi, Jakow. *Ein Verbrechen gegen die Justiz; über denn antijugoslawischen und antidemokratischen Prozess gegen Rajk und seine Mitangeklagten.* Belgrade, 1950.

Lovrenović, Stjepan. *Ekonomska politika Jugoslavije.* Sarajevo, 1956.

[Lukić, Radomir]. *Materijal za izučavanje teorije države i prava.* Belgrade, 1952.

———. *O narodnoj državi.* Belgrade, 1948.

———. *Teorija države i prava.* Belgrade, 1953–1954. [2nd ed., 1955]. 2 vols.

Mao ce tung [Mao Tse-tung]. *Govori i članci.* Belgrade, 1949.

Marković, Dragan; Mimica, Miloš; Ristović, Ljubiša. *Fabrike radnicima— Hronika o radničkom samoupravljanju u Jugoslaviji.* Belgrade, 1964.

Marković, Ljubisav. *Državni kapitalizam.* Belgrade, 1953.

Marković, Mihajlo. *Revizija filozofskih osnova marksizma u Sovjetskom savezu.* Belgrade, 1952.

Marković, Moma and Laća, Ivan. *Organizacioni razvitak Komunističke partije Jugoslavije (SKJ).* Belgrade, 1960.

Marković, Moma. *Osvrt na razvitak Narodnog Fronta Jugoslavije.* Belgrade, 1948.

Materijal za proučavanje linije KP Jugoslavije: Članci, rezolucije i proglasi KPJ do 1941 godine. [Belgrade], 1946.

Mates, Leo. *Nesvrstanost.* Belgrade, 1970.

Milatović, Mile. *Slučaj Andrije Hebranga.* [Belgrade], 1952.

Miljević, Dj., Blagojević, S., and Nikolić, M. *Razvoj privrednog sistema FNRJ.* Belgrade, 1955, 2nd ed.

Mirković, N. *Socijal-demokratija u Skandinavije.* Belgrade, 1953.

Morača, Pero, and Bilandžić, Dušan. *Avangarda 1919–1969.* Belgrade, 1969.

Narodna skupština FNRJ. Stenografske beleške, 31 Jan 1946– 11 Mar 1954. Belgrade, 1946–1954. 13 vols.

Narodni Front i komunisti. Jugoslavija, Čehoslovačka, Poljska 1938–1945. Belgrade, 1968.

Narodni Front Jugoslavije. Drugi kongres Narodnog Fronta Jugoslavije. Belgrade, 1947.

Nedeljković, Dušan. *Naša filosofija u borbi za socijalizam.* Belgrade, 1952.

O kontrarevolucionarnoj i klevetničkoj kampanji protiv socijalističke Jugoslavije. [Belgrade], 1949–1950. 2 vols.

O neistinitim i nepravednim optužbama protiv naše partije i naše zemlje. Belgrade, 1948.

Perović, Mirko. *Prelazni period od kapitalizma ka komunizmu.* Belgrade, 1953.

Petranović, Branko. "Metodologija i organizacija rada na istoriji SFRJ (prilog pitanju)." *Istorija radničkog pokreta. Zbornik radova-1:* 333–396. Belgrade, 1965.

_____. *Političke i pravne prilike za vreme privremene vlade DFJ.* Belgrade, 1964.

Pijade, Moša. *About the Legend That the Yugoslav Uprising Owed Its Existence to Soviet Assistance.* London, 1950.

_____. *Izabrani govori i članci, 1941–1947.* [Belgrade], 1948.

_____. *Izabrani govori i članci, 1948–1949.* Zagreb, 1950.

_____. *Pet godina narodne države.* Belgrade, 1948.

_____. *Veliki majstori licemerja. Članci povodom budimpeštanskog procesa.* Zagreb, 1949.

Pisma CK KPJ i pisma CK SKP(b). Belgrade, 1948.

Plenča, Dušan. *Medjunarodni odnosi Jugoslavije u toku drugog svjetskog rata.* Belgrade, 1962.

Pregled istorije Saveza komunista Jugoslavije. Belgrade, 1963.

Pregled posleratnog razvitka Jugoslavije (1945–1965). Belgrade, 1966.

Priručnik za istoriju medjunarodnog radničkog pokreta. Belgrade, 1964.

Ranković, Aleksandar. *Izabrani govori i članci, 1941–1951.* [Zagreb], 1951.

Romac, P., and Franić, J. *Workers' Self-Management in Factories.* Belgrade, 1962.

Rukovodioci i štampa SSSR-a o NOB-i i socijalističkoj izgradnji u Jugoslaviji (pre rezolucije IB). Belgrade, 1951.

Savez komunista Jugoslavije. *Borba komunista Jugoslavije za socijalističku demokratiju. VI kongres KPJ (Savez komunista Jugoslavije).* Belgrade, 1952.

_____. *Odluke V kongresa Komunističke partije Jugoslavije.* Zagreb, 1948.

_____. *V kongres Komunističke partije Jugoslavije. Izveštaji i referati.* Zagreb, 1948.

_____. *V kongres Komunističke partije Jugoslavije, 21–28 jula 1948. Stenografske bilješke.* Zagreb, 1949.

_____. *Program i Statut Komunističke partije Jugoslavije.* Belgrade, 1948.

_____. *VI kongres Komunističke partije Jugoslavije (Saveza komunista Jugoslavije) 2–7 novembra 1952; stenografske beleške.* [Belgrade], [1952].

_____ . *Yugoslavia's Way: The Program of the League of Communists of Yugoslavia.* New York: All Nations Press, 1958.

_____ . Centralni komitet. *Istorijski arhiv Komunističke partije Jugoslavije.* Belgrade, 1949–1952.

Savez sindikata Jugoslavije. *Drugi kongres Saveza sindikata Jugoslavije; Zagreb 6–8 oktobra 1951 godine.* Belgrade, 1951.

Sinko, Ervin. *A mi mašodik forradalmunk.* Novi Sad, 1953.

Sirotković, Jakov. *Novi privredni sistem FNRJ; osnove, organizacioni oblici i metodi upravljanja.* Zagreb, 1954.

Slovenska akademija znanosti in umetnosti. *Letopis. Tretja knjiga, 1948–1949.* Ljubljana, 1950.

Šnuderl, Makso, ed. *Dokumenti o razvoju ljudske oblasti v Sloveniji.* Ljubljana, 1949.

Socijalistički savez radnog naroda Jugoslavije. *IV kongres Narodnog Fronta Jugoslavije (Socijalističkog saveza radnog naroda Jugoslavije) 22–25 februara 1953.* Belgrade, [1953].

The Soviet-Yugoslav Dispute. London: Royal Institute of International Affairs, 1948.

Stamenković, Radoš. *O nastanku i karakteristikama državnog kapitalizma.* Belgrade, 1953.

Strugar, Vlado. *Jugoslavija 1941–1945.* Belgrade, 1970, rev. ed.

Stvaranje i razvoj Jugoslovenske Armije. Belgrade, 1949–1952.

Teslić, Vlado. *Kineska revolucija i Moskva.* Belgrade, 1953.

Testimonies That Cannot be Refuted. Statements by Refugee Soldiers of the Soviet Satellite Armies. [Belgrade] : Yugoslav Newspapermen's Association, [1952].

Tito, Josip Broz. [*Dela*]. [Belgrade], 1947–1957. 9 vols.

_____ .*Govori i članci.* Zagreb, 1959–.

Todorović, Mijalko. *O problemima zadrugarstva i odnosima na selu.* Zagreb, 1951.

_____ . *Za pravilan odnos prema općim poljoprivrednim zadrugama.* Zagreb, 1950.

Van Bergh, Hendrek, ed. *Genosse Feind.* Bonn: Berto Verlag, 1962. (Translation of *Zločinstva pod plaštom socijalizma.* Belgrade: Narodna armija, 1953.)

Veselinov, Jovan. *Obražlozenje predloga zakona o poljoprivrednom zemljišnom fondu.* Belgrade, 1953.

Vinterhalter, Vilko. *Tito. Der Weg des Josip Broz.* Vienna: Europa, 1969.

Vlahović, Veljko. *Planovi američkih imperijalista za svetskim gospodstvom i obnovom fašizma.* Belgrade, 1948.

_____ . *Šest godina postojanja narodne države.* Belgrade, 1949.

Vranicki, Predrag. *Historija marksizma.* Zagreb, 1961.

_____ . *O nekim pitanjima marksističke teorije u vezi sa ždanovljevom kritikom Aleksandrova.* Zagreb, 1950. ⁓

_____ . *Prilozi problematici društvenih nauka.* Zagreb, 1951.

Vujanović, Nikola. *O podizanju svijesti radničke klase.* Belgrade, 1953.

Vukmanović-Tempo, Svetozar. *Revolucija koja teče. Memoari.* Belgrade, 1971. 2 vols.

_____ . *Six Years of the Yugoslav Army.* Belgrade, 1947.

White Book on Agressive Activities by the Goverments of the USSR, Poland, Czechoslovakia, Hungary, Rumania, Bulgaria, and Albania towards Yugoslavia. Belgrade, 1951.

Zbornik o radničkom samoupravljanju. Belgrade, 1957.

Ziherl, Boris. *Članci i rasprave.* [Belgrade] , 1948.

_____ . *Dijalektički i istorijski materijalizam.* Belgrade, 1949–1951. [2nd ed., 1952] .

Zogović, Radovan. *Na poprištu.* Belgrade, 1947.

*Periodicals**

Anali Pravnog fakulteta u Beogradu (Belgrade).

Arhiv za pravne i društvene nauke (Belgrade).

Borba (Belgrade and Zagreb).

Ekonomist (Belgrade).

Ekonomski pregled (Zagreb).

Filosofski pregled (Belgrade).

Jugoslovenski istorijski časopis (Belgrade).

Jugoslovenski pregled (Belgrade).

Književne novine (Belgrade).

Komunist (Belgrade). (Title changed to *Naša stvarnost* in 1953.)

Medjunarodna politika (Belgrade). (English edition: *Review of International Affairs.*)

Medjunarodni radnički pokret (Belgrade).

*Full references to articles are to be found in the notes.

Naprijed (Zagreb).

Narodna država (Belgrade).

Naša reč (Belgrade).

Naša zakonitost (Zagreb).

Nova misao (Belgrade).

Oslobodjenje (Sarajevo).

Osvit (Belgrade).

Partiska izgradnja (Belgrade). (Title changed to *Komunist* in 1953.)

Politika (Belgrade).

Praxis (Zagreb).

Pregled (Sarajevo).

Putevi revolucije (Zagreb).

Rad (Belgrade).

Republika (Zagreb).

Sindikati (Belgrade).

Službeni list FNRJ (Belgrade).

Socialist Thought and Practice (Belgrade).

Socijalistička poljoprivreda (Belgrade).

Svedočanstva (Belgrade).

Vjesnik (Zagreb).

Vojnopolitički glasnik (Belgrade).

Other Sources and General Works

Books and Pamphlets

Adamić, Louis. *The Eagle and the Roots.* Garden City, N.Y.: Doubleday & Co., 1952.

Armstrong, Hamilton Fish. *Tito and Goliath.* New York: Macmillan Co., 1951.

Auty, Phyllis. *Yugoslavia.* London: Longmans, Green, & Co., 1965.

Avakumović, Ivan. *History of the Communist Party of Yugoslavia* 1. Aberdeen: Aberdeen University Press, 1964.

Bass, Robert, and Marbury, Elizabeth, eds. *The Soviet-Yugoslav Controversy 1948-1958: A Documentary Record.* New York: Prospect Books, 1959.

Bauer, Otto. *The Austrian Revolution*. London: Leonard Parsons, 1925.

Benseler, Frank. *Die Diktatur des Proletariats in der Verfassung der Föderativen Volksrepublik Jugoslawien*. Regensburg, 1958.

Black, Cyril E., and Thornton, Thomas P., eds. *Communism and Revolution: The Strategic Uses of Political Violence*. Princeton, N.J.: Princeton University Press, 1965.

Bobrowski, Czeslaw. *La Yougoslavie socialiste*. Paris: Librairie Armand Colin, 1956.

Bombelles, Joseph T. *Economic Development of Communist Yugoslavia, 1947–1964*. Stanford, Calif.: Hoover Institution, 1968.

Borkenau, Franz. *European Communism*. London: Faber & Faber, 1953.

Brashich, Ranko M. *Land Reform and Ownership in Yugoslavia, 1919–1953*. New York: Free Europe Committee, 1954.

Brzezinski, Zbigniew K. *Ideology and Power in Soviet Politics*. New York: Praeger Publishers, 1962.

_____ . *The Soviet Bloc: Unity and Conflict*. Cambridge, Mass.: Harvard University Press, 1967, rev. ed.

Brzezinski, Zbigniew, and Huntington, Samuel P. *Political Power: USA/USSR*. New York: Viking Press, 1965.

Cady, John F. *A History of Modern Burma*. Ithaca, N.Y.: Cornell University Press, 1958.

Campbell, John C. *Tito's Separate Road*. New York: Harper & Row, 1967.

Cattell, David T. *Communism and the Spanish Civil War*. Berkeley and Los Angeles: University of California Press, 1955.

Clissold, Stephen. *Whirlwind: An Account of Marshal Tito's Rise to Power*. London: Cresset Press, 1949.

Cohen, Arthur A. *The Communism of Mao Tse-tung*. Chicago: University of Chicago Press, 1964.

Conquest, Robert. *Power and Policy in the USSR*. New York: St. Martins, 1961.

Daniels, Robert V. *The Conscience of the Revolution*. Cambridge, Mass.: Harvard University Press, 1960.

_____ . *A Documentary History of Communism*. New York: Vintage Books, 1962. 2 vols.

Degras, Jane, ed. *The Communist International 1919–1943 Documents*. London: Oxford University Press, 1956–1965. 3 vols.

Denisov, A. I. *Osnovy marksistsko-leninskoi teorii gosudarstva i prava.* Moscow, 1948. (Yugoslav edition: *Osnovi marksisti*č*ko-lenjinisti*č*ke teorije dr*ž*ave i prava.* Belgrade, 1949).

_____ . *Sovetskoe gosudarstvennoe pravo: Uchebnik dlia iuridicheskikh shkol.* Moscow, 1947.

Deutscher, Isaac. *Heretics and Renegades.* London: Hamish Hamilton, 1955.

_____ . *The Prophet Outcast: Trotsky, 1929-1940.* New York: Vintage Books, 1965.

_____ . *The Prophet Unarmed: Trotsky, 1921-1929.* London: Oxford University Press, 1959.

Dimitrov, Georgi. *Govori, *č*lanci i izjave.* Belgrade, 1947.

_____ . *Sachineniia* 12. Sofia, 1954.

Dobb, Maurice. *Soviet Economic Development Since 1917.* London: Routledge & Kegan Paul, 1960, 5th ed.

Dragnich, Alex N. *Tito's Promised Land, Yugoslavia.* New Brunswick, N.J.: Rutgers University Press, 1954.

Draskovich, Slobodan M. *Tito, Moscow's Trojan Horse.* Chicago: Henry Regnery Co., 1957.

Ehrenburg, Ilya. *European Crossroad.* New York: Alfred A. Knopf, 1947. (Yugoslav edition: Erenburg, Ilja. *Putevima Evrope.* Zagreb, 1946.)

Eudin, Xenia, and North, Robert C., eds. *Soviet Russia and the East, 1920-1927: A Documentary Survey.* Stanford, Calif.: Stanford University Press, 1957.

Fabre, Michael Henry. *Théorie des démocraties populaires: contribution à l'étude de l'Etat socialiste.* Paris: A. Pedone, 1950.

Fainsod, Merle. *Smolensk under Soviet Rule.* Cambridge, Mass.: Harvard University Press, 1959.

Farberov, N. P. *Gosudarstvennoe pravo stran narodnoi demokratii.* Moscow, 1949.

Farrell, Robert Barry. *Yugoslavia and the Soviet Union, 1949-1956: An Analysis with Documents.* Hamden, Conn.: Shoe String Press, 1956.

Fetjö, François. *Histoire des démocraties populaires.* Paris: Editions de Seuil, 1952.

Fisher, Jack C. *Yugoslavia: A Multinational State.* San Francisco: Chandler Publishing Co., 1966.

Freedman, Robert Owen. *Economic Warfare in the Communist Bloc.* New York: Praeger Publishers, 1970.

Fundamentals of Marxism-Leninism. Moscow, 1961.

George, Alexander. *Propaganda Analysis: A Study of Inferences Made from Nazi Propaganda in World War II.* Evanston, Ill.: Row, Peterson & Co., 1959.

Gomułka, Władysław. *Artykuły i Przemówienia.* Warsaw, 1962–.

Gottwald, K. *Deset let.* Prague, 1948.

Griffith, William E. *Albania and the Sino-Soviet Rift.* Cambridge, Mass.: M.I.T. Press, 1963.

———, ed. *Communism in Europe* 1. Cambridge, Mass.: M.I.T. Press, 1964.

Guillebaud, C. W. *The Works Council: A German Experiment in Industrial Democracy.* Cambridge: University Press, 1928.

Halperin, Ernst. *The Triumphant Heretic.* London: Heinemann, 1958.

Hamilton, F. E. Ian. *Yugoslavia: Patterns of Economic Activity.* London: G. Bell, 1968.

Hemberger, A. *Das historisch-soziologische Verhältnis des westeuropäischen Anarcho-Syndikalismus zum Marxismus.* Heidelberg, 1963.

Hodgkinson, Harry. *Challenge to the Kremlin.* New York: Praeger Publishers, [1952].

Hoffman, George W., and Neal, Fred Warner. *Yugoslavia and the New Communism.* New York: Twentieth Century Fund, 1962.

Hoffman, Walter. *Marxismus oder Titoismus? Titos Versuch zur Neuordnung gesellschaftlicher Beziehungen im Staate.* Munich: Isar Verlag, 1956.

Hondius, Frits W. *The Yugoslav Community of Nations.* The Hague: Mouton, 1968.

Hunt, R. W. Carew. *The Theory and Practice of Communism.* New York: Macmillan Co., 1960.

Iatrides, John O. *Balkan Triangle: Birth and Decline of an Alliance Across Ideological Boundaries.* The Hague: Mouton, 1968.

International Labour Office. *Workers' Management in Yugoslavia.* Geneva: ILO, 1962.

Joll, James. *The Anarchists.* Boston: Little, Brown & Co., 1964.

Jukić, Ilija. *Tito Between East and West.* London: Demos, 1961.

Kalvoda, Josef. *Titoism and Masters of Imposture.* New York: Vantage Press, 1958.

Kartun, Derek. *Tito's Plot Against Europe: The Story of the Rajk Conspiracy.* New York: International Publishers Co., [1950].

Kase, Francis J. *People's Democracy.* Leyden: A. W. Sijthoff, 1968.

Kautsky, John H. *Moscow and the Communist Party of India.* Cambridge, Mass., and New York: Technology Press of M.I.T. and John Wiley & Sons, 1956.

Kirsavov, V. *IUgoslavskii narod pod vlast'iu fashistskikh naimitov amerikanskogo imperializma.* Moscow, 1950.

Kjosseff, Dino G. *Tito ohne Maske.* [East] Berlin, 1953.

Klugmann, James. *From Trotsky to Tito.* London: Lawrence & Wishart, 1951.

Kolaja, Jiri. *Workers' Councils: The Yugoslav Experience.* New York: Praeger Publishers, 1966.

Kopecký, V. *KSČ & ČSR.* Prague, 1957.

Korbel, Josef. *Tito's Communism.* Denver: University of Denver Press, 1951.

Kousoulas, D. George. *Revolution and Defeat.* London: Oxford University Press, 1965.

Labedz, Leopold, ed. *Revisionism: Essays on the History of Marxist Ideas.* New York: Praeger Publishers, 1962.

Lapena, Ivo. *State and Law: Soviet and Yugoslav Theory.* New Haven: Yale University Press, 1964.

Lazlo Rajk and His Accomplices before the People's Court. Budapest, 1949.

Lenin, V. I. *State and Revolution.* New York: International Publishers Co., 1932.

Leonhard, Wolfgang. *Die Revolution entlasst ihre Kinder.* Berlin: Kippenheuer & Witsch, 1955. (Abridged English translation: *Child of the Revolution.* Chicago: Henry Regnery Co., 1958.)

———. *Sovjetideologie Heute II Die politischen Lehren.* Frankfurt and Hamburg: Fischer Bucherei, 1962.

Lewis, Flora. *Red Pawn: The Story of Noel Field.* Garden City, N.Y.: Doubleday & Co., 1965.

McClellan, W. D. *Svetozar Marković and the Origins of Balkan Socialism.* Princeton, N.J.: Princeton University Press, 1964.

Macesich, George. *Yugoslavia: The Theory and Practice of Development Planning.* Charlottesville: University Press of Virginia, 1964.

McKenzie, Kermit E. *Comintern and World Revolution, 1928-1943.* New York: Columbia University Press, 1964.

Maclean, Fitzroy. *Tito.* New York: Ballantine Books, 1957.

McVicker, Charles P. *Titoism: Pattern for International Communism.* New York: St. Martin's Press, 1957.

Mao Tse-tung. *Selected Works.* New York: International Publishers Co., 1954.

Markert, Werner, ed. *Jugoslawien.* Cologne: Böhlau Verlag, 1954.

Marx/Engels. *Ausgewählte Schriften.* [East] Berlin, 1954. 2 vols.

Meier, Viktor. *Das neue jugoslawische Wirtschaftssystem.* Zurich and St. Gallen: Polygraphischer Verlag, 1956.

Meister, Albert. *Socilisme et Autogestion L'Experience Yugoslave.* Paris: Editions du Seuil, 1964.

Meyer, Alfred G. *Leninism.* Cambridge, Mass.: Harvard University Press, 1957.

Milenkovitch, Deborah D. *Plan and Market in Yugoslav Economic Thought.* New Haven: Yale University Press, 1971.

Mitrany, David. *Marx against the Peasant.* Chapel Hill: University of North Carolina Press, 1951.

Moore, Barrington, Jr., *Soviet Politics: The Dilemma of Power.* New York: Harper & Row, 1965.

Neal, Fred Warner. *Titoism in Action: The Reforms in Yugoslavia after 1948.* Berkeley and Los Angeles: University of California Press, 1958.

Novak, Bogdan C. *Trieste, 1941-1954.* Chicago: University of Chicago Press, 1970.

O'Ballance, Edgar. *The Greek Civil War, 1944-1949.* London: Faber & Faber, 1966.

Ochab, E. *Wieś polska na nowych drogach.* Warsaw, 1946.

O sovetskom sotsialisticheskom obshchestve. Moscow, 1949.

Overstreet, Gene D., and Windmiller, Marshall. *Communism in India.* Berkeley and Los Angeles: University of California Press, 1959.

Pejovich, Svetozar. *The Market-Planned Economy of Yugoslavia.* Minneapolis: University of Minnesota Press, 1966.

Pipes, Richard. *The Formation of the Soviet Union.* Cambridge, Mass.: Harvard University Press, 1954.

Reale, Eugenio. *Avec Jacques Duclos Au Banc des Accusés à la Réunion Constitutive du Kominform à Szklarska Poreba.* Paris: Librairie Plon, 1958.

Rosenberg, Arthur. *A History of Bolshevism.* New York: Russell & Russell, 1965. (Translation of *Geschichte des Bolschevismus* [1932].)

Rubinstein, Alvin Z. *Yugoslavia and the Nonaligned World.* Princeton, N.J.: Princeton University Press, 1970.

Sanders, Irwin T., ed. *Collectivization of Agriculture in Eastern Europe.* [Lexington, Ky.] : University of Kentucky Press, [1958] .

Schleicher, Harry. *Das System der betrieblichen Selbstverwaltung in Jugoslawien.* Berlin: Duncker & Humbolt, 1961.

Schurmann, Franz. *Ideology and Organization in Communist China.* Berkeley and Los Angeles: University of California Press, 1966.

Schweissguth, Edmund. *Die Entwicklung des Bundesverfassungsrechts der Föderativen Volksrepublik Jugoslawien.* Frankfurt: Verlag für internationalen Kulturaustausch, 1960.

Seton-Watson, Hugh. *The East European Revolution.* New York: Praeger Publishers, 1951.

Shachtman, Max, ed. *The New Course: The Struggle for the New Course.* Ann Arbor: University of Michigan Press, 1965.

Shoup, Paul. *Communism and the Yugoslav National Question.* New York: Columbia University Press, 1968.

Shulman, Marshall D. *Stalin's Foreign Policy Reappraised.* Cambridge, Mass.: Harvard University Press, 1963.

Spulber, Nicolas. *The Economics of Communist Eastern Europe.* Cambridge, Mass., and New York: Technology Press of M.I.T. and John Wiley & Sons, 1957.

Stalin, I. V. *Problems of Leninism.* Moscow, 1954.

_____ . *Sochineniia* 10. Moscow, 1948.

_____ . *Works* 12. Moscow, 1953.

Sturmthal, Adolf F. *Workers Councils: A Study of the Workplace Organization on Both Sides of the Iron Curtain.* Cambridge, Mass.: Harvard University Press, 1964.

Tomasic, Dinko. *National Communism and Soviet Strategy.* Washington, D.C.: Public Affairs Press, 1957.

Trotsky, Leon. *The Revolution Betrayed.* New York: Pioneer Publishers, 1945.

Tucker, Robert C., and Cohen, Stephen F., eds. *The Great Purge Trial.* New York: Grosset & Dunlap, 1965.

Ulam, Adam B. *Titoism and the Cominform.* Cambridge, Mass.: Harvard University Press, 1952.

U.S., Congress, Senate, Committee on the Judiciary. *Yugoslav Communism: A Critical Study* [by Charles Zalar] . Washington, D.C.: Government Printing Office, 1961.

U.S., Department of State, Office of Public Affairs. *Yugoslavia: Titoism and U.S. Foreign Policy.* Washington, D.C.: Government Printing Office, 1952.

Varga, E. *Izmeneniia v ekonomike kapitalizma v itoge vtoroi mirivoi voiny.* Moscow, 1946.

Vucinich, Wayne S., ed. *Contemporary Yugoslavia.* Berkeley and Los Angeles: University of California Press, 1969.

Warriner, Doreen. *Revolution in Eastern Europe.* London: Turnstile Press, 1950.

Waterston, Albert. *Planning in Yugoslavia.* Baltimore: Johns Hopkins Press, 1962.

Wolff, Robert Lee. *The Balkans in our Time.* Cambridge, Mass.: Harvard University Press, 1956.

Wolter, Hans Henning. *Die Entwicklung der kommunistischen Bewegung Jugoslawiens. Der Kampf um die Machtergreifung und den Ausbau der sozialistischen Ordnung.* Munich, 1960.

Yugoslavia. New York: Free Europe Committee, 1957.

Zagoria, Donald S. *The Sino-Soviet Conflict, 1956–1961.* Princeton, N. J.: Princeton University Press, 1962.

Zaninovich, M. George. *The Development of Socialist Yugoslavia.* Baltimore: Johns Hopkins Press, 1968.

Zhdanov, A. *O mezhdunarodnom polozhenii.* [Moscow], 1947.

Zilliacus, Konni. *Tito of Yugoslavia.* London: Michael Joseph, [1952].

Articles

Adamiak, Richard. "The 'Withering Away' of the State: A Reconsideration." *The Journal of Politics* 32, no. 1 (February 1970): 3–18.

Auty, Phyllis. "Popular Front in the Balkans: 1. Yugoslavia." *Journal of Contemporary History* 5, no. 3 (1970): 51–67.

Bell, Daniel. "Ideology and Soviet Politics" [with comments by George Lichtheim and Carl J. Friedrich]. *Slavic Review* 24, no. 4 (December 1965): 591–621.

———. "Ten Theories in Search of Reality: The Prediction of Soviet Behavior in the Social Sciences." In Alexander Dallin, ed., *Soviet Conduct in World Affairs.* New York: Columbia University Press, 1960.

Bosnitch, Sava D. "The Significance of the Soviet Military Intervention in Jugoslavia 1944–45." *Review* (Study Center for Yugoslav Affairs) no. 8 (1969): 695–710.

Brown, Giles T. "The Dialectic Gulf between Tito and Moscow." *World Affairs Quarterly* 28, no. 4 (January 1958): 377–397.

Byrnes, Robert F. "Heresy in Yugoslavia." *Current History* 33, no. 191 (July 1957): 16–21.

Carpenter, Donald L. [Review of *Ustavno pravo FNRJ*, by Jovan Djordjević]. *American Slavic and East Eurpoean Review* 13, no. 4 (December 1954): 609–612.

Comey, David. "Marxist-Leninist Ideology and Soviet Policy." *Studies in Soviet Thought* 2, no. 4 (December 1962): 301–320.

Daniels, Robert V. "The State and Revolution: A Case Study in the Genesis and Transformation of Communist Ideology." *American Slavic and East European Review* 12, no. 1 (February 1953): 23–43.

Dean, Vera Michels. "Yugoslavia: A New Form of Communism?" *Foreign Policy Reports* 27 (May 1, 1951): 38–47.

Dragnich, Alex N. "How Different Is Tito's Communism?" *American Political Science Review* 6, no. 1 (March 1957): 112–114.

_____ . "Recent Political Developments in Yugoslavia." *Journal of Politics* 20, no. 1 (February 1958): 114–126.

Fischer, Ruth. "Tito contra Stalin." *Der Monat* 1, no. 7 (April 1949): 44–57.

_____ . "Tito und Trotzki." *Der Monat* 2, no. 16 (January 1950): 398–409.

Griffith, William E. "On Esoteric Communications." *Studies in Comparative Communism* 3, no. 1 (January 1970): 47–54.

Hammond, Thomas Taylor. "The Djilas Affair and Yugoslav Communism." *Foreign Affairs* 33, no. 2 (January 1955): 298–315.

_____ . "The Origins of National Communism." *Virginia Quarterly Review* 34 (Spring 1958): 277–291.

Handler, M. S. "Communist Dogma and Yugoslav Practice." *Foreign Affairs* 30, no. 3 (April 1952): 426–443.

Helm, Paul. "Yugoslavia and the Afro-Asian Bloc." *Review* (Study Center for Yugoslav Affairs) no. 7 (1968): 618–642.

Hilferding, Rudolf. "State Capitalism or Totalitarian State Economy." *Modern Review* 1, no. 4 (June 1947): 266–271.

"Ideology and Power—a Symposium." In Abraham Brumberg, ed., *Russia under Khrushchev.* New York: Praeger Publishers, 1962.

Lasky, Melvin J. "Balkan Tagebuch." *Der Monat* 3 (December 1951): 261–269; 4 (January 1952): 345–356.

Lens, Sidney. "Yugoslavia's 'New Socialism,'" *Foreign Policy Bulletin* 33: 5–7.

Lopandić, Dušan. "Die Agrarpolitik Jugoslawiens." *Sudosteuropa-Jahrbuch* 1 (1956): 179–196.

Lowenthal, Richard. "Djilas Crisis," *Twentieth Century,* April 1954, pp. 316–326.

_____. "Modellfall Jugoslawien." *Der Monat* 5 (November 1953): 125–134.

_____. "Titos grosses Experiment." *Der Monat* 4 (October 1952): 39–48.

Macdonald, H. Malcolm. "Marxism and Revisionism: The Case of Yugoslavia." *Il Politico* 29, no. 1 (1964): 89–102.

Macridis, Roy. "Stalinism and the Meaning of Titoism." *World Politics* 4, no. 2 (January 1952): 219–238.

Meier, Viktor. "Impressions from a Recent Visit to Yugoslavia." *Swiss Review of World Affairs*, August 1955, pp. 10–13.

Monicelli, Mino. [Interview with Djilas and others on 1948 events]. *L'Espresso*, June 30, July 7, 1968.

Neal, Fred Warner. "The Reforms in Yugoslavia." *American Slavic and East European Review* 13, no. 1 (April 1954): 227–244.

_____. "Titoist Theory and Titoist Practice." *Journal of International Affairs* 15, no. 2 (1961): 115–124.

_____. "Yugoslav Communist Theory." *American Slavic and East European Review* 19, no. 1 (February 1960): 42–62.

_____. "Yugoslav Communist Theory." *American Universities Field Staff Reports*, FWN-5-1954.

Petrovich, Michael Boro. "The Central Government of Yugoslavia." *Political Science Quarterly* 62, no. 4 (December 1947): 504–530.

Plamenatz, John. "Deviations from Marxism." *Political Quarterly* 21, no. 1 (January–March 1950): 40–55.

Pollack, Stephen W. "Tito's Peasants." *New Statesman and Nation*, July 11, 1953, pp. 38–39.

Raditsa, Bogdan. "The Sovietization of the Satellites." *Annals of the American Academy of Political and Social Science* 271 (September 1950): 122–134.

_____. "What Price Tito?" *American Mercury* 74, no. 341 (May 1952): 33–43.

Rossi, A. "Théorie des démocraties populaires." *Preuves*, May 1953, pp. 61–68.

Roucek, Joseph S. "Titoism and the Growth of a New National Communistic Movement," *World Affairs Quarterly* 20, no. 3 (October 1949): 233–240.

Schwartz, Benjamin. "China and the Soviet Theory of People's Democracy." *Problems of Communism* 3, no. 5 (September–October 1954): 8–15.

Sharp, Samuel L. "People's Democracy; Evolution of a Concept." *Foreign Policy Reports* 26, (January 1, 1951): 186–188.

Sherman, A. "The Yugoslav Dilemma." *Twentieth Century*, August 1951, pp. 133–145.

Skilling, H. G. "People's Democracy in Soviet Theory." *Soviet Studies* 3, no. 1 (July 1951): 16–33; 3, no. 2 (October 1951): 131–149.

_____. "People's Democracy, the Proletarian Dictatorship and the Czechoslovak Path to Socialism." *American Slavic and East European Review* 10, no. 2 (April 1951): 100–116.

Sperber, Manès. "Milovan Djilas." *New Leader*, July 9, 1962, pp. 11–17.

Togliatti, Palmiro. ["Journey to Yugoslavia."] *Rinascita*, February 1, 1964.

Tucker, Robert C. "The Deradicalization of Marxist Movements." *American Political Science Review* 61, no. 2 (June 1967): 343–358.

Ulam, Adam B. "Titoism." In Milorad M. Drachkovitch, ed., *Marxism in the Modern World*, Stanford, Calif.: Stanford University Press, 1965.

Ward, Benjamin, "Workers' Management in Yugoslavia" [and comments]. *Journal of Political Economy* 65, no. 5 (October 1957): 373–386; 67, no. 2 (April 1959): 194–200.

Warriner, Doreen. "Urban Thinkers and Peasant Policy in Yugoslavia, 1918–1959." *Slavonic and East European Review* 38 (1959): 59–81.

Werth, A. "Tito's Fifth International." *Nation*, November 5, 1949, pp. 412–414; November 12, 1949, pp. 461–464.

Zaninovich, M. George. "Yugoslav Party Evolution: Moving Beyond Institutionalization." In Samuel P. Huntington and Clement H. Moore eds., *Authoritarian Politics in Modern Society*. New York: Basic Books, 1970.

Other Periodicals

Bol'shevik. (Moscow).

Chieh Fang Jih Pao [Liberation Daily] . (Shanghai).

Die Neue Zeitung. (Munich).

Einheit. (East Berlin).

For a Lasting Peace! For a People's Democracy! (Belgrade and Bucharest).

Fourth International. (New York).

Mirovoe khoziaistvo i mirovaia politika. (Moscow).

Nowe Drogi. (Warsaw).

Planovoe khoziaistvo. (Moscow).

Pravda. (Moscow).

Rabotnichesko Delo. (Sofia).

Radio Free Europe Research. (Munich).

Sovetskoe gosudarstvo i pravo. (Moscow).

Társadalmi Szemle. (Budapest).

Voprosy istorii. (Moscow).

Unpublished Material

Croan, Melvin. "Dependent Totalitarianism: The Political Process in East Germany." Ph.D. dissertation, Harvard University, 1960.

Duisin, Dusko I. "The Impact of United States Assistance on Yugoslav Policy 1949–1959." M.A. essay, Columbia University, 1963.

Dunn, William N., "Yugoslavia: National Communist Ideology and Political Integration." Ph.D. dissertation, Claremont College, 1969.

Free Europe Committee. "Changes in Yugoslavia since 1948: 'The Yugoslav Road to Socialism.' " New York, 1956.

Kuic, Vukan. "The Titoist Deviations from the Orthodox Bolshevist Doctrine." Ph.D. dissertation, University of Chicago, 1959.

McCagg, William O. "Communism and Hungary." Ph.D. dissertation, Columbia University, 1965.

Spencer, Frank W. "Origins, Theory, and Practice of Communism in Yugoslavia, 1948–1952." M.A. essay, Columbia University, 1952.

Ward, Benjamin N., Jr. "From Marx to Barone: Socialism and the Postwar Yugoslav Industrial Firm." Ph.D. dissertation, University of California (Berkeley), 1956.

Other Sources

Personal interviews with Wolfgang Leonhard. Manderscheid/Eifel, West Germany, October 1965 ; New Haven, Conn., June 1966.

Personal interview with Ilse Spittmann. Cologne, West Germany, October 1965.

Index

Action program,1, 2, 4
Administrative socialism, 148, 149
Agriculture
  collectivization of, 176–186
    abandonment of, in 1953, 186–189,
    193
    criticism of, within CPY, 177–186
    demoralization of CPY cadres due to
      abandonment of, 188–189
    initiation of, in 1949, 76
    peak of, in 1951, 182
  — peasant resistance to, in 1950–1951,
    181
    reservations about, in Croatia, 192
  cooperatives of, 37, 76, 176–193
  doctrine on socialization of, 37,
    176–193, 229–230
  droughts of 1950–1952, 81, 82
  — role of individual peasant in, 36–37,
    188–191
Albania, 10, 24, 48, 65, 81, 96
Allen, George, 126
Anarcho-syndicalism, 171
Anti-Dühring (Engels), 154
Asian Socialists, 136
Austria, 126
AVNOJ (Anti-Fascist Council of the
    People's Liberation of Yugoslavia),
    25, 28

Bakarić, Vladimir, 95n.80, 178, 179,
    183, 185, 189, 235
Balkan federation, 51, 65
Balkan Pact, 126
Bierut, Bolesław, 15, 74
Brezhnev Doctrine, 241
Brzezinski, Zbigniew, 1, 2, 4
Building socialism, 9, 10, 17, 30,
    40–43, 45, 46
Bukharin, Nikolai, 92n.30, 237
Buković, Ivan, 194n.10, 194n.22
Bulgaria, 9, 15, 48
Bureaucratic degeneration of USSR,
    101–103, 112
Burma, 135, 142n.55
Burnham, James, 119n.70

Calcutta Youth Conference, 61n.132
Capitalism, 127–131
Capitalist encirclement, 44
Chetniks, 24, 25
China, People's Republic of, 98, 99,
    122–124
Chinese Revolution and the Chinese

Communist Party, The (Mao), 12
Church, reconciliation with, 144
Citizens' committees, 150
Civil War in France (Marx), 170
Class structure, 16, 17, 37–40
Collectivization of agriculture. *See*
    Agriculture, collectivization of
Cominform
  inaugural meeting of, 30, 32, 41, 45,
    50, 52
  Zhdanov speech at, 18
  resolution of 1948 condemning
    Yugoslavia, 26, 65, 70
  resolution of 1949 condemning
    Yugoslavia, 66
Cominformists, 69
Comintern, 45
  Fourth Congress of, 20n.9
  Second Congress of, and national
    question, 45
  Seventh Congress of, and popular
    fronts, 12
Committee for Assistance to the Greek
    People, 61n.132
Communes, 168
Communist Party, leading role of, 38,
    39, 132–134, 169
  differing CPY views on, after Sixth
    Congress, 209–215
  impact of Stalin's death on, 214, 215
  initial CPY reevaluation of, 199–202
  interpretation of, at Brioni Plenum
    (1953), 214, 215
  Leninist-Stalinist doctrine of, 197,
    198
Concerning Questions of Leninism
    (Stalin), 198
Concessions to popular sentiment after
    1949, 144
Constitutional Law of 1953, 144
Constitution of 1946, 31, 35
Cooperatives, agricultural. *See* Agricul-
    ture, cooperatives of
Councils of producers, 153, 168
CPSU (Communist Party of the Soviet
    Union), Tenth Congress ban on
    factions, 198
CPY (Communist Party of Yugoslavia),
    24, 212, 213
  Brioni Plenum (1953), 213–215
  CC (Central Committee) directive
    (June 22, 1950) on role of, 199
  CC directive (November 24, 1951) on
    agriculture, 181